Schriftenreihe des
EUROPA-KOLLEGS HAMBURG
zur Integrationsforschung

Herausgegeben von
Prof. Dr. Peter Behrens
Prof. Dr. Thomas Bruha
Prof. Dr. Thomas Eger
Prof. Dr. Armin Hatje
Prof. Dr. Gert Nicolaysen
Prof. Dr. Stefan Oeter
Prof. Dr. Wolf Schäfer
Prof. Dr. Thomas Straubhaar

Band 58

Heinz Rieter/Joachim Zweynert (Eds)

Economic Styles in the Process of EU Eastern Enlargement

Nomos

Die Deutsche Nationalbibliothek verzeichnet diese Publikation in
der Deutschen Nationalbibliografie; detaillierte bibliografische
Daten sind im Internet über http://www.d-nb.de abrufbar.

Die Deutsche Nationalbibliothek lists this publication in the Deutsche
Nationalbibliografie; detailed bibliographic data is available
in the Internet at http://www.d-nb.de

ISBN 978-3-8329-4684-5

1. Auflage 2009
© Nomos Verlagsgesellschaft, Baden-Baden 2009. Printed in Germany. Alle Rechte, auch die des Nachdrucks von Auszügen, der fotomechanischen Wiedergabe und der Übersetzung, vorbehalten. Gedruckt auf alterungsbeständigem Papier.

This work is subject to copyright. All rights are reserved, whether the whole or part of the material is concerned, specifically those of translation, reprinting, re-use of illustrations, broadcasting, reproduction by photocopying machine or similar means, and storage in data banks. Under § 54 of the German Copyright Law where copies are made for other than private use a fee is payable to »Verwertungsgesellschaft Wort«, Munich.

Editors' Introduction

The present volume is the final outcome of a research project on *The Historical and Cultural Path Dependence of the Transition Processes in the Baltic Sea Region and its Significance for the Enlargement of the European Union*. The papers collected in this book were presented at the main project conference which took place on 31 March and 1 April 2006 at the Hamburg Institute of International Economics.

The project was pursued jointly by the Institute of Economic Systems, Economic History and the History of Economic Thought of Hamburg University and the Hamburg Institute of International Economics (HWWI) under supervision of Prof. Dr. Heinz Rieter (University of Hamburg) and Prof. Dr. Thomas Straubhaar (HWWI and University of Hamburg) between 2004 and 2007. Within its funding initiative *Unity amidst Variety? Intellectual Foundations and Requirements for an Enlarged Europe* the VolkswagenStiftung generously supported our research. Apart from the financial support, we would like to express our gratitude to the foundation for the very pleasant atmosphere of cooperation. In parts of the projects we co-operated with the Walter Eucken Institute (Freiburg im Breisgau) and the Europa-Kolleg Hamburg and would like to thank our colleagues at both institutions for what we felt was a very stimulating exchange of ideas. We should also like to thank Dr. Inga Fuchs for her help with the technical production of this volume, a task that due to the high number of figures and illustrations was much more difficult and time-consuming than anyone of us had expected. Johannes Bryde (Europa-Kolleg Hamburg) supervised the final production and made some last corrections.

The basic idea of the project was that despite the increasing interest in culture and history as determinants of growth and development, there is still a lack of studies applying recent insights of cultural economics to problems of actual economic policy. We hold that the Baltic Sea Region offers a particular suitable starting point for studying the impact of culture and history on economic integration. For this area traditionally has been a focal point of economic interaction and integration between Western and Central/Eastern Europe. Especially the joint history of the Hanse does not only provide a historical blueprint of successful economic integration, it also offers possibilities to construct – by historical 'story-telling' – a common identity which might give an important stimulus to economic integration.

Our methodological starting-point was the concept of economic styles, which was developed by German economists in the 1920s to 1940s and aimed at achieving a 'third way' between neoclassical economics which tended (and still tends) to neglect historical and cultural specificity, and the younger historical school which over-emphasised specificity and thus neglected general theory. The main idea of the theory of economic styles was to devise ideal types containing the typical characteristics of an economic system existing at one particular time and at one particular place (e.g. Spiethoff 1932; see also the contribution by Carsten Herrmann-Pillath). Certainly, there is much to be criticised about the original design of the theory of economic styles. In particular, inductivism and the almost complete lack of empirical underpinning were severe shortcomings hampering the development of the concept. However, the increasing problems of today's mainstream economics in explaining the problems of economic change in developing and emerging countries clearly demonstrate the significance of a research agenda trying to come up to historical and cultural specificity without neglecting general theory. Due to the above mentioned shortcomings, we explicitly do not argue in favour of simply reviving the style-theoretical concept of the 1920s to -40s. Rather, we hold that, first, it needs to be brought together with newer institutional and evolutionary ideas, and, second, that there is an urgent need to empirically underpin the style-theoretical research agenda.

The volume is organised in four parts reflecting all aspects of our research agenda: The first part consists of three papers inquiring into the "Theoretical Foundations" of the project. It starts with an essay on "Time, Style and Institutions: An Evolutionary Approach to Institutional Diversity" by one of the pioneers of econocultural transition research (in German: Wirtschaftskulturelle Transformationsforschung), Carsten Herrmann-Pillath.[1] His evolutionary re-consideration of the theory of economic styles is based on a combination of Gestalt theory and Veblenian institutionalism. Institutional variety, then, can mainly be explained by the cognitive dimension of path dependence and the emergence of Eigen times which, according to Herrmann-Pillath, are the key to understanding multi-level selection in economic systems. In his article "How to Integrate Culture into Economics?" Rainer Klump, co-editor of a book series on Kulturelle Ökonomik analyses how economists of the past and present have been trying to integrate culture into economic theory. Discussing various aspects of culture, such as culture as a determinant of preferences, as a capital good and as a source of network effects, and reporting on different attempts to measure culture, he concludes that theorising and measuring the impact of culture on growth and economic performance shares many structural problems with money. His forecast that the similarities between culture and money will become more visible when the Monetary Union will be extended to new member states, leads directly into Bertram Schefold's contribution "Enlargement and the European Monetary System: Foundation or Precondition of a Common European Economic Style". In the best tradition of German historicist economics, Schefold, who in the context of the German nuclear power debate of the 1970s was the first author to revive the theory of economic styles, in some detail looks at historical precedents of today's monetary union before then reflecting the general theoretical and macroeconomic perspective. He concludes by bringing these aspects together, arguing that the main danger to monetary integration stems from divergent economic interests among different countries becoming associated with differing overall conceptions of how social and political life should be organised. For the time being, Schefold concludes,

---

1   See e.g. his 1999 essay "What is and how should one pursue econo-cultural transition research" (Was ist und wie betreibt man wirtschaftskulturelle Transformationsforschung?).

within the enlarged EU no such conflicts are in sight, so that there is reason for optimism regarding the future of Europe's monetary union.

Part two, "Poland's and Latvia's Economic Cultures and Enlargement of EU", provides two case-studies on the impact of cultural factors in the accession process in the Baltic Sea Region. Unfortunately, Vladimir Avtonomov (State University Higher School of Economics, Moscow) was not able to deliver a written version of his exciting talk on "'Russian Economic Man': An Obstacle for Russia's Westernising Reforms?". This is why this section of the volume is somewhat shorter than the other parts. In their paper on "Material Interests versus Perceptions of Christian Values in Poland's Path to the EU", Bozena and Mikolaj Klimzcak question the image prevailing among Western intellectuals and politicians of Poland as a successful transition country. It must not be overlooked, the authors argue, that the values that had been basic to the liberation movement, and namely that of individual freedom, have been discredited by politicians and businesspeople exploiting these values for the sake of their vested interests. Partly as a result of this experience, Klimczak and Klimczak hold, Polish society is in a deep identity crisis. According to them, fundamental Catholicism and uncritical imitation of the Western life style can be seen as a result of this crisis. All in all, the authors conclude, it is still an open question whether the informal institutions necessary for a transition into an open society have gained strong enough a foothold in Poland to ensure a more or less smooth development towards this aim. A rather less gloomy picture is provided by Raita Karnite in her contribution "The Baltic Countries as Mediators in the Clash between Western European and Post-Soviet Economic Cultures? A Latvian Perspective". First of all, Karnite draws attention to the sponginess of the concept of "economic culture" and to the serious measurement problems it brings about. The existing differences in values and norms between the 'old' and the 'new' Europe, she argues, are not likely to cause conflicts and will diminish with increasing integration. According to her, it should not be overlooked that over the last years the accession countries were much more successful in pursuing reforms than the EU-15. Therefore, the new member states might even become engines rather than subjects of reforms. Nevertheless, she concludes the Baltic countries could indeed contribute to improving the mutual understanding between Russian and Western Europe.

Part three, "In Search of Empirical Evidence: Attitudes towards the Extended Order", consists of four papers, one study based on representative surveys we have conducted in Latvia, Poland, and Russia, and three case studies based on in-depth interviews with entrepreneurs (mostly owners of small and medium companies) in the three countries. In their article "Measuring the Attitudes towards the Extended Order in Latvia, Poland and Russia: The Extended Order Index", Joachim Zweynert and Robert Wyszyński start from an ideal-type distinction between holistic and extended orders inspired by the ideas of Friedrich August von Hayek. According to them, transition can be seen as a development from a holistic to an extended society with 'holisticness' and 'extendedness' manifesting themselves at the levels of the micro-, meso-, and macro-level of social relations. The hypothesis that not least due to religious affiliations, at all three levels 'extendendness' should be highest in Poland and lowest in Russia with Latvia taking an intermediate position, has been largely confirmed by their research. However, as Friederike Welter points out in her comment, it remains to be seen whether the chosen ideal-type construction really comes up to the legacy of economic styles: For obviously, it bears the risk of turning too complex a concept into a too simplistic one.

In a less strict sense than in the paper by Joachim Zweynert and Robert Wyszyński, the idea of holistic and extended orders was also basic for the in-depth interviews conducted in Latvia, Poland and Russia. Alexander Chepurenko, who also assisted us in developing the questionnaire for the representative survey, developed the interview basic to the three individual case studies. The resulting papers clearly show that there are similarities as well as differences between the countries. What all Baltic entrepreneurs – but probably not only the Baltic ones – have in common is a contradictory attitude of businesspeople towards the state, which is typical not only of transition countries: In all three countries the respondents are calling for a lean state not interfering with the market, yet at the same time they would like the state to be more sensitive to their specific needs and demands. As Inese Šūpule shows, Latvian businesspeople feel that over the last years the national business environment has significantly improved particularly due to the reforms of the State Revenue Service. At the same time, they are pretty critical about the introduction of EU regulations they regard to be potentially harmful to the growth dynamics of a rapidly developing transition economy. Ideological pragmatism seems to be the key characteristic of Russian businesspeople who according to Nina Oding and Lev Savulkin are neither prone to Soviet nostalgia, nor to what the authors call "market romanticism". Being generally interested in 'Westernising' reforms, Russian businesspeople are pessimistic that the Russian traditional values they do not share themselves can be changed in the short to medium run. This is the main reason why they believe that Russia will be forced to choose a somewhat special development path. In contradiction to common prejudices about the ideological orientations of businesspeople, Polish entrepreneurs have much more sympathy for welfare states like Sweden and Germany than for the economically freer version of the market as prevailing in Great Britain or the USA, reports Oskar Kowalewski in his case study. Maybe precisely due to the fact that they have the more 'socially' oriented market economies in mind when speaking of the 'West', they have the most positive attitude towards the Western countries among the surveyed societies.

The fourth and last part of the volume deals with "Economic and Cultural Integration in the Baltic Sea Area" focusing on historical and cultural interchange and its impact both on economic development in certain countries and in the region as a whole. In his contribution "Factors influencing Integration of the Baltic Sea Region. With special Focus on the Spatial and Economic Dimensions" Jacek Zaucha convincingly argues that regarding economic links the Baltic Sea Region is not yet a region in the functional sense and is – and this second part of the argument is certainly controversial – unlikely to become one in the future. Despite this, Zaucha claims, integration around the Baltic Sea bears a huge growth potential still vastly lying idle.

The most important means to better exploit this potential, the author argues, would be investments in infrastructure and communication, as well as administrative support for network building. Very much in line with the recent "Variety of Capitalism" argument, in her short but very rich paper "Cultural Factors of Competitiveness in the Baltic Sea Region" Anna Barbara Kisiel-Łowczyc on the example of the region demonstrates that despite increasing economic and social integration globalisation brings about, the specific dispositions people in a society have are still decisive for the question of what kind of formal institutions will improve a country's international competitiveness. In his paper "Latvia and the Baltic Sea Region: The Historical Context of Trade and Investment" Viesturs Pauls Karnups compares economic interaction between Latvia and its neighbours in the two periods of independence: the inter-war period (1925-1939) and the years since the declaration of independence from the Soviet Union in 1992. Although some common patterns can be detected, there is a basic difference between the two periods, Karnups argues, as in the inter-war period Latvia was mainly a primary producer, whereas, not least due to large Soviet investments (particularly into the Riga region), today products of metal and light industry enrich the traditional basket of export goods in which forestry still plays an important role. Gennadiy Fedorov's and Valentin Korneyevets' paper "Russia and the Baltic Sea Region: Perspectives for the Integration of Kaliningrad" analyses the prospects of the Russian exclave and 'special economic zone' Kaliningrad and its possible role for Russia's interaction with the Baltic Sea Region. Referring to the Finnish economist Urpo Kivikari, the authors are optimistic that the region around Kaliningrad might indeed become a focal point combining investments from Sweden, Denmark and Germany, labour from Poland and the Baltic Countries and raw materials from Russia.

Hamburg, 9 March 2009

Heinz Rieter
Joachim Zweynert

Content

Editors' Introduction   5

Content   11

Part 1: Theoretical Foundations   13

Time, Style and Institutions: An Evolutionary Approach to Institutional Diversity   15
Carsten Herrmann-Pillath

How to Integrate Culture into Economics? Some Reflections on an Old
and still Challenging Research Agenda   55
Rainer Klump

Enlargement and the European Monetary System: Foundation or Precondition
of a Common European Economic Style   69
Bertram Schefold

Economic Styles and European Integration (Comment)   97
Hans-Jürgen Wagener

Part 2: Poland's and Latvias's Economic Cultures and Enlargement of EU   103

Material Interests versus Perceptions of Christian Values
in Poland's Path to the EU   105
Bozena Klimczak & Mikolaj Klimczak

The Baltic Countries as Mediators in the Clash between Western European
and Post-Soviet Economic Cultures? A Latvian Perspective   127
Raita Karnite

Historical and Cultural Specificity (Comment)   143
Karl-Heinz Schmidt

**Part 3: In Search of Empirical Evidence:
Attitudes towards the Extended Order**   147

Measuring the Attitudes towards the Extended Order
in Latvia, Poland and Russia: The Extended Order Index   149
Joachim Zweynert & Robert Wyszyński

Attitudes towards the Extended Order
in Latvia, Poland and Russia (Comment) 181
Friederike Welter

The Business Environment: Case Study Latvia 185
Inese Šūpule

The Approach of Russian Entrepreneurs towards the Extended Order 219
Nina Oding & Lev Savulkin

The Entrepreneurial Approach to the Extended Order: Case Study Poland 241
Oskar Kowalewski

All happy Families are happy in the same Way: Some Remarks
concerning Baltic Entrepreneurs and Extended Order (Comment) 251
Alexander Chepurenko

Part 4: Economic and Cultural Integration in the Baltic Sea Area 259

Factors influencing Integration of the Baltic Sea Region.
With special Focus on the spatial and economic Dimensions 261
Jacek Zaucha

Cultural Factors of Competitiveness in the Baltic Sea Region (BSR) 293
Anna Barbara Kisiel-Łowczyc

Latvia and the Baltic Sea Region: The Historical Context
of Trade and Investment 303
Viesturs Pauls Karnups

Russia and the Baltic Sea Region: Perspectives
for the Integration of Kaliningrad 325
Gennadiy Fedorov & Valentin Korneyevets

Comment on Country Studies:
Poland, Latvia, and Russia in the Baltic Sea Area 339
Konrad Lammers

Affiliations 343

Part 1: Theoretical Foundations

Time, Style and Institutions: An Evolutionary Approach to Institutional Diversity

Carsten Herrmann-Pillath

1. The problem of time in the analysis of institutions

1.1 Institutional diversity is a fact of life

The divergence of institutions across economic systems is a simple empirical fact which seemed to become obsolete during the early stages of post-socialist transition. Catchwords such as the "Washington consensus" highlighted the belief that the evolution of institutions is convergent in the long-run, i.e. that it is a process of continuous melioration in the sense of achieving "best-practice" institutions, right in the same way as economies are supposed to grow towards a moving technology frontier. However, today post-socialist countries manifest a widely diverging performance and pathways of transition, in spite of sharing a common starting point and a common destiny, namely the market economy. This fact has become a textbook case of divergence of economic performance *cum* institutions (Bowles 2004: 4ff.), just like North's (1990) favourite example of South and North America after the transfer of constitutional designs from North to South. Indeed, convergence might only hold valid if a very abstract and general idea of the market economy is maintained, and if all "real existing market economies" are just subsumed under this broad concept. Within its scope, various countries may end up with very different specific manifestations of this idea, as it has happened in the long-run divergence between the Japanese, the German and the US-American economy with regard to the structure of capital markets, labour markets and corporate governance (Aoki 1988; Abelshauser, 2003). Generally speaking, economists tend to emphasize convergence, whereas political scientists, historians and sociologists emphasize divergence (e.g. Berger and Dore, 1996).

The convergence argument is a clear example of a "long run" argument in economics. To explain observed divergence, one simple strategy is to refer to divergent starting conditions, which has been presented as an explanation, for example, for the stark differences between gradualist strategies in China and the "big bang" approaches in Eastern Europe by Sachs, amongst others (for a survey, see Woo 1999). In the long run, convergence will prevail. As with all "long run" arguments, they remain irrefutable unless a binding statement about the time horizon is made. In fact, so-called transitional phenomena may have a systemic status in the sense that they may stabilize for a very long time, with far-reaching effects on economic performance. "Transitional" phenomena such as the long-run troubles with policies and institutions in some Latin American countries may be conceived as stable institutional regimes, unless a very long-run perspective were adopted, which would allow for radical changes in a distant future. Similar conditions may apply for important cases such as China and Russia, so that the conclusion may be legitimate that in the less-than-the-very-long run we will have to deal with institutional divergence analytically. Furthermore, there is a theoretical argument which treats institutional diversity as a source of gains in specialization (Aoki, 1996; Grossman and Maggi, 2000; Herrmann-Pillath, 2004). This would imply that convergence of economic performance presupposes institutional divergence, but not convergence to the identical set.

Since the days of the "Methodenstreit", economics has not found a proper way how to deal with this diversity of institutions through time and space. After the demise of the planned economies, we are still missing a convincing "medium level" typology which might help to systematize the diversity within the broad setting of market economies with predominantly private ownership and strong governments. Contemporary attempts to classify the diversity of nations mostly apply lists of distinctive features, such as the "Bertelsmann transformation index" (Bertelsmann Stiftung 2005), and they are based on some general normative statements, such as that a democracy should manifest separation of law and religion. Evidently, those classifications presuppose a particular benchmark, so that they start out from the convergence assumption. They classify the state of countries in terms of a multidimensional distance from this benchmark. Interestingly, the Bertelsmann researchers reach the conclusion that institutional change seems to be highly context-dependent. By this, they try to deal with the fact that countries differ in terms of speed in different dimensions (for example, a country might be slow in democratization but fast in terms of building a professional bureaucracy, resulting in strong macro-management potential, such as Singapore). This raises the question how far institutional change is dependent of contextual change. In other words, we face the problem of analyzing different speeds of change in different parts of the entire socio-economic system, and we need to understand their interaction. This is the challenge of time-dependent analysis which this paper ventures to tackle.

1.2 Biology offers the template for a time-dependent typology to deal with institutional diversity

Building on earlier work (Herrmann-Pillath, 1997), in this paper I propose a theoretical framework to deal with the problem of time in the typology of (socio)economic systems. This is a first step, so I will not end up with an explicit proposal of a complete typology. I concentrate on the theoretical foundations to build one. The failure of the historical school was to remain within the limits of a historically contingent typology, and just trying to overcome the tight spot of the individual cases by formulating theories about directed institutional change in terms of "stages" (e.g. Bücher 1914). Thus, it followed an essentialist methodology, which, paradoxically, remained time- and spaceless. I wish to argue that we need a time-dependent typology. Time-dependent typologies are very rare in the social sciences, because the formation of typologies mostly takes place in the framework developed by influential authors such as Hempel and Lazarsfeld, who emphasize the analytical role of spaces of properties which are themselves dependent on the research question, hence being mostly synchronic or time-independent in nature (surveyed in Kluge 1999). Max Weber is also towering about the issue, who related "ideal types" clearly to reconstructions based on the concept of rationality of action ("Zweckrationalität"). The resulting typologies are time-independent, only to be applied on historical phenomena.

Time-dependent typologies are the outcome of evolutionary theories in the strict Darwinian sense, i.e. which adopt both the population approach and the concept of lines of descent. The archetypical case is the taxonomy of biological descent, i.e. the phyletic tree. Evolutionary Economics largely forgets the central role of taxonomy in the edifice of the biological theory of evolution (Mayr 1982: 209ff.). In the biological nomenclature, there is a reference to certain sets of joint characteristics of phylae, species etc., however, these are only a secondary result of grouping certain classes of animals and plants together according to common descent. Actually, common characteristics in the present serve as an indicator of common descent and are hence relegated to surface phenomena, with the evolutionary sequences being the deeper phenomena, only to end up into a certain synchronic distribution of species and their properties. At the same time, there are criteria to delimit those classes, mainly in the context of the application of definitions of species. In particular, the idea of reproductive isolation implies that classes in biology are grounded in certain engineering principles of the reproductive process, which either lead towards successful reproduction (which entails categorial merger across types, i.e. the emergence of new species) or the failure to reproduce at all (which manifests genetic incompatibility across types, and hence manifests the border between species). These principles finally go back on the selective pressures of the environment, i.e., as Mayr (1982: 275) has it, reproductive isolation and niche specialization are "simply two sides of the same coin". That means, a biological time-dependent type is defined firstly, according to its viability through time and secondly, according to the scope of its reproductive capacity in relation to all other species. These criteria need to match the reconstruction of descent via the phylogenetic taxonomy. The biological typology does not operate with a closed state space, but with an evolving open design space (Dennett, 1995: 124ff.).

How could we use this biological methodology in the context of socio-economic systems? I think it makes sense to postulate that

- *firstly*, there is an historical descent of systems in the sense of an historical continuity of the series of changing properties in time;

- *secondly*, for all systems viability is a criterion and hence the question whether a particular combination of systems properties can be reproduced through time;

- *thirdly*, in all systems there are phenomena of institutional match and mismatch in the sense of different degrees of institutional complementarity. This refers to the self-stabilizing and mutually reinforcing nature of many institutions (Aoki, 2001, is a systematic approach on this);

- *fourthly*, all systems manifest institutional novelty through time.

The crucial question results to be, what can be the descriptive equivalent to the biological taxonomic concepts. Subsequently, I will argue that this is the neglected concept of "economic style".

2. Time-dependent typologies in evolutionary economics

2.1 Most time-dependent typologies in economics relate to technological evolution

The theoretical setting for the development of time-dependent typologies in economics is evolutionary economics. However, so far attempts have been only fragmented, because the issue of taxonomy has never played a strong role in its development. One of the most important contributions certainly is the research related to the *"long wave"* theory. This is pertinent for our topic, because theorizing about long waves refers to the idea of demarcating certain socio-economic patterns of the use of technology, and to identify lines of descent between basic innovations and branches of applications. In most recent versions of this field of research, the original idea of long waves being something similar to the business cycle, but on a larger time-scale, has been substituted by the concept of complex socio-economic regimes following each other, punctuated by basic innovations and possibly related political events (Freeman and Louçã, 2001).

A kindred approach has been developed in French *regulation theory* which emphasizes the punctuation of socio-economic regimes by crises which cause a transition between different regimes. Thus, a regime such as "Fordism" can be described as part of a time-dependent typology of economic systems, because it is not simply describing some general characteristics of economic systems, but a complex interaction between technological, organizational and institutional forms, which are clearly related to historical events triggering their emergence. As a result, regulation theory ends up with the analysis of individual trajectories of change through time, where two different temporal states are distinguished: One is the stage of institutional stability, which might nevertheless manifest "crises endogène ou cyclique", the other is the time of changing the trajectory, or of "crises structurelles" (Boyer and Saillard, 1995: 65ff.). This comes close to what I regard to be a time-dependent typology.

Long wave theorizing does not pay strong attention to spatial patterns of economic systems as compared to temporal patterns. It writes economic history in terms of a global economic history, which is a result of its emphasis on universally applied technologies. Space may play a role because it determines the specific way how technological diffusion takes place, but these are only transient phenomena. Regulation theory is much more explicit on spatial patterns because it concentrates on the interaction between the political and the economic system, with the political system mainly being defined in terms of the nation state. More recently, the role of regional systems of production has been also recognized (Benko & Lipietz, 1995). Still, a regime such as Fordism is defined as a spaceless pattern, because it spreads across countries just as technologies diffuse.

This oscillation between time and space can be also observed in other attempts to construct typologies, with the foremost one being the *national systems of innovation approach* (Edquist 1997). The NIS approach inherently emphasizes the spatial integration of institutions and routines of innovation, whereas the descent through time is treated more accidentally, especially across different NIS. This results in fuzzy boundaries between national, regional, sectoral or global systems of innovation. The specific shape of an NIS in the present is related to its historical emergence, but the lines of descent between NIS and their relation to the unified evolutionary trajectory of technological development are not scrutinized in more detail, presumably because technology is in the centre of the analysis, similar to the long wave literature that we touched upon previously. Still, the NIS certainly is an important contribution to developing a time-dependent typology. Indeed, in analytical elaborations such as Cimoli and Dosi (1995) the concept of technological trajectory is linked up with the notion of the organizational and institutional embeddedness, resulting in the conception of technological evolution unfolding in systematic patterns of time and space. Those patterns would be in the centre of attention in constructing a time-dependent typology.

To summarize, there are promising steps towards time-dependent typologies in evolutionary economics, which seem to be mostly related to the fact that the underlying technological change can be conceived as unfolding through the evolutionary mechanism of variation, selection and retention (Ziman, 2000). However, this interrelation between evolutionary mechanisms and the macro-evolution under scrutiny is not yet made explicit. Thus, the nascent typology remains an essentialistic one.

2.2 The methodologically most advanced time-dependent typologies can be found in industry studies

Most recently, an explicit attempt at transferring biological approaches to analyzing phyletic trees has been made in industry studies. This clearly shows that one problem with the aforementioned approaches is that they still stay in the essentialist tradition and do not take the crucial step towards population thinking, because they operate on a very high level of aggregation. One of the most promising areas is the transfer of *cladistic methods* in biology onto the methodology of industry classification proposed by Andersen, Ridgway and others. This argument mainly rests on the assumption that behind industry structure there is an evolving structure of knowledge which can be dissected into basic units, akin to genetic programs. Cladistic methods allow for a precise determination of the distance between different kinds of knowledge. Knowledge units may be identified by the observer by means of a familiarity with the techno-organizational building blocks of the industry (McCarthy et al., 2000), or they may be treated as implicit in the input-output relations between industries (Andersen, 2002). As a result, industries can be arranged in a tree-structure which may simultaneously reveal their phyletic relatedness and their current distribution. This is a clear example of developing a time-dependent typology. However, there is strong emphasis on the dimension of similarity and less on common descent, which is crucial for cladistics in biology.

One crucial problem in these classifications is that they cannot simply refer to observable characteristics of industry, but would need to uncover the unobservable determinants of those surface phenomena. The industrial tree is a tree of knowledge, which means that we talk about a bi-modal approach to typology: There is the mode of knowledge and the mode of technological or industrial artefacts. The driving forces of evolution are located in the first mode, which is, however, difficult to observe directly. This becomes even more evident if the fact is recognized that the application of technology is deeply enmeshed with practicing certain organizational forms.

Indeed, in their approach to *industrial demography* Carroll and Hannan (2000) introduce a fully-fledged bimodal approach in arguing that organizational forms are basically cultural phenomena in the sense that organizational patterns and practices go back on certain ideas about organizations. Remarkably, their approach drives disaggregation towards an even lower level, because industries are disaggregated into populations which are patterned according to a number of competing organizational forms, such as brewing industry with microbreweries, brewpubs etc. These forms go back on particular entrepreneurial inventions, and they stabilize via intraorganizational and extraorganizational interactions and linkages. One crucial mechanism is the legitimacy of an organizational form in the context of markets and society, which also involves cultural factors, i.e. manifest the bimodal nature of the classification. From these different causal forces, the organizational form emerges as one of the most important determinants of the social identity of single individuals in the population. As a result, industrial demography ends up with a detailed study of the emergence, the diffusion and also spatial distribution of organizational forms through time, which are carried on by the individuals of the population of firms in the industry.

The bimodal approach implies that there is a direct relation between what anthropologists call the "emic" and the "etic" dimension of the analysis of human social organization (Headland et al. 1990). Whereas the aforementioned cladistics of industry just assume that the external observer is able to identify the elements of industrial organization that are constantly reshuffled during industrial evolution (which is the etic approach), industrial demography also relies on the internal perception and endogenous construction of elements in the observed socio-economic system (hence including the "emic" perspective) (Carroll and Hannan, 2000: 60ff.). This approach to "forms" as cultural objects has important consequences for the evolution of industries because the diffusion process also becomes bimodal: A form can spread without direct competitive interaction on the markets, just by observation and imitation.

Industrial demography is a most promising archetype of developing a time-dependent typology in economics, because it makes the ecology of industrial evolution more explicit, which is missing in the cladistic approaches (just as in the original biological treatment of the method). However, there is a lack of a precise reference to evolutionary mechanisms in the sense of universal Darwinism as proposed by Hodgson (2002).

Concluding our brief survey, we note that time-dependent typologies are already a lively research topic, however mostly at the fringes of economics as a discipline, and with a small number of contributions which even do not put the issue of typology as such into their centre. The most advanced approaches can be found in industry research, whereas higher-level typologies still bear a strong mark of essentialism.

What can we learn for our problem of the typology of economic systems? First, we need to make clear what the population approach would mean in this context, second, we need to identify evolutionary mechanisms, and third and foremostly, we need to develop a bimodal analytical framework. Let us turn to the third aspect first, revisiting one of the rare explicit attempts at developing a time-dependent typology of institutions in economics.

2.3 "Economic style" is the most important precursor of time-dependent institutional analysis

In the wake of the "Methodenstreit", some German-language economists developed an early conception of a time-dependent typology which aimed at bridging general theory and historical singularity. I do not want to go into the details here, but only note three important points (for more on style, see Klump 1996; Zweynert 2002).

The first one is that many authors treat style as equivalent to "types" in the sense of submitting a certain list of properties according to which a particular economic system can be classified (e.g. Spiethoff 1932). This, however, stays in a certain tension with the claim that the style should refer to time-dependent characteristics: Spiethoff clearly argued that economics should be divided into two methodologically different parts, the time-independent one relying on universal laws, and the time-dependent one, which rests on theoretical constructs specific to time and space (the "geschichtliche Theorie"). Historically, this attitude goes back to the critique of the theories of stages produced by the Historical School. As we have remarked previously, those typologies relied on general classes of economic systems which were in turn neutral to time, such as the "urban economy". The younger style theorists tried to remedy the problem of arbitrariness of classification by means of referring to a complete and time-independent set of criteria of classification (for a concise summary in English, see Ebner 1999). In our context, this raises the issue how idiosyncratic factors can be grasped in a systematic fashion that prove to be crucial for a developmental trajectory to emerge. In the style-theorists' work, this tension became obvious in the simultaneous emphasis on the individual characteristics of a particular economic system, which cannot possibly be reflected in the time-independent classification.

This methodological contradiction also inheres the second point, which is that style is clearly related to the theoretical claim that ideas impact on the economic system, such as religions. This is a statement that is independent from the stance in the first dimension, i.e. even if there is a series of time-independent properties of systems, this does not imply that the specific shape of the system is not time-specific, because of the contingent impact of ideas. In other words, there is a strong interaction between the history of ideas and the institutional evolution of a system. Since the ideas show a strong historical context-sensitivity, this applies to the systems as well. It should be emphasized that the style-theorists put much emphasis on an holistic approach to ideas in the sense that the systematic effect does not primarily reside in particular ideas about particular institutions, but in the interrelatedness of a set of ideas which cumulates into a certain "spiritual stance" (Geisteshaltung), as in Sombart (1930). Hence, style theorists directed a lot of attention to phenomena of complementarity among ideas and institutions.

My third point is that there is an explicit consideration of the relation between the observer and the observed in the construction of a style. This reflects the fact that the "style" concept is a borrowing from the humanities, in particular the arts, where style is a category to grasp the subjective dimensions of the relation between two kinds of observers, i.e. the current participating observers and the external academic observer (Bechtel 1930). The latter tries to define certain perceptions of convergence of esthetic standards within a certain period of time, which need to converge with the perceptions of the participating observers who perceive ruptures and changes in prevailing standards. This is very much related to our second point because single ideas and characteristics certainly do not suffice to identify the unity of a style in the sense of a dominant feature during a particular period of time. Hence, the concept of style can be related to the concept of "epoch", which implies that the unity of style is also a clear demarcation in historical time which separates systemic states from each other.

Taking these three points under consideration, we realize that the concept of style is partly related to the defining features of a time-dependent taxonomy which we distilled from the biological approach. This assessment also illustrates that the major deficiency in the older style-theoretic approaches is precisely their reliance on a time-independent set of properties, i.e. a static state space. At the same time, they neglect the category of common descent, which could have naturally resulted from an explicit consideration of the history of ideas. Further, style-theorists certainly refer to the category of viability, if only because historical continuity implies an idea of institutional resilience. And finally, style-theorists obviously emphasize complementarity of institutions.

Thus, within the limits of scientific knowledge of their time, the style theorists prepared a fertile ground for developing a time-dependent typology, because they proposed to concentrate on the interaction between ideas and institutions. However, they had no concept of evolution, and they could not link up the macro-phenomena with micro-mechanisms. This requires, apart from the evolutionary dimension, a reformulation of their cultural science approach in terms of modern cognitive sciences.

2.4 Two strands interweaving in a modern reformulation of style: Gestalt theory and Veblenian institutional economics

The style-theoretic approach has never been further developed in a systematic fashion. Its "Geisteswissenschaften" methodology simply did not fit into the turn to natural science as a methodological template for economics. In contemporary economics, I see two possibly related strands of thought, which might help to overcome this cleavage.

One is Schlicht's much more recent attempt at applying Gestalt theory to institutional analysis (Schlicht 1998; for a related approach, see Kubon-Gilke 1997). In a nutshell, Schlicht argues that institutional resilience is based on the general psychological attitude of people to complement imperfect phenomena to certain ideal forms and shapes. This can be an important determinant of the human capacity to create rules, in the sense that the construction of ideal forms goes back on a close interaction between induction and deduction. With reference to institutions, induction operates via the extension of observed regularities into mutual expectations of behaviour, and deduction works via a given set of ideas about regular behaviour which causes individuals to subsume behaviour to classes of "good behaviour". Both forces concur in the creation of ideal forms, which then strongly supports the commitment of people to a particular set of institutions. This Gestalt theoretic argument also applies for institutional complementarity (i.e. sets and the implied patterns of institutions), so that precisely the main theoretical claim of the style theorists can be easily reduced to some general principles of human cognition. In other words, human cognitive tendencies towards ideal forms support the emergence of clusters of ideas and institutions, which are stabilized through the feedback loop with cognition, leading to a stronger potential of reproduction and viability because of lower costs of implementing and maintaining the institutions, given the stronger commitment of the individual agents to follow those institutions along their ideal forms.

This matches precisely the main idea of the elder style-theorists. We recognize that the ensuing task for research would be to reconstruct those ideal forms and to analyze the underlying cognitive processes. Those ideal forms would be put into a line of descent. Evidently, this is a far cry from simply applying a given set of time-independent classifications. Therefore, a modern application of the concept of style has to reject this legacy and has to focus on the cognitive and historical dimension of style. In the context of the bimodal approach to typology, we extract from Gestalt theory the cognitive micro foundation of a time-dependent typology.

The other strand of thought relates to recent developments in American institutionalism which introduced the concept of "cultural species". Indeed, Veblen himself has to be regarded as an important precursor of time-dependent typologies because he emphasized the interaction between "habits of thought" and institutions, emphasizing the embeddedness of institutions into schemes of life. Most importantly, he adopted a population approach centering on individual behavioural variation, which in turn is rooted in some universal behavioural drives in human beings, such as curiosity. Hogdson (1999) rightly emphasizes that Veblen may be regarded as the most advanced precursor toward a universal Darwinian methodology in evolutionary economics (in a similar vein, see Herrmann-Pillath, 1996). In modern institutional approaches, this has been condensed into the concept of "cultural speciation", as proposed by Jennings and Waller (1994) (for an application, see Herrmann-Pillath, 2006). Cultural speciation is ultimately rooted in the interpretive and creative activity of human agents, but takes place via the emergence of coherent interpretive patterns. The intermediate processes follow a mechanics of cumulative causation which links up individual variety with the larger stable patterns. The most important methodolological difference to evolution as depicted in biological accounts of natural selection is the systematic inclusion of hermeneutics in the explanatory model. This means that the whole of culture is continuously recreated and changed via the interpretive activity of the single agents, with interpretation, however, simultaneously relying on the cultural repertoire. Out of this, "speciation" events and cultural species evolve with stable properties, which separate different cultures from each other, even though the underlying mechanism shows strong features of individual variation within fluid populations. This view is supported by modern evolutionary approaches in anthropology, foremostly in the work of Richerson and Boyd (2005). It clearly relates to Schlicht's Gestalt approach which shows how larger patterns might be stabilized via universal cognitive mechanisms on the individual level, and adds a precise idea about the interaction between the individual and the population level.

In conclusion, we can say that the interaction between ideational and material aspects of human action lies in the core of constructing time-dependent typologies, just as has been presaged by the style theorists. There are already many promising approaches which await methodological and theoretical integration. Time-dependent typologies are needed on different levels of aggregation and with different time-scales, also integrating population-level phenomena with individual life-cycle phenomena. This implies that evolutionary economics needs to synthesize the two realms distinguished since Dilthey, namely the "Geisteswissenschaften" and the "Naturwissenschaften", "Verstehen" and "Erklären". The task is to develop an explanatory framework which allows to integrate interpretive human action, which in turn can only be accessed scientifically via the Geisteswissenschaften route.

3. Ideas and institutions: Some insights of the recent literature and the concept of cognitive path-dependence

3.1 The role of ideas is reinstated in recent theorizing about institutions in economics

It is interesting to observe that in the more recent economic literature on institutions a strong interest in ideas has revived. This is mainly related to the fact that in modelling approaches to institutional change a dependence of equilibria on ideas could be clearly demonstrated: In his grand survey on comparative institutional studies,

Aoki (2001), amongst others, builds on the fundamental notion that all social interaction is shaped by the external structures of pay-offs in games and internal representations of those structures. In a similar vein, North's (1990, 2005) work culminated in the emphasis on "shared mental models" for the diffusion and stabilization of particular institutions. This is precisely building a bimodal analytical framework.

On the most abstract level, these ideas can be connected to the ubiquitous "framing" effects in rational decision making (the classic is Thaler 1994), which in turn can be explained by Schlicht's Gestalt approach. Ideas affect the way how certain situations are perceived, in particular in terms of the assessment of outcomes. As a result, behaviour can differ considerably, even if the pay-off structure seems to be the same from the viewpoint of the external observer. This is true even for very simple constellations, and hence even more so for more complex issues such as the determination of institutions (Mantzavinos 2001). The concept of frames clearly introduces the distinction between participant and scientific observer, because it can no longer be assumed that the cognitive models that describe the setting of choice are the same across all kinds of observers. To fully explain an observed behaviour, the external observers need to reconstruct the frames that actually determine the perception of that setting on part of the observed agents. These phenomena are well-documented on the micro-level of individual decisions. However, there is no easy way to proceed to the aggregate level of institutions.

One way is to realize that many institutions are public goods, so that insights of behavioural economics on the individual tendencies to contribute to the production of public goods can be extended to aggregate phenomena (for a survey of this literature, see Bowles 2004: 116ff.). Simple economic models of strategic dilemmata cannot explain the plain fact that human societies have discovered a multitude of institutional solutions for the production of public goods in seemingly similar circumstances (Ostrom 1990 is a classic). This is precisely grasped in the recent approaches towards social capital and civil society as determinants of successful economic performance in the long run (Dasgupta and Serageldin 1990). However, this literature so far focuses on the quantitative analysis of growth factors, which is already implied in the use of the term "social capital" and its "capital" metaphor. There is still a lack of precise connections to the very general concepts about the impact of "mental models" or "cognitive schemata" on institutional change in the aggregate. Further, there is no explicit attempt at clarifying the causal structures. In general, this causal structure is seen as being rooted in the mechanism of path-dependence, as has been proposed by North (2005).

3.2 Only cognitive path-dependence can explain the historicity of institutional change

In a recent paper (Herrmann-Pillath 2007), I have proposed to distinguish between two different notions of path-dependence, namely context-specific and context-unspecific path-dependence (cf. Ackermann, 2001). The latter refers to the exclusive working of particular external incentives on the propagation of institutions.

Taking the simple example of the institutional phenomenon of corruption as a workhorse for the subsequent arguments, and summarizing the observations in fig.1:

- Firstly, the spread of corruption is a frequency-dependent phenomenon because the individual preference for corruption will depend on the perceived prevalence of corruption in a society, such that the individual benefits from corruption also depend on that (type A path-dependence in fig. 1).
- Further, there can be network effects in the sense that corruption networks can be self-reinforcing because the benefits depend on the frequency of collaborating with other corrupt people (type B path-dependence in fig. 1).
- Finally, both kinds of path dependence need to be distinguished from cognitive path-dependence when path-dependent processes work on two different ontological levels, namely the real economy and the world of ideas (type C path-dependence in fig. 1). Thus, the frequency of corruption will depend on moral persuasions of the people.

The latter interrelation between ideas and incentives leads to the emergence of context-specific path dependence. Context-specific path dependence implies that the meaning of institutions depends on the evolution of ideas, which in turn manifests autonomous path-dependence, so that the effects of external incentives on institutions become ambiguous. It is context-specific path-dependence that constitutes historicity through singular causation in open systems and the complexity of the interactions between different kinds of path-dependence.

Fig. 1: Historicity and kinds of path-dependence

Historicity of institutional change	
Path dependence o Type A: Frequency-dependence and critical mass effects o Type B: Network effects and Institutional complementarity o Type C: Bimodality of institutions and cognition	**Singularity** in multi-level systems with open state spaces and novelty
Dynamics: ⇨ singular events trigger path dependent processes ⇨ Type A-C PD interact	

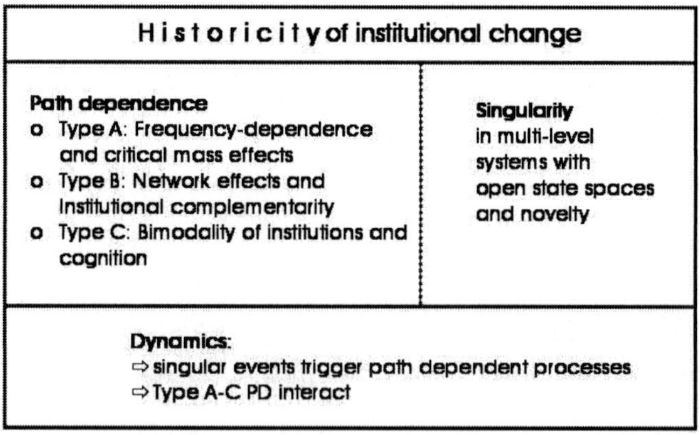

In many treatments, the first two kinds of path-dependence are seen as the main causes of historicity in economic change, because they turn systems non-ergodic in the sense of small initial events causing lasting effects on the system state at later stages. Add singularity in the sense of truly accidental events in complex systems of human interaction, and we can indeed imagine to fully explain historicity. However, at the same time this kind of path dependence does not preclude the possibility to invest a certain effort to get the system out of the track laid by the initial events. Following the results of the discussion about network externalities in technology (Liebowitz and Margolis, 1994), the fallacy of sunk cost applies here, because human agents will always be able to switch if the present relation between costs and (expected) benefits make a change attractive. Past initial events are totally irrelevant for deliberate human choice in the present.

Once we introduce a bimodal methodology, things turn out very differently. This is because the present perception of costs and benefits of institutions will also depend on a particular set of mental models and ideas that emerges simultaneously with the spread of the behavioural patterns in the population. Changing a mental model cannot possibly be done by considering the costs and benefits of the model, because the individual cannot bootstrap herself out of her own cognitive system. If you believe that you get into hell if you do not follow a certain institution, you cannot simply choose a belief that might appear to be less costly, because your identity as a person is dependent on that belief. This implies that in matters of institutions with human agency, only the bimodality of cognition and institutions can explain lasting effects of path-dependent processes.

The final brick of our conceptual building is added if we pay respect to the Northian point that mental models need to be shared to be effective in supporting the coordinating role of institutions (Denzau and North, 1994). This implies that the diffusion of mental models and ideas itself can show patterns of path-dependence. Path-dependence can occur in both realms of bimodality, and the interesting question is how the two interact. This opens up many degrees of freedom and possible behavioural constraints at the same time. For example, people might just adapt to a certain "modern" behaviour like drinking Coke, because many others do it, and still stick to very traditional beliefs about religious aspects of marriage. In particular, mental models show network effects and phenomena of complementarity of their own vintage, which means that cognitive path-dependence gives rise to a systematization of ideas into more coherent wholes.

The first two kinds of path-dependence have in common that they can be fully described in the etic dimension, i.e. there is no immediate need to make the interpretive activity of agents explicit. The third kind is different, because it requires the transition to an emic approach to be fully able to explain observed phenomena. In particular, the emic approach is necessary to understand the reflexive nature of cognitive phenomena. Ideas are not simply direct causes of behaviour, but they are actively related to each other via human thought. That means, agents rely on ideas to think over ideas. This kind of reflexivity opens up ways to break out of the forces of path dependence because of the myriads of permutations possible within the cognitive realm. Institutional change is driven by new ideas, and not so much by changing costs and benefits, which, after all, are perceived via the filter of ideas.

I propose to describe cognitive path-dependence as "culture" on the aggregate level. Culture refers to a particular pattern of mental models / cognitive schemata that emerges from the interaction of type A and B path dependence on the level of cognition, and from the reflexivity that inheres any process of cognition which includes the way how people themselves refer to their ideas. This conception of culture as a pattern of elementary cognitive schemata follows the established use of cognitive science, in particular in the so-called "connectionist" approach (e.g. DiMaggio, 1997; Strauss and Quinn, 1997). As a pattern, culture implies as series of further developmental constraints on new ideas, because, for example, there are requirements for consistency, coherence and avoidance of contradictions. Our definition seems to be an advance over existing definitions in the economic literature, because it relates culture to certain processes, and hence renders it into a dynamic category. For example, in North's (2005: 48ff.) treatment of path-dependence culture is just the intergenerational transfer of ideas and values, which leaves open how cultural change operates and interacts with institutional change.

This interaction is depicted in fig. 2, where two forces are seen to drive institutional change in the economy. The first force could be treated as exogenous, though being not exogenous in essence, namely the imposition of institutional change by policy makers. This is institutional design. The other force is culture. Both are related to each other because it is the human agent who is at the centre of interpretive action (which is the engine of cultural change) and who may be at the same time the agent that imposes institutional design. This second connection implies that institutional design becomes endogenous. This is not necessarily the case because change agents might act from within a totally different cultural setting (such as in colonialism), or because we might imagine of complex societies as consisting of many subcultures, so that institutional design might be partially exogenous with regard to a particular subculture (e.g. government imposing laws on drug trade).

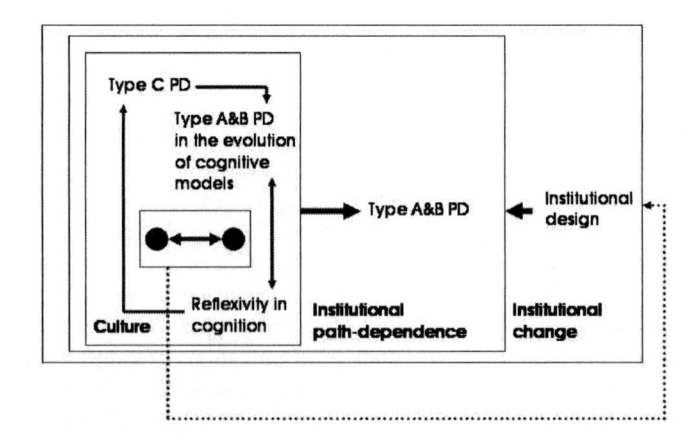

Fig. 2: Culture and path-dependence

Culture in the sense of cognitive path dependence works through different layers of causality, building on the fundamental fact of the cultural embeddedness of interaction between human agents (visualized with the two circles at the centre). The minimum distinction is between the two ontological realms itself, i.e. the world of ideas and the real economy. The important issue here is how cognitive path-dependence impacts on institutional path-dependence, which are precisely the "framing" effects that are discussed in more abstract models of behaviour. Institutional path-dependence relates to the etic dimension of institutional analysis, cognitive path-dependence to the emic.

How can we relate this conceptual framework to the previous idea of a time-dependent typology, i.e. the concept of "style"? The core intuition is to relate the concept of time to the concept of structural hierarchy and to draw on concepts of hierarchical selection theory to distinguish between different levels of aggregation. This allows to identify trajectories of institutional cum cultural change, which would become the conceptual elements of a time-dependent typology.

4. Style and order in an evolutionary framework

4.1 Eigen times are the key to understand the dynamics of multi-level selection in economic systems

To start out from a simple observation, the traditional economic belief of cultural irrelevance assumes that ideas are just adapting to real economic incentives so that cultural inertia is only possible in areas without any pressures to change, which then are at the same time irrelevant for economic processes (Jones 1995). This is tantamount to assuming a very high speed of cultural change, akin to Marx's idea of the determination of superstructure by infrastructure. So the most simple approach to relate institutional change to cognitive path-dependence is to assume that the latter operates on the level of lower-speed processes. A straightforward explanation may be that cultural change normally operates via generational change, so that certain mental models only change within a 30-years rhythm at the minimum. A more sophisticated approach may relate to cohorts of people with similar experiences in historical time (implying, e.g. a ten-year rhythm) (cf. Braungart and Braungart, 1986). In the context of evolutionary theory, these differences of speed can be designated as differences in the "Eigen times" of different kinds of processes.

The concept of Eigen time is closely related to the biological concept of a demographic clock, hence emphasizes the rhythmic nature of time which results from certain mechanisms in the reproduction of phenomena (for the application in industrial demography, see Carroll and Hannan 2000: 109ff.). In demography, different species reproduce with different speed, hence showing different Eigen times in evolution. In our context, this concept is of crucial importance. Clearly, it implies a rupture with common treatments of time in economics which rely on the unilinear arrow of physical time. Even in evolutionary economics, this is only enlarged to in clude irreversibility. However, there is a relation to the theory of capital, because different technologies of roundabout production imply different Eigen times of the reproduction of capital. Other examples of Eigen times in economics include the much-debated speed differences in the adaptive processes of global capital markets and national production systems, or the impact of the electoral cycle on the business cycle.

In institutional change, Eigen times have two most important consequences:

- First, as I have stated previously, they imply a hierarchy of relatively stable constraints which can be ordered according to the relative speed of change. Formally, this idea has been proposed and fully developed in synergetics where the so-called "order parameters" constrain the movement of higher speed variables, however, at the same time emerging out of the higher speed processes. Slower changing mental models which are bimodally related to institutions therefore might constrain higher-speed processes of institutional design.

- Second, if we envisage processes of different Eigen times to happen simultaneously, they themselves constitute a structured pattern where possibly moments of simultaneity play a crucial role in determining the further evolution of the entire system. That is, different Eigen-times might coalesce into a higher-order temporal pattern which I propose to designate as "epoch". This is most evident from cultural and political history, as well as implicit to modern conceptions of "long waves" which emphasize simultaneous changes in different spheres of the socio-economic system. Epochs would be prime candidates for elementary units in a time-dependent typology.

Thus, different Eigen times give rise to particular hierarchies of selection in the sense that institutional change operates under certain constraints which themselves change with a slow speed, and which precisely causes their selective potential. This argument is similar to arguments on the long-term impact of real economic phenomena such as the topography and location of a country. This comparison also shows that all these constraints are relative to the capabilities of the people to change their effects, i.e. there is no absolute hierarchy of Eigen times. Rather, the structure of Eigen times is a temporal phenomenon on its own, i.e. it evolves through time. For example, the environmental constraints can be analyzed both in the emic and the etic dimension, which means that there are physical determinants of the selective effects as well as cognitively intermediated effects which are determined by the specific human response to the observed physical effects. Hence, the concept of Eigen time does not imply a determinism of slow parameters, such as the material environment. Indeed, as we shall see later, human agency itself may cause a reversal of Eigen times, firstly, because of its potential to create true novelty even on the level of slow-changing variables, and secondly, because it can be endowed with different potentials for action. In the context of institutions, this relates to the fundamental social category of power. Powerful agents can impose institutional design on a socio-economic system, thus speeding up institutional change. Clearly, the main is sue here is that power itself is an institutional phenomenon. That is, the evolutionary process might lead to the emergence of positions of power which enable individuals to change the pattern and direction of evolution in substantial ways.

In sum, we can say that Eigen times plus human agency imply a heterarchic approach of variation, selection and retention of institutions. Following Veblen, variation relates to interpretive human agency as well as to random phenomena such as cultural drift. Selection and retention are closely related to each other, because retention is implied in the emergence of slow-changing parameters, in the sense of structural stabilization. For example, in cultural history certain ideas and values often form constitutive principles of human societies, which at the same time carry on cultural patterns ("retention") and select fast-changing variants on the level of the population of creative human agents. A classic study on this is Hallpike (1986), which, interestingly, is written with the intention to falsify Darwinian approaches to culture. Hallpike argues that the main difference between biological and social evolution lies in the strong forces of directedness governing the latter. However, this is precisely what we expect to emerge in a multi-level system of variation, selection and retention (Knudsen, 2002; Hodgson and Knudsen, 2006). Hallpike's "core principles" of cultures operate as slow-changing order parameters on institutional change, as, for example, the civilian nature of hierarchy in the Chinese state which has persisted for two millenia until today.

4.2 The distinction between internal and external selection opens the way for developing a time-dependent typology based on the concept of style

In order to further specify the effects of differing Eigen times in economic systems I propose to distinguish between two different kinds of selection and different levels of selection, the latter implying a differentiation between Eigen times. Regarding the former, I introduce the distinction between internal and external selection, following the precedent of the so-called "systems theory of evolution" (Wuketits, 1987; for a detailed elaboration, see Herrmann-Pillath, 2002, chapter III, 3). External selection refers to the standard conception of a neat system / environment distinction, with the latter being a source of selective pressures which impact on differential systems reproduction (and is hence related to the viability dimension mentioned at the end of first section). Internal selection operates via endogenous structural constraints which arise from certain limits to an arbitrary combination of properties within a system (and which is related to the dimension of complementarity). To take a simple example, an economic system might experience external selection via locational competition in the world economy, whereas internal selection works via the complementarity of particular institutions (for example, democracy and market economy might co-determine each other in the long run, which is the assumption in the Bertelsmann index).

Clearly, the distinction between internal and external selection is not an absolute one but in turn depends on relative Eigen times. Slower variables may operate as a selector on fast changing variables, assuming the role of a quasi-environment. This is very useful to establish an analytical boundary between behaviour and institutions. Let us take observed individual behaviour as the starting point, for example, a series of instances of corruption. This behaviour is determined by two forces, one is the spontaneous action on the level of the individual, the other is the impact of institutional regularities which are imposed via a series of sanctions and other mechanisms. Both forces cannot be distinguished unequivocally in terms of observational data. Their relation is disentangled via the differentiation of three levels of selection:

- The first is internal selection of variations in individual behaviour through institutions and their direct effect on individual preferences, such as via Gestalt effects, via forces of conformity or via complementarities. This gives rise to clusters of institutions and preferences, which classically have been dubbed "habits of thought" by Veblen (for a more modern version of this idea, see Bowles 1998). We call the institutions of this level primary institutions. For example, societies may have different conceptions of the role of personal relations and gift exchange in business, which draws different border lines between corruption and socially approved interaction. On this level, we observe cognitive path-dependence interacting with institutional path-dependence.

- The second is external selection of institutions via other secondary institutions governing the sanctions that maintain certain behavioural patterns. Typically, these are institutions related to government and politics. If they change slower than the primary institutions, they operate as a constraint. In our example, independent from social attitudes toward gift exchange the political system might impose tough penalties on corruption. This is the impact of institutional design, which is in turn dependent on a particular distribution of power in a society.

- The third level is external selection through environmental forces, such as locational or military competition, which might in turn be influenced by determinants such as climate and geography. These forces may be long-run stable, but not necessarily so. For example, a country might have a rugged landscape with many obstacles to transport and communication, which allows local communities to continue with local customs of gift exchange. Thus, imposing government sanctions may turn out to be too costly to suppress corruption entirely. As a result of the interaction of selective forces, formal institutions sanctioning corruption coexist with informal institutions and subcultures supportive of corruption.

As we see from this example, heterarchic interaction implies that the relative speed of change depends on the particular circumstances. For example, a singular event such as a natural catastrophe can change the environmental determinants into a fast-changing parameter, possibly releasing certain constraints on the behavioural level. Of more interest is the impact of powerful action on secondary institutions, as in the case of a revolution. Here, as has been shown in classics of social history such as Skocpol (1979), primary institutions might emerge as slow-changing parameters constraining voluntaristic political action, even providing the basis for such fundamental institutions like the state. For example, a puristic revolutionary government might attempt at eradicating corruption, but might fail to overcome strong forces of custom in society.

What are the implications for developing a time-dependent typology? One starting point is the observation that a typology certainly might refer to a subset of slow-changing parameters, which are themselves temporal phenomena. Insofar as these can be spatially circumstricted, we have the starting point for a time-space typology which had been also requested by the style theorists. The other is that we explicitly include the interpretive activity of the agents into consideration, which means that the typology need to include the emics of the systems dynamics. In other words, a typology needs to include both institutions and ideas in a time-dependent fashion. Let us try to link this general points with the classical conceptions of style.

4.3 Merging time-independent and time-dependent typologies: order and style

I now propose the following conceptual distinction. In the older German language literature on institutional economics there are frequent attempts at distinguishing style from "order", mostly as mutually excluding alternatives (a classic is Eucken 1939). Both concepts share commonalities, in particular in the sense that both refer to entire arrangements of institutions on the level of economic systems. I propose that we can employ both concepts precisely to distinguish between time-dependent and time-independent typologies of economic systems.

The style would refer to a pattern of behaviour and institutions which has crystallized into a Gestalt during a certain period of time, whereas the "order" is a set of institutions that makes up a time-independent system of constraints and incentives/sanctions that govern behaviour. Here, time-dependence refers to the observation that behavioural patterns in a population of actors are culturally embedded, whereas time-independency means that these patterns are explained by time-invariant, universal regularities of behaviour (which just takes up Spiethoff's previously mentioned distinction). In order to describe a style it is necessary to understand the interaction between individual cognition and institutions, which requires the reconstruction of the meaning of institutions for the individuals in the sense of the framing of behavioural responses to incentives and sanctions. This analysis is necessarily time-dependent because the underlying cognitive schemata, i.e. the ideas, change through time. In contrast, the analysis of order is based on a generalized conception of the individual such as the rational choice paradigm and refers to intersubjectively invariant characteristics of institutions on both the primary and the secondary level. Style would require an emic access to the perceptions and interpretations of the individuals, whereas order would rely on universal regularities of human behaviour. Thus, in the case of corruption the two perspectives of cultural anthropology and economics would be merged into one systematic evolutionary approach.

For example, the analysis of the Soviet centrally planned economy can adopt the perspective of order which means that it tries to understand the structure of incentives and sanctions that work on rational individual behaviour. This might result into a more specific characterization of that system, such as the "shortage economy" and the "shadow economy". Thus, the widespread existence of the shadow economy would be regarded as a part of the economic order of the Soviet state, which is explained via reactions of economic agents on price controls and rationing. These systems effect result into behavioural phenomena such as corruption. Approaching the same system from the viewpoint of style would require to relate the Soviet economy to the evolution of ideas and cognitive schemata that co-determine the behaviour of people under the institutional constraints, such as the lack of institutional trust emerging from the shadow economy, finally resulting in a criminalization of the economy, which in turn harmonizes with the culture of mistrust and control pervading the security apparatus. This interacts with pre-existing cultural patterns such as ethnic and religious identities, imprinting the Soviet shadow economy with a peculiar cultural shape. The latter was then an important factor in the persistence of exchange networks after the break-up of the Soviet Union, resulting in a strong ethnicization of certain sectors of the Russian economy, in particular trade.

Fig. 3: Basic structure of heterarchical selection and time in institutional change

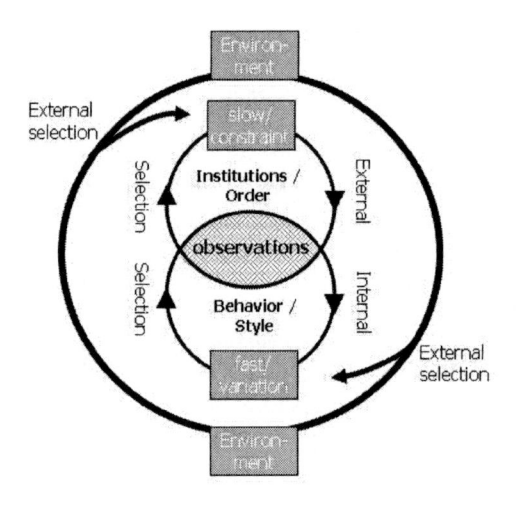

I summarize my argument in fig. 3. Observations on behavioural patterns in a population of actors are the basic elements of the construction of a typology. These are condensed into phenomenological regularities (such as the widespread existence of a shadow economy in the Soviet economy). These regularities are explained in a bimodal way. Firstly, we assume that variants of behaviour are subject to external selection of institutions as a part of order (second level selection). For example, the diffusion of the shadow economy depends on the intensity and frequency of sanctions by the government authorities. We subsume that in the normal case these institutions change relatively slowly, thus acting as a constraint with selective force. On the other pole, individual variation occurs much faster. However, it is constrained by forces of internal selection which result from cognitive path-dependence, as for example, forces of institutional complementarity working on the interaction between traditional ethnic customs and the functional requirements of the shadow economy, e.g. in networking activities (first-level selection). Thus, style is mostly related to internal selection, and order to external selection. Beyond this, order and style are heterarchically embedded into structures of external selection which delineate a moving border between the environment and the economic system. For example, since 1917 the actual role of the shadow economy in the Soviet Union was also determined by the extent of the war economy.

4.4 Culture emerges as a force of external selection separate from style

The approach outlined so far is only a first approximation, however. In particular, the relation between culture and style is not sufficiently clear, possibly conflating both. In order to achieve conceptual clarification, I propose to distinguish between culture as a force of external selection and specific endogenous amalgates of cognitive schemata and behaviour, which are in turn cultural phenomena. In fig. 4, this distinction can be related to different Eigen times of the respective processes, and to the different levels of individual behaviour and population phenomena.

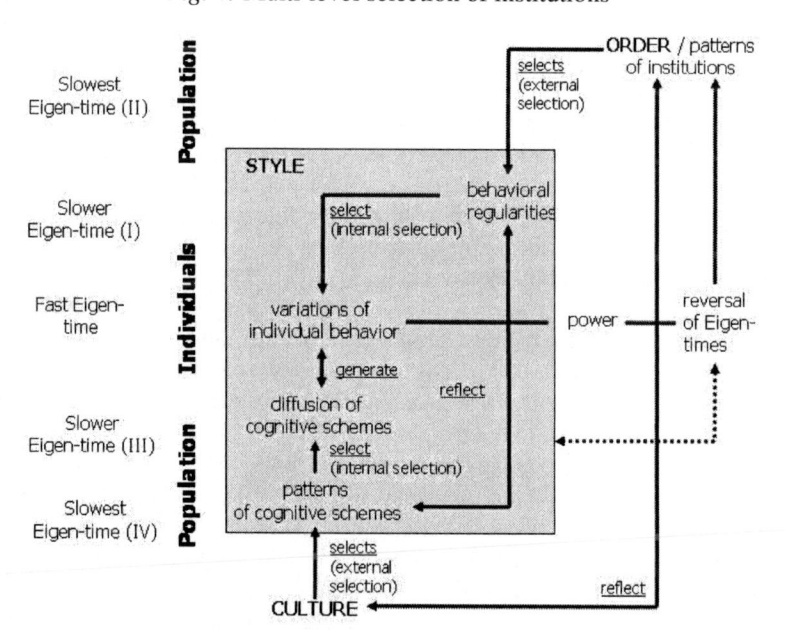

Fig. 4: Multi-level selection of institutions

There is a broad consensus that some aspects of cognition may change slowly, even though they work on the individual level. This is the very concept of cultural inertia, which results from many different causes, such as the complementarity of sets of ideas, a general bias of conformity in human behaviour, or the simple fact that cultural meaning is not fully accessible to individual deliberation and choice, and therefore cannot be changed in a voluntaristic fashion. Further, institutions and ideas are both phenomena on the level of the population, because ideas are also stabilized and disseminated via the communication among the individuals. In culturally advanced societies, these population level phenomena are themselves the object of institutionalization, beginning with the introduction of the script. This implies, however, that certain cultural phenomena attain a similar status as phenomena of order, in the sense that particular patterns of culture are fixed, for example, in holy scriptures, constitutions, or legal texts. Typically, apart from political and administrative actors who impose sanctions on deviant behaviours, these societies also manifest a group of actors who are especially in charge of maintaining and interpreting the cultural tradition. Thus, culture partly becomes a force of external selection on the second level. In fig. 4, I include this special relation between order and culture by means of explicitly considering the fact that culture directly reflects order. Both order and culture are population-level phenomena because almost by definition they encompass the entire society or economic system which they are related to. Culture is related to the individual level via the complex interactions of cognitive path-dependence. As we see, culture as a force of external selection relates to culture as a pattern of cognitive schemata, which in turn interacts with the process of the diffusion of cognitive schemata via internal selection, from which the directedness of cultural change results.

As a result, individual behaviour is actually embedded into population-level phenomena in two dimensions. Culture and order emerge as intersubjective phenomena for different reasons. In distinction to the previous definition of order, culture is a phenomenon which is accessible via an objective hermeneutics, such as the analysis of texts and interpretations of texts. Objective hermeneutics comes close to an etic approach, because there is the potential for an universal agreement of internal and external observers about the meaning of texts (Ingold, 1993). For example, understanding Muslim economic behaviour may rely on both the analysis of the institutions governing credit markets (and hence, order), and the objective-hermeneutic analysis of commentaries on the Koran where certain authoritative statements on credit can be found. The results of this analysis, however, need to be related to the interpretations by the agents themselves, which are context- and time-dependent, and hence require the transition to the emic perspective.

We arrive at a more complex description of cognitive path-dependence as related to institutions, because we take heed of the fact that culture itself has institutional properties. Precisely because of these fuzzy borders, "style" becomes a crucial analytical category. As we see in fig. 4, style would especially refer to the interaction between behavioural regularities, the diffusion of cognitive schemata and the related patterns, hence to that part of cognitive path-dependence which is endogenously determined. The approach to the respective cultural phenomena would accordingly oscillate between an objective and subjective hermeneutics, which is also precisely where cultural creativity happens. Take the example of corruption, again. There is the possibility that aside of the legal system of a country a written cultural tradition exists which makes explicit and formal distinctions between insiders and outsiders, therefore allowing for corruption especially in external economic relations. This tradition has to be distinguished from the perceptions and values governing the individual behaviour, which, of course, are strongly imprinted by official culture. Methodologically, the former is accessed via the study of texts, whereas the latter requires interviews, participant observation and fieldwork.

In this perspective, cultural change itself operates in the threefold structure of internal and external selection. The diffusion of cognitive schemata takes place in the tension between behavioural regularities and formal culture. Behavioural regularities and cognitive schemata continuously interact, with culture directly selecting the expression of cognitive schemata through the formal cultural repertoire, and behaviour being selected by institutionalized sanctions.

Individual behavioural variations can impact on external selection mainly via two channels. Firstly, individuals may attain positions of power which allow them to change the formal institutions with high speed, and secondly, individuals may create new interpretations of a given cultural repertoire. For the latter channel we may assume that normally the resulting speed of change might be slower than in the former case, because rarely individuals can impact directly on the existing diffusion of cognitive schemata in a society. This means, that even in the case of institutional change which is strongly supported by ideological transformation, the reversal of Eigen time resulting from powerful action almost always implies that style becomes a constraint or selecting force on order. In addition, powerful action directed at changing properties of entire systems, i.e. order, is itself embedded into ideas and cognitive schemata prevailing in a population, unless the action is imposed from the outside, as in colonialism. In the case of endogenous power, features of style may in fact exert a strong influence on the actually emerging order. Thus, although powerful individual action may cause a reversal of Eigen times, this will mainly take place between order and style, with style becoming a slow-changing parameter assuming a selective force, mainly in the sense of the internal selection of powerful action.

Summarizing, we can identify economic style as a particular part of the complex system of interacting forces in institutional change. In fig. 4, style encompasses that part of the picture where individual behaviour links up with cognitive schemata on the one hand and clusters of cognitive schemata and institutions on the other hand, which we have identified as behavioural regularities. Culture, power and order remain outside the conceptual scope of style, which is important for empirical analysis. The different phenomena have different reach as far as the distinction between individual-level and population-level processes is concerned, and they operate with different speeds, i.e. Eigen times. Empirical research must pay particular attention to the interaction of selective processes on different hierarchical levels and hence, with different Eigen times. This constitutes style as a time-dependent phenomenon, because processes with a slow Eigen time delimit larger stretches of time which reach back into the past.

The conclusion for our problem of a time-dependent typology is close at hand. Within the evolutionary context, we can reinstall style as an analytical category by which a time-dependent typology can be developed. The crucial ingredient is to concentrate on cognitive schemata and culture in their relation to individual behaviour that is governed by institutions, which are in turn arranged into the pattern of order. Only the explicit inclusion of cognition and culture can render a typology time-dependent. This is especially important for constructing lines of descent. Cultural history and historical anthropology are crucial research disciplines for constructing a time-dependent typology. This results into a dynamic conception of the interaction between historical research into economic behaviour and the objective hermeneutics of cultural history.

5. First steps towards applied analysis: Constructing styles

So far, we have developed a broad conceptual framework of a time-dependent typology of institutions. I shall now explicate some first steps towards an application, without being able to present a full taxonomy at the moment. Simultaneously, I will complete several missing pieces in my analytical tool case.

5.1 Population thinking in style-theoretic analysis takes "institutionally guided behavioural patterns" as basic units

Two main ideas have to be borrowed directly from evolutionary taxonomy in biology: Founder events and lines of descent. Before detailing the conceptual transfer, however, we need to further clarify the relevance of the population concept in institutional taxonomy. Evidently, treating entire styles as units of a population of "economic systems" would be seriously misleading, because the number of existing economic systems is very small, and styles are highly aggregate phenomena. What is the basic unit of the taxonomy and hence, economic selection of styles? Following the structure outlined in Fig. 4, I propose to identify "institutionally guided behavioural patterns", henceforth IGBP, to be such units, which I conceive to be the micro-elements and single instantiations of style. This refers to observable regularities in the behaviour of economic agents which can be explained as the effects of stable institutions and their corresponding cognitive schemata, and which reproduce through time. IGBPs are the micro-units in path-dependent institutional change, that is, they are the results of dynamic lock-in effects in individual behaviour. On first sight, this is another analogy to the gene concept, as such analogies have been proposed in the context of other related approaches, such as the organizational "routines"(which could be understood as IGBPs in an organisational setting) (Nelson and Winter, 1982; Aldrich, 1999: 35ff.).

This is not the place to open the Pandora's box of discussing the advantages and disadvantages of transferring the gene concept to other scientific fields. Suffice to state here, that there are important arguments in the context of the debate over "memes" that render the assumption plausible that beyond biological evolution there are domains where the general concept of a "replicator" may be applied usefully (see Dennett, 1995: 335; Hull, 2000; Knudsen, 2002). Thus, constructing a time-dependent taxonomy in economics would entail the identification of replicators, which dynamically reproduce observed regularities making up a distinctive style in their entirety. However, at a closer look even the biological conceptual model relies on observational data which are independent from identifying the replicators, i.e. the biological taxonomy mainly builds on identifying observational similarities between the single entities that make up the observed populations (such as similar body shape). Thus, in the first step it is perfectly possible to concentrate on the phenomenology of institutions and leaving the analysis of the generative forces aside, which would be entailed by the focus on replicators. This implies that IGBRs are not replicators and analogues to genes, but to phenotypical regularities, hence to phenomena on the level of the interactors. In identifying IGBPs, we concentrate on structural similarities across interactors, leaving the question open which underlying mechanism causes these regularities. We can speculate that these might be replicators of the kind of "memes" in the sense of cognitive schemata (Aunger, 2000), but we do not need to fix our thought here, because in order to construct a time-dependent taxonomy phenomenological regularities suffice, just as Darwin did not need to understand the gene mechanism, which was yet to be discovered in his times.

IGBPs are, for example, particular ways to arrange labour relations between workers and capitalists, specific institutionalized interactions between government officials and entrepreneurs, or widely observable attitudes towards income inequality. How do we distil those patterns out of observations? This is the onerous task of comparative economic systems in the sense of identifying patterns which make up a difference in functioning and performance of economic action in different systemic contexts. That is, we adopt a performance-based criterion for identifying IGBPs, which again follows the biological model in the sense that economic efficiency and efficacy are concepts closely related, if not almost identical, to the evolutionary concepts of adaptation and fitness. A classic example for this kind of work is Aoki's (1988) comparison between the American and the Japanese economy in the 80ies, which was built on the observation of distinct behavioural patterns in the economy, such as different approaches to the organization of work and related training systems and the different degrees of mobility on the labour market. In all these cases it was relatively straightforward to show how these IGBPs determine the specific and relative performance of the Japanese and the American economy.

With this basic unit of our time-dependent typology, it jumps to the eye that larger units correspond to the larger units in the biological taxonomy, in particular the species concept in a most general sense. In this first application, I do not systematically discuss the elaboration of higher-level taxonomic units, but just propose that we treat the style to be a conceptual equivalent to the species in biology. This implies that there is no necessary relation between a certain style and particular IGBPs.

IGBPs, most generally, are "traits" which might be found in different economic systems being assigned to different styles. The crucial difference between IGBPs and styles, hence, is that the style is a systematic pattern of a set of IGBPs, or, in Schlicht's words, a Gestalt. This clearly reveals that the analysis of styles has to rely on the interaction between the emic and the etic approach, as the cognitive forces of the unity of styles reside in the participant observers of the economic system. This has to be balanced with the etic perspective, and as we have developed in the previous section, the property of the systematicity of styles reflects the selective forces of the their two main determinants that I treated as exogenous, i.e. culture and order:

- Order can be related to what has been called "Baupläne" in some strands of evolutionary thought, as it refers to particular engineering principles of economic systems that can be equated with non-situational laws of economics. Picking up Aoki's comparative study again, Aoki (1988) has argued that a low level of labour mobility in Japan requires a matching pattern in the capital market, i.e. a bank-dominated system of corporate governance with a long-term horizon in financing decisions. This institutional match is explained by considerations of economic efficiency, i.e. reflects criteria of optimal social engineering. As is well known, this governance pattern itself is an IGBP, and has been compared very often to the "Rhenish" capitalism of Germany. In Germany, a similar relation between long-term employment and bank-dominated governance can be observed, which might be regarded as a case of evolutionary convergence that manifests the workings of universal economic laws in this sense of engineering principles (see also Aoki, 2001: 307ff.).

- Culture is related to the cognitive realm, i.e. the role of ideas in shaping styles. Again, the reference are not single ideas, but it is the impact of a systematic pattern among ideas that counts for the description of styles. For example, just treating the idea of loyalty as being one determinant of the stability of labour relations in Japan would not be sufficient, unless this idea is linked up with other notions in Japanese culture that make up an integrated system of meanings, which has to be related also to some external references of culture, such as indigenous texts that establish this system. That is, cultural analysis has to make the entire mechanism of cognitive path-dependence explicit, in particular the interaction among style A, B and C path dependence within the cognitive realm (a classic on pre-crisis Japan is Iwata, 1992).

Thus, we end up with a basic conceptual structure with IGBPs making up the populations that can be arranged into styles and which are subject to the selective forces of order and culture, in the first place. In order to further develop this taxonomic methodology, we have to differentiate the role of selective forces along the lines of the distinction between internal and external selection.

5.2 Founding events, order and culture: How to build bridges between past and present

We can now outline the first empirical steps toward setting up a time-dependent taxonomy. This starts out from a preliminary collection of observations about economic systems as they stand in the eye of the pre-theoretical observer. Mostly, this will be countries as political units, given that many institutions depend on government enforcement. However, even on this level there can be already intricate questions such as whether the post-colonial African states are the proper starting point for the analysis, given the distorted relations between their artificial borders and the related ethnically fragmented societies (Leeson, 2005). One important criterion for the identification of the starting point is therefore the existence of an internal discourse and set of concepts that relate to the identity of the economic system as being separate from others, i.e. we have to pay explicit attention to the perspective of the participant observers. Switches between the emic and the etic perspective are necessary methodological devices in order to generate taxonomical hypotheses. For example, the recent controversies in Germany over the "locusts" (i.e. hedge funds etc.) that aim at unravelling the stable network of relations between banks and corporations in Germany reveal that many outsiders and insiders perceive a clear identity of the German economic system which might change with the increasing role of the stock markets in corporate take-overs.

At the same time, there are preliminary conjectures regarding the impact of order and culture, which already shed light on the emerging role of styles. An illuminating example is the grouping of countries under the heading "centrally planned economies", which in the 80ies included such diverse cases as the Soviet Union and China. The Centrally Planned Economy is a kind of order with particular formal institutional features that generate lawlike economic effects, such as the "shortage economy" analyzed by Kornai in his classics (Kornai, 1980, who already adopted a methodological focus on behavioral regularities). Shortage-conditioned behaviour is a clear instance of IGBPs that could be met in both economies, such as the strong investment drive in the two economies, or the important role of "grey market traders" in making up for coordination failures in the central plan. China and the Soviet Union certainly shared these features, but at the same time there were stark institutional differences, which exerted a strong impact on the subsequent transition to a market economy. These differences had been arranged by many observers under the heading of "culture", already in the political culture literature that started to emerge in the 1960ies. For example, China and the Soviet Union clearly diverged very early in the role assigned to regional units in administrating the economy, which led an astute observer as Granick (1990) to claim that China reveals a distinct property rights regime, i.e. "regional property rights". This difference can be explained by profound, culturally imprinted differences in political culture, at least partly (Herrmann-Pillath, 1991; 2006).

With these comparative exercises, preliminary hypotheses about the synchronic distribution and groupings of IGBP can be generated. These are, however, still a far cry from a time-dependent taxonomy, because it is just a synchronous snapshot on the current distribution of potentially important IGBPs across economic systems, mostly political units. In contrast, a time dependent taxonomy has the two previously mentioned distinguishing features, i.e. it refers to a founding event and it makes lines of descent explicit.

Regarding the former, hypotheses can be generated by analyzing the history of the preliminary classification generated in the first step. Founding events must be somehow related to as many IGPRs as possible, which also show up in the most recent stage of institutional evolution. The major problem is the role of political design and intervention, i.e. power, in shaping economic systems. For example, we may be inclined to regard 1917 as being the founding event of the Soviet economic system. But precisely in this context the concept of "style" shows its analytical value. Most large-scale political interventions refer to the design of the order of an economic system, that is, they do not directly effect the elementary classification into styles. Indeed, in case of the Soviet Union one might regard the transition to Stalinism at the end of the 1920ies to be the founding event of a particular style, which might be tentatively labelled as "Soviet command economy" which persisted until the collapse of the Soviet Union the latest, attempts at perestroika notwithstanding. Thus, the identification of founding events will already loosen up the seemingly tight connection between styles and political units.

The historical depth of styles can differ considerably, depending on the relative weight given to the stable and to the varying features. For example, in the case of the United States one might be inclined to regard the Declaration of Independence as a founding event, as the causal forces driving the political process were closely related to fundamental economic issues which remained a leitmotif of American history up to the present. On the other hand, there are important turning points such as the abolishment of slavery after the Civil War and the New Deal in the 20th century, which changed some fundamental IGBPs that had been characteristic for the US economy for decades. Thus, the question arises how we can deal with those junctures in constructing a typology.

Other cases might be more easy to make the procedure clear. For instance, in the case of Germany it is relatively straightforward to identify the national unification under the auspices of the Bismarck era as the founding event, where many important IGBPs emerged, such as the corporatist arrangements between industry and government and the peculiar approach to social welfare. However, it still remains open to debate how to deal with the strong political interventions of the Nazi era, and of the resulting separation of ways in the GDR and the FRG. In the case of the latter, many observers would also assign the post-WWII Erhard policies the status of a founding event, namely of the "Social Market Economy", which is a concept that comes very close to a style intuitively, as it is clearly linked to a particular time, place and set of ideas. Interestingly, this style today interacts strongly with another political factor which can also be related to a most recent founding event, i.e. the establishment of the common European market, possibly best marked by the Maastricht Treaty of 1992. This shows that styles can be mixed through political changes in the environment, similar to the blending of species through interbreeding.

These considerations lead us to further enhance complexity of our basic concept and to introduce a distinction that rings familiar to the biological distinction between species and genera. It seems clear that the US economy still shows a lasting impact of the 1776 founding event until today. On the other hand, there have been crucial junctures related to major political events, that introduced important new institutional patterns into the general framework of the US economy, such as the New Deal. From this we might conclude that there are different epochs of institutional development with changing styles, however, all these remain connected to the same initial founding event. This larger pattern spanning the entire period of the US economy may be referred to broader conception of style that is similar to the role of genera in biology. Thus, we end up with a more specific conjecture, namely that styles are grouped around "meta-styles". For example, the southern slave economy between 1776 and 1865 is a style belonging to the meta-style US economy, and the Social Market economy 1949-present is a style belonging to the meta-style "German economy" related to the founding events of 1873.

On the other hand, we might also further differentiate established styles into sub groupings. This is familiar in evolutionary economics, where "regional innovation systems" have received much attention, as a special case of the NIS that we discussed in the second section of this paper. For example, the German economy post-1949 might be further analyzed into regional sub groupings, with Baden-Württemberg having received a lot of analytical attention in the context of economic geography (Herrigel, 1992). In this case, we observe a lasting impact of cultural factors, in particular a specific religious background related to Protestant pietism with a strong emphasis on diligence and trust. This might be compared to North-Rhine-Westfalia, which has a strong political culture of regional alliances between large corporations and trade unions. Thus, the style of the German economy post 1949 can be further dissected into subtypes, which is very important to understand the evolution of styles, because subtypes can be starting points for divergent evolution, or they may tend to dominate the style after some time elapsed, or they may trigger convergent evolution across the political borders.

5.3 Slow-changing selective forces maintain "family resemblances" between different states of an economic style through time

We realize that a time-dependent typology refers to specific segments in time and space, which is mostly reflected in current approaches to distinguish political and societal units. However, the proof of the pudding rests on the construction of lines of descent. For this, it is essential to apply the concept of Eigen times on the historical data, which means, more specifically, to distinguish between slow and fast changing determinants of institutional change. In our context, I would just like to point out four possible slow changing determinants:

- geography,

- culture,
- ideology, and
- political culture.

Geography can shape the long-run evolution of institutions in a direct way, because it is a slow-changing determinant of economic aspects of political control and integration. To name just a few examples: The stronger inclination towards liberalism in Britain has been related, amongst other reasons, to the fact that the British Isles could mainly rely on the navy as core military unit, whereas in continental Europe large standing armies played a crucial role in the centuries-long military competition over political dominance (Rokkan, 1975). Large standing armies require a much stronger extractive role of the state, which might explain the emergence of more interventionist approaches to economic policy in most larger continental states. It is also very illuminating to compare the geographic factors in the long-run development of Russia and America, with Russia being mainly a continental power with very long open borders to strong rivals in power, resulting in a very different pattern of a frontier society, as compared to America (White, 1987). As in the case of Britain, these geographical factors intermingle with the geopolitical and military environment, which can be a slow-changing determinant, too. For example, maintaining the unity of Russia in the face of the centrifugal economic tendencies in its Far East, together with the simple fact of a low share of the Russian population living there, has always been one of the driving forces of the recurrent reinstatement of central political power also in the economy (which we observe precisely today).

Culture is another slow-changing variable, as compared to order which can be reset by political fiat. This interrelates with the role of ideas, but does not concur with that. Ideas are especially important in their occurrence as ideologies, which makes them more resilient to change, and hence, turns them into slow-changing determinants. This is because an ideology is a coherent system of ideas in which single ideas may be very difficult to change, because otherwise the unity of the ideology may be jeopardized, which is particularly important for maintaining a certain identity as public actor. People who have attached themselves to a particular ideology may therefore manifest a strong conservativism in their political attitudes (cf. Kuran, 1995).

However, ideologies are clearly different from cultures, Communism emerged as an ideology after Marx had created his scientific theory about economic systems, and it diffused all over the world. If a political party defines itself as being a communist one, this imposes certain constraints on institutional change over the long run. For example, until the 2004 constitutional amendment, the Chinese Communist Party was reluctant to express a full constitutional guarantee to private property, and still the property in land remains non-private in China. This is a major constraint for institutional evolution, even though there are many ways to circumvent the ideological fetters. Still, this results into peculiar IGBPs, especially on the Chinese countryside. At the same time, China did never fully adopt the Communist ideology in its

Soviet interpretation, which was dominating the Communist world in the Stalinist and the post-Stalinist times. The peculiar Chinese way of communism is deeply imbued by certain cultural factors, which, amongst others, include the Confucian belief that the individual is a morally responsible person that can be shaped by education almost without any limit (Pye, 1988). This idea was in direct contradiction to the Marxist theory of the dominant causal role of the material infrastructure, as compared to the ideological superstructure. Hence, the Chinese communists adopted what has been called by the Soviets a "voluntaristic" approach to economic change, especially pronounced during the Cultural Revolution, when economics was turned into a moral category. Paradoxically, the same ideational stance can help to understand the shift towards "pragmatism" under Deng Xiaoping.

Finally, political culture is a more specific way to identify the patterns that result from the interaction of the previously mentioned determinants, with special reference to the way how power is managed in a society. For example, most observers agreed that the success of the East Asian countries in development mainly relates to a specific political culture which causes a distinctive divergence in the performance of institutions which otherwise might be analyzed in terms of the same causal relations underlying their arrangement into an order (Wade, 1990; Amsden, 1991). The most conspicuous case is the effects of subsidies and other policy measures in administrating external economic relations. Standard political economy would just expect that these end up in a state with rampant corruption and lack of dynamism. Although the East Asian countries certainly also manifested this kind of performance, this was by far outweighed by the fact that there was a strong political culture keeping the government aloof from the people, and supporting a performance based approach to subsidies, which is very different from the interest-group politics of Western countries. Generally speaking, political cultures embed the political bargaining process into long-run stable patterns of behaviour at the interface between the economy and the state.

Based on these observations and the analysis of other slow-changing variables (such as religion, ethnic composition of the population etc.), we are enabled to identify constraints on institutional change that link up founding events and the present state. Their "channelling" effect should be recognizable in "family resemblances" between institutional states and the related IGBP across different points in time. Those resemblances are the main indicator for unearthing lines of descent in the historical data. Again, this is a very complex issue, and I only wish to pinpoint a couple of observations related to the empirical identification of resemblances. These are, in particular:

- Continuities of IGBPs across economic crises affecting the entire economy for a longer time span,

- Continuities of IGBPs across periods of political redesign affecting the entire economic order,

- Spread of IGPRs beyond the political units which are hypothesized to link up the founding event and the present state, in particular into contexts with a different political, cultural and societal context, and continuing observability.

Starting with the last point first, an intriguing example is the continuity of certain IGPRs of Chinese economic behaviour in as different contexts such as the PR China, Taiwan, Singapore and Hong Kong, adding even diaspora communities of the Chinese. For example, the special role of the family enterprise in Chinese business culture clearly manifests close resemblances in all these cases, with a direct interaction e.g. with institutional patterns in the capital market and banking, i.e. the governance structures. This becomes even more obvious if political culture is also transferred, especially evident in the case of the competing systems of Mainland China and Taiwan, where the antagonistic parties in the 1950ies tended towards very similar institutional designs of the economy, only diverging afterwards along the lines of the military conflict, with the Mainland pushed towards the Soviet model and Taiwan towards the US-model. Still, precisely the reforms under Deng Xiaoping seem to follow a developmental trajectory that rings familiar to the Taiwanese case, such as the role of informal bureaucratic coordination between government and industry, with a clearly exalted role of the government official that is rooted in traditional Chinese conceptions of the superiority of the government to business.

This example also shows how continuities might prevail over radical political transformations. In the case of China, many observers have emphasized the special role of the intermediary political organizations, in particular the county, in both the traditional and the modern body politic of China (e.g. Shue, 1988). This seems to be related to political culture, specifically with relation to administrative values and approaches. Generally speaking, radical political transformations in agrarian societies are a very illuminating case for the strength of cultural factors in determining economic styles. In this context, a major difference between China and the Soviet Union is precisely the extermination of rural society under Stalin, whereas in China even the Cultural Revolution did not substantially interfere with the cultural traditions.

Crises are very often transformative events, that is, they might trigger the emergence of new styles. We have already mentioned the role of the New Deal in American history, which reflects the impact of the Great Depression. Thus, crises are litmus tests in both directions, because some cases may just manifest the deeper continuities. In the case of Germany, one cannot simply assert that the political unification of the "Deutsches Reich" in 1871 is the founding event, but 1873, because only in the aftermath of the "Gründerkrise" did the transition to the corporatist market system of modern Germany take place. Thus, the crisis marks a transformative event. On the other hand, the Nazi system, also a result of a deep economic crisis, partly just accentuates the government pole in the corporatist structure established in the Bismarck era, which is evident from the peculiar mix of planned economy elements and private-sector industry organization in preparing for the war economy.

5.4 A simple result: Germany 1949-present is an economic style deducible from taxonomic analysis

Let us continue with the example of Germany to complete our first steps to an application of the proposed methodology. In brief, we have the following ingredients for constructing an economic style.

Current state: Despite a strong impact of the European Union, Germany still seems to retain important distinguishing features of corporatism. Main recent observations include the strengthening of the coordinative role of government in the health care system and the continuing conflicts over the so-called "Deutschland AG", i.e. the close networks between banks and large corporations in corporate governance. Thus, we can state a preliminary list of IGBPs which seem to be distinctive for the contemporary German economy (Abelshauser 2003: 99):

Highly-qualified long-term employment relations; long and formally specialized professional education, also related to widespread industry standardization; well-developed public welfare systems with high ancillary wage costs; universal banks and long-term corporate finance; corporatist regional economies with strong interaction between corporate and political leaders.

This style can be briefly characterized as "democratic-liberal corporatist welfarism".

Founding event: Economic historians trace this pattern back to the early decades of a unified Germany up to WW I. Main family resemblances with the present include (Abelshauser, 2003: 93ff.): A strengthening role for permanent employees, state-sponsored social security; long-term relations between universal banks and companies with a relatively weak development of the stock market, few hostile takeovers, strong industry associations. This style can be briefly characterized as "authoritarian-liberal corporatism".

Order: Rooted in the 19th century liberal traditions, German style mainly was influenced by the market economy type of order, with the Nazi rule stepwise strengthening the command economy elements. After WWII, the economy of the GDR followed closely the model of the planned economy, resulting in a stark structural divergence between the two Germanies. After unification, there was a swift transfer of the market economy order to the eastern part of Germany. However, observers agree that there are still vestiges of the old system in behavioural and attitudinal patterns of the eastern population (Alesina / Fuchs-Schündeln, 2006). Recently, there is an increasing impact of the EU on further liberalizing the economy, weakening corporatist market closures (e.g. in the energy sector).

Culture: The German economy reflects a strong impact of cultural determinants that had emerged in the 18th and the 19th century, in particular affecting the specific interpretation of liberalism in Germany (in comprehensive detail, see Armbrüster, 2005). Up to the present, German liberalism concentrates on the economy and the law, leaving issues of social liberalism aside. Traditionally, there is a strong emphasis on public order and strong government, with a peculiar interpretation of freedom as being related to personal development and education, and less on entrepreneur ship. German political culture today manifests this convergence among the main political parties, leaving the "economic liberals" and the "social liberals" being split into two entirely different groups (today, the Liberal Party and the Greens). The idea of freedom as personal development has been a shaping force of labour relations for two centuries, because central ideas such as the "profession" (Beruf) being a lifelong feature of individual identity, foster preferences for long-term employment relations.

Lines of descent: Based on this brief analysis of determining factors, we can propose a preliminary version of taxonomic relations that fit different types of the German economy into a genealogical tree. The main aspect is the distinction between two epochs, i.e. the epoch of 1873-1945 (with the founding event) and the epoch of 1945-present, which are marked the by two styles featured above. Thus, we have a meta-style "Germany$_{1873\text{-present}}$" which has evolved in two distinct styles "Germany$_{1873\text{-}1945}$" and "Germany$_{1949\text{-present}}$". The impact of order, triggered by military defeat in WWII, gave rise to another style, "Germany$_{1949\text{-}1989}$", which is the special case of the planned economy in the GDR. Recently, there is a blending with institutions of the EU, which might lead towards a new style that is embedded into a newly emerging meta-style "Europe$_{1992\text{-present}}$". The German meta-style, in turn, is embedded into a larger taxonomic area, if only because the impact of culture is mediated via historical developments that reach back into the 18th century. However, it remains to be investigated in more detail how far this style is itself a blend of other styles, such as a Prussian style that evolved since the early 19th century, or a "Hanse style" prevailing in the northern members of the Deutsche Bund in the 19th century. Today, such taxonomic strands can be discerned in the existence of sub styles of Germany1949-present, such as the Baden-Württemberg regional economy.

6. Conclusion

Our final example in applying a time-dependent taxonomy of institutions may appear to be a bit sobering, as it is very simple and does not produce a new insight beyond the ways how observers, especially historians, so far would have classified Germany as an economic system. However, this example was chosen for convenience, as the more complex cases would have required an extensive discussion of historical and institutional details. The lesson learned from the example is that a basic unit of a time-dependent taxonomy is a style which refers to a particular socio-economic unit constrained in time and space. Compare this with common approaches to economic systems, which normally start out from very general, theoretically based features, such as ownership structures and allocative mechanisms. Even recent attempts at reviving the style conception remain on a very high level of abstraction and use time-independent categories (e.g. Zweynert, 2002).

The analysis of styles ultimately rests on the identification of traits, but this does not imply, as in the case of the elder style theorists, a closed list of traits. The design space of economic systems is evolving through time, which is the essential reason why a time-dependent taxonomy is needed. For example, the IT industry and the evolution of the internet/WWW have given rise to new conceptions of intellectual property rights in the context of open-source software and digital media. This emergence of new institutional traits may finally end up with the crystallization of new styles. As this is especially vigorous in the United States, we might consider the possibility of the emergence of an "$US_{2.0}$" style in the near future.

The sobering effect of my taxonomic exercise also results from the fact that I refer to simple political units within a certain time span. This is a necessary result of the fact that in recent historical times, formal institutions have mostly been set by national governments, and formal institutions exert a strong impact on style. However, this seemingly simple picture would become much more complex when turning to examples where styles compete and even clash within the confines of a national system (such as the Civil War in the United States), or when we deal with a strong interaction between national systems and transnational styles, as in the case of Africa. There is the fascinating research issue whether there is an Islamic style, because there are clear economic prescriptions in Muslim thought, as on interest payments and on welfare, which mix with national institutions across countries with a strong Muslim population. Further, taxonomic work will be much more demanding when dealing with pre-modern societies, such as the European Middle Ages.

One fundamental insight is important to notice, namely that these taxonomic exercises will presumably shake the economist's natural inclination to think of institutional evolution as being similar to technological evolution in the sense that there is continuous institutional progress. Dissecting styles into institutionally guided behavioural patterns does not necessarily imply that there is a progression of styles towards an "improvement" in whatever sense. There is certainly a continuous emergence of new IGPRs and hence a flux of styles, but at the same time old IGPRs persist in modified versions, adapting to the environment. An evolutionary approach to institutions takes diversity as a basic fact, and following Darwin's famous advice, should be cautious in assessing institutions as being on a "higher or lower" level of development.

References

Ackermann, Rolf (2001): Pfadabhängigkeit, Institutionen und Regelreform, Tübingen: Mohr Siebeck.

Amsden, Alice (1991): Diffusion of Development: The Late-Industrializing Model and Greater East Asia, in: American Economic Review, Vol. 81, 282-286.

Armbrüster, Thomas (2005): Management and Organization in Germany, Aldershot / Burlington: Ashgate.

Abelshauser, Werner (2003): Kulturkampf. Der deutsche Weg in die Neue Wirtschaft und die amerikanische Herausforderung, Berlin: Kadmos.

Aldrich, Howard (1999): Organizations Evolving, London: Sage.

Alesina, Alberto / Fuchs-Schündeln, Nicola (2006): Good-bye Lenin (or not?): The Effect of Communism on People's Preferences, http://www.economics.harvard.edu/faculty/alesina/papers/goodbyelenin-0606.pdf.

Andersen, Esben (2002): The Tree of Industrial Life: An Approach to the Systematics and Evolution of Industry, http://www.business.aau.dk/evolution/projects/phylo/

Aoki, Masahiko (1988): Information, Incentives, and Bargaining in the Japanese Economy, Cambridge et al.: Cambridge University Press.

Aoki, Masahiko (1996): An Evolutionary Parable of the Gains from International Organizational Diversity, in: Landau et al. (1996), 247-263.

Aoki, Masahiko (2001): Toward a Comparative Institutional Analysis, Stanford: Stanford University Press.

Aunger, Robert, ed. (2000): Darwinizing Culture: The Status of Memetics as a Science, Oxford: Oxford University Press.

Bechtel, Heinrich (1930): Der Wirtschaftsstil des deutschen Spätmittelalters, Breslau.

Benko, G. and Lipietz, A.: "De la régulation des espaces aux espaces de régulation", in: Boyer and Saillard (1995b), 293-303.

Berger, Suzanne / Dore, Ronald, eds (1996): National Diversity and Global Capitalism, Ithaca et al.: Cornell University Press.

Bertelsmann Stiftung (2005): Bertelsmann Transformation Index 2006. Auf dem Weg zur Marktwirtschaftlichen Demokratie, Gütersloh: Verlag BertelsmannStiftung.

Bowles, Samuel (1998): Endogenous Preferences: The Cultural Consequences of Markets and other Economic Institutions, in: Journal of Economic Literature, Vol. XXXVI, 75-111.

Bowles, Samuel (2004): Microeconomics. Behavior, Institutions, and Evolution. New York and Oxford: Russell Sage Foundation and Princeton University Press.

Boyer, R. and Saillard, Y. (1995a): "Un précis des la regulation", in: Boyer and Saillard (1995b), 58-68.

Boyer, R. and Saillard, Y., eds (1995b): Théorie de la régulation. L'état des savoirs, Paris (La Découverte).

Braungart, Richard G. / Braungart, Margaret M. (1986): Life-Course and Generational Politics, in: Annual Review of Sociology, Vol. 12, 205-231.

Bücher, Karl (1914): Volkswirtschaftliche Entwicklungsstufen, reprinted in: Schachtschabel (1971), 77-104.

Carroll, Glenn R./Hannan, Michael T. (2000): The Demography of Corporations and Industries. Princeton: Princeton University Press.

Cimoli, Mario/Dosi, Giovanni (1995): Technological Paradigms, Patterns of Learning and Development: An Introductory Roadmap, in: Journal of Evolutionary Economics, Vol. 5, 243-268.

Dasgupta, Partha/Serageldin, Ismail, eds (1999): Social Capital. A Multifaceted Perspective, Washington: World Bank.

Dennett, Daniel (1995): Darwin's Dangerous Idea. Evolution and the Meanings of Life, London et al.: Penguin Press.

Denzau, Albert T. / North, Douglass C. (1994): Shared Mental Models: Ideologies and Institutions, in: Kyklos, Vol. 47, 3-32.

DiMaggio, Paul (1997): Culture and Cognition, in: Annual Review of Sociology, Vol. 23, 263-287.

Ebner, Alexander (1999): Understanding Varieties in the Structure and Performance of National Innovation Systems: The Concept of Economic Style, in: Groenewegen/Vromen (1999), 141-169.

Edquist, Charles, ed. (1997): Systems of Innovation. Technologies, Institutions and Organizations. London/Washington: Pinter.

Eucken, Walter (1939): Grundlagen der Nationalökonomie, Berlin: Springer.

Freeman, Chris & Louçã, Francisco (2001): As Time Goes By. From the Industrial Revolutions to the Information Revolution, Oxford: Oxford University Press.

Granick, David. Chinese State Enterprises. A Regional Property Rights Analysis. Chicago: University of Chicago Press, 1990.

Groenewegen, John/Vromen, Jack, eds (1999): Institutions and the Evolution of Capitalism: Implications of Evolutionary Economics, Cheltenham/Northhampton: Edward Elgar.

Grossman, Gene M. / Maggi, Giovanni (2000): Diversity and Trade, in: American Economic Review, Vol. 90(5), 1255-1275.

Hallpike, Christopher R. (1986): The Principles of Social Evolution, Oxford: Clarendon.

Headland, Thomas N./Pike, Kenneth, L./Harris, Marvin, eds (1990): Emics and Etics. The Insider/Outsider Debate, Newbury Park, London, New Dehli: Sage.

Herrigel, Gary B. (1993): Power and the Redefinition of Industrial Districts: the Case of Baden-Württemberg. In Gernot Grabher, The Embedded Firm. On the Socioeconomics of Industrial Networks. London, New York: Routledge, 227-251.

Herrmann-Pillath, Carsten (1991): Institutioneller Wandel, Macht und Inflation in China: Ordnungstheoretische Analysen zur Politischen Ökonomie eines Transformationsprozesses. Baden-Baden: Nomos.

Herrmann-Pillath, Carsten (1996): Thorstein Veblen's Menschenbild: Theoretische Grundlagen und empirische Relevanz, in: R. Penz/H. Wilkop, Hrsg., Zeit der Institutionen - Thorstein Veblens evolutorische Ökonomik, Marburg: Metropolis, 83-132.

Herrmann-Pillath, Carsten (1997): Wettbewerb als ontologische Universalie: Natürliche Arten, wettbewerbliche Interaktionen und Internalisierung, in: U. Fehl/K. von Delhaes, Hrsg., Dimensionen des Wettbewerbes, Stuttgart/Jena/New York: G. Fischer, 321-356.

Herrmann-Pillath, Carsten (2002): Grundriß der Evolutionsökonomik, München: Fink (www.evolutionaryeconomics.net)

Herrmann-Pillath, Carsten (2004): The Evolutionary Perspective on Institutional Divergence and Competitive Advantage, in: Werner Pascha, ed., Systemic Change in the Japanese and German Economies. Convergence and differentiation as a dual challenge, New York: RoutledgeCurzon, 51-84.

Herrmann-Pillath, Carsten (2006): Cultural Species and Institutional Change in China, in: Journal of Economic Issues, XL(3), 539-574.

Herrmann-Pillath, Carsten (2007): China's Path-dependent Transition: Culture Mediating Between Market and Socialism, forthcoming in: Qian Yingyi, ed., Market and Socialism in China and Vietnam, IEA.

Hodgson, Geoffrey M. (1999): Evolution and Institutions. On Evolutionary Economics and the Evolution of Economics, Cheltenham and Northampton: Edward Elgar.

Hodgson, Geoffrey M. (2002): Darwinism in Economics: From Analogy to Ontology, in: Journal of Evolutionary Economics, Vol. 12 (3), 259-282.

Hodgson, Geoffrey M. / Knudsen, T. (2006): The Nature and Units of Social Selection, in: Journal of Evolutionary Economics, 16(5), 477-490.

Hull, David L. (2000): Taking memetics seriously: Memetics will be what we make it, in: Aunger (2000): 43-67.

Ingold, Tim (1993): "The Art of Translation in a Continuous World." In Beyond Boundaries. Understanding, Translation and Anthropological Discourse, edited by Gísli Pálsson, Oxford/Providence: Berg, 211-30.

Iwata, Ryushi (1992): The Japanes Enterprise as A Unified Body of Employees: Origins and Development, in: Kumon / Rosovsky (1992), 170-197.

Jones, Eric L. (1995): Culture and Its Relationship to Economic Change, in: Journal of Theoretical and Institutional Economics, Vol. 151 (2), 269-285.

Kluge, Susann (1999): Empirisch begründete Typenbildung. Zur Konstruktion von Typen und Typologien in der qualitativen Sozialforschung, Opladen: Leske + Budrich.

Klump, Rainer, Hrsg., (1996): Wirtschaftskultur, Wirtschaftsstil und Wirtschaftsordnung, Marburg: Metropolis.

Knudsen, T. (2002): Economic Selection Theory, in: Journal of Evolutionary Economics, 12(4), 443-470.

Kornai, Janos (1980): The Economics of Shortage, Amsterdam / New York / Oxford: North Holland.

Kubon-Gilke, Gisela (1997): Verhaltensbindung und die Evolution ökonomischer Institutionen, Marburg: Metropolis.

Kumon, Shumpei / Rosovsky, Henry, eds (1992): The Political Economy of Japan. Vol. 3: Cultural and Social Dynamics, Stanford: Stanford University Press.

Kuran, Timur (1995): Private Truths, Public Lies. The Social Consequences of Preference Falsification, Cambridge / London: Harvard Unversity Press.

Landau, Ralph/Taylor, Timothy/Wright, Gavin, eds (1996): The Mosaic of Economic Growth, Stanford: Stanford University Press.

Leeson, Peter T. (2005): Endogenizing Fractionalization, in: Journal of Institutional Economics, 1(1), 75-98.

Liebowitz, S.J./Margolis, Stephen E. (1994): Network Externality: An Un-common Tragedy, in: Journal of Economic Perspectives, Vol. 8, No. 2, 133-150.

Mantzavinos, Chrysostomos (2001): Individuals, Institutions, and Markets, Cambridge et al.: Cambridge University Press.

Mayr, Ernst (1982): The Growth of Biological Thought. Diversity, Evolution, and Inheritance. Cambridge & London: Belknap.

Mayr, Ernst (1999): Interview of Ernst Mayr by Bill Charlesworth, in: Human Ethology Bulletin, Vol. 14(3), 1-9

McCarthy, Ian/Ridgway, Keith/Leseure, Michel/Fieller, Nick (2000): Organisational Diversity, Evolution and Cladistic Classifications, in: Omega 28, 77-95.

Müller-Armack, Alfred (1940/1971): Zur Geneaologie der Wirtschaftsstile, reprinted in: Schachtschabel (1971), 156-207.

Nelson, Richard R./Winter, Sidney G. (1982): An Evolutionary Theory of Economic Change, Cambridge/London: Belknap.

North, Douglass C. (1990): Institutions, Institutional Change, and Economic Performance, Cambridge et al.: Cambridge University Press.

North, Douglass C. (2005): Understanding the Process of Economic Change, Princeton and Oxford: Princeton University Press.

Ostrom, Elinor (1990): Governing the Commons. The Evolution of Institutions for Collective Action. Cambridge et al.: Cambridge University Press.

Panther, Stephan (2002): Kulturelle Faktoren in der Transformation Osteuropas in: Thomas Eger, Hrsg., Kulturelle Prägung, Entstehung und Wandel von Institutionen, Berlin: Duncker und Humblot.

Pascha, Werner, ed. (2002): Systemic Change in the Japanese and German Economies, Convergence and Differentiation as a Dual Challenge, London/New York: Routledge.

Pye, Lucian W. (1988): The Mandarin and the Cadre: China's Political Cultures. Ann Arbor: University of Michigan.

Richerson, Peter J. / Boyd, Robert (2005): Not By Genes Alone. How Culture Transformed Human Evolution. Chicago: University of Chicago Press.

Rokkan, Stein (1975): Dimensions of State Formation and Nation-Building: A Possible Paradigm for Research on Variations within Europe, in: Tilly, 1975, 562-601.

Schachtschabel, Hans G., Hrsg. (1971): Wirtschaftsstufen und Wirtschaftsordnungen, Darmstadt: Wissenschaftliche Buchgesellschaft.

Schlicht, Ekkehard (1998): On Custom in the Economy, Oxford: Clarendon.

Shue, Vivienne. The Reach of the State. Sketches of the Chinese Body Politic, Stanford: Stanford University Press, 1988.

Siewing, Rolf, Hrsg. (1987): Evolution. Bedingungen – Resultate – Konsequenzen. Stuttgart/New York: Gustav Fischer.

Skocpol, Theda (1979): States and Social Revolutions. A Comparative Analysis of France, Russia and China, Cambridge: Cambridge University Press.

Sombart, Werner (1930): Die drei Nationalökonomien, München.

Spiethoff, Arthur (1932/1971): Die allgemeine Volkswirtschaftslehre als geschichtliche Theorie. Die Wirtschaftsstile, reprinted in: Schachtschabel, 1971, 123-155.

Strauss, Claudia/Quinn, Naomi (1997): A Cognitive Theory of Cultural Meaning, Cambridge et al.: Cambridge University Press.

Thaler, Richard H. (1994): Quasi-Rational Economics, New York: Russell Sage.

Tilly, Charles, ed. (1975): The Formation of National States in Europe, Princeton: Princeton University Press.

Wade, Robert (1990): Governing the Market. Economic Theory and the Role of Government in East Asian Industrialization, Princeton: Princeton University Press.

White, Colin (1987): Russia and America. The Roots of Economic Divergence, London / New York / Sydney: Croom Helm.

Woo Wing Thyy (1999): The Real Reasons for China's Growth, in: The China Journal 41, 115-138

Wuketits, Franz (1987): Evolution als Systemprozeß: Die Systemtheorie der Evolution, in: Siewing, 1987, 453-474.

Ziman, John, ed. (2000): Technological Innovation as an Evolutionary Process, Cambridge et al.: Cambridge University Press.

Zweynert, Joachim (2002): Eine systemtheoretische Neuformulierung des Wirtschaftsstilkonzepts – Geldwirtschaft und Machtwirtschaft als stiltheoretische Idealtypen, in: Schmollers Jahrbuch, 122, 415-444.

How to Integrate Culture into Economics? Some Reflections on an Old and still Challenging Research Agenda[*]

Rainer Klump

1. Introduction

General interest in the cultural determinants of economic behaviour and economic development has always been characterized by remarkable cycles. This is certainly true for the last wave which started at the same time when the Soviet empire broke down which also marked the victory of market capitalism over state-controlled socialism. This new wave reached a first upper turning point in 1994 when "Foreign Affairs" enthusiastically declared: "Culture is in. From business consultants to military strategists, people talk about culture as the deepest and most determinative aspect of human life." (Zakaria 1994, 125) Only one year later, the same journal launched an intensive debate about the significance of culture by publishing Samuel Huntington's investigation of a possible "clash of civilizations" (Huntington 1995), and Francis Fukuyama (1995) came out with his provocative study of the "underestimated influence of culture on economic development."

The world wide victory of capitalism over socialism also set an end to the common practice of international comparative economics of regarding the question of the distribution of property rights and the centralization or decentralization of decisions as the main elements of analysis. A world of market economies which all allow for private property needed some other analytical tools to help shed light on the still remarkable differences between countries and their economic systems. At the same time, the still ongoing East Asian miracles seemed to underline that models other than the "Western" capitalist market economies not only existed, but even performed better. It became therefore of interest to study the specific elements of the "Asian" model or models of capitalism including the potential influence of their specific cultural traditions (Klump / Menkhoff 1995). After September 2001 the violent confrontations between "Western" and Islamic cultural traditions and their repercussions on political, social and economic relationships with Islamic countries has further increased the academic interest in this subject. And it also plays a major role when Europeans are currently trying to define possible limits of integration given that with the latest round of enlargement and the negotiations with future

---

[*] An earlier version of this paper has been published under the title "The Role of Culture in Economic Theorizing and Empirical Economic Research" in *H.H. Nau und B. Schefold* (Eds), The Historicity of Economics. Continuieties and Discontinuities of Historical Thought in the 19th and 20th Century Economics, Berlin u.a. (Springer) 2002, 207 - 224.

members seem to increase significantly the cultural heterogeneity of the European Union.

The task to integrate elements of culture into a comparative economic perspective is a major challenge for future economic research. This paper aims at defining the challenging task more precisely. It starts with a short review of the eminent role which cultural elements had played in earlier theories of economic development. An overview is then presented of how elements of culture are integrated into modern theories of economic development. Four different channels are distinguished by which culture can influence economic actions: It can determine preferences, it can work as a capital good which then is regarded as an additional factor of production, it can create positive network effects which reduce social and economic transaction costs, and it can finally shape common rules of games for individual interactions. After a brief look at some of the empirical studies in which an attempt has been made to test and quantify the role of culture in economic development, the paper ends with some conclusions with a special view of the European Union.

2. Culture in early theories of economic development

It is not surprising that after the end of the Cold War comparative economics began to rediscover the methodological complexity for which it was known before the antagonism between capitalism and socialism dominated everything else. Notably in pre World War II Germany, the different Historical Schools had inspired generations of economists with the view that cultural elements, such as a particular "economic spirit" (Wirtschaftsgeist), were just as important for economic development as physical factors of production (Klump 1995). Since the Historical Schools and their influence on modern economic theory are widely covered elsewhere, I will concentrate on another historical reference for the present debate on culture and development. When the Historical Schools developed during the 19th century, Asia was no longer considered an economic rival for Europe. Comparative analyses were concentrated on defending the hypothesis that market economies in Continental Europe with cultural traditions other than the British variant could progress at a high and steady rate. As little as one century earlier, however, the situation with reference to Asia had been different.

Economics as a modern science began to develop after an era of increasing worldwide trading activities, the global mercantilism of the late 17th and early 18th centuries, which may even be considered a first period of globalisation. In this particular period, encounters between civilizations via trade and other forms of international communications, such as the reports of missionaries or adventurers increased, and gave Europe and Europeans the opportunity to gain new insights and knowledge about civilizations on other continents, particularly those in Asia, whose economies showed a comparable or even higher level of wealth (Osterhammel 1998). The obvious fact that the economic development in the Asian empires was based perhaps on the same economic principles, such as free trade or investment in agriculture, but relied in any case on different cultural roots, was reflected in works of early economists. The influence of this "Asian encounter" is especially notable in the writings of French physiocrats including those of Quesnay, where it is apparent that culture was considered to have an important role in economic life. Comparative studies of various cultures and civilizations became popular among the French "philosophes" in this period, with Montesquieu analyzing "L'esprit des lois" (1748) in different countries and Voltaire comparing "Les moeurs et l'esprits des nations" (1756). Turgot (1970) set up his main economic work, les "Réflexions sur la formation et la distribution de la richesse" (1766) as a guide for two young Chinese which had been educated in France by the Jesuits and were being sent back to Canton. At the same time, Turgot became one of the founders of comparative universal history, postulating the progress of mankind as proceeding in stages which were much more strongly influenced by cultural elements than by physical ones – a view that contrasted sharply with Montesquieu's.

Turgot and the French pyhsiocrats with their particular view of a political economy necessary for development (Gömmel / Klump 1994) are thus representative of a period of time in the history of economics in which different views of how to analyze the causes of the wealth of nations coexisted peacefully and even supported each other. The beginning of the industrial revolution and the emergence of a dominant English school of economics changed this coexistence enormously. While in England the role that the cultural dimension in the analysis of the wealth of nations played declined steadily, it was given a particularly high importance in the Historical Schools on the continent. Karl Marx was perhaps the last who tried to reconcile both strands in a unique synthesis. With the emergence of neoclassical economics it became more and more difficult to integrate cultural aspects in formal models. It later became the most important achievement of new institutional economics to succeed in bridging this gap of disconnected communication between two very successful branches of economic analysis.

3. The role of culture in modern theories of development

3.1 Culture, economic sociology and new institutional economics

Modern attempts to integrate elements of culture into economic theories follow the paths of their predecessors in one direct and one more indirect way. The direct way, which leads us into modern sociology, points out the "embeddedness" (Granovetter 1985) of all economic actions in a social structure strongly influenced by cultural traditions. Peter Berger's theory of economic culture, his inquiry into the nature of the "capitalist spirit" and his search for a "religious ethic of wealth creation" (Berger 1990) is perhaps the most prominent example of this approach. Berger postulates that "economic institutions do not exist in a vacuum but rather in a context of social and political structures, cultural patterns, and indeed, structures of consciousness (values, ideas, belief systems). An economic culture then contains a number of elements linked together in an empirical totality. The question concerns the manner of the linkage." (Berger 1986, 25)

Berger's concept of economic culture, evidently inspired by Max Weber, laid the theoretical foundations for Gordon Redding's investigation into the "Spirit of Chinese Capitalism" (Redding 1993). This study tries to prove that the common culture of Chinese communities throughout Southeast Asia, in particular in all the miracle economies of the 1980's and early 1990's, contributed significantly to their economic strength The study is based on interviews with Chinese entrepreneurs and managers and reveals the existence of powerful networks spanning over the whole region and establishing a strong basis for trade and investment activities.

The "embeddedness" approach of economic sociology can be criticised for its lack of greater theoretical specification about how the different elements of an economic culture are linked and how they influence economic actions (Smelser / Swedberg 1994). In contrast to this, the indirect way of integrating culture into economics tries to avoid these difficulties by making use of the insights of new institutional economics. Transaction costs, incomplete contracts and agency problems are used as methodological concepts in order to establish culture as a meaningful factor in economic life (Richter / Furubotn 1996). Once the model of perfect competition in a world of perfect information and costless contracting is challenged, there is plenty of room for integrating various aspects of culture in models of economic behaviour. Culture then, is regarded as a social institution, "a regularity in social behaviour that is agreed by all members of society, specifies behaviour in specific recurrent situations and is either self-policed or policed by some external authority." (Myhrman 1989, 49)

It is not clear yet whether new institutional economics should be regarded as rather supplementing or replacing the neoclassical mainstream. However, the new institutionalism opens the door for the consideration of cultural factors with the instruments of economic analysis in a very specific sense, in addition to those instruments which are taken from sociology and other social sciences. Given that Friedrich List had developed an early theory of transaction costs and recognized their significance for the emergence of institutions (Müller 1986) he can be regarded as a direct predecessor of the new institutionalism. This brings, via the concept of transaction costs, the tradition of a more historically oriented economics back into the modern mainstream of the profession.

3.2 Possible operationalizations of culture

Before going into more detail, it is worth noting that the concept of culture includes a multitude of different elements. Attempts to integrate culture in economic models which per se focus on relations between some very specific elements have to make clear what exactly is meant by the term "culture" in this context. From this definition of culture one can then deduce a specification of those cultural factors which influence economic development in one way or the other.

Eric Jones (1995, 281) defines culture as "consisting of learned behaviour reflecting socialization and persisting after the events that gave rise to it". For Ekkehard Schlicht (1993, 182) culture is reflected in "the prevailing set of customs and interpretations." And William O'Mally (1988, 328) refers to the "sharing among a people of values, norms, expectations and interpretations ... that ties individuals together through integrated patterns of behaviour..." Traditionally, religion was considered a central element of culture. Today it still continues to influence social life even though it no longer plays a very active role in most people's daily life, at least compared to the prominent role it played in pre-modern times.

As to elements of culture other than religion, it is somehow difficult to decide what should or should not be included. Several features, however, are common to every definition of culture. First, culture concerns the subjective evaluation of the world and can in this regard be related to specific parameters of preferences, in particular if they are formulated on a collective level. Second, because of its long lasting character, culture has qualities of a capital good with little decay and can therefore be regarded as an additional factor of production. Third, culture manifests itself in collective actions and is typically characterized by strong positive network effects which improve the functioning of social contacts by reducing transaction costs defined in a very broad sense. And finally, we can regard culture as a set of rules in a game theoretic framework.

3.3 Culture as a determinant of preferences

Cultural traditions may be considered to be determinants of a people's work and saving ethics or its collective support and regard for human capital formation. In the context of a neoclassical model of growth this can be translated into culturally determined parameters such as a rate of time preference, a preference for leisure or work, and a particular preference for human capital. From this perspective, every possible parameter of a representative individual's utility function could be, at least partly, influenced by culture. Attention should be directed to those parameters, however, which also play an important role in the explanation of other elements of economic life. This is the case with the rate of time preference which is a major determinant of the real rate of interest (Klump 1995) and is also of great importance for the stability of social arrangements as can be deduced from dynamic games of cooperation.

In addition to the pure rate of time preference culture can influence individual or collective utility functions in other ways. One important way is the existence of particular preferences for social status (Fukuyama 1995) which then is related to other economic variables such as real wealth or real capital. Since through this channel one can construct a direct dependence of utility on capital stock, it is used here to introduce the concept of a Weberian "spirit of capitalism" into a simple neoclassical growth model. Considering a high direct preference for real capital basically leads to the same results as assuming a very low rate of time preference – it reduces current consumption, increases saving and investment and fosters growth. In the particular model by Zou (1994) it is (under very restrictive assumptions) even possible that the "spirit of capitalism" is sufficiently high for an economy to move from steady growth equilibrium on to a continuous growth process.

3.4 Culture as a capital good

Culture as a capital good could be termed "cultural capital" as it was called by Pierre Bourdieu (1983). However, in the new institutionalist literature the term "social capital" (Platteau 1994) is used in this context which in Bourdieu's terminology would be identical with human capital. Social capital was defined by James Coleman (1988, 95) as "the ability of people to work together for common purposes in groups and organisations"; in the institutionalist literature it is more precisely related to trust und reliability in social interactions. As with human capital it is acquired by individuals over a long period of time; but in contrast to human capital it is impossible to replace once acquired.

The modelling of social capital in institutionalist theories of growth and development is very similar to the treatment of human capital. It can be regarded as an additional factor of production that somehow can substitute for real capital inputs and can increase productivity as well as some other measures implemented to advance technological progress (Paldam / Svendsen 2000). The costs of accumulating social capital representative of a particular culture could even be considered to be a kind of tax which is collected for the purpose of financing public goods. This could then also imply that an optimal tax rate and an optimal size of culture exists (Dorner 2000, 206 ff.).

3.5 Culture, transaction costs, and network effects

As an alternative to the treatment of culture as an additional factor of production one could make it a determinant of the level of social transactions costs (Paldam / Svendsen 2000). In the world of new institutional economics a positive level of transaction costs symbolizes the existence of some kind of incomplete contracts. The role of culture would then be to develop mechanisms to overcome long lasting quarrels over the interpretation and enforcement of such contracts. This would lead to a lower level of transaction costs in a particular society and could generate positive growth performance in its economy.

Avner Greif (1993) presented the historical example of the group of Magribi traders for which a system of cultural rules specified the rules of behaviour for every group member. "Culture may substitute for comprehensive contracts by specifying ex ante systematic rules of behaviour. These cultural rules indicate what members of the organization should do after an unforeseen state of affairs occurs. Hierarchy and culture, however, differ substantially. While culture requires ex ante learning of rules but no ex post communication, hierarchy does not require ex ante learning but requires ex post information transmission between the parties." (Greif 1993, 542 f.). Greif's example shows that culture as a non market institution is necessary for a proper functioning of the market and a certain degree of market integration.

Transaction costs in the broader sense can also be regarded as one reason for making culture one determinant of preferences. It has been shown (Cole / Mailath / Postelwaite 1992) that the preference for social status associated with real capital or real wealth can be regarded as a useful device which lowers transaction costs in the process of the allocation of "social" goods which are normally not traded on markets at all. As an example, one can think of the search for marital partners, the successful outcome of which can be increased by status considerations. In the formal model in which different devices of allocating "social" goods are compared, one can derive the same qualitative results as in simple growth models where real capital is considered as an additional determinant of preferences.

The idea that trust and reliability which a culture can provide to a community's members reduce social transaction costs can be further developed to also include the existence of strong network effects. Positive network effects, implying that with a growing number of group members the advantages of membership increase dramatically for every member, should be regarded as one central reason for the strong path-dependency of culture. Indeed, one can typically observe the evolution of culture only over very long intervals of time (Williamson 2000, 596). This long term inflexibility of culture, which is a direct result of its short term network effects, may account for the different evaluations of specific cultures in distinct periods of time. It is normally not culture that changes, but rather the very nature of contract enforcement problems which culture originally helped solve. On the other hand, in a period of successful economic development in which the division of labour proceeds quickly, recourse to a traditional culture may be one relatively easy way of stabilizing social relations. This was widely practiced in the Asian miracle economies.

3.6 Culture and the common rules of games

It is interesting to note that the most recent advances in modern microeconomics which is the victory of a game-theoretic analysis of individual strategic behaviour has also created an innovative approach to incorporate culture into economics. As Bednar / Page (2002) can show, if individual agents have cognitive constraints and face an ensemble of games, the ensemble's composition may influence behaviour in individual games in ways that suggest the emergence of culture. If people living in different climates or followers of different religions or citizens of various political institutions daily face different mixes of strategic situations, they may be led to evolve different practices in common games, hence distinct behavioural cultures.

In the game-theoretic framework cultures depend on the frequency in which agents are confronted with different games. This frequency may depend on a given state of nature or on pure coincidence or on the working of particular institutions. This last set of determinants leaves some room of manoeuvre for economic policy interventions in the process of creating or reshaping a particular cultural behaviour.

The approach by Bednar / Pages is also capable of explaining both stickiness of cultural behavior and cultural path dependency, and even predicts the inevitability of clashes between cultures. Clashes emerge if societies with developed cultures must share access to a new common resource such as a newly opened trade route. Trade creates new strategic interactions between individuals who are embedded in their traditional cultures. In this context it is not clear which strategy will win or whether there can be the emergence of a third, somehow overarching culture. This insight of the model fits very well with the empirical evidence on today's globalized world markets and in competing and evolving cultures.

4. Empirical studies on cultural determinants of economic development

4.1 Religion and growth

Over the last decade, a number of empirical studies in different fields of economics and business administration, making use of various methods of testing, tried to investigate the supposed nature and the actual impact of cultural determinants on economic development. The most simple approach as represented by Dülfer (1997, 325 ff.) still follows Weber's methodology and simply contrasts the dominant religious belief in a country with the same country's per capita income. The results seem to indicate that Protestant countries on average are much more highly developed than Catholic or Islamic countries. However, it is unclear how countries like Israel, Japan or Thailand fit this explanation of economic development.

A contribution to the international management literature by Berger (1994) presented anecdotal evidence concerning the positive influence of some Protestant sects on the economic development of various Latin American countries. This seemed to underline the Weberian conjecture that a deeply rooted work and accumulation ethics is an excellent prerequisite for growth. Anecdotal evidence was also used in most of the studies of the potential relationship between the East Asian growth miracles and the Confucian tradition in the miracles countries. Vogel (1991) coined the expression of an "industrial neo-Confucianism" which supposedly prevailed in the East Asian societies and manifested itself in a powerful and efficient bureaucracy, a high esteem of human capital formation and a strong reliance on network structures.

4.2 Cultural dummies

More sophisticated approaches of testing cultural influences on growth have emerged from the new interest in empirical determinants of growth. Cultural dummies were included in the set of potential variables whose potential contributions to growth were statistically tested in cross-country regressions. Levine and Renelt (1992) investigated the robustness of variables significantly related to economic growth in various empirical studies. They identified only two robust variables as general determinants of growth: the share of investment in GDP and the initial income level, the latter being justified by the neoclassical convergence hypothesis. But surprisingly, regional dummies for countries in Latin America and Sub-Saharan Africa turned out to be statistically robust as well. Romer (1989), Romer (1990) as well as Grier and Tullock (1989) also found statistical significance for regional country dummies.

Using the same testing method Sala-i-Martin (1997) discovered only one really robust variable significantly correlated with growth: the fraction of the population with Confucian religion. Since this variable takes the value zero for most countries with the exception of the East Asian growth miracle economies, "this acts pretty much a dummy for East Asian miracle economies."(Sala-i-Martin 1997, 9) Accepting weaker standards for statistical significance, Sala-i-Martin also found other regional variables supportive to growth, among them absolute latitude, indicating that lying far away from the equator is good for a country's growth potential. Moreover, he confirmed the relevance of religion as a variable, such as e.g. Confucianism, Buddhism and Islam (with a positive growth impact) and Protestantism as well as Catholicism (with a negative growth impact). He pointed out that most of these variables tend to be regional dummies acting as proxies for some other regional phenomenon. The Islam variable for example may be strongly correlated with oil production.

The relevance of cultural variables was also confirmed by studies of economic convergence. De Long (1988) discussed the convergence hypothesis which can be derived from the standard neoclassical growth model and concluded from his regression analyses that samples of countries, adequately grouped according to their ex-ante growth chances, have not converged. "Growth since 1870 is unrelated to income in 1870. There is no convergence. Those countries with income edges have on average maintained them." (De Long 1988, 1145) At the same time he found a significant ex-ante association between growth performance between 1870 and 1979 and the dominant religion in a country. A dummy with the value one for protestant countries, zero for catholic countries and one half for mixed countries is significantly correlated with growth performance. Despite these results, De Long pointed out that the interpretation of the results is somewhat problematic because the Protestantism variable is positively correlated with a variety of phenomena such as early specialization in manufacturing, high investment rates and northern latitude. Therefore economic success cannot be explained by religion alone. But in general he had to accept that the dominant religion is a surprisingly good proxy for a country's social capability to absorb and to adopt modern technology.

For Grier (1997) religion can contribute to explaining the poor growth performance of Latin American countries. Grier conducted a cross-sectional study to analyze whether Protestantism is positively correlated with growth and whether religion can help to explain the poor growth performance of former Spanish compared to former British colonies in Latin America. He also used dummies for the dominant religion. Grier showed that the former Spanish and French colonies – all with Catholic tradition – grew on average at a significantly lower rate than the former British colonies. Moreover he found that the expansion rate of Protestantism was positively correlated with the growth rate of real GDP and the expansion level was positively correlated with the level of per capita income.

4.3 Culture and factors of production

Instead of relating culture and growth directly Leff and Sato (1993) analyzed the influence of cultural variables on saving and investment rates. From a sample of 82 countries they concluded that international differences in saving and investment behaviour could be explained by international heterogeneity of preferences. This implied "...that sociocultural conditions matter for international differences in economic performance." (Leff / Sato 1993, 219) On the other hand, Carroll, Rhee and Rhee (1994) studied the saving and investment behaviour among immigrants to Canada and could not find strong evidence for culturally determined differences. Only investment in human capital was found to be significantly higher for Asian immigrants than for others.

An important study on the interaction between social capital and economic development was presented by La Porta, Lopez-de-Silanes, Shleifer and Vishny (1997). It revealed a statistically significant influence of trust in anonymous transaction partners on the growth of income per capita as well as on some indicators of industrial structure. The authors found that countries with a population reporting a higher degree of general trust have a significantly higher level of wealth and that the market share of big firms is higher. Great regional differences coincided in this respect with religious and cultural borderlines. The study's data base was the 1994 *World Values Survey* for which people from 40 countries had been interviewed. The highest values for general trust in other people were found in the Scandinavian countries whereas a lot of countries with the lowest values of trust were located in South America. The authors concluded that, "in sum, trust enhances economic performance across countries." (LaPorta / Lopez-de-Silanes / Shleifer / Vishny 1997, 336)

In a further analysis in the same study the trust variable was correlated with the proportion of people adherent to a hierarchic religion in a country, in particular Catholicism, the Greek Orthodox Church and Islam. The correlation was found to be strictly negative implying that "hierarchical religion and distrust may both reflect some underlying basic "factor" in a society that is detrimental to the performance of large organizations. This factor may reflect dysfunctional institutions in a society, but if so, this is largely a long-term dysfunctionality associated in part with a hierarchical religion (and not just with recent events). Interestingly, this factor does not reflect the ethnic heterogeneity in a society, which might be viewed as a source of distrust. ... Despite economists´ scepticism, theories of trust hold up remarkably well when tested on a cross section of countries." (LaPorta, Lopez-de-Silanes, Shleifer and Vishny 1997, 337)

The statistical significance of cultural variables for macroeconomic performance has also spurred analyses of the impact of culture on the functioning of specific markets with a particular importance for the process of economic development. The one example deals with stock markets, whereas the second example analyzes the functioning of labour markets. Bakshi and Chen (1996) studied the impact of a particular "spirit of capitalism", a preference for relative status in a society related to relative wealth positions, on the pricing of stocks and bonds. Using various testing methods they found strong evidence to support the claim that "incorporating the spirit of capitalism, or concerns about status, into the investor's preferences improves the ability of the asset-pricing model to explain both stock and bond price movements."(Bakshi / Chen 1996, 153) In sum they conclude that a concern for status makes investors more conservative in risk taking, more frugal in consumption spending and stock prices more volatile.

Yang and Lester (2000) presented an analysis of the determinants of unemployment in OECD countries. The authors introduced two index variables representative for a "national character" into a regression analysis: neuroticism, representing the level of anxiety, and extroversion, measuring the degree of socialization. They found that the index of extroversion is significantly correlated with unemployment. Moreover, when it is introduced into the regression, it changes the set of significant variables so that neuroticism becomes a variable as significant as union coverage. The authors' core conclusion can be summarized by saying that "the greater the nation's index of extraversion (that is, the less well socialized it is), the higher the unemployment rate." (Yang / Lester 2000, 289)

From this overview it can be concluded that significant correlations exist between cultural variables and indicators of economic development. Even if the causality is not always clear, one finds that the inclusion of cultural variable in empirical studies of growth improves the ability of models to predict real world behaviour. One should be cautious to make culture the only or at all events a dominant determinant of growth, but it may contribute through one channel or other to an improved growth effect of the standard variables. "Societies cannot become rich merely by espousing or proclaiming appropriate beliefs but the "right" kind of beliefs will increase that likelihood." (Jones 1995, 280)

5. Conclusions

Culture has been recognized as a potential determinant of economic actions by economic science since its early days. Periods of increased global trade have always been times in which not only new theories of development were proposed, but also in which the economic importance of foreign cultures was extensively studied. The renewed interest in the most recent wave of globalization was characterized by the parallel attempt to use not only different elements of economic sociology but also new institutional economics to establish the links between different cultures and comparative economic performance. As the empirical studies revealed, culture seems to have an economic importance, albeit an indirect one, contributing to an improved performance of the classical growth determinants.

Compared with other possible determinants of growth, culture shares many structural problems with another highly debated variable, money. This, of course, is no coincidence, but rather a sign of the cultural dimensions of money. Culture, like money, is difficult to integrate into modern, and, in particular, into modern neoclassical theories of development. Due to its complex nature, culture can be considered an element of a representative individual's utility function, a capital good serving as an additional factor of production, a positive network externality which reduces transaction costs in social and economic life (Klump 1993) and a system of rules for common games. Like with money, one is easily convinced that culture could have significant effects on economic actions and one is surprised that empirical studies do not find more pronounced evidence of its influence.

It is the European Union where these similarities between culture and money will materialize very visibly in the near future when not only further enlargement of the EU is on the agenda, but also the further enlargement of the European Monetary Union will be discussed. And one can be sure that issues of cultural homogeneity or heterogeneity will become a focal point in both discussions. This will put even more pressure on economists to develop new and better approaches of how to introduce culture into economics.

References

Bakshi, G. S. / Chen, Z. (1996), The spirit of capitalism and stock-market prices, in: American Economic Review, 86, 133-157.

Bednar, J. / Page, S. (2002), Can game(s) theory explain culture?, Updated Working Paper, Unversity of Michigan.

Berger, P. L. (1986), The capitalist revolution, New York.

Berger, P. L. (1990), The capitalist spirit. Toward a religious ethic of wealth creation, San Francisco.

Berger, P. L. (1994), The gross national product and the gods, in: McKinsey Quarterly, 1994/1, 97-110.

Bourdieu, P. (1983), Ökonomisches Kapital, kulturelles Kapital, soziales Kapital, in: Kreckel, R. (Hrsg.), Soziale Ungleichheiten (Soziale Welt, Sonderband 2), Göttingen, 183-198.

Caroll, C. D. / Rhee, B.-K. / Rhee, C. (1994), Are there cultural effects on saving? Some cross-sectional evidence, in: Quarterly Journal of Economics, 59, 685-699.

Cole, H. L. / Mailath, G. J. / Postlewaith, A. (1992), Social norms, savings behavior, and growth, in: Journal of Political Economy, 100, 1092-1125.

Coleman, J. (1988), Social capital in the creation of human capital, in: American Journal of Sociology, Supplement, 95-S120.

De Long, B. (1988), Productivity growth, convergence, and welfare: Comment, in: American Economic Review, 78, 1138-1154.

Dorner, K. (2000), Kultur und Wachstum. Eine institutionenökonomische und wachstumstheoretische Analyse kultureller Einflüsse auf das Wachstum von Volkswirtschaften, Ulm.

Dülfer, E. (1997), Internationales Management in unterschiedlichen Kulturbereichen, 5. Aufl., München / Wien.

Fershtman, C. / Weiss, Y. (1993), Social status, culture and economic performance, in: Economic Journal, 103, 946-959.

Fukuyama, F. (1995), Trust. The social virtues and the creation of property, New York.

Gömmel, R. / Klump, R. (1994), Merkantilisten und Physiokraten in Frankreich, Darmstadt.

Granovetter, M. (1985), Economic action and social structure: the problem of embeddedness, in: American Journal of Sociology, 91, 481-510.

Greif, A. (1993), Contract enforceability and economic institutions in early trade: The Magribi trader's coalition, in: American Economic Review, 83, 525-548.

Greif, A. (1994), Cultural beliefs and the organization of society: A historical and theoretical reflection on collectivist and indivualist societies, in: Journal of Political Economy, 102, 912-950.

Grier, K. (1997), The effect of religion on economic development: A cross national study of 63 former colonies, in: Kyklos, 50, 47-62.

Grier, K. / Tullock, G. (1989), An empirical analysis of cross-national economic growth, 1951-1980, in: Journal of Monetary Economics, 24, 259-276.

Herrmann-Pillath, C. (1994), Endogenes Wachstum, Externalitäten und Evolution: Industriekulturen und gesamtwirtschaftliche Entwicklung im evolutionsökonomischen Paradigma – Eine Einführung, Diskussionsbeiträge des Fachbereichs Wirtschaftswissenschaft der Gerhard Mercator-Universität GH Duisburg, Nr. 213.

Huntington, S. P. (1994), The clash of civilizations?, in Foreign Affairs, 74, 22-49.

Jones, E. L. (1995), Culture and its relationship to economic change, in: Journal of Institutional and Theoretical Economics, 151, 269-285.

Klump, R. (1993), Geld, Währungssytem und optimales Wachstum. Ein Beitrag zur monetären Wachstumstheorie, Tübingen.

Klump, R. (1995), On the institutional determinants of economic development: Lessons from a stochastic neoclassical growth model, in: Jahrbuch für Sozialwissenschaft, 46, 138-151.

Klump, R. (1996), Hrsg., Wirtschaftskultur, Wirtschaftsstil und Wirtschaftsordnung. Methoden und Ergebnisse der Wirtschaftskulturforschung, Marburg.

Klump, R. / Menkhoff, L. (1995), Die Wirtschaftswunder in Ostasien. Eine Suche nach Erklärungen, in: IFO-Studien, 41, 271-287.

La Porta, R. / Lopez-de-Silanes, F. / Shleifer, A. / Vishny, R. W. (1997), Trust in large organizations, in: American Economic Association, Papers and Proceedings, 87, 333-338.

Leff, N. H. / Sato, K. (1993), Homogeneous preferences and heterogeneous growth performance – International differences in saving and investment behavior, in: Kyklos, 46, 203-223.

Levine, R. / Renelt, D. (1992), A sensitivity analysis of cross-country growth regressions, in: American Economic Review, 82, 942-963.

Müller, A. (1986), List als Vorläufer der Transaktionskostenökonomik: Zur jüngst entdeckten Preisschrift von 1837, in: List-Forum, 13, 341-345.

Myhrman, J. (1989), The new institutional economics and the process of economic development, in: Journal of Institutional and Theoretical Economics, 145, 38-59.

O'Malley, W. J. (1988), Culture and industrialization, in Hughes, H. (ed.), Achieving industrialization in East Asia, Cambridge, 327-343.

Osterhammel, J. (1998), Die Entzauberung Asiens. Europa und die asiatischen Reiche im 18. Jahrhundert, München.

Paldam, M. / Svendsen, G. T. (2000), An essay on social capital: Looking for the fire behind the smoke, in: European Journal of Political Economy, 16, 339-366.

Platteau, J.-P. (1994), Behind the market stage where real society exists – Part II: The role of moral norms, in: Journal of Development Studies, 30, 753-817.

Rauscher, M. (1997), Protestant ethic, status seeking, and economic growth, Thünen Series Working Papers, No. 9, University of Rostock.

Redding, G. (1993), The spirit of Chinese capitalism, Berlin / New York.

Richter, R. / Furubotn, E. (1996), Neue Institutionenökonomik, Tübingen .

Romer, P. M. (1989), Human capital and growth: Theory and evidence, NBER Working Paper No. 3173.

Romer, P. M. (1990), Capital, labor, and productivity, in: Brookings Papers on Economic Activity, Special Issue, 337-420.

Schlicht, E. (1993), On custom, in: Journal of Institutional and Theoretical Economics, 149, 178-203.

Smelser, N. / Swedberg, R. (1994), Introduction, in: The Handbook of Economic Sociology, Princeton.

Turgot, A. R. J. (1970), Ecrits économiques, Paris.

Vogel, E. (1991), The four little dragons – The spread of industrialization in East Asia, Cambridge / London.

Williamson, O. E. (2000), The new institutional economics: Taking stock, looking ahead, in: Journal of Economic Literature, 28, 595-613.

Yang, B. / Lester, D. (2000), An exploration of the impact of culture on the economy: An empirical study of unemployment, in: Journal of Socio-Economics, 29, 281-290.

Zakaria, F. (1994), Culture is destiny. A conversation with Lee Kuan Yew, in: Foreign Affairs, 73, 109-126.

Zou, H.-F. (1994), The spirit of capitalism and long-run growth, in: European Journal of Political Economy, 10, 279-293.

Enlargement and the European Monetary System: Foundation or Precondition of a Common European Economic Style[*]

Bertram Schefold

1. Introduction: The problem of European integration

Will the cohesion of the European Union be fostered or endangered by the superimposition of a monetary union on its pre-existing economic and political institutions? This was the question when Euro-land was created. And it continues to be the question when the accession states have to decide whether they should adopt the Euro as their currency earlier or later. According to general agreement, there is no simple answer, since a monetary union creates both cohesive and divisive forces, as we shall see in detail below on the basis of historical precedents and of theoretical reflections.

The problem is that economic integration and the creation of a monetary union mean both a program (we want to unite!) and a variety of mechanisms (in particular a system of free trans-national exchange within a framework of agreed rules). The best concept I know for catching this ambiguity is the one chosen by the organisers of this workshop: that of economic style, for it combines the systemic elements of economic reproduction with people's vision of how it should be done.

I first came across this concept in the late seventies, when proponents of nuclear energy and of 'soft' energies confronted each other in a passionate political debate. It clearly transcended the field of economics of energy: on the one side there were the proponents of continued industrial production in the developed nations of a liberal economic order within a strong national state and the existing form of society, on the other we found the proponents of a shift towards services and less energy-intensive sectors of the economy, of policies to encourage energy saving devices and possibly also towards more agrarian forms of production, towards less commercialised forms of consumption, these proponents being ready to experiment with new social forms.[1]

Spiethoff, the first important progenitor of the concept of economic style, had spoken of five dimensions in which it should be analysed: the economic spirit (this

---

[*] An early draft of this paper was presented at the Institute for Economic Research, Taipeh (Taiwan), September 2004. I am very grateful to my assistant Mr. Alexander Klein, Dipl.-Vw., Dipl.-Pol., for his support in writing the successive versions. I should like to thank the organisers and participants of the HWWA workshop on Economic Styles and Eastern Enlargement of the EU for helpful comments.

[1] Schefold 1981, Schefold 1986.

is the programmatic aspect), the natural and technical conditions (like population or the energy system), the economic constitution (the economic order), the social constitution (like the family structures) and the dynamic of the economy (e.g. mainly driven by successful exports or by domestic consumption).[2] The characteristics of an economy, seen as an economic style, were interdependent: a more entrepreneurial spirit would correspond to a stronger economic dynamic, but neither might flourish except within a liberal order or certain forms of state capitalism etc. Spiethoff has used the concept mainly to interpret historical transformations such as that in the late Middle Ages. The programmatic aspect of the economic style emerges strikingly, if one considers the classical Athenian economy of the 5th and the 4th century BC with its peculiar institutions, in particular the liturgies as a mean to finance the state: the orators (Pericles' oration for the dead, the speeches by Lysias and Demosthenes) and the historians (Herodotus, Thukydides) then appear to differentiate between their view of an Athenian economic style and that of despotic Persia or aristocratic and warrior-like Sparta.

If economies are different as styles, they are probably also different as systems, and vice versa. We were educated to compare the Unites States and the Soviet Union as economic systems in order to focus on efficiency and welfare and in order to abstract from ideology, but when we are dealing today with the prospects of European unification, the real question is whether the rapid imposition of common economic institutions and the growing importance of similarly imposed social reforms are compatible with the inertia and the spontaneity of what Spiethoff called the economic spirit.

The theory of economic styles is discussed in other papers in this volume; for my own account, more directed towards an interpretation of the historical genesis of the concept, see Schefold.[3] Here, it is a matter of applying the concept to the concrete problem of the monetary union in Europe.

The economist who deals with problems of European integration should never forget that the independent nation-states relinquish part of their sovereignty primarily for political, not for economic reasons. The program – not universally popular – was first imposed from above. The foundation for the European Community was laid by France, Germany and Italy as 'large' states, with the Netherlands, Belgium and Luxemburg as smaller ones, in order to overcome a dramatic experience of the two World Wars and to unite Europe against the communist block. It is therefore not surprising that the process of integration was slowed down when the tensions between East and West eased. Integration intensified again to the extent that the former great powers of Europe realised the supremacy of the United States and of the Soviet Union. A new phase of integration has now been reached with the enlargement towards Eastern Europe, while the earlier enlargements can be regarded

---

2   Spiethoff 1932.
3   Schefold 1994, 1994a, 1995, 1995a.

as accomplished facts. Today, the challenges of globalisation provide the main impetus.

Integration is not achieved in one step but sequentially. At times, it is more a matter of solidifying the political, economic and social structures of the Union in its actual composition (the main issue at present being the new Constitution proposed for Europe). At other times, it is again a question of extending the Union and defining new borders. There is a remarkable cultural unity to the European Union in its present state. It can be described best in terms of old religious borderlines: the frontier basically now follows the demarcation between the catholic and protestant West on the one hand, the Eastern orthodox church and the Islamic world on the other (with orthodox Greece and Cyprus perhaps being on the Western side, because of the old ties which developed between Greece and the West, when Greece fought to get free from the Ottoman Empire and when the Romantics, most notably the poet Lord Byron, supported the liberation movement). This looks like a surprising confirmation of Müller-Armack's[4] approach to economic styles, based on Max Weber's sociology of religion. Müller-Armack held that the difference between the church of the East and the Catholicism and Protestantism in the West was at the root of important differences in economic styles.[5]

The origins of the European idea are quite old. Reference is usually made to the Roman Empire and Augustus, to the Carolingian Empire and Charles the Great, to the Holy Empire and Charles V. The Habsburg Empire remained trans-national, while colonialism and imperialism followed national ideas. Churchill, who identified with the traditions of the British Empire, gave on 19 September 1946 the most important single stimulus to European unification in a speech in Zurich where he proposed a partnership between France and Germany.[6] Economic integration became the instrument of this political goal. It started with the European Coal and Steel Community (ECSC) of 1950 which lead to the Treaty of Paris in 1951. At a time when heavy industry still dominated economic development, the idea was to introduce a joint control in both countries, thus helping to prevent a new arms race between the participating states. A Council of Ministers was to link the national governments and the High Authority in charge of investment and competition policies. Italy and the BENELUX-countries were part of the ECSC, but European defence was based on other organisations (NATO and WEU).

The next step then consisted in the inclusion of other economic sectors. The European Economic Community (EEC) was founded in 1957 in Rome; it called for a co-ordination of economic policies, the elimination of customs duties, freedom of movement not only for goods, but also for persons, a common policy in agriculture and transport, and it created a commission which was to implement decisions taken

---

4   Müller-Armack 1941.
5   Schefold 1999a.
6   Schefold 2000, 13-38.

by the Council of Ministers, in consultation with the European Parliament, and subject to a control by the Court of Justice.

This concept of integration prevailed over other attempts to promote Europe as a free trade area. The ECSC, the EEC and EURATOM were joined in the European Community (EC) in 1967. Many events took place affecting the integration process during the next thirty years, for instance the downfall of the Bretton-Woods-System, German reunification combined with the end of the Eastern Bloc, Maastricht Treaty. Nevertheless, the process of integration proceeded in the second half of the 20th century without conquest, civil war or violence. It was and is based on the use of economic mechanisms to create cohesion, but there have also been direct processes of political, and to a lesser extent, of social integration. Schuman, one of the founders of the European movement, wondered towards the end of his life whether it would not have been better to start with cultural unification. One must speak of an original primacy of political ideas in so far as the visions of the founders revolved around ideas of a European federation or a European federalist state, and they then discovered how economic integration might serve as an instrument.[7]

The institution of the European Central Bank was created during the second stage of the European Monetary Union, the first having resulted in the Maastricht Treaty. It began with the establishment of the European Monetary Institute (EMI) which helped to strengthen Central Bank co-operation and to prepare for the establishment of the European System of Central Banks (ESCB). The single currency came into the existence on 1 January 1999; the exchange rates of the currencies of the 11 Member States initially participating in the Monetary Union had been agreed upon and were now maintained by a central authority. This entailed the conduct of a single monetary policy under the responsibility of the European Central Bank. The Bank of Greece joined the system on 1 January 2001. The transition to a tangible single currency, the Euro, with the issue of coins and notes, was a subsequent step of tremendous symbolic value, but the Euro really had been created by the previous fixing of the exchange rates.[8]

At present, one must distinguish between Euro-land (the members of the European Union who have adopted the Euro as a single currency) and the European Union of now 25 states. The 10 accession states are committed to adopt the Euro. They do not have the freedom to be members of the Union and to retain an own currency such as have, at present, Great Britain, Denmark and Sweden. The only questions are how they will make the transition and when they will join (whereas Great Britain and Denmark, but not Sweden, could in principle stay outside Euro-land indefi-

---

[7] As an example, we may mention Luigi Einaudi whose early ideas seem to have anticipated the later logic in the sequence of events; cf. Sarcinelli 2004.
[8] European Central Bank 2004a.

nitely).[9] The European Central Bank therefore has two governing bodies. The General Council, comprising the President and Vice-President of the European Central Bank plus the governors of the National Central Banks of the 25 Member States of the EU, may be regarded as a transitional institution, carrying out tasks taken over from the European Monetary Institute in preparation of the extension of the Euroland. The Governing Council of the European Central Bank, by contrast, consists of the 6 members of the Executive Board and of the governors of all the National Central Banks from the 12 Euro-area countries. The Governing Council adopts the guidelines and takes the decisions necessary to ensure the performance of the tasks entrusted to the Euro-system and formulates the monetary policy for the Euro-area. It usually meets twice a month at the Eurotower in Frankfurt am Main.

The Euro is now as old as a schoolchild. Inflation has been kept under control and the tensions arising from differences in growth rates and inflation rates in different countries and regions so far have proved tolerable. The introduction of the common currency proceeded swiftly and without incidents. The Euro has become a leading financial currency, second only to the Dollar. To this extent, the Euro is a great success. But will it last or will the tensions due to different inflation rates increase? Integration is a political goal in itself, it certainly helps to promote internal free trade in goods and services, and monetary integration adds an important symbolic dimension. It contributes directly by facilitating transactions and increasing homogeneity, but the loss of the autonomy of national monetary policies implies the loss of the most direct instrument to fight inflationary tendencies and also of an important tool to steer the process of accumulation through changes of the interest rate. Some argue that the preservation of monetary autonomy has helped the United Kingdom to show a better economic performance than the large European countries within Euro-land.

I wish to discuss historical precedents, certain key facts and theoretical arguments in order to assess the chances of the Euro to survive in the long run. If one likes, it is the question, whether there exists a European economic style into which the Euro might fit.

2. Historical precedents

The European Monetary Union seemed a novel and unconventional idea, but the first monetary unions were created thousands of years ago. We know that in the 6th century BC, less than 200 years after the introduction of coinage, Greek cities found it convenient to share their mints, for to create a mint was expensive for the small

---

[9] The United Kingdom and Denmark are not obliged to replace their national currencies with the Euro but Denmark keeps the Danish krone within narrow bands in the EMU's transitional exchange rate mechanism ERM2, while Sweden is, like the accession countries, committed sooner or later to adopt the Euro.

Greek city states, and it was also expensive to maintain a metallic currency in circulation, since seigniorage did not automatically suffice to cover the cost of worn-out old coins. The existence of such unions can be inferred from the names of the cities inscribed on the coins. In other cases, the similarity of coins originating from different cities indicates at least some form of monetary cooperation. The most famous monetary union existed between the cities of Asia Minor around 500 BC, presumably connected with the attempt on the part of those cities to emancipate themselves from Persia. In another, later case the treaty leading to the establishment of a monetary union has been preserved (between Phocaea and Mytilene). The Romans unified coinage in their time. Unions between private traders emitting knife-money seem to have existed in old China.[10]

More direct precedents were found in the 19th century, national and multinational ones. A national, with a complicated history, was the monetary union of the United States where a central bank with a lender of last resort function was established only in the 20th century, and national were also the monetary unions of Italy and Germany which were each closely connected with nation building, with central banks being created some time after national unification (1893 in Italy and 1875 in Germany). While the details are involved, the basic conclusion seems clear: Monetary unions serve on a path of transition from the creation of the national state to the introduction of a unified currency.

But there have also been trans-national monetary unions, between states, which clearly had no intention to amalgamate.[11] The Latin Monetary Union between France, Belgium, Switzerland and Italy was established in 1865. It originated because these nations had used their coins mutually even earlier on an informal basis. The Union then set standards for the coins according to the principles of a bimetallic standard. The Union experienced various difficulties because of different economic conditions in the different countries, but it functioned up to the First World War. These monetary or rather currency unions were occasionally remembered as possible models for the European Community, when the process of integration had slowed down. When Edgar Salin had his last conference of the List Society organised, in 1972, after the break-down of the Bretton-Woods system, he returned to such a suggestion, and a Federal Trust Report, discussed at the conference, made a case for creating a European Bank and a new international monetary unit, the Europa.[12]

It is a fascinating aspect of monetary economics that distant historical parallels can be illuminating as in hardly any other field of our discipline. I should like to add another earlier example based on own research in the history of economic ideas. Saxony was a major producer of silver in Europe in the late Middle Ages, and the

---

10 Burns 1927 [1965].
11 Bordo and Jonung 1999.
12 Schefold 1972.

silver coins minted there circulated widely.[13] The Dukedom of Saxony was divided around 1485 for dynastic reasons; one part was ruled by the dynasty of the Albertines, the other by the dynasty of the Ernestines. Successive heirs of the two dynasties decided not to divide the silver mines, however, but to exploit them jointly and to share the proceeds from selling silver and from minting. They thus formed a Monetary Union of the two Saxonies. Their policy had been, down to 1525, to maintain a stable currency. In that year the Albertine ruler was Duke George (Georg) and the Ernestine duke was John (Johann der Beständige). The latter was an ardent Protestant, a friend and admirer of Luther, while Duke George had remained catholic. Both met in the city of Zeitz in 1526 in order to discuss the proposal of Duke John to debase. Since they could not agree after apparently heated discussions, Duke John began to mint his own coins with a lesser silver content; to reach this form of independence, the two dukes now partitioned the silver, not the proceeds from minting. This led to a public discussion of the move in printed anonymous pamphlets. The first appeared in 1531 and defended the point of view of the Catholic Albertine Duke George, the second in the same year was longer and expressed the less orthodox ideas of Duke John; a rejoinder by the Albertine came a little later. Again a few years later, the Monetary Union was at least temporarily tried again on the basis of a silver content of the coins which represented a compromise.

We are here not interested in the historical detail, but in the arguments put forward by the anonymous pamphleteers which are of extraordinary interest because they contain perhaps the earliest expressions of mercantilist ideas, written in the plain, simple and colourful language of the German of the Reformation, prior to the formation of all formal economic concepts and embedded in the religious ideas of the times.[14] And yet there appears a surprising understanding of economic interest and economic logic. It is hard to say whether practitioners had had a similar understanding earlier, so that the novelty now consisted in the form of publication, or whether both the ideas and their appearance in print were new.

The Albertine begins with God's creation of a social order which leads to prosperity, even for the poor, as can be seen by looking at the improvements of buildings – this is how he perceives economic growth. The coinage of good money is a precondition of this order – hence the necessity of great expenses on the mines – and the mines generate employment, employment allows to sell more, population increases which in turn leads to an extension of cultivation and of handicraft. The Albertine admits that part of the good coins minted by his duke are exported – insofar, one might say that he knows what we call Gresham's law: the traders recognise the good coins, carry them away to places where they fetch more, but this trade benefits the country. The debasement would lead to higher prices. The inflation of the 16th century is observed by both pamphleteers, but both regard it as domestic and do not

---

13   The Denomination "Dollar" is derived from the German "Taler", this was derived from "Joachimsthaler", and this in turn was derived from the name of the city Joachimsthal, in the Erzgebirge, close to Saxony, in the region where the silver coins originated.
14   Vgl. Schefold 2000a.

connect it with the discovery of the New World although there is much talk of colonies; we are in 1531 only at the beginning of that inflow, and there is agreement among economic historians that a great inflation began prior to the discovery of the New World and was therefore fuelled, but not initially caused, by its consequences.

The Albertine believes that the value of the coins is estimated according to their metal content. To mint good coins is to preserve good economic order in the country, to export the silver and therefore to give employment to traders. A debased coin would lead to rising prices at home. He realises that a seigniorage associated with the debasement is equivalent to a form of taxation, but he fears the distributive implications, he believes that the debasement would have to be repeated because of anticipations of the price rise, and the incomes derived from the coins brought abroad would disappear.

The Ernestine advocates debasement, yet he is aware of the danger of inflation and recommends to avoid "excessive minting" ("Übermünzung"). He cannot deny that the debasement is meant to increase the seigniorage (it may be added that Duke John spent much on the Protestant movement), but he advances some other motives as well. The debasement would allow to keep the coined silver in the country. It would also mean a devaluation of the currency and it would render domestic goods cheaper for foreigners. It is not easy for the Ernestine to express these complicated relationships in plain language – not only because he must argue without having modern concepts at his disposal, but also because there are contradictions between his economic logic and his valuations. His intention is in fact not to promote the export of goods other than silver, but rather to restrict the import of luxury goods. He here speaks as a Lutheran Protestant to whom foreign luxury goods are evil.

If this attitude seems backward, he is on the contrary very advanced in his interpretation of the economic motives of the great trading nations like England, Venice and France who wish to sell their colonial wares and their domestic products in Saxony in order to get hold of the Saxon silver. The Ernestine here formulates the mercantilist policy of acquiring the precious metals as means of circulation through a favourable balance of trade in a critical perspective, before the English mercantilists like Thomas Mun put it down in writing as a laudable conception. The Ernestine in effect denounces the one-sided development of Saxony as a silver producer for export. But he does not draw the conclusion that Saxony should diversify its production for export and foster domestic growth on that basis. Rather, he seems to be in favour of a modest and autarchic development, and, to achieve it, he advocates controls like the prohibition of luxury imports. He regards debasement as a more subtle mean to render such imports difficult.

The Albertine, in his second pamphlet, then is able to point out the inconsistencies and shortcomings of the analysis of the Ernestine, and later interpreters have praised him for the clarity of his advocacy of a stable currency. However, the pamphlet of the Ernestine, with its mercantilist and Keynesian and interventionist trends, contains the germs of conceptions which later played important roles, and it is also an early expression of the cameralist attitude to promote small principalities by means of administrative measures, balancing the interests of the local ruler and the lower population engaged in agriculture and handicraft.

The example deserves to be discussed here at some length because it illustrates beautifully how a disagreement about a seemingly isolated point of monetary policy may in fact be connected with different views about economic policy, which in turn result from different ideas about the functioning of the economy and from different valuations of different patterns of development. The "liberalism" of the Albertine and the "cameralism" of the Ernestine are connected with their religious confessions, hence the passionate character of their writings. One might say that they agree on certain traits of the economic style of Saxony but differ in the programs (which, as each claims, correspond to the mentality of the populace) as to how the style should and could be developed. If the disagreement had only concerned technical measures, they might have found a satisfactory common solution. But the adoption of the Reformation by the followers of Duke John, the reaction against it by the followers of Duke George had inspired them with different visions of the Good Life and of the right economic means to support it. The combination of the difference of spirit and of economic goals was the dynamite which let the currency union explode.

When the members of the European Union had to decide whether they wanted to join the Monetary Union, their visions of how they should continue their national paths of economic development likewise played a decisive role, with modifications, of course, according to the political parties which were able to exert a relevant influence in each case. Nearly a decade after the creation of the ECB, the discussion has become more technical and the advantages of a unified currency are weighed more soberly against the disadvantages by comparing what can be achieved with the instrument of a unified currency in a large union with what monetary authorities can do in small countries. To retrace the agitated discussions of the 90s, it suffices to look at one of the books which helped to prepare the decisions for a broad public; now there are textbooks on how the Monetary Union actually works, based on new theories and recent experience, and many research institutions have contributed to the analysis. We shall discuss each approach in turn.[15]

3. Cohesive and disruptive forces of integration: the general perspective

Whenever I return to a European country which I last visited when I was young, I am impressed by three associated changes. The first concerns modern consumer goods and equipment. When I accompanied my parents to Southern Italy or Greece 45 years ago, rural life was simple, donkeys being used everywhere, and the cities were poor, while Switzerland, where I had been growing up, was economically ad-

---

15 The two kinds of publication may be represented by Pitchford / Cox (eds) 1997 and Grauwe 2003.

vanced and Germany was catching up fast. These differences have narrowed considerably and been reversed in some cases. It was very useful in those days to know a few words of modern Greek in order to find one's way. Today, if one does not speak the national language with some fluency, almost all communication switches to English quickly. But what is most impressive now is so suddenly to be able to use the Euro, therefore to have only one wallet, not one for each currency, and prices of shirts and lunches abroad can be compared with those at home without mental acrobatics. The first change may sometimes be regretted by a tourist who misses old traditions and sees picturesque landscapes industrialised. The second also sometimes generates misgivings: Why English? Is it not a pity that we do not try to learn more about a country by learning also the national language? The third transformation, however, simply is innocent progress insofar as it is a convenience to use everywhere the same means of payment and measure of value. At the same time, this experience infuses a sense of communality across Europe which seems entirely compatible with a certain degree of regional cultural diversity.

Indeed, in the past, "money may have played a role in the formation of an imagined community and the consolidation of the nation state".[16] The Euro was introduced first as an imaginary unit of account when the national moneys of the nation states in Euro-land began to keep exchange rates fixed on 1 January 1999 under the supervision of a central authority, but the tangible Euro today has been created to enhance this feeling of community. Since antiquity, coins have two sides: one with an economic denomination like a figure for a number of Euros today or the owl which became a sign for the Drachma in ancient Athens, and another side for a possible religious symbol of the state, some sacred or earthly authority, like the goddess Athena or a Roman emperor. The Euro, however, being the currency of a Monetary Union, is curiously mixed. One side of the coin is national. The Italians have used it for symbols of their magnificent cultural achievements, showing e.g. the head of the poet Dante, the Germans have preserved e.g. the oak leaf, the symbol of the holy Germanic tree. The side with the economic symbol of e.g. 20 Cent therefore must also carry the symbol of European identity: a stylised map of Europe. The Euro-Notes leave no room for national symbols; they show European maps and architecture.

Money as a symbol of trust also creates trust, if it is well managed. At this level, the general feeling is that the European identity has in fact been better established in the minds of people.

But let us now look at the doubts voiced prior to the introduction of Euro. The Germans thought the French wanted to stimulate their economy by means of deficit spending, to avoid harsh measures to limit the rise of money wages, to undervalue the currency in order to promote exports, and they suspected them of being prepared to tolerate inflation in order to achieve those ends. The French government had accepted the principle of the independence of the European Central Bank which was to

16   Kaelberer 2004.

be created, but a fairly general French desire remained to keep the option of a political intervention in monetary policy. And an interventionist policy seemed not only to be in the national interest: it was defended as one of the instruments needed to regain the influence one thought was due to Europe. The German wish to aim at stable prices independently of other considerations was regarded as retrograde in this perspective – an attempt to mimic the gold standard.[17]

The French position was therefore similar to that of Keynes who had analysed the causes and the devastating effects of the great inflations of the early 20th century but who was more relaxed with regard to moderate inflations which might reduce the weight of the public debt and hence increase the possibilities of action of the government by helping to reduce real interest rates and hence to stimulate investment. On the other hand, the same Keynes had toyed with the idea that money wages could be kept fixed and productivity increases would be passed on through *falling* prices. The logic of such an arrangement is discussed in the General Theory, but, in the end, Keynes regarded deflation as worse than inflation and thought that the rigidity of money wages was a good thing. For it prevented a deflationary spiral in which investors would be completely discouraged because the prices at which the investors had hoped to sell their products would fall – possibly below the costs of production already incurred. Real balance effects – of which Keynes was aware – seemed less relevant. Keynes was therefore happy to see that the fetters of the old gold standard were being shaken off and that there was now more freedom for economic policy. The position of the French was Keynesian in this sense.

But the Germans after unification were not orthodox either. Using various words to cover up their policy, they were pursuing something like an extremist Keynesian program insofar as their transfers to East Germany were so massive that every single East German could have lived on welfare payments, had the transfers been used in total for that purpose. The first phase of unification therefore was characterised by a boom which was terminated by a rise of higher interest rates, caused partly by the conditions in international capital markets, partly by the policy of the Bundesbank when rising demand, production and employment had led to excessive wage claims. The Treaty of Maastricht was necessary to limit the tendency of these Keynesian measures to expand - not, of course, because one was against growth, but because of the fiscal consequences. The limits favoured by German politicians to prevent France, Italy and later the accession countries from following Keynesian policies leading to unsustainable deficit spending must now be applied to Germany whose industry and services have been less quick to use the opportunities created by the New Economy so that growth is slow and revenues are inadequate to cover necessary expenditure on social services – they therefore have to be curtailed. Some argue that unification was not a dead-weight on the West German economy but stimulated it, because the boom induced by unification could have been made to last

---

17 I described the discussion of the beginning of the 90s in retrospect with more details in: Schefold 1999. Padoa-Schioppa 2000 [1994].

if monetary policy had not dampened it, with rising interest rates as a cost contributing to the rise of prices. In my opinion, this argument underestimates the pressures of wages which arose at that time, forcing the Bank to act. But it is true in any case that the growth potential was not realised, with consequences that cannot easily be reversed.[18]

Maastricht criteria require to limit the deficit to 3% of the gross domestic product, while the debt ratio shall not rise above 60% of the gross domestic product; these two rates are sustainable indefinitely according to Domar's theory, if the nominal growth rate is always greater or equal to 5%, for $3\% = 5\% \cdot 60\%$. Germany and France have been in conflict with these limits for several years. The European Commission therefore initiated procedures against Germany in November 2002 and against France in April 2003, and the European Court has decided against the Council of the Ministers of Finance of the EU (Ecofin) that Ecofin had no right to prevent the commission from imposing sanctions. As a matter of fact, the debt ratio in Euroland as a whole is well beyond 60% which implies that the limit on deficit spending should be lowered, e.g. from 3% to 2.5%. But Germany and France still hope to be spared the sanctions. Nobody denies that there is arbitrariness in the limits imposed; the point is to have some, to try harder to achieve more growth and then to reduce the debt ratio. The European Central Bank admits that fiscal consolidation reduces government demand but argues that fiscal consolidation in a framework of credible long-term structural expenditure reforms will lead to an increase of confidence and support growth.[19]

The main immediate consequence of the introduction of the Euro has been the creation of a common European capital market. Interest rates on long-term treasury bills in Italy or Spain were still five to six percentage points above the level of German interest rates even in 1995, because of high-risk premia, and intermediate conditions reigned in other countries. This means that firms in the peripheral countries can now raise credit at rates similar to those which had earlier been accessible only to firms operating in Germany, Austria or the Netherlands. Germany thus has lost a comparative advantage, which may help to explain the slowness of growth in the largest nation state within the European Union.

---

18 See for instance: Bibow 2003.
19 Issing 2004b.

Convergence of Long-Term Interest Rates

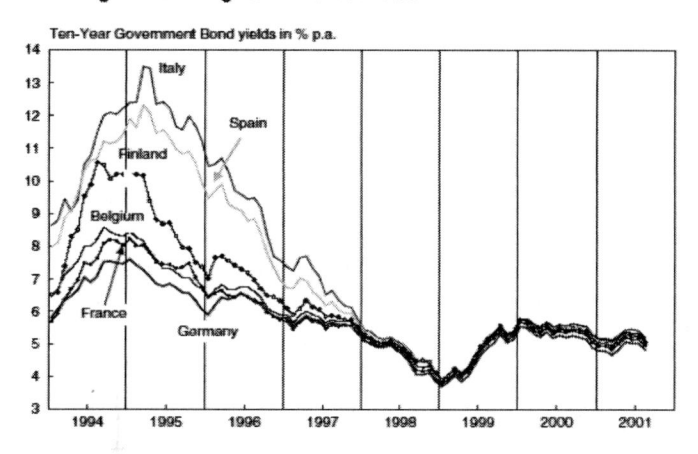

Source: Sinn 2004, 25.

The convergence of interest rates intensifies competition among national governments to provide attractive locations for investors. The Germans have tried since 1987 to tax interest income. When, in the first attempt, a source tax on interest income was imposed in autumn 1987, considerable amounts of capital were exported and Germany was forced to rescind the law only four months after its introduction. After other attempts, the taxation of interest now is to be based on European agreements, but there remain safe havens outside the Union. There is a similar competition to reduce corporation income tax, with Ireland being a forerunner with a corporation income tax rate of only 10% for an increasing number of sectors. Since capital is more mobile than labour, taxation shifts to wages; there is a growing share of taxes on labour in the OECD, as the following chart shows.

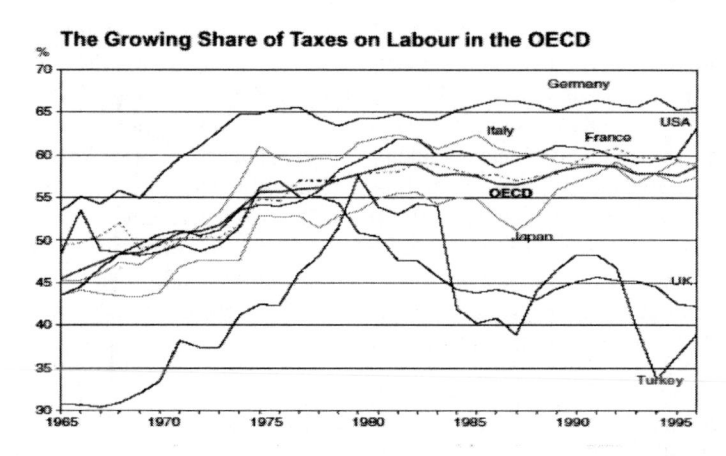

The Growing Share of Taxes on Labour in the OECD

Source: Sinn 2004, 27

Migration will increase with integration; countries which traditionally were relatively homogenous become immigration countries, and the countries of Western Europe try to be less attractive to immigrants which will be net recipients of government benefits by scrutinising their social welfare systems. At present, immigrants in Germany are net recipients of government benefits during their first ten years of residence, insofar as each of them receives on average about 2.300 Euros more in terms of public goods and transfers per year than he or she pays in taxes and fees.[20] The welfare state must be adapted but – even from a merely utilitarian point of view – not beyond limits where misery becomes a danger for social cohesion. Similar considerations apply to the provision of infrastructure and to regulation in sectors such as banking where there is a trade-off between the growth-inducing effects of liberal arrangements and the safety of tighter supervision.

The imposition of fiscal discipline, the loss of the interest advantage, the induced shift in taxation and the pressure of migration have mainly hit the core countries of the EU, where people are ready to accept a burden for the sake of unification, even if accompanying advantages are not so readily perceived. While the European Monetary Union is as such directly concerned with intensifying competition only in special cases like the regulation of banking, the common currency facilitates comparisons in many areas and helps to increase the mobility of factors. The historian of economic thought is reminded of the discussions of the cameralists, at the time when Germany was still divided into hundreds of small principalities in the 17th and 18th centuries, each trying to procure locational advantages by following ideas which are still being pursued. But we now turn to the macroeconomic problems in the European Union and their analysis in terms of some simple models.

4. Cohesive and disruptive forces in the monetary union: macroeconomic analysis

We begin with a classic consideration taken from the theory of optimum currency areas.[21] Suppose there is full employment in countries A and B which are joined in a currency union, and suppose that demand shifts to some extent from the goods of country A to the goods of country B. If labour and capital are not mobile to follow the demand shift, an inflationary tendency develops in country B which might be controlled by means of monetary policies, if the countries still had independent monetary authorities, accompanied by a rise of the exchange rate, but these instruments are not available so that only the flexibility of wage rates remains for an adjustment to take place: If wages are lowered in country A and raised in B, with corresponding movements of product prices, demand for the goods of country A will again increase relatively to that for the goods of country B. Hence the current insis-

---

20 Sinn 2004.
21 Pitchford and Cox (eds) 1997.

tence on more flexibility of wage rates, given a certain factor immobility in the core countries of Europe.

Asymmetric shocks of this kind can also be corrected by means of transfers. Very considerable national transfer systems exist, Germany being a prime example, and the European Union is engaged in different schemes of redistribution, but the differences of income levels in Western and Eastern Europe are too large to be corrected merely by such means. Differences in the inclinations of countries to permit inflation, differences in labour market institutions and legal systems also are reasons not to create a monetary union according to the optimum currency area theory. Seigniorage as a percentage of GNP was of the order of magnitude of half a percent in Germany prior to unification and as large as 3 % to 4% in the 1980s in some Southern European countries.[22] This revenue is equalised in the Monetary Union.

Growth rates continue to differ considerably within Euro-land. It may then be a problem that faster growing countries and regions will experience a slower growth of their exports to the slow growing regions with a common currency, while a lowering of the exchange rate might help with sticky prices, as long as national currencies remain. Similarly, the imports of the faster growing countries will grow faster in line with their faster growing incomes. This effect again can be corrected by an exchange rate mechanism, as long as it is in place, or else prices and wage rates must be sufficiently flexible.

Average yearly growth rates of GDP in the EU, 1981 – 2001

Country	%
Austria	2.30
Belgium	2.05
Denmark	1.94
Finland	2.55
France	2.12
Germany	1.99
Greece	1.60
Ireland	5.36
Italy	1.92
Luxembourg	4.66
Netherlands	2.55
Portugal	2.98
Spain	2.72
Sweden	1.99
United Kingdom	2.48

Source: EU Commission, European Economy, various years

22 Grauwe 2003, 21.

The defenders of Monetary Union have various answers to the optimum currency area theorists. It may be pointed out that asymmetric demand shocks are not frequent and likely, because goods and services of key sectors are being produced and supplied in several countries – car production, for instance. The trend to regional concentration may be smaller in the service sector which is now the largest in advanced economies. Differences in the behaviour of trade unions may be reduced in the face of a common monetary policy, and governments have other instruments to compensate for different wage setting behaviours in different countries, apart from monetary policy. Capital markets are clearly becoming more similar in that the structures of long-term and short-term indebtedness of governments and large private borrowers become more similar. The argument that different growth rates might create trade imbalances is not of crucial importance either. First of all, if the exports of faster growing regions grow less than their imports, growth rates overall tend to get equalised, which is good from the point of view of the union. But the outcome does not necessarily follow, to the extent that faster growth is based on greater diversification, and income elasticities for production of the new goods produced by the more innovative regions may be higher than the income elasticities for the imports of those regions, so that their advantages in their growth potential may be preserved, as Krugman has emphasised.[23]

There basically remains the question of the effectiveness of monetary policies to stimulate demand and employment. According to monetarist analysis, these policies are of no avail in the long run, since Phillip's curves eventually are vertical. The natural rate of unemployment is given so that independent monetary policies only change the rates of wage increases and of inflation. To form a monetary union then is no disadvantage. The costs of forming a monetary union in terms of employment-creating policies that must be missed is low because such policies operate only in the short run.

I doubt this monetarist analysis: The short-term losses in terms of employment and demand may be transformed into long-term losses because opportunities to innovate are lost, the skills of the labour force may suffer and the trend of the growth of effective demand may be permanently lower than if moderate and intelligent demand management helps to overcome slumps with their hysteresis-effects. But monetary policy is only one instrument to achieve this goal, and the opportunities created by a unified market may be more important than the maintenance of this particular tool for national economies.

The discussion recently has focussed on the Balassa-Samuelson-effect, in relation to the accession countries. Unlike the United Kingdom and Denmark, the accession countries cannot opt out of the European Monetary Union, as we saw above. They are therefore granted a transitional period in which they are supposed to fulfil criteria for convergence on sustainable growth paths. Any succession country has to fulfil the requirement of the Maastricht Treaty, regarding fiscal deficits, and its rate

---

23   Krugman 1989.

of inflation must not exceed the average rate of inflation of the three most stable states in the European Union by more than 1.5% in the year preceding the check of whether it qualifies. Similarly, their rates of interest should not exceed the rates of interest of the three most stable countries by more than 2%, and their exchange rates must have stayed within a band of 15% within the exchange rate mechanism of the European Monetary Union. This condition seems more generous in that the band allows a fluctuation of plus or minus 15% within the last 2 years. Different policies to achieve such convergence may be pursued to which we shall return.

But here the Balassa-Samuelson-effect comes in: The prices of non-tradable goods (mainly services) differ between countries. These prices are generally higher in more advanced countries because they enjoy a higher productivity in the sector of tradable goods (mainly industrial goods). They therefore have a higher level of real wages in the sector of tradable goods which leads to similarly higher levels of wages in the sector of non-tradable goods (if their labour markets are integrated). The relatively backward countries will enjoy a rapid growth of productivity and hence of wages in their sectors of tradable goods, but the prices of tradable goods will follow world market trends. Hence prices of tradable goods will not decline with productivity in the countries catching up so that there will be room for more than average increases in wage costs in the industrial sector, hence correspondingly higher increases of prices in the service sector. Higher rates of inflation in those countries therefore seem unavoidable; the relatively high rate of inflation of Ireland in the decade around 1990 has thus been explained; productivity there grew in the sector of tradables by 6%, in the sector of non-tradables by a little less than 2%. The exact difference was measured as 4.23%, while the same difference in Germany was only 0.34%.[24]

The German Bundesbank has concluded that, as a consequence of this Balassa-Samuelson-effect, the rate of inflation of the accession countries will be higher by 2 - 2.5% than that of the core countries, and still stronger differences in rates of inflation are to be expected because of the necessary liberalisation of administrated prices as remnants of the socialist past. Some have argued that too early an accession to the European Monetary Union would thus be a disadvantage for the accession countries themselves. For the Balassa-Samuelson-effect would contribute to overall inflation in the Euro-area but, as far as the core countries are concerned, this is not really to be feared because of the low weight of the accession countries in the Union as a whole. However, early accession and even the preparation of accession by means of the maintenance of stable exchange rates may create permanent competitive disadvantages for the accession countries themselves. If it is a reasonable policy to maintain a rate of inflation of 2% in the core countries of the Monetary Union, this may not be so for the periphery.

Especially German authors therefore have feared that pressures to relax the strong inflation criterion of the European Central Bank would arise in consequence

---

24 Ruckriegel and Seitz 2003.

of the accession of the new members, and there has been considerable debate about the voting rules to be adopted in the governing council of the ECB. Others have doubted the importance of the Balassa-Samuelson-effect, since it may be counterbalanced by more centralised wage bargaining and since the main assumption of the argument in its application to the accession countries is doubtful: the tradable goods produced by the accession countries may not have the same quality as the tradable goods in the world market. Moreover, empirical investigations have not found large inflation differentials in the accession countries which could confidently be ascribed to the Balassa-Samuelson-effect.[25]

The overall conclusion is that the criticism of optimum currency area theory of the conception of a large Monetary Union cannot be entirely dismissed. Its success will depend on the efficiency of accompanying policies to create more homogeneous market conditions and homogeneous economic policies of governments. This implies that national governments will have to cede still more of their power to supranational European authorities and, since a European monster State is undesirable, also to local and regional bodies in order to decentralise where that is feasible. But whether this will happen is not clear: The identification of the citizen with the national State will be stronger in a Union composed of more nations.

These long-run worries contrast with undeniable short-term success, especially in the monetary area. The rate of inflation in the European Monetary Union has stayed close to the target of an inflation rate just below 2%.

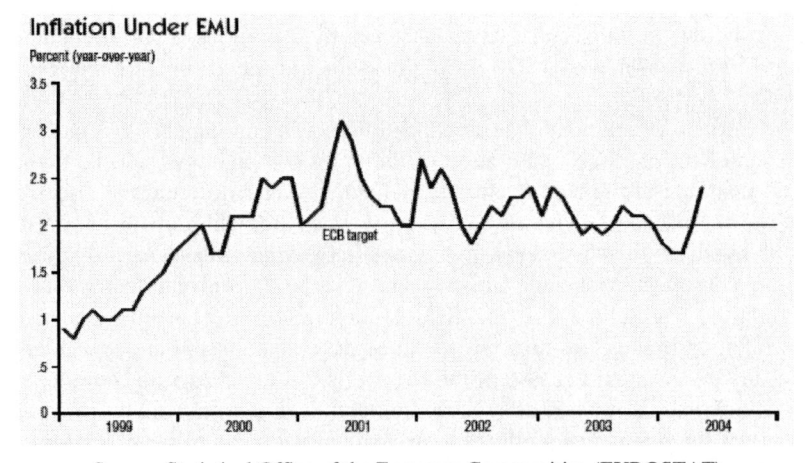

Inflation Under EMU

Source: Statistical Office of the European Communities (EUROSTAT)

Growth was lower than in the US, but the lagging-behind of the Euro-area as a whole could still turn out to have been only cyclical.

---

25   Lommatzsch and Tober 2002.

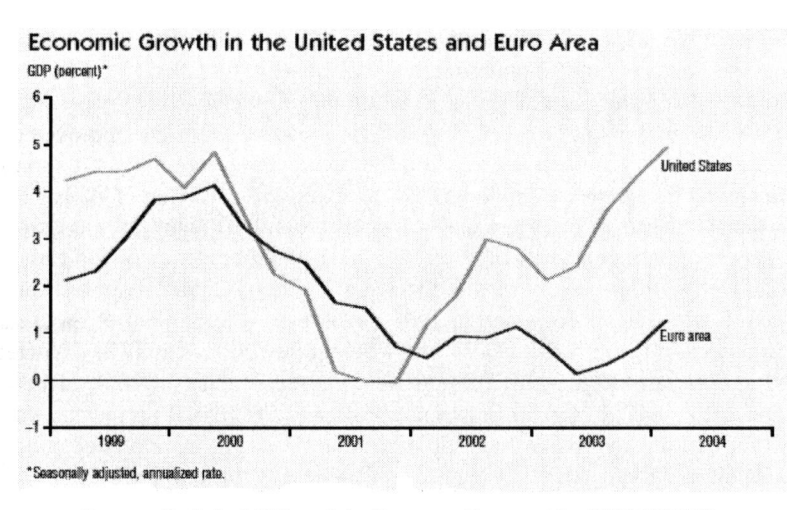

Economic Growth in the United States and Euro Area

Sources: Statistical Office of the European Communities (EUROSTAT);
US Bureau of Economic Analysis

Smaller countries like Ireland and Portugal have benefited considerably. On the other hand, the UK, which opted out, has shown a better record both in terms of inflation and growth than the Euro-area as a whole.[26]

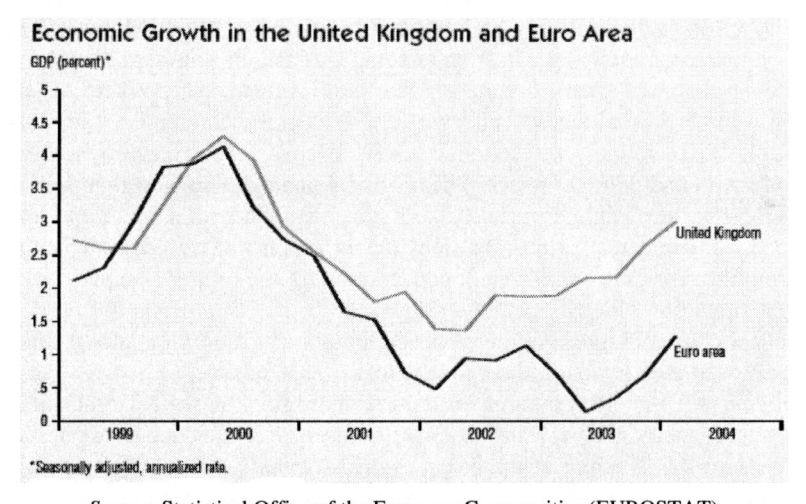

Economic Growth in the United Kingdom and Euro Area

Source: Statistical Office of the European Communities (EUROSTAT)

---

26   Alm 2004 (Internet).

The Euro has survived and is firmly established as a stable currency.[27] The ECB has combined an economic and a monetary analysis (the so-called two pillars of the ECB-strategy) in order to achieve its inflation target which is not zero-inflation – there are many reasons not to seek zero-inflation, among them the improvement of the quality of goods – but a low level of inflation; some believe it is a little too low. It has achieved transparency on the basis of an extensive gathering of statistical material which first had to be organised, it has successfully fought price rises (of oil prices between the second half of 1999 and 2001 and a tendency of food prices to rise in 2001) by progressively raising the interest rate by 225 basis points. Interest rates were lowered again from spring 2001 onwards to take account of shocks such as those related to the terrorist attacks on 11 September 2001. The ECB expected an average annual rate of growth of the gross domestic product in 2004 of between 1.4% and 2.0%, and in 2005 of between 1.7% and 2.7%, based on increases in the demand for exports, on higher domestic investment and also more private consumption expenditure. The dynamic of employment was thought to improve in 2005.[28] In fact, GDP rose in 2005 by 1.4 %.

5. Perspectives for the enlargement of the European monetary union

I tried to show by means of analogies in my historical introduction that the menace to the cohesion to the European Union is not so much that there will be a technical failure in macroeconomic coordination of some kind which would cause a country to move away from the Union despite binding treaties under the pressure of popular opinion – rather, a real dissent, relevant to a democratic community, can only develop, if a divergent view on economic perspectives is accompanied by a divergent view on social and political issues. The historical analogies suggest that such divergences develop not within a time-span of a few years but within one or two generations and a major threat to a union does not follow from mere dissatisfaction but only from the emergence of different conceptions for the future, associated not with different strata but with different countries or groups of countries within the union. Theoretical considerations and the empirical trends which so far could be observed do not allow to identify major disruption forces.

Of course, there are economic challenges and pitfalls in the enlargement of the European Monetary Union. The accession countries cannot expect to be carried away by a strong dynamic of the core countries of the European Union where the low inflation rate does not provide a stimulus to spending.[29] Unemployment in July

---

27 Issing 2004a (Internet). For an early analysis of how market perceptions of the monetary policy of the ECB have effected (enhanced) its reputation, see Goldberg / Klein 2005.
28 European Central Bank 2004.
29 On Deflationary Dangers see Krupp / Cabos 2003.

2004 in Germany was at the highest level since unification, with 4.36 millions unemployed,[30] it rose in 2005 to 4.8 millions.

On the one hand, the accession countries wish to join the Monetary Union fast. It is a matter of prestige to do so, but there is also an economic motivation: as long as the accession countries tie their currencies to the Euro by means of "soft pegging" or managed floating, they risk a financial instability of their currency as the experience of the Asian crisis shows. If they therefore take the irreversible step of introducing the Euro quickly, they have to reach a rapid alignment of the inflation rates and of the nominal interest rates for long-term borrowing, and they have to conform to the Maastricht criteria. On the other hand, their GDP is on average only at one third of the level of the European Union; to reduce this discrepancy requires considerable time. Political pressure will arise to grant similar privileges to the poor and the unemployed as in the core countries, but this would not be feasible and entails disadvantages, as German unification has shown.[31] Inflation was higher, fiscal deficits were less well controlled in recent years in the accession countries than in the Euro-area as a whole. They therefore should not join too early.

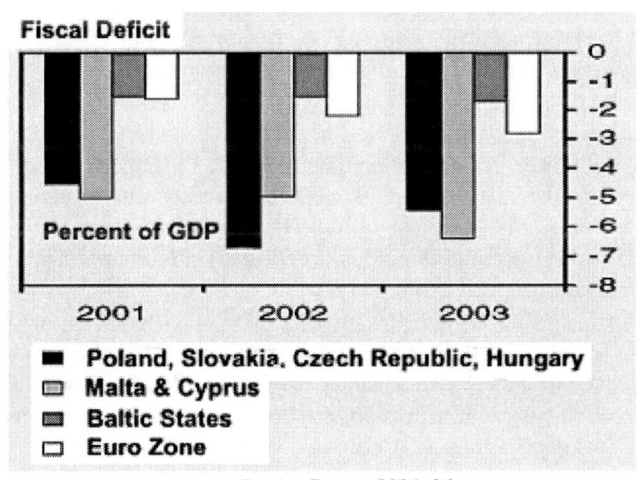

Fiscal Deficit

Percent of GDP

2001   2002   2003

■ Poland, Slovakia, Czech Republic, Hungary
□ Malta & Cyprus
▨ Baltic States
□ Euro Zone

Source: Berger 2004, 26

---

30 FAZ 2004.
31 Wagner 2002.

Inflation Rate in Selected Acession Countries

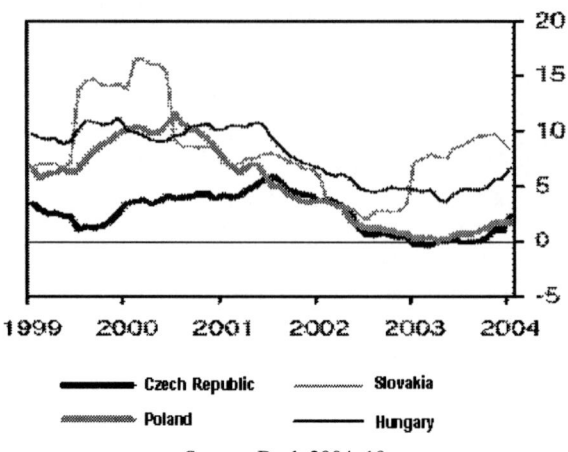

1999 2000 2001 2002 2003 2004

— Czech Republic   ⋯ Slovakia
▨ Poland   — Hungary

Source: Beck 2004, 10

The accession means an increase of population of about 20%, but the increase of the GDP amounts only to 4.8% at actual exchange rates, a smaller percentage increase than when Spain and Portugal acceded in 1986 and when Finland, Austria and Sweden acceded in 1995. However, the increase is one by 9.2% if it is measured using purchasing power parity and the data of 2002.[32] Productivity per head diminishes and similarly the share of exports while the average rate of unemployment increases; it is considerably higher than in the United States and in Japan. The higher public deficits in the acceding countries do not markedly change the average of all the countries in the European Union.

In anticipation of accession, the trade between the countries of the European Union and the acceding states has been rising as a share of total external trade. This is the consequence of the relative advantages in trade liberalisation which proceeded by steps and which has, with accession, now been completed irrevocably. One now expects gains from an increasing division of labour and scale effects. One also expects migration towards core countries because of the differences in wage rates. However, since the growth of employment at the centre is only slow, another tendency is perhaps more remarkable and, in the interest of integration, beneficial: the share of foreign direct investment in the acceding countries has been rising rapidly, indeed dramatically in the last years.

---

32   For the data, see: European Central Bank 2004b.

FDI flows from the EU-15 to the new Member States
(as a share of total extra EU-15 FDI flows)

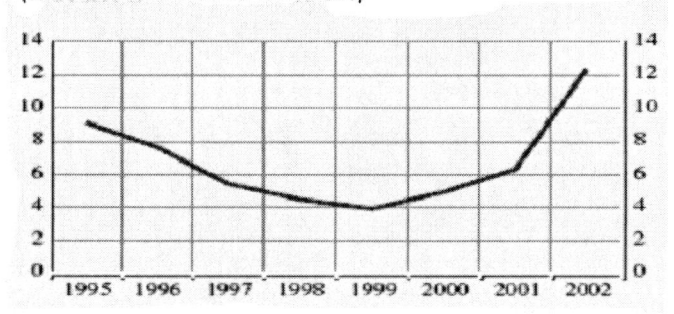

Source: Statistical Office of the European Communities (EUROSTAT)

The statistics of the European Central Bank underestimate the income levels in the accession countries, insofar as the shadow economy is not represented. A recent estimate of the shadow economy in 110 countries shows that it generally attends to be larger in poor countries, but exists in rich countries as well, and it is growing. The following table shows the size of the shadow economy for 23 European countries (1999/2000, % of GDP):

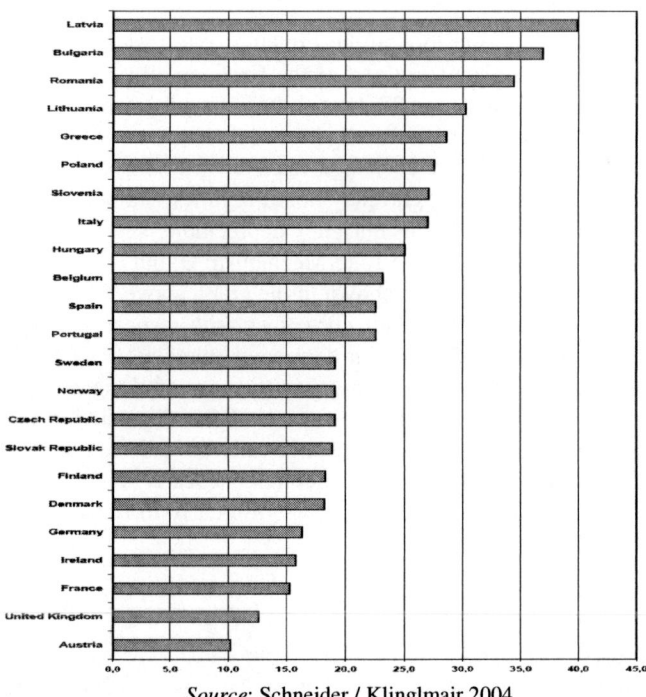

Source: Schneider / Klinglmair 2004

It is clear that we are faced with considerable distortions if the size of the shadow economy is in-between 10% and 40%.

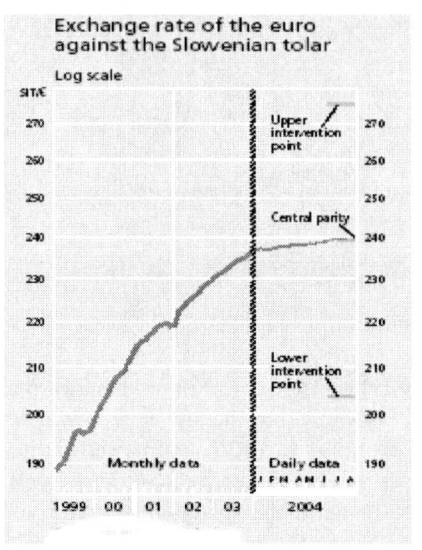

Exchange rate of the euro against the Slowenian tolar

Source: Deutsche Bundesbank 2004, 20

It remains to take a closer look at the exchange rate systems. The currencies of Estonia, Lithuania and Slovenia are part of the Exchange Rate Mechanism II of the European Monetary Union (since 27 June 2004). This formally implies a band of 15%. Estonia and Lithuania previously had fixed their currencies to the Euro, using a currency board regime. Those exchange rates are now the central rates; Estonia and Lithuania want to keep their currency board regimes without obliging the European Central Bank. Slovenia had its currency depreciating since 1999; Slovenia can credibly participate in the Exchange Rate Mechanism II, but only if the trend to depreciation can be reversed.[33] This is shown in the graph above.

Latvia and Malta have fixed their currencies with respect to a basket of other currencies. Cyprus and Hungary let their currencies float within the band of plus and minus 15%; the variations have been larger in the case of Hungary. Poland and the Czech Republic have flexible exchange rates, but the depreciation in the case of Poland is much larger. Charts of how exchange rates have altered in the last five and a half years show surprisingly different pictures.[34] Clearly, there is great diversity among the chosen strategies, and it is perhaps too early to draw conclusions as to which will be the most successful.

---

33 Deutsche Bundesbank 2004.
34 Deutsche Bundesbank 2004; Deutsche Bundesbank 2004a; European Central Bank 2004c.

The provisional conclusions of Otmar Issing, Chief economist of the European Central Bank, are as follows: Fixed exchange rates are appropriate for small open economies if goods and labour markets are sufficiently flexible, but several countries have softened their pegs and adopted a more independent monetary policy in the years immediately preceding accession. They then adopted inflation targeting. There has been a tendency for most accession countries to let their real exchange rate appreciate. This may in part be due to the Balassa-Samuelson-effect which implies that the price level of accession countries increases relative to that of the Euro-area and is not sufficiently counteracted by the movement of the nominal exchange rate, for strong nominal devaluations would increase the inflationary pressure. There is therefore no strategy which would be valid in all cases. Issing points out that it will be important well to guide the timing of entry into the Exchange Rate Mechanism II and later into the European Monetary Union – not all countries have joined the exchange rate mechanism yet, let alone decided when they would adopt the Euro. The European Central Bank continues to insist that the independence of the Central Banks of the acceding countries must remain guaranteed, but that monetary policy alone cannot create the prerequisites for monetary unification.[35] Given the conditions which have been fixed, it will be in the interest of the Union as a whole, if the accession countries manage the transition towards the adoption of the common currency well and if they chose their date of entry according to their needs and possibilities.

We may conclude by stating that the European monetary system has been established successfully and the European Central Bank has achieved the necessary authority in the few years of the existence of the Euro. Problems like asymmetrical shocks, unequal regional rates of inflation and different growth performances within the Union have so far not led to substantial imbalances and political difficulties, and the countries participating in the Union learn to adapt to it. The historical experience of monetary unions teaches that they cannot survive without political cohesion and that a real danger for them arises as soon as divergent economic interests in different countries become associated with different conceptions of how the economic future is to be shaped. Such differences in conceptions are more dangerous, if they are not confined to the economic sphere alone but also express hopes for different lifestyles. No major economic movement of this kind has become visible in recent years. We may thus assert that a common European economic style is in the making.

The accession countries present a less clear and more varied picture, and swings to political extremes are not so easily ruled out. But the very variety among those countries lets it appear likely that deviations would be confined to at most a small number of States which could not seriously disrupt the Union at large and which would therefore probably find it wise to conform to the majority. For the desire to seek protection by the large community has deep roots, it is supported by the mechanism of redistribution of the European Union as a whole, and the acceptance

---

35 Issing 2004.

of the common currency is now a *conditio sine qua non* for being part of it. The process of European monetary integration as part of general European integration therefore will proceed safely in the coming years, even if there is no lack of concrete problems in the management of the new currency.

References

Alm, R. (2004). "Five Years of the Euro: Successes and New Challenges", Federal Reserve Bank of Dallas Journal "The Southwest Economy", July 2004, 13-18.
(http://www.dallasfed.org/research/swe/2004/swe0404c.html, 9/2/2004).

Beck, R. (2004). "EWU-Erweiterung: Kein Big-Bang", DB Research EU-Monitor, Nr. 12, 19. März 2004, 9-17.

Berger, H. (2004). "The Economic Challenges of EMU Enlargement". Frankfurt: Deutsche Bank. Deutsche Bank Research EU-Monitor [engl.], No. 12, April 2, 2004, 24-32.

Bibow, J. (2003). "On the 'Burden' of German Unification", Banca Nazionale del Lavoro Quarterly Review 56, No. 225, 137-169.

Bordo, M. D., Jonung, L. (1999). The Future of EMU: What Does the History of Monetary Unions Tell Us? Cambridge, MA: National Bureau of Economic Research. NBER Working Paper Series, Working Paper 7365.

Burns, A.R. (1927 [1965]). Money and Monetary Policy in Early Times, London: Paul a.o. 1927; Repr.: New York: Kelly 1965, 90-92.

Deutsche Bundesbank (2004). Aufnahme neuer Währungen in den WKM II. Frankfurt: Deutsche Bundesbank. Deutsche Bundesbank Monatsbericht August 2004, 19-20.

Deutsche Bundesbank (2004a). Wechselkurssysteme der neuen Mitgliedsländer der EU und Wechselkursentwicklung gegenüber dem Euro. Frankfurt: Deutsche Bundesbank. Deutsche Bundesbank Monatsbericht Mai 2004, 39-40.

European Central Bank (2004). Von Experten des Eurosystems erstellte gesamtwirtschaftliche Projektionen für das Euro-Währungsgebiet. Frankfurt: Europäische Zentralbank. Monatsbericht Juni 2004, 69-74.

European Central Bank (2004a). The Monetary Policy of the ECB. Frankfurt: European Central Bank, 101-103.

European Central Bank (2004b). Die Wirtschaft der EU nach dem Beitritt der neuen Mitgliedstaaten. Frankfurt: Europäische Zentralbank. Monatsbericht Mai 2004, 53-60.

European Central Bank (2004c). "Der Wechselkursmechanismus II (WKM II) – Konventionen und Verfahren". Frankfurt: Europäische Zentralbank. Monatsbericht Juli 2004, 43-44.

FAZ (2004). "Die Arbeitslosigkeit steigt ungebremst". Frankfurter Allgemeine Zeitung, 5. August 2004, 11.

Goldberg, L.S., Klein, M.W. (2005). Establishing Credibility: Evolving Perceptions of the European Central Bank. New York: Federal Reserve Bank of New York. Staff Reports No. 231.

Grauwe, P. de (2003^5). Economics of Monetary Union, Oxford: University Press.

Issing, O. (2004). "Considerations on Monetary Policy Strategies for Accession Countries", in: Szapáry, G. and Hagen, J. von (eds), Monetary Strategies for Joining the Euro, Cheltenham: Elgar, 23-32.

Issing, O. (2004a). The ECB and the Euro – the First Five Years. Mais Lecture, City University Business School, London, 12 May 2004 (http://www.bis.org/review/r040521f.pdf, 9/2/2004).

Issing, O. (2004b). "The Stability and Growth Pact: The Appropriate Fiscal Framework for EMU", International Economics and Economic Policy, No.1, 9-13.

Kaelberer, M. (2004). "The Euro and European Identity: Symbols, Power and the Politics of European Monetary Union", Review of International Studies 30, 161-178.

Krugman, P. (1989). "Differences in Income Elasticities and Trends in Real Exchange Rates", European Economic Review 33, 1031-1046.

Krupp, H.-J., Cabos, K. (2003). "Zu den Risiken einer Nullinflation als geldpolitisches Ziel", in: Köhler, C., Rohde, A. (eds), Geldpolitik ohne Grenzen. Berlin: Duncker und Humblot. Veröffentlichungen des Instituts für Empirische Wirtschaftsforschung 39, 105-120.

Lommatzsch, K., Tober, S. (2002). Monetary Policy Aspects of the Enlargement of the Euro Area. Frankfurt: Deutsche Bank. Deutsche Bank Research August 7, 2002. Research Notes. Working Paper Series 4.

Müller-Armack, A. (1941). Genealogie der Wirtschaftsstile. Die geistesgeschichtlichen Ursprünge der Staats- und Wirtschaftsformen bis zum Anfang des 18. Jahrhunderts, Stuttgart: Kohlhammer.

Padoa-Schioppa, T. (2000 [1994]). The Road to Monetary Union in Europe. The Emperor, the Kings, and the Genies, Oxford: University Press.

Pitchford, R., Cox, A. (1997) (eds). EMU Explained. A Guide to Markets and Monetary Union, London: Kogan Page.

Ruckriegel, K., Seitz, F. (2003). "EU-Erweiterung, Währungsunion und Balassa-Samuelson-Effekt", WiSt 2, 94-100.

Sarcinelli, M. (2004). "Europe's Federation and Currency: the Contribution of Luigi Einaudi", Banca Nazionale del Lavoro Quarterly Review 57, no. 229, 109-130.

Schefold, B. (1972) (ed.). Floating. Realignment. Integration, Basel: Kyklos, und Tübingen: Mohr (9. Gespräch der List Gesellschaft).

Schefold, B. (1981). Wie möchten wir in Zukunft leben? München: Beck (Die Sozialverträglichkeit von Energiesystemen, Bd. 1, (Beck'sche Schwarze Reihe, Bd. 242).

Schefold, B. (1986). Grenzen der Atomwirtschaft, München: Beck 1986.

Schefold, B. (1994). "Nationalökonomie und Kulturwissenschaften: Das Konzept des Wirtschaftsstils", in: Deutsche Geisteswissenschaften zwischen Kaiserreich und Republik. Zur Entwicklung von Nationalökonomie, Rechtswissenschaft und Sozialwissenschaft im 20. Jahrhundert; hg. von K.W. Nörr, B. Schefold u. F. Tenbruck, Stuttgart: Steiner, 215-242.

Schefold, B. (1994a). Wirtschaftsstile Bd. 1: Studien zum Verhältnis von Ökonomie und Kultur. Frankfurt am Main: Fischer Taschenbuch Verlag.

Schefold, B. (1995). Wirtschaftsstile Bd. 2: Studien zur ökonomischen Theorie und zur Zukunft der Technik. Frankfurt am Main: Fischer Taschenbuch Verlag.

Schefold, B. (1995a). "Theoretical Approaches to a Comparison of Economic Systems from a Historical Perspective", in: The Theory of Ethical Economy in the Historical School, ed. by P. Koslowski. Berlin et al.: Springer, 221-247.

Schefold, B. (1999). "Der Euro: Barriere oder Brücke auf dem Weg zu einem föderalistischen Europa?" in: Nölling, W., Schachtschneider, K.A. and Starbatty, J. (eds), Währungsunion und Weltwirtschaft, Stuttgart: Lucius & Lucius, 155-163.

Schefold, B. (1999a). "Vom Interventionsstaat zur Sozialen Marktwirtschaft. Der Weg Alfred Müller-Armacks", in: Vademecum zu einem Klassiker der Ordnungspolitik (Hg. B. Schefold).

Kommentarband zum Repr. von Alfred Müller-Armack: Wirtschaftslenkung und Marktwirtschaft. [Hamburg: Verlag für Wirtschaft und Sozialpolitik 1947]. Düsseldorf: Verlag Wirtschaft und Finanzen. Klassiker der Nationalökonomie, 5-42.

Schefold, B. (2000): "The Problem of European Integration: Implications for Economic Methodology, Research and Teaching", in: Bertram Schefold (ed.): Economic Interests and Cultural Determinants in European Integration. Bozen: Europäische Akademie. Schriftenreihe der Europäischen Akademie, Nr. 21, 13-38.

Schefold, B. (2000a). Wirtschaft und Geld im Zeitalter der Reformation, in: Schefold, B. (ed.), Vademecum zu drei klassischen Schriften frühneuzeitlicher Münzpolitik. Kommentarband zum Reprint: Die drei Flugschriften über den Münzstreit der sächsischen Albertiner und Ernestiner: a) Gemeyne stimmen von der Muntz (Dresden 1530); b) Die Müntz Belangende. Antwort und Bericht (o.O. 1530); c) Gemeine Stymmen Von der Müntze: Apologia ... und Vorantwortung (Leipzig 1548). Düsseldorf: Verlag Wirtschaft und Finanzen. Klassiker der Nationalökonomie, 5-46.

Schneider, F., Klinglmair, R. (2004). Shadow Economies Around the World: What Do We Know? München: Ifo Institute for Economic Research e.V., CESIFO Working Paper No. 1167.

Sinn, H.-W. (2004). "The New Systems Competition", Perspektiven der Wirtschaftspolitik 5, 23-38.

Spiethoff, A.A.K. (1932). "Die allgemeine Volkswirtschaftslehre als geschichtliche Theorie. Die Wirtschaftsstile", Schmollers Jahrbuch 56, 51-84.

Wagner, H. (2002). Pitfalls in the European Enlargement Process – Financial Instability and Real Divergence. Frankfurt: Deutsche Bundesbank. (Discussion Paper 06/02, Economic Research Center of the Deutsche Bundesbank, February 2002).

Economic Styles and European Integration (Comment)

Hans-Jürgen Wagener

Three quite different, but stimulating papers were presented in the first session of the workshop. I see my task in pulling together what seems to be loose ends, but what fits together very well with the general topic of the workshop "Economic Styles and Eastern Enlargement of the EU", as you will see in a moment. My comment will come in three parts: the first dealing with the concept of economic style, the second dealing with institutional variety and culture, and the third dealing with harmonisation in the European Union. Clearly, the first part refers mostly to Carsten Herrmann-Pillath's paper, the second to Rainer Klump's and the third to Bertram Schefold's paper.

To begin with, there is a language problem. "Wirtschaftsstile" is a German concept which has not found acceptance with the English speaking profession. The same is true of "Wirtschaftsordnung" which, however, has become the subject of constitutional economics. Comparative economics is working with institutions and policies and, more recently, culture under which heading we subsume such divergent items as ideologies, beliefs, mental models, visions, behavioural regularities, traditions, habits and the like. Typical combinations of individual elements may be combined to economic or cultural systems by the observer. I shall come back to that operation in a moment.

First, we have to concentrate on the operation called "Verstehen", another of those untranslatable German concepts which, according to Arthur Spiethoff (1932/1971: 129), means "bestimmte geschichtliche Tatbestände wesensgemäß ausschöpfen" (to render exhaustively the essence of certain historical facts). For it is by way of "Verstehen" that economic styles can be discerned. At least, that is what I understand from Spiethoff (1932), Müller-Armack (1940), and Schefold (1994), while Herrmann-Pillath attempts to offer a logical construction of economic styles. "Stil ist die in den verschiedensten Lebensgebieten einer Zeit sichtbare Einheit des Ausdrucks und der Haltung" (Müller-Armack 1940/1971; style ist he unity of expressions and habitus visible in the most diverse spheres of life of a period). To perceive the unity of expression and comportment or the essence of things or phenomena is an ideational method of cognition and not an analytical method as is more commonly applied in economics. Without judging the productivity of the concept it should be clear that incorporating economic styles in analytical operations may cause tensions. With Imanuel Kant's *Kritik der Urteilskraft* (1790/1968: 420) I should like to plead for a clear distinction of the two approaches:

"Zwar gibt es zweierlei Art (modus) überhaupt der Zusammenstellung seiner Gedanken des Vortrags, deren die eine Manier (modus aestheticus), die andere Methode (modus logicus) heißt, die sich darin von einander unterscheiden: daß die erstere kein anderes Richtmaß hat, als das Gefühl der Einheit in der Darstellung, die andere aber hierin bestimmte Prinzipien befolgt."

"Manier", the Italian "maniera" and the English "manner", the way things are made by hand, is at the basis of what in German art history is called style. It is produced by individual "genial" artists (Rembrandt vs. Caravaggio) whose example leads to school forming and, hence, may characterise epochs (gothic vs. renaissance) or geographical areas (Italian vs. Weser renaissance), but also recurrent manners of artistic expression (classicism vs. romanticism). In economic life, things are also made or operated in different ways: exchange for cash or for credit, old age provisions by way of individual insurance or social security, corporate control via the market or via banks, in-firm vocational training vs. external training. These things are rarely innovated by genial persons, but evolve over time. There are certain complements to individual manners, epochs and local styles in economics such as individual policy styles (Thatcherism, Reagonomics), policy paradigms (Keynesianism, monetarism) and local models (Anglo-American model, Rhenanian model). If we called such differences instances of economic styles (which is usually not done), it would be by way of analogy and not because we think them being conceived by a *modus aestheticus*.

Schefold (1994) has a certain predilection for the manner of *modus aestheticus* in "anschauliche Theorie" (again there is no exact English complement, but in a wider sense it is phenomenology) as against what he called "the barren concepts of order and system" (ibid.: 81) that have been developed in the *modus logicus* of comparative economics. Of course, it all depends on what we want to explain. The major task of comparative economics is to find causes for differences in economic outcome or simply to answer the question "why growth rates differ". Any factor influencing welfare production is of interest. Traditionally, we start with primary factors of production, capital and labour, and technical progress. This leaves a major part of growth differences unexplained for. Hence the search for additional factors.

Since Marx and the institutionalists it has become clear that institutions matter. Let me assume that we know what we mean by institutions. Now you can try to trace the impact of individual institutions upon welfare. Alternatively you can think in orders and conceive economic systems as Walter Eucken (1943) did. This implies that institutions cannot be combined according to the cafeteria principle, but will show a certain internal coherence. Hierarchies and complementarities of elements of economic systems may not be logically compelling, as is the case with Eucken. At least they show certain empirical regularities. The difference stems from the ontological status of these phenomena. Eucken's orders are real world phenomena, while the systems of modern systems theory are constructs by the observer. A similar distinction has been made with economic styles: while Spiethoff, and now Herrmann-Pillath, consider styles as constructs of the observer, Müller-Armack thought them to be real world phenomena. The distinction will have consequences for propositions about causal relations.

There is an interesting recent literature on differences among capitalist economic systems which tries to group individual economies into different varieties of capitalism, capitalist economic systems or systems of economic regulation (the French regulation school is very productive in this respect). Whether they discern two (Michel Albert 1991, Peter Hall and David Soskice 2001), three (Gösta Esping-Andersen 1990, Vivien Schmidt 2002), four (Robert Boyer 1997) or five (Bruno Amable 2005) models of capitalism or social systems of innovation and production, as the regulationists call them, they all follow – unwittingly – Eucken's methodology and select typical institutions from different fields of economic coordination: coordination of production, industrial relations, financial intermediation, corporate governance, social protection, and educational regimes. Comparing outcomes of these different systems typically reveals that they may be equally satisfactory. There is no apparent optimal system. As, for instance, Hall and Soskice (2001) show, their two varieties of capitalism, the liberal market economy and the coordinated market economy, produce different comparative advantages and, hence, result in different structures of production and trade. Well operated they both may lead to similar levels of welfare.

If we define economic order as those institutions that can be deliberately constituted and changed, such varieties or systems of capitalism are analysed on the level of order. This leaves aside most informal institutions and other factors which we have subsumed under the term of culture. In particular transformation has taught us that such things also matter. In the first instance, transformation from socialist planning to capitalist markets is a problem of economic constitution or economic order. What is necessary, has been described in Eucken's 1952/1990) constitutive elements of a competitive system or in the, for the greater part equivalent, elements of the Washington consensus. Certain variations are possible, but there is little room for national idiosyncrasies: the Romanian model of a market economy was a disaster. Cultural factors become immediately visible, when it comes to explain why some countries are quick transformers and others are lagging and why similar models of a competitive market order yield satisfactory results in some countries and less satisfactory ones in others.

As Klump has told us, there is an interesting recent literature trying to spot some of the cultural influences upon transformation and economic outcomes in general. Religion, for instance, immediately catches the eye. The borderline between more and less successful transformers in Eastern Europe coincides with the border line between latin Christianity on the one side and orthodox Christianity and Islam on the other. The eight new member states of the first round of eastern enlargement are all "latin" countries, the two countries of the second round are both orthodox, catholic Croatia will join much earlier than orthodox Serbia or Muslim Bosnia. To explain the obvious is much more difficult (I have made an attempt in Wagener 2001).

Another approach dwells upon the concept of governance. Governance is an aggregate of institutional and cultural factors which can be grouped in clusters describing good governance and bad governance, such as voice and accountability vs.

political instability and violence, government effectiveness vs. regulatory burden, and rule of law vs. graft. The last two, for instance, comprise enforceability of contracts, predictability of courts and respect of the institutions on the one side and corruption, state capture and rent seeking on the other (see Kaufmann, Kraay, Zoido-Lobatón 1999). Other conceptualisations are, of course, possible. The measurement of the variables and their aggregation into six clusters is a complicated procedure performed by a World Bank team. It allows to correlate governance with economic outcomes, in particular welfare levels and growth of welfare, but also transformation success. The result is quite clear: governance matters and transformation success is due to good governance (see Wagener 2004). The theoretical problem, of course, is the transmission mechanism by which good governance produces good outcomes.

Correlation is not causality. Systems, models, governance, culture, and, if necessary, economic styles are aggregates and as such cannot enter causal relationships. They are, as said, products of the observer. Only if they are perceived by the actors of the economic game, they may become part of mental models, ideologies, visions with normative value that influence their decisions. As is the case in normal macroeconomics, causal analysis with institutional aggregates needs a micro-foundation. Such are the prescripts of methodological individualism. We may perhaps be able to explain why corruption has detrimental effects upon economic growth, for bad governance as such this is not possible. We may be able to show how price stability influences investment, for Eucken's competitive market order as such it is not possible either. If, however, the elements of the aggregates turn up in clusters and have strong complementarities, it will be impossible to trace their individual impact directly. It happens that theoretical causal relationships can only be tested in blocks.

There are considerable differences in governance among the old EU-15. It is interesting to note that being member of the EU reduces the negative influence of bad governance. We may conjecture the existence of two cultures, a national and a European one, the second superimposing the first and levelling national differences. The governance record of the new member states, and of the transformations countries in Eastern Europe in general, is markedly lower than in the old EU-15. Governance has been one of the criteria that qualify for membership. Hence, the new member states of the first round have a higher standard than those of the second round and the rest of Eastern Europe . By way of analogy it would make sense to speak of national governance styles. However, terms like cultural or social capital or infrastructure are more in use. The crucial problem of transformation is the question what time does it take to build up such capital and to change it. Putnam (1993) considers the social infrastructure as result of cultural development over centuries. There are other indications, like the influence of EU membership, suggesting that things may change rather quickly. The fact that candidates have to fulfil the Copenhagen criteria containing political and legal values and have to adopt the so called *acquis communautaire*, a huge body of rules and regulations, cannot leave their culture untouched. The philosophy behind these rules and regulations will surreptitiously be smuggled into the new member states.

This brings me to my third and final point, the question whether European integration is possible with different national models of capitalism that may engage in systems competition or whether it harmonises deliberately or automatically economic models and economic behaviour. Going back to the varieties of capitalism approach already mentioned above, we see that the different models have representatives within the Union: England is always mentioned as example of the Anglo-American liberal market economy, Scandinavia exhibits the model of a social-democratic market economy, continental Europe stays for the Rhenanian corporatist variety and the Mediterranean member states have a strong etatist tradition. As may be expected, the differences are strongest in those fields of economic and social policy that remain predominantly in the competency of the member states. This is the case, above all, with social policy. Nevertheless, many authors speak of a European social model (Hartmut Kaelble and Günther Schmid 2004, e.g.), and seen from a greater distance, from Japan or from America, it may very well exist.

The paper of Schefold shows the opposite case, a policy field in the sole competency of the Community, the monetary union. It implies perfect harmonisation of monetary and exchange rate policies and a far reaching institutional centralisation. The road into the monetary union was paved by convergence, the famous Maastricht convergence criteria. They refer, as we know, not only to central banking, monetary policy and exchange rate regimes, but also to fiscal policy which is not centralised. We see that monetary union has consequences for other policy fields and this not only for fiscal policy. Another field which is closer to what may be called economic style is wage setting. Before monetary convergence set in, Italy and France were used to a specific, rather inflationary way of solving wage setting disputes that were accommodated by the central bank and led to higher inflation than in Germany, Austria, and the Netherlands. Exchange rate realignments within the European Monetary System tried to redress the loss in international competitiveness. In a monetary union, all this is not possible any more, and collective bargaining behaviour as well as government and central bank policy have to adapt to the new situation. As Schefold correctly has stressed, the adoption of the Euro, i.e. full integration, may not be desirable for certain new member states in the short run.

Compared to other common markets of similar size like, for instance, the United States, the European Common Market exhibits a large variety of product specifications and a large diversity of preferences and habits. *Unité dans la diversité* is the slogan of the Community. Subsidiarity as its basic organisational principle is meant to preserve this diversity. Nevertheless, within the wider process of globalisation European integration has strong convergence effects, institutional convergence, political convergence, cultural convergence. So I come to the conclusion: whatever the historical and cultural specificities, whatever the institutional and behavioural legacies of the past that may be identified during this workshop, membership of the European Union, sooner or later, will erode the differences and result in convergence. This does imply neither centralisation nor perfect unification, but rather the evolution of a kind of federal European economic culture. There will be a European way of doing things and an American way of doing things and others. At the same time, the importance of regional difference in Europe will be greater than in the United States manifesting itself, for instance, in a much lower degree of inter-state labour mobility.

References

Albert, M. (1991). Capitalisme contre capitalisme, Paris: Seuil.

Amable, B. (2005). Les Cinq Capitalismes. Diversité des systèmes économiques et sociaux dans la mondialisation, Paris : Seuil.

Boyer, R. (1997). French Statism at the Crossroads, in: Colin Crouch, C., Streeck, W. (eds), Political Economy of Modern Capitalism. Mapping Convergence & Diversity, London: Sage, 71-101.

Esping-Andersen, G. (1990). The Three Worlds of Welfare Capitalism, Princeton: Princeton University Press.

Eucken, W. (1943). Die Grundlagen der Nationalökonomie, 3rd ed., Jena: Gustav Fischer.

Eucken, W. (1952/1990). Grundsätze der Wirtschaftspolitik, 6. Aufl., Tübingen: Mohr Siebeck.

Hall, P.A., Soskice, D. (eds) (2001), Varieties of Capitalism: The Institutional Foundations of Comparative Advantage, Oxford, Oxford University Press.

Kaelble, H., Schmid, G. (ed.), Das europäische Sozialmodell. Auf dem Weg zum transnationalen Sozialstaat, WZB Jahrbuch 2004, Berlin: Edition Sigma.

Kant, I. (1790/1968). Kritik der Urteilskraft, in: Werke in 10 Bänden (W. Weischedel ed.), Band 8, Darmstadt: Wissenschaftliche Buchgesellschaft.

Kaufmann D., Kraay, A., Zoido-Lobatón, P. (1999). Governance Matters, Policy Research Working Paper 2195, Washinton D.C.: The World Bank.

Müller-Armack, A. (1940/1971). Genealogie der Wirtschaftsstile. Die geistesgeschichtlichen Ursprünge der Staats- und Wirtschaftsformen bis zum Ausgang des 18. Jahrhunderts, in: Schachtschabel, H.G. (ed.), Wirtschaftsstufen und Wirtschaftsordnungen, Darmstadt: Wissenschaftliche Buchgesellschaft, 156-207.

Schefold, B. (1994). Nationalökonomie und Kulturwissenschaften: Das Konzept des Wirtschaftsstils, in: Schefold, B., Wirtschaftsstile, Band 1, Frankfurt a.M.: Fischer Taschenbuch, 73-110.

Schmidt, V. (2002). The Futures of European Capitalism, Oxford: Oxford University Press.

Spiethoff, A. (1932/1971). Die allgemeine Volkswirtschaftslehre als geschichtliche Theorie. Die Wirtschaftsstile, in: Schachtschabel, H.G. (ed.), Wirtschaftsstufen und Wirtschaftsordnungen, Darmstadt: Wissenschaftliche Buchgesellschaft, 123-155.

Wagener, H.-J. (2001). "Warum hat Russland den Zug verpasst?", Leviathan. Zeitschrift für Sozialwissenschaft 29-1, 110-140.

Wagener, H.-J. (2004). Good Governance, Welfare, and Transformation, European Journal of Comparative Economics 1-1, 127-143 (online at http://eaces.liuc.it).

Part 2: Poland's and Latvias's Economic Cultures and Enlargement of EU

Material Interests versus Perceptions of Christian Values in Poland's Path to the EU

Bozena Klimczak & Mikolaj Klimczak

1. Introduction

15 years since the transition towards a market economy has begun, Poland is still perceived as an example of successful transformation. In confirmation of this thesis, it is usually stated that the main goals of this process have been achieved: membership of NATO and the EU, hard budget constraints and the formal framework of market economy institutions.[1] There has been a continuous improvement of the official indicators of economic and general well-being.[2] In comparison with other Eastern European countries in the Orthodox tradition, Poland's Latin tradition made it "fertile cultural ground"[3] of the consistent implementation of westernising reforms. As an explanation of why the transformation process has been so diverse in CEEC, this hypothesis seems to be quite potent and plausible. Integrity and economic freedom indices are favourable for Poland and adverse for Russia and other "Orthodox" countries. Formally, the rule of law, fundamental freedoms and human rights are part of the Polish constitution. The Roman Catholic Church has strong roots in Polish society, not only because of tradition, but also due to the role played by the first Polish Pope and the Polish Church in the collapse of the centrally planned economy and the communist state. One could maintain that the success of Poland's transition is a result of such informal institutions based on Christian values, which created the foundation for the transfer to or introduction of formal market institutions. Yet, to defend such a hypothesis would require a series of comparative studies. Hence, before one can discuss the question of whether the cohesion of formal and informal institutions is the source of Polish transition, it is necessary to do the following first.

Dismiss the assumption about the transfer of formal institutions. Polish re-modernisation and sovietisation was not so deep. Fundamentals of civil law had been preserved from the time before the Second World War, and commercial law, private ownership of agricultural land and some markets still existed. Broadly speaking, the

---

[1] "When governments have built new institutions they have met with varying success. Contrast Poland and Russia in 1990s. To promote market development, Poland's government moved quickly to clarify property rights between the state and private actors. It imposed hard budget constraints on enterprises and promoted a dynamic class of entrepreneurs", *Building Institutions for Markets. World Development Report 2002*, World Bank, 2002.

[2] This was confirmed by the results of research *Social Diagnosis 2005* (*Diagnoza społeczna 2005*: http://www.diagnoza.com/).

[3] J. Zweynert, N. Goldschmidt, "The Two Transitions in Central and Eastern Europe as Processes of Institutional Transplantation", *Journal of Economic Issues* 40, 2006, p. 898.

so-called shock therapy of 1989–1993 did not touch formal institutions but focused on institutional changes that create rapid real advancements in the economy: liberalisation of markets and monetary policy. Institutional change proceeded gradually after 1993, in the enactment of the Constitution in 1997.

Dismiss the perception of the Polish transition as institutional success. Procrastinated enactment of the constitution and the appointment of the Constitutional Tribunal together with the weakness of the administration of justice are perceived as the main reasons for failing to fulfil the prerequisites for a truly democratic state based on the rule of law.

Dismiss the notion that the Polish transition was an economic success. Despite favourable economic indicators, unemployment in Poland is very high and the public finances poor, subjective indices of poverty are high and the country's ranking on the Transparency International Corruption Perception Index has been falling year after year.

This view of the Polish transformation inclines towards the hypothesis that the informal background for formal institutional change was internally incoherent and hampered modernisation processes. Formal and informal institutions in Poland were not homogeneous and constituted a bundle of "Christian" and "liberal" values that have resulted from political compromise and trade-offs. Quotation marks are used because, although those values were manifested as Christian or liberal, they concealed private interests. In this paper, it is only possible to present some of the phenomena within the political market and on the micro-level.

The paper is organised in six sections. Following this introduction, the second section presents an overview of the constitutional framework of Poland as a democratic state based on the rule of law – essential for the development of a market economy. The third part deals with the functioning of the state. In section Four we discuss ownership, entrepreneurship and labour, which formed the informal institutional background of the Polish transition. In this part we also consider the lack of axiological cohesion in the informal institutions and their connections with the formal institutions. Section Five presents some general conclusions. The annex includes several maps of tendencies and attitudes in Polish society.

2. Creation of the institutional framework

Polish politics is a result of the compromise of the Round Table that lasted from 6 January to 5 April 1989. The negotiations between the communist regime and the opposition established the conditions and degree of inclusion of the latter party in official public life while allowing the former party to retain power. The conditions for legalising the independent labour union *Solidarnosc* and holding free, but not truly democratic elections were gradual institutional transformation and the protection of the interests of the communist authorities and the Polish Communist Party (PZPR). Various factors contributed to this compromise. Firstly, the geopolitical situation, i.e., the presence of the Soviet Union, and of Soviet troops in Poland, forced the opposition to be prudent. Secondly, the communist authorities were in charge of the army, police and security service. Thirdly, the opposition had no consistent concept for institutional change.

Legal and institutional transformation in Poland proceeded by gradually supplanting the laws of the Polish People's Republic partly with laws that had been in force in pre-Second World War, partly with the common law of Anglo-Saxon countries and partly with statute law the of continental European countries and the European Union. For example, the Polish Civil Code of 1964 was amended in 1990 to remove regulations typical of centrally planned economies and introduced the rules of civil law: freedom of contracts, protection of property and responsibility. Commercial law, bankruptcy law, law of corporate reorganisation, the law on registering companies and the Bill of Exchange Act were based on their pre-war equivalents of 1934.[4] The antitrust law of 1990 was based on common law principles, whereas the Law on the Public Trading of Securities and the stock exchange were organised along continental European lines.

During the shock therapy, it was essential to abolish central planning regulations, as was done by the 1989 law on state enterprises, central bank and banking. Two regulations of 1988 played a special role: the Law on Economic Activity and the Law on Economic Activity of Foreign Persons. They both went into effect on 1 January 1989, i.e., just before the Round Table negotiations. They put various forms of enterprises on an equal footing – including those with foreign capital. Those laws governed not only business operations by private entities, but also the transfer of state property to private companies. Article Four of those laws became a fundamental tenet and part of the public consciousness:" Enterprises may, within the frames of their economic activity, perform actions and practices that are not forbidden by the law."[5]

After 1994, the Polish legal system began adjusting to the requirements of the European Union and its related international standards of freedom and human rights. However, owing to the gradual character of this transformation under successive governments of different political persuasions, Polish law is overly detailed, inconsistent and incoherent. Legislation was rushed and needed constant amendment. In addition, protracted court cases and difficulties in enforcing verdicts created the opinion that Poland lacked some features of the rule of law.

One of the most important outcomes of the Round Table was the communist authority's agreement to submit to the rule of law. On the 7 April 1989, the communist Constitution of 1952 was amended to allow free elections and to remove the possibility of eliminating the opposition. The amendment introduced in December 1989 eliminated regulations defining the state as the instrument of the communist

---

4   During the Second Republic (1918 – 1939) Civil Codes were not unified – old legislation inherited from the time of partition was still in force.

5   *Journal of Legislation*, 28 December 1988, No. 41, item 324 (Dz.U z 28 grudnia 1988 r., nr 41, poz. 324).

party and defined Poland as the Republic of Poland – "a democratic state based on the rule of law that implements the principles of social justice". The amended Constitution of 1952 contained the minimum of fundamental rights needed to carry out the transition. For example, Chapter 8 – "Rights and obligations of citizens" – included the prohibition of discrimination, the right of free association and the right to privacy. These freedoms and rights had been regularly violated before. It should be noted that institutions are not only principles, norms and rules but also a system of enforcement consisting of formal organisations and informal structures creating a so-called social mirror. The Constitutional Tribunal serves an important function in the system of formal safeguards.[6] Nevertheless, the administration of justice and informal institutions seems to have carried out its functions rather poorly.

The amended Constitution of 1952 remained in force until 1997. The Parliamentary Constitutional Commission and social initiatives had been working on the draft of a new constitution since 1992. Already prior to 1992, 11 different drafts for the constitution had been presented to the public; after that year the Constitutional Commission worked on seven projects. Due to coalition disputes, cabinet crises and election campaigns, the Commission's work continued until 1997. A constitution has normative character – it is a collection of norms and rules that form the foundation of a democratic state based on the rule of law that fulfils the principles of social justice. Constitutional provisions are applied directly; therefore, it is not self-evidently axiological. However, constitutional principles have very strong elements of compromise between axiological and socio-economic options. The axiological aspect is based on the concepts of human dignity, freedom and solidarity. These are included in the Preamble written by Tadeusz Mazowiecki, in which one can find reference to the transcendental sources of human dignity and the Christian heritage. Freedoms, rights and peoples' obligations are inspired by international covenants such as the Universal Declaration of Human Rights of 1948 and the European Convention on Human Rights and Fundamental Freedoms of 1950, which also refer to the dignity of human being.

There is a certain equilibrium between human rights and responsibilities to the community in the Christian concept of human dignity. The principle of solidarity, which is part of the Preamble, is not included in the general freedoms and rights. Instead, the limits on freedoms and rights are determined by liberal axiology: "Everyone shall respect the freedoms and rights of others. No one shall be compelled to do that which is not required by law".[7] An example of an axiological eclecticism is the rule governing property rights, which does not include the principle of using property for the common good.[8]

---

6   The amended Constitution of 1952 did not contain the rule that the findings of the Constitutional Tribunal are final. They could be evaluated and overruled by the Parliament.
7   The Constitution of the Republic of Poland of 2 April 1997, Art. 31, *Journal of Legislation* (Dziennik Ustaw) No. 78, item 483.
8   Cf. the Constitution of Germany, Art. 14.

The socio-economic element is based on social justice. The Constitution consists of a catalogue of social and economic rights built on political compromise. It includes, among others things, the right to health care, publicly financed medical treatment, free education and employment. These rights, unlike fundamental and economic freedoms, are not constitutionally protected. Their contents are described in the separate acts, and their implementation is a matter of political responsibility rather than legal obligation.[9]

3. Functioning of the state

A constitutional framework for institutions is a necessary but not a sufficient condition for an effective system of norms. According to D. North, "Institutions are not necessarily ... created to be socially efficient; rather they ... are created to serve the interests of those with the bargaining power to devise new rules".[10] This statement shows that institutions function effectively only if the actions of a state are based on the rule of law, i.e. are subject to the provisions of the constitution. The quality of legislation, of the executive and the judiciary, influences the level of transaction costs, market activity and the level of trust. The functioning of the state was very weak during the period of transition in Poland. Legislation, the civil service and the judiciary were influenced by political interests and special interest groups with short-term objectives, regardless of the common good. Not even parties with a majority in parliament showed respect for the rule of law, looking only to their own political gain. The voters were quick to notice this phenomenon, as reflected in voter turnout since the first free elections in 1989 (Table 1). Voters generally do not decide on the details of government; however they legitimise the political system and determine the framework of politics.

Table 1: Voter turnout for elections from 1989 to 2005

No	Year	Election	Turnout
1	1989	Parliamentary elections – round 1	62.0%
		Parliamentary elections – round 2	25.3%
2	1990	Local government elections	42.3%
3	1990	Presidential elections – round 1	59.7%
		Presidential elections – round 2	25.3%
4	1991	Parliamentary elections	43.2%
5	1993	Parliamentary elections	52.8%
6	1994	Local government elections	33.8%

9 M.Wyrzykowski, *Prawa człowieka i obywatela*, in: W. Kuczyński (ed.), *Dziesieciolecie Polski Niepodległej 1989 – 1999*, United Publishers and Productions.
10 D. North, *Institutions, Institutional Change and Economic Performance*, Cambridge University Press, Cambridge 2004, p. 16.

7	1995	Presidential elections – round 1	64.7%
		Presidential elections – round 2	68.2%
8	1996	Referendum on privatisation and bestowing property	32.4%
9	1997	Constitutional referendum	42.8%
10	1997	Parliamentary elections	47.9%
11	1998	Local government elections	45.5%
12	2000	Presidential elections	61.1%
13	2001	Parliamentary elections	46.3%
14	2002	Local government elections	44.2%
15	2003	Referendum on the accession to the EU	58.9%
16	2004	European parliamentary elections	20.9%
17	2005	Parliamentary elections	40.6%
18	2005	Presidential elections – round 1	49.7%
		Presidential elections – round 2	51.0%

Source: K. Jasiewicz, *Polskie wybory*, in: W. Kuczyński (ed.), *Dziesieciolecie Polski Niepodleglej 1989–1999*, United Publishers and Productions, Warsaw, 2001; www.pkw.gov.pl

In Poland, around 40–45% of registered voters do not vote and have no interest in politics. A similar proportion of Poles do not read daily newspapers and do not watch TV news. According to L. Kolarska-Bobinska "convergence of this group with the so-called silent majority is significant".[11] This group consists mainly of unskilled workers and farmers, older people, the unemployed, villagers and others. This group feels marginalised and increasingly excluded from jobs, education and health care. Freedoms and human rights seem to be lower in their hierarchy of values then equality and distributive justice. Active voters, on the other hand, appear to support politicians more interested in realising their own private interests, which does not secure the rule of law. There are several indicators for this. Firstly, between 1999 and 2003, the democratisation index (DEM) and the rule of law index (ROL) worsened from 1.44 to 1.63 and 1.88 to 2.00, respectively.[12] Secondly, the corruption perception index (CPI) also deteriorated – from 4.8 in 1997 to 3.4 in 2005 – and is the lowest among the transition countries of Central Europe.[13] Surprisingly, the index of economic freedom (EFI) shows that Poland is "mostly free", as the EFI decreased from 3.51 in 1995 to 2.49 in 2006,[14] which may indicate that freedom without morality or law enforcement may lead to corruption. Thirdly, acceptance of the current economic and social order (i.e., legitimisation) is the lowest among

---

11 L. Kolarska – Bobinska, *Polskie wybory*, in: W. Kuczyński (ed.), *Dziesieciolecie Polski Niepodleglej 1989–1999*, United Publishers and Productions, Warsaw, 2001.
12 *Nations in Transit 2003. Democratization from Central Europe to Eurasia*, Freedom House, New York – Washington, 2003, pp. 14–15.
13 Transparency International: http://transparency.org/policy_and_ research/surveys_indices/cpi.
14 The smaller number, the freer the surveyed country is. http://www.heritage.org/research/features/index/index.cfm.

European countries surveyed in 2002.[15] The legitimisation index is based on surveys about satisfaction with the state of the economy, actions of government and the functioning of democracy. In Poland the result was approximately half that in Denmark and other Scandinavian countries. The survey also looked at trust in politicians and other people. Other studies show that the climate of trust is highly correlated with legitimisation, the level of education and the corruption perception. A comparison of the legitimisation index and the corruption perception index of Transparency International confirms the results:

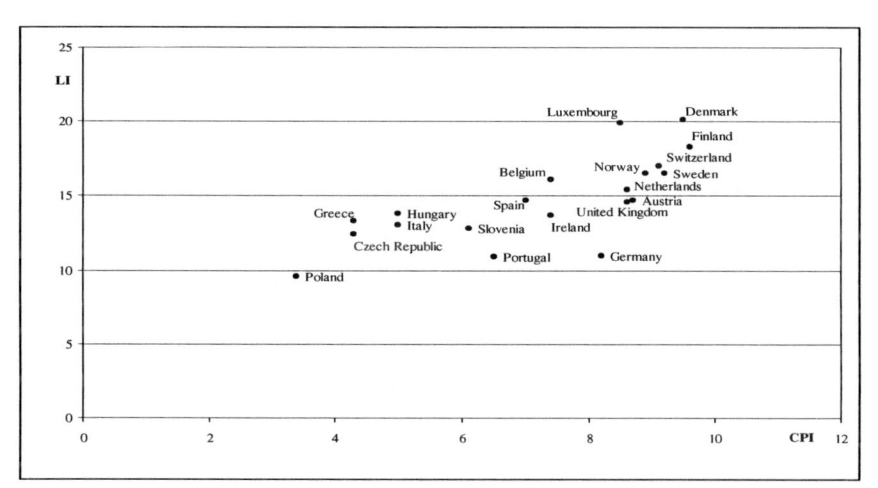

Fig. 1: Interdependence between corruption level (CPI) and legitimisation index (LI)

Source: Own interpretation, based on CPI Transparency International and European Social Survey 2002.

Fourthly, the checks on executive power and the legislature are not fully independent of political influence. In Poland, the controlling bodies include the Constitutional Tribunal, the Ombudsman, the National Council of the Judiciary, the Supreme Chamber of Control and the National Council of Radio Broadcasting and Television. Some of them existed prior to the transformation, though their range of operation and authority gradually changed after 1989. Table 2 provides general information about the above-mentioned bodies and the opinion of society about their functioning.

---

15 European Social Survey: http://ess.nsd.uib.no/index.jsp?year=2003&module=main&country=.

Table 2: Controlling authorities in Poland

Authority	Date of appointment	Scope of activity	Form of politicising	Opinion (% of positive opinions)
Constitutional Tribunal	1985 – 1997	Compliance of the law with the Constitution.	Inadequacy of rulings.	40–50%
	1997 –	Compliance of the law with the Constitution; compliance of the Polish legislation with international conventions; considers constitutional complaints.	Politicians appointed as members.	40–50%
Ombudsman	1988	Protection of freedom, human and citizen rights.		40–50%
National Council of the Judiciary	1989	Protection of the independence of the judiciary; evaluation of candidates for judges; protection of professional ethics	Procedure of the appointment of members.	No data
Supreme Chamber of Control	– 1989		Reports to the prime minister; parliament appoints the chairman.	No data
	1989 –	Control over the utilisation of public funds, including the budget		No data
National Council of Radio Broadcasting and Television	1993	Protection of the freedom of speech; safeguards the right to information	Appoints supervisory boards of public television companies; issues broadcasting licences.	No data

Source: Constitution of the Republic of Poland of 1997; A. Mateja, J. Strzałka, Tygodnik Powszechny, 19 February 2006; M. Wenzel, *Opinions on the activities of public bodies*, CBOS, Warsaw 2005; www.cbos.pl

Opinions of specialists and independent experts indicate that there have been numerous attempts to politicise these bodies. Firstly, it was done through acts that regulate the scope of competencies. In case of the National Council of Radio Broadcasting and Television, this body has been given the power to nominate supervisory boards in all public television companies, issue broadcasting licences and redistribute radio, television and broadcasting fees. The body's power to control the media was granted by a parliamentary majority. Secondly, it was done through nominations of chairpersons and members by parliament – in such situations the majority might have supported candidates with similar beliefs and preferences to those of the political majority. Since 1997, the Constitutional Tribunal and the Ombudsman have been the most independent bodies thanks to the strong personalities of their chairpersons – professional and reliable. Members of other bodies have been selected in accordance to the interests of major parties, and specialists have questioned their reasons. The relatively high percentage of positive opinions in the survey equals the percentage of people who have no opinion about the surveyed bodies and do not care about them at all.

It seems to confirm the hypothesis of a silent majority in Poland – a group of citizens that does not take part in public life and has no interest in policy-making and politics. A survey of democracy in Poland shows that members of this group believe that it does not matter whether the government is democratic or not.[16] Prior to the elections of 2005, the Polish bishops appealed to this group to vote.

The aforementioned indicators and the opinions about the weakness of public institutions are confirmed by developments in the areas of ownership, entrepreneurship and labour.

4. Attitudes and behaviour at the microeconomic level

4.1 Ownership

The transition of property rights has been achieved in Poland both formally and informally. In accordance with the Act on Deregulation of State Enterprises and further constitutional protections of property rights, a formal framework for specific processes of the transfer and redistribution of property rights has been created as a result of the state's withdrawal from the economy. The macroeconomic effect of privatisation, as measured by the growth of private sector participation in GDP and estimates of the impact of privatisation on GDP growth appear to be favourable.[17] However, differences among social groups and regions and between the poor eastern parts and the wealthy western parts of Poland did not narrow. The latter has better fundamental conditions thanks to circumstances that have long existed favouring entrepreneurship and foreign direct investment (see Annex – Figs. B and C). Investment and property transfer were greatest in the agglomerations of Warsaw, Poznan, Wroclaw, Gdansk, Cracow and Szczecin.[18] Relatively, the central and eastern regions – characterised by small-scale, inefficient agriculture, poorly developed infrastructure and low urbanisation – benefited least. These patterns have not really

---

16 L. Kolarska-Bobinska, op. cit.
17 The private sector accounted for more than 60% of GDP in 2000 and provided around 70% of total employment in Poland. From 1992 to 2001, around a quarter of productivity growth was a result of privatisation. If one takes investment's impact on productivity as 1, the share of privatisation equals 0.63 (J. J. Sztaudynger, *Wzrost gospodarczy a kapitał społeczny, prywatyzacja i inflacja*, PWN, Warsaw, 2006, pp. 56 – 57).
18 G. Gorzelak, *Regional and Local Potential for Transformation in Poland*, Euroreg, Warsaw, 1998.

changed after 15 years of privatisation and still have a negative impact on public support for privatisation.[19] Accounts of serious flaws in some big privatisation processes, the influence of state security services on these and other large capital investments, and the role of foreign companies has deepened the negative perception of property transfer.[20] The redistribution of property rights in favour of special interest groups linked to politics does little to strengthen the average Pole's perception of legitimate property rights, particularly when the rights of large groups of citizens who lost their property due to the change of the country's eastern borders, nationalisation, agricultural reform and restrictions on private property have been ignored.

The decline in the pace of privatisation is connected with benefits for politicians' clients in the form of positions on boards of management and supervisory boards. Political interest is also involved in the transfer of ownership and supervisory functions in large enterprises, subject to profit sharing for the treasury. Sometimes, such situations clearly conflict with the public interest.

This dysfunctional privatisation of state enterprises is the result of valid and formal political decisions taken under existing laws and reflects a particular perception of property rights that is rooted in the communist system. This attitude consists of, on one hand, distrust and aversion toward persons who try to increase their wealth not only legally, but also honestly. On the other hand, this view creates a mistrust of authorities and their agencies and inclines people to conceal ownership. An example of this is the number of unregistered agricultural properties, dating from the 1940s. It has been diminishing since Poland joined the EU and adopted the Common Agricultural Policy. It is worth noting that the reasons for this phenomenon go back to the nineteenth century, when property rights accumulated through three partitions and annexations, and subsequently were not unified during the Second Republic. Thirdly, the perception of property rights is influenced by the irresponsibility of property owners with limited real rights. Such dead capital that exists in Poland is very interesting for various interest groups: managers of housing cooperative societies and cottage allotments.

The above-mentioned circumstances have resulted in a situation in which large groups of people with limited rights of ownership call for fair redistribution of property and income. Both right and left-wing parties try to exploit this need with slogans of social justice. Citizens who see their chance to increase their private capital treat property rights as indefeasible rights without any obligations.

A good example of this is the continuous struggle between two different groups of people in Poland. On the one hand, a group of landowners in the Tatra Mountains wish to retain their rights. Highlanders are very averse to change and seem to be very attached to the land. On the other hand, there are entrepreneurs who wish to utilise mountain slopes during winter. As the development of property rights continues, this particular situation remains unsolved. The utilisation of the property in

---

19　W. Dereszczynski, *Opinions on the privatisation*, CBOS, 2005.
20　M. Jarosz, *Władza, przywileje, korupcja*, PWN, Warsaw, 2004.

exchange for the monetary equivalent is an action for the common good which brings benefits for a wider group of people, too. This is the case here – business connected with winter sports is beneficial not only for ski-lift owners, but also for other businesspersons: providers of lodging, catering, rental services, skiing schools and ski instructors and many others. The group of landowners does not seem to grasp the wider implications of this phenomenon: without tourism in the region there is a very strong possibility of them loosing income even from other activities. Nevertheless, this situation will remain unsolved as long as any legislation to settle the dispute is not compliant with the constitution. Only after the amendment of this primary document will it be possible to resolve this argument. The fact that the 2005-2006 winter brought bankruptcy to several small entrepreneurs in the area, where almost all ski lifts were closed due to unregulated property obligations, failed to teach a lesson.

4.2 Entrepreneurship

In Poland, the greatest wealth is not a result of entrepreneurship in Schumpeter's sense, although there are many entrepreneurial Poles. Creativity and ingenuity were not awarded under the centrally planned economy. Nonetheless, it was important to posses the ability to "arrange" deficit goods, an ability based on informal connections, acquaintances and exchange of non-economic benefits. In the informal economy, e.g. currency market, the main sources of income were differences in prices. That particular type of entrepreneurship survived the transition and even developed some specific forms. One of the types of entrepreneurship during the transition is based on profits from price differentials together with the ability to create these differentials thanks to influence on the legislation process and political connections. Disparities in prices were result of objective and subjective differences in indirect taxation. In some cases, it was claimed that the names of several companies exploiting this situation were known. Another form of transitional entrepreneurship was intermediation between buyers of companies being privatised and the treasury or government. Polish privatisation is not transparent and there are no strict procedures. Foreign investors hire intermediaries to deal with "bureaucratic obstacles". One well-known representative of this group of "businessmen" sought to create an image of himself as an honest entrepreneur, active member of the local community and a friend of the church hierarchy. Other "businessmen" of this type prefer to avoid the spotlight because of direct or indirect connections with state security services under the former regime. This entrepreneurship has features similar to the mob-like activities under communist rule.

Apart from big ventures, tens of thousands of Poles also became entrepreneurs during first period of transition. They established small family companies that for the most part imitated the technology and products of developed economies. Small enterprises was a subject of a sociological study between 1999 and 2000[21] that identified the main development factors and entrepreneurial style of small companies.

According to the study, the main factors in the development of small companies are diligence, innovativeness, creativity, initiative – but only in evading the law and exploiting legal loopholes – and ruthlessness towards contractors and employees. The survey indicates that the main reason for breaking the law is legal inconsistencies and uncertainty, especially in tax law.[22] L. Balcerowicz, the chairman of the National Bank, and A. Zoll, its Ombudsman, also drew attention to this in 2004. L. Balcerowicz's diagnosis of the Polish economy highlighted the waste of potential due to ineffective institutions.[23] A. Zoll stated that the legal system is incoherent, full of uncertainties and dysfunctional and does not defend commonly accepted values.[24] The state administration acts arbitrarily and without responsibility and is still influenced by politics. Both Balcerowicz and Zoll highlighted the inefficiency of the courts. Their comments on faulty legislation and weak law enforcement confirm the research on small companies. Thus, entrepreneurship in Poland is influenced not only by the flawed traditions of the socialist system, but also by the political and legal imperfections of the newly established system. However, treating business as a contest with the state – a contest, moreover, without rules – eventually results in the widespread view that breaking the law is a trivial matter. J. Gandawski points out the similarity between these attitudes and J.W. Coleman's descriptions of white-collar crime.[25]

Special forms of entrepreneurship may also be observed in groups of professionals that enjoy public confidence. These groups of professionals have the constitutional right to establish independent organizations that "shall concern themselves with the proper practice of such professions in accordance with, and for the purpose of protecting, the public interest".[26] This article serves to limit access to these occupations and creating privileges for families of members. For example, the quality of legal services fell as the number of professionals declined. CBOS research indicates that there is less interest in other professions as people try to qualify for the public trust professions.[27] The research also pointed to the need for the rules of professional ethics to be established by independent specialists of ethics and science or by the

---

21 The research was representative. J. Gardawski, *Przedsiębiorcy: beneficjenci czy przegrywający*, in: M. Jarosz (ed.), *Manowce polskiej prywatyzacji*, PWN, Warsaw, 2001.
22 According to the Central Statistical Office (GUS), at least half of all small enterprises commit tax fraud (P. Kozlowski, *Gospodarka nieformalna w Polsce*, Ziggurat, Warszawa, 2004, s. 76 – 77).
23 L. Balcerowicz, "Tygrys w klatce", *Tygodnik Powszechny*, 1 February 2004.
24 A. Zoll, "Złe prawo – złe państwo", *Tygodnik Powszechny*, 25 January 2005.
25 J. W. Coleman, *Motivation and Opportunity. Understanding the Causes of White-Collar Crime*, in: G. Geis, R. F. Meier, L. M. Salinger, *White-Collar Crime. Classic and Contemporary Views*, The Free Press, New York, 1995.
26 Constitution of Poland of 1997, Art. 17.
27 B. Badora, B. Roguska, *Opinia społeczna na temat zawodów zaufania publicznego*, CBOS, 2004.

government. Half of those surveyed stated that access to the professions should not be controlled exclusively by the professional bodies, but also regulated by the government.

The examples of entrepreneurship during Poland's transition presented above are far from Schumpeter's concept of business and also from Kirzner's ideas.[28] An entrepreneur in Kirzner's definition is an intermediary who discovers new possibilities of exchange, thanks to his knowledge and skills in the field of information. The particular entrepreneurship of transition comes closest to Baumol's concept of unproductive business activity. Those with access to information about the formal functioning of institutions in the system benefit from the system.[29] During the transition in Poland, formal rules directed entrepreneurship toward unproductive behaviour.

4.3 Labour

The creation of a labour market in Poland after a half a century of socialist rule has been the main factor shaping a new attitude to work. It is worth remembering that the concept of the value of labour was not strong in Poland. Compulsory work in agriculture was first abolished in the area annexed by Prussia and later in the Russian parts of Poland. The influence of Protestantism was quite weak and visible only in the area annexed by Prussia where people practised the German teaching of hard work to fight for their own national, cultural and economic identity. Unemployment in the nineteenth century and during the Second Republic was the main cause of large migration to Western Europe and America. During the Second World War, forced labour was reintroduced and had features of exploitation and slavery. The turtle was a symbol of resistance to Nazi occupation among members of the underground Polish state. During the communist regime, which produced employment for everybody, turtle tactics were the most rational form of survival. The value of labour was low due to a sense of pointlessness and the state's non-compliance with workers' fundamental rights. On several occasions, citizens showed their discontent of this situation, for the first time in Poznan, a capital of a region known for hard workers, in 1956, then in Gdansk in 1970, again in Gdansk in 1976 and in Radom, Wroclaw, Szczecin and Upper Silesia in 1980. Worker revolts, strikes and other forms of protest were one of the main reasons for the disintegration of the communist, centrally planned state in Poland. The paradox of transition was that workers that were heavily involved in breaking down the previous system seemed to suffer the greatest welfare losses. They suffered greatly from unemployment and poverty, especially in relatively undeveloped regions with extensive state-controlled agriculture. At the beginning of the 1990s, workers often went on strike to protect

---

28 I. M. Kirzner, *Competition and Entrepreneurship*, Chicago University Press, Chicago 1973.
29 W. Baumol, "Entrepreneurship: Productive, Unproductive and Destructive", *Journal of Political Economy*, 1990, No. 98.

their rights – the largest protest brought together some 750,000 people in 1992.[30] Since 1993, the number of strikes has decreased and other forms of protest have been developed. At the same time, the role of labour unions diminished as a result of their politicisation, their submission to the boards of enterprises and the involvement of union leaders in private businesses. In a 1999 survey, over 54% of interviewees stated that no one represented their interests at work.[31] Workers in newly established small and medium enterprises and foreign capital businesses were not organised. In these two groups, there have been a number of cases of threats to lay off workers unless they agreed to more burdensome conditions of work. In 2003 research on employers showed that one in six employees highlighted a lack of respect on the part of his or her employer and one in eight was not paid on time; 45% of employees were not paid for overtime or were paid with a delay; only 45% of those surveyed co-operated with labour unions.[32]

The survey on the informal economy in Poland stated that there are 1.5–2 million unregistered workers.[33] Thus, around 15% of all gainfully employed are deprived of social rights and benefits. According to another indicator, the informal economy in Poland accounted for 27.6% of GDP in 1999/2000, which is at least twice as high as in western countries.[34]

Concern about unemployment is a basic factor defining attitudes to work. Research in 2004 showed that employment is one of the most important values in life, after family life, health, love and friendship.[35] Difficulty in finding employment, shameful conditions of work and very slow increases in incomes are the main factors behind higher crime (homicide, theft, robbery) during the transition. The number of these crimes increased from 14 per 1000 inhabitants in 1989 to 36 per thousand in 2001. Research on the effect of crime on economic growth by J. J. Sztaudynger[36] showed that the increase in crime from 1992 to 2001 decreased labour productivity by 0.7% each year and halved the positive influence of privatisation (in its absence productivity would have increased by around 1.4% a year). The survey revealed a strong correlation between the increase in crime and the increase in unemployment together with the increase of real income. Therefore, one can state that changes in system of property ownership and interconnected changes in the level and structure of incomes are directly linked with the increase in crime. Moreover, this was confirmed by regional differences in crime levels: crime was highest in Pomerania, Western Pomerania, Lubusz and Lower Silesia and lowest in

30   R. Towalski, *Instytucjonalizacja konfliktu przemysłowego w Polsce*, SGH, Warsaw, 2000.
31   J. Gardawski et al, *Rozpad bastionu?Związki zawodowe w gospodarce prywatyzowanej*, Instytut Spraw Publicznych, Warsaw, 1999.
32   *Co polacy myślą o odpowiedzialności biznesu?*, Magazyn Odpowiedzialnego Biznesu, No. 3, April 2003.
33   P. Kozłowski, *Gospodarka nieformalna...*, op. cit., pp. 76–77.
34   F. Schneider, R. Klinglmair, *Shadow Economies Around the World: What Do We Know?*, Center for Research in Economics, Management and Arts, Working Paper No 2004 – 03.
35   J. Lewandowska, M. Wenzel, *Polacy o swoim zatrudnieniu*, CBOS, 2004.
36   J. J. Sztaudynger , *Wzrost gospodarczy a kapitał społeczny...*, op. cit.

Lower Carpathia, Swietokrzyskie, Lublin, Lesser Poland and Lodz. It is also reflected in the amount of communist state farmland taken over by the treasury: the largest areas are in voivodships with the highest crime levels.[37] These regions are also the areas of highest unemployment.

This tendency goes hand in hand with the lack of perspectives for a better life offered by work in less developed regions. Mob-like businesses and crime make it difficult for millions of Poles to utilise economic freedoms and take their destiny into their own hands. The above-mentioned CBOS research shows that all those surveyed would like to take part in training if they were provided free. Every third person surveyed thought that the only reason to work was the need to make money and that no one would work unless they had to.

In conclusion, it could be stated that the transition period further weakened the working ethos, but under circumstances quite different from those of the communist system. This phenomenon can be found not only among employees, but also among the self-employed and small entrepreneurs. Distinct regional differences appear to be the legacy of nineteenth-century annexations.

5. Conclusions

The transition from the centrally planned economy to the market economy has been a very complex process. More important, this phenomenon has had its own inner dynamics, influenced by the past. The impact has been affected by ongoing changes and it is now very difficult to generalise about the factors that influenced transition. The changes in the informal and formal institutional background in Poland have implications for development.

The institutional framework is the result of intentional actions only in the broadest sense. It is changing as the rule of law develops and as the interaction between different interests change axiologically. Preparing a constitutional framework for institutions confirms this process.

The Constitution of 1997 has a natural rather than a positive character. Both the Preamble and specific norms refer to principles above the law – freedom, justice, solidarity and the common good. However, such rules can be variously interpreted and apprehended. Moreover, they may be used to disguise economic interests and a struggle for power. Personal freedom is a rule typical of both Christianity and liberalism. In the 1980s, in liberal intellectual circles it was very common to interpret the principle of freedom in terms of Christian traditions and Christian values.[38] Nevertheless, the instrumentalisation of this rule by left-wing politicians and the existence of mob-like businesses discredited this principle. A special feature of this phenome-

---

37 M. Jarosz (ed.), *Prywatyzacja bezpośrednia*, Instytut Studiów Politycznych PAN, Warsaw, 1998.
38 M. Dzielski, *Credo*, Znak, 1990, pp. 425–426.

non is the separation of economic freedom and responsibility, with the result that the former has become identified with wilfulness and lawlessness. The principle of justice went through a similar process. In a situation of subjective perceptions of a lack of opportunity and disproportional distribution of the costs of transition, justice begins to mean equality and becomes a tool of revendication and redistribution. It is exploited by both left and right-wing politicians for their temporary goals. In the homeland of John Paul II and the independent self-governing trade union *Solidarnosc*, the rule of law, defined as the creation in solidarity of durable institutions of political, social and economic order, has not become deeply rooted. This interpretation of justice demands reference to either brotherly love or social contract. In both cases, it is necessary to adequately interpret freedom in the context of individual and social responsibility.

Phenomena presented in the fourth part, usually described by economists as rent-seeking or opportunism, consist of cunning and misleading actions for personal gain without breaking the law. German philosopher and economist Goetz Briefs defined these actions as a marginal morality (*Grenzmoral, Gegen-Ethos*) in 1921.[39] Described as such, this behaviour seeks the lowest possible limit of permitted actions. At first, they are committed by individuals or single groups. After a while, they start to spread and find imitators. The result is a decline in the general level of morality. In the dynamic approach, marginal morality becomes an ideal type, one of the forms of ethos, rather different from communal morality. The concept of marginal morality was developed from studies of market behaviour, but it is valid for social life as a whole. One the one hand, marginal morality can be identified in the market economy by studying interest groups that tend to acquire private or group goods at the expense of weaker, less organised participants in economic life. On the other hand, marginal morality also appeared to be the means of survival in the centrally planned economy, a way of dealing with shortages and restrictions on freedom; it was based on self-defence and self-help and helped to soothe the irrationality of economy.[40] The rejection of that system was built on traditional values: nation, family and religion, not on modernist ones.[41] Familism[42] as a form of marginal morality spread widely during the transition and became amoral, taking the form of nepotism, corruption and mob-like entrepreneurship.

It is quite clear that Poland is in an identity crisis. Poles are unsure whether to hold on to tradition, whose continuity has been disturbed, or to imitate the West. It

---

39   G. Briefs, *Untergang des Abendlandes. Christentum und Sozialismus. Eine Auseinandersetzung mit Oswald Spengler,* Freiburg, 1921; G. Briefs, *Grenzmoral in der pluralistischen Gesellschaft*, in: *Gewerkschaftsprobleme in unserer Zeit. Beiträge zur Standortbestimmung*, Frankfurt/M, 1968, pp. 197–207.
40   A. Dylus, *Morlaność krańcowa jako problem dla katolickiej nauki społecznej*, Pallotinum, Warsaw 1992, p. 111.
41   M. Ziółkowski, *Przemiany interesów i wartości społeczeństwa*, Humaniora, 2000.
42   Here familism is defined as a form of social organization in which all values are determined by reference to the maintenance, continuity, and functions of family group.

has led on the one hand to fundamental Catholicism and on the other to ill-considered acceptance of foreign ways. These attitudes have occurred in private as well as professional, social and political life. Interests are catalysts for this process, against the background of an ageing society with a low level of education and scientific knowledge. In both cases, there is no understanding that an action for the common good need not be contradictory with an action for the personal good – common benefits create suitable conditions for obtaining personal gains. The chief result of this outlook is transient interpretations of primary values, both liberal and Christian, to suit one's interests. This approach is quite common in various spheres of public life. The main paradox of this is that social justice is a measure used by both liberals and Christians and is by each group to suit its goals. As a result, most Poles have little trust in other people and in institutions – a survey shows that only one person in ten trusts most people, whereas in Norway such opinions are seven times more frequent.[43] The lack of trust is caused by, besides axiological frustration, the lack of transparency in public life, political scandals, corrupt public officials, unemployment, social and economic diversity and conflicts of interest between the beneficiaries of transition.

Maps that are included in the Annex show clearly enough that Poland is divided between the entrepreneurial west and conservative east. It seems to be a legacy of the partition of Poland in the nineteenth century, developments in the Second Republic and socialism. In the nineteenth century, the western and northern parts that were under the influence of Prussia (see Fig. B) adopted typical Prussian virtues: perfect organization, sacrifice and the rule of law. Since the beginning of the transition, the western parts of Poland have received all investment thanks to their location. The eastern parts of the country were always under-invested, less entrepreneurial and more agricultural, and gave conservative and populist parties majorities (see Figs. A and D). This part of Poland is also the poorest region not only of Poland, but also of the EU (see Fig. C) which makes for even more fertile ground for social and populist policies.

Do these implications allow us to draw firm conclusions? One may say that the past has had a strong impact on transition in Poland. On the one hand, the political powers in the political market used it to negotiate specific institutional arrangements to benefit group interests. On the other hand it could be seen as an erosion of informal institutions that lack the basis of formal institutions. The consequence of this influence of the past is high transaction costs, and opportunity costs that tend to slow down the process of modernisation and economic development. For 15 years, Poland's transformation has taken place within specific institutional arrangements. These arrangements have reproduced the disparities of wealth and power and the social role of the former regime in the new institutional framework.[44] In conclusion,

---

43   P. J. Zak, S. Knack, "Trust and growth", *The Economic Journal*, April 2001, pp. 295 – 321.
44   M. Aoki, *Institutional evolution as punctuated equilibria in institutions, contracts and organisations (ed. C. Ménard),* Edward Elgar, Cheltenham 2000, J. Staniszkis, *Postcommunism*, Institute of political studies, Polish Academy of Sciences, Warsaw 1999.

one may say that the unsatisfactory effects of the Polish transition are the outcome of a strong system of interests inherited from the centrally planned economy and weak institutions that have not been able to provide enough axiologically grounded rules, either Christian or liberal.

Annex

Fig. A: *Percentage of voters against accession to the EU in regions*

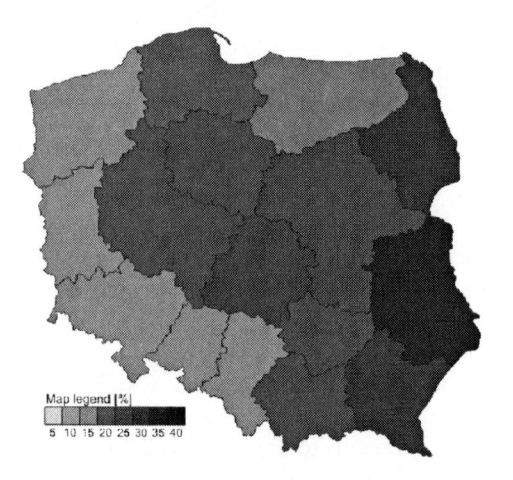

Source: own; data from http://referendum.pkw.gov.pl/sww/kraj/indexA.html

Fig. B: *Borders of Prussia, Russia and Austria – the partition of Poland*

Source: own; after http://pl.wikipedia.org/wiki/Królestwo_Kongresowe

Fig. C: *The poorest regions in Poland*

Source: own; after Eurostat 2005, *Sustainable development indicators*

Fig. D: Presidential elections 2005 – majority on each candidate in regions

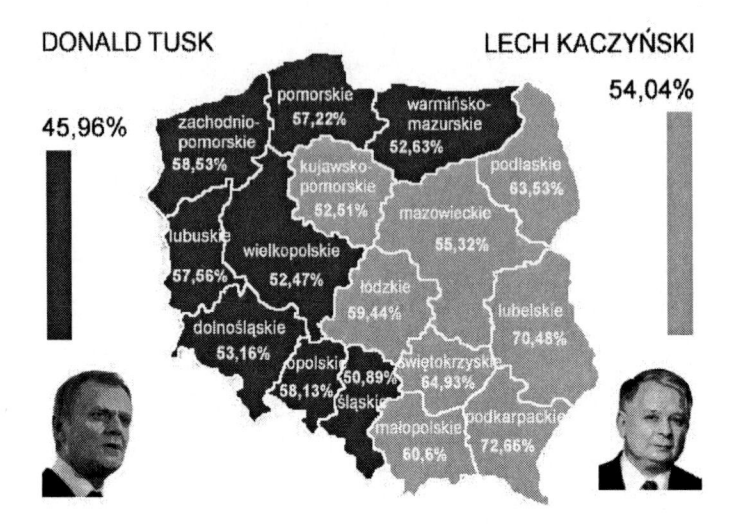

DONALD TUSK — 45,96%

LECH KACZYŃSKI — 54,04%

- pomorskie 57,22%
- warmińsko-mazurskie 52,63%
- zachodniopomorskie 58,53%
- kujawsko-pomorskie 52,51%
- podlaskie 63,53%
- lubuskie 57,56%
- wielkopolskie 52,47%
- mazowieckie 55,32%
- łódzkie 59,44%
- lubelskie 70,48%
- dolnośląskie 53,16%
- opolskie 50,89%
- śląskie 58,13%
- świętokrzyskie 64,93%
- małopolskie 60,6%
- podkarpackie 72,66%

Source: http://pl.wikipedia.org/wiki/Grafika:Wybory_2005_w_wojewodztwach.png

References

Aoki, M. (2000). Institutional evolution as punctuated equilibria in institutions, contracts and organisations (ed. C. Ménard), Cheltenham: Edward Elgar.

Badora, B., Roguska, B. (2004). Opinia społeczna na temat zawodów zaufania publicznego, CBOS.

Balcerowicz, L. (2004). "Tygrys w klatce", Tygodnik Powszechny, 1 February 2004

Baumol, W. (1990). "Entrepreneurship: Productive, Unproductive and Destructive", Journal of Political Economy 98.

Briefs, G. (1968). Grenzmoral in der pluralistischen Gesellschaft, in: Gewerkschaftsprobleme in unserer Zeit. Beitrage zur Standortbestimmung, Frankfurt/M.

Briefs, G. (1921). Untergang des Abendlandes. Christentum und Sozialismus. Eine Auseinandersetzung mit Oswald Spengler, Freiburg.

Coleman, J.W. (1995). "Motivation and Opportunity. Understanding the Causes of White-Collar Crime", in: Geis, G., Meier, R.F., Salinger, L.M. (ed.), White-Collar Crime. Classic and Contemporary Views, New York: The Free Press.

Co polacy myślą o odpowiedzialności biznesu?, Magazyn Odpowiedzialnego Biznesu, No. 3, April 2003.

Dereszczynski, W. (2005). Opinions on the privatisation, CBOS.

Dzielski, M. (1990). Credo, Znak.

Dylus, A. (1992). Morlaność krańcowa jako problem dla katolickiej nauki społecznej, Pallotinum, Warsaw.

Eurostat 2005, Sustainable development indicators.

Gardawski, J. et al. (1999). Rozpad bastionu? Związki zawodowe w gospodarce prywatyzowanej, Instytut Spraw Publicznych, Warsaw.

Gardawski, J. (2001). "Przedsiębiorcy: beneficjenci czy przegrywający", in: Jarosz, M. (ed.), Manowce polskiej prywatyzacji, PWN, Warsaw.

Gorzelak, G. (1998). Regional and Local Potential for Transformation in Poland, Euroreg, Warsaw.

Jarosz, M. (ed.) (1998). Prywatyzacja bezpośrednia, Instytut Studiów Politycznych PAN, Warsaw.

Jarosz, M. (2004). Władza, przywileje, korupcja, PWN, Warsaw.

Jasiewicz, K. (2001). "Polskie wybory", in: Kuczyński, W. (ed.), Dziesieciolecie Polski Niepodleglej 1989 – 1999, United Publishers and Productions, Warsaw.

Kirzner, I.M. (1973). Competition and Entrepreneurship, Chicago: Chicago University Press.

Kolarska-Bobinska, L. (2001). "Polskie wybory", in: Kuczyński, W. (ed.), Dziesieciolecie Polski Niepodleglej 1989 – 1999, Warsaw: United Publishers and Productions.

Kozłowski, P. (2004). Gospodarka nieformalna w Polsce, Ziggurat, Warsaw.

Lewandowska, J., Wenzel, M. (2004). Polacy o swoim zatrudnieniu, CBOS.

Mateja, A., Strzałka, J. (2006). Tygodnik Powszechny, 19 February 2006.

Nations in Transit 2003. Democratization from Central Europe to Eurasia, New York, Washington: Freedom House.

North, D. (2004). Institutions, Institutional Change and Economic Performance, Cambridge: Cambridge University Press.

Schneider, F., Klinglmair, R. (2004). Shadow Economies Around the World: What Do We Know?, Center for Research in Economics, Management and Arts, Working Paper No. 2004–03.

Staniszkis, J. (1999). Post-communism, Institute of political studies, Polish Academy of Sciences, Warsaw.
Sztaudynger, J.J. (2006). Wzrost gospodarczy a kapitał społeczny, prywatyzacja i inflacja, PWN, Warsaw.
Towalski, R. (2000). Instytucjonalizacja konfliktu przemysłowego w Polsce, SGH, Warsaw.
Wenzel, M. (2005). Opinions on the activities of public bodies, CBOS, Warsaw.
World Development Report 2002. Building Institutions for Markets, World Bank 2002.
Wyrzykowski, M. (2001). "Prawa człowieka i obywatela", in: Kuczyński, W. (ed.), Dziesieciolecie Polski Niepodleglej 1989 – 1999, Warszawa: Fundacja Księgi Dziesieciolecia Polski Niepodległej; United Publishers & Producton.
Zak, P.J., Knack, S. (2001). "Trust and growth", The Economic Journal, April 2001.
Ziółkowski, M. (2000). Przemiany interesów i wartości społeczeństwa, Humaniora.
Zoll, A. (2005). "Złe prawo – złe państwo", Tygodnik Powszechny, 25 January 2005.
Zweynert, J., Goldschmidt, N. (2006). "The Two Transitions in Central and Eastern Europe as Processes of Institutional Transplantation", Journal of Economic Issues 40, 895-918.

Internet Resources:
European Social Survey 2002: http://ess.nsd.uib.no/index.jsp?year=2003&module=main&country=
http://pl.wikipedia.org/wiki/Królestwo_Kongresowe
http://pl.wikipedia.org/wiki/Grafika:Wybory_2005_w_wojewodztwach.png
http://referendum.pkw.gov.pl/sww/kraj/indexA.html
http://transparency.org/policy_and_research/surveys_indices/cpi
Social Diagnosis 2005 (Diagnoza społeczna 2005: http://www.diagnoza.com/*)*
http://www.heritage.org/research/features/index/index.cfm
www.pkw.gov.pl

The Baltic Countries as Mediators in the Clash between Western European and Post-Soviet Economic Cultures? A Latvian Perspective

Raita Karnite

1. Introduction

Some of the differences in the ways in which similar economic activities are accomplished in different countries cannot be explained by the tools of economic theory. For lack of better explanations, many authors refer to notions such as "national economic culture" and "economic style" and related theories. Despite extensive theoretical discussion on the topic, the notion of economic culture is not clearly defined, and there is no agreement on its origin. Some authors (Zver et al. 2004) think that it was inspired by Almond's notion of political culture and developed by Peter L. Berger in the mid-1980s and later at the Boston University's Institute for the Study of Economic Culture and by other researchers. Others (Noland 2003, referring to Anderson 1988) refer to a much earlier period, namely Adam Smith's argument in the *Wealth of Nations* that participation in the religious sects could potentially have economic advantages for adherents, as well as to Max Weber's theories and more recent developments.

Despite these differences, most authors agree that economic culture is an interdisciplinary concept. Whatever aspect is taken to define economic culture, it reflects the relationship between economics and culture, where culture is understood in the wider sense – as a life style, set of skills, customs, and norms of conduct. It can also be understood in a more narrow sense as a "way of doing things in economics" (Plaschke 1994), economic relations, or industrial relations, or in a more general sense as a value system (Zver et al. 2004).

Reference to economic culture to explain divergent economic performances is based not only on the empirical findings in the field of political culture – that a close relation exists between democratic political culture and democratic political systems (Almond and Verba 1965, as cited in Zver et al. 2004) – but also on the concept that human resources are the main factor in production and in economic development. Further logical steps depend on prioritization – does culture play the central role in determining people's value orientations, or do values play the central role in determining people's cultural orientations?

In theories of economic culture, many researchers argue that religious belief has an impact on behavioural outcomes and that religious activity can affect economic performance at the individual, group and national level, while others strongly oppose these views (Noland, 2003).

The role of economic culture in different continents, economic regions, countries, local territories, time periods and concepts is widely discussed in the literature.

During the last decade the concept of economic culture has been used to explain existing or apparent divergences in the development of transition economies. These studies help to explain part of the differences in economic performance between diverging economic cultures. However, despite numerous attempts to develop a typology of the economic cultures, there are no clear definitions of the Western European and the post-Soviet economic cultures. Nor are determinants of diversity in economic culture (whether historical and geographical background, national, administrative, regional or ethnical peculiarities, social or economic conditions, or others) assessed. The image of Western European economic culture is related to the acceptance of common basic values. The majority of research findings are based on the provisional perception that in terms of the market economy and economic development post-Soviet economic culture is something unfavourable, even wrong. Yet in the absence of reliable quality and impact measurement methodologies it is impossible to make proper comparisons of different economic cultures.

This article seeks answers to several questions: Is there a clash between Western European and post-Soviet economic cultures, and if so, what is the impact of such a clash; what is position of the Baltic States in relation to the Western European and post-Soviet economic cultures; if and how the Baltic States could be mediators in the clash of Western European and post-Soviet economic cultures. In this article the author assesses the impact of post-Soviet economic culture from a less traditional angle.

2. Is there a clash between Western European and post-soviet economic cultures, and what is the impact of such a clash?

There is strong belief among researchers that Western European and post-Soviet economic cultures differ and this has an impact on economic development. The origins of the divergence between Western European and post-Soviet economic cultures lies in the history of the relevant socio-economic systems – democratic society and market economy in the former and one-party state and planned command economy in the latter.

In the theoretical discourse it is argued that democracy removes social and economic barriers to the development of creative human resources and enables people to work for their own gain and profit. There is a common understanding that the one-party state and command economy has the opposite effect and therefore performance and output must be different. This raises a number of questions: what are the differences, might they be classified as constituting a clash, and how sustainable are they? More specifically, how does post-Soviet economic culture meet the needs of a modern capitalistic society and economy, what are the consequences of the coexistence of different economic cultures in the context of the transformation to a market economy and, particularly, of EU enlargement, which leads to the closer integration of societies and economic systems with different economic cultures. Last but not least, we need to understand how such integration influences the further development of the enlarged European Union.

Let us take a look at the first question: what kind of differences appear? The decisive role of cultural differences in economic development is discussed in many publications of post-Soviet researchers. Vitaly Aleshchenko (2008) argues that cultural practice acts as an informal institution and by virtue of its nature has a stronger impact on the economic development of the region than formalised institutes, which lack the cultural support of economic agents and a population. Essential progress in economic development and increasing competitiveness can be achieved only by undertaking measures to increase economic culture and change of dated views and customs, which dominate people's psychology, simultaneously and together with technological improvements.

A team of Slovenian authors (Zver, Zivko, & Bobek 2004) argue that while normative and behavioural patterns and organisational and institutional structures can be "standardised" relatively quickly in favourable conditions, structural adaptation is more complex at the level of the cultural core, i.e. in respect of value systems.

It is argued that the cultural differences appear in value systems, views (more often than not out of date), customs and habits, the relationship between formal and informal institutional systems and distorted religious traditions. Countries of the former Soviet Union have weak religious traditions. In the Soviet state, religion was not totally prohibited, but not encouraged, either. Even now, when people in former Soviet countries return to the church, for many of them belief in God means something different than in countries with sustained religious traditions, and the impact of religion on individuals' behaviour and in forming of economic culture is much weaker.

Slovenian authors (Zver et al. 2004) identify several variables that mark the cultural economic value orientations. This identification is based on the definition of economic culture as a combination of economic values and beliefs, which guide economic behaviour. Indicators of economic culture include the degree of acceptance of democracy, market economy, free initiative, self-responsibility and the disapproval of tax evasion. It is assumed that the weaker these indicators, the less compatibility there is with the standards of democracy and market economy in western countries.

Based on statistical data from the World Values Survey (1999), Table 1 presents calculations, and consequent conclusions regarding differences between EU countries and the CEEC, including the Baltic States:

- differences between EU countries and the CEEC are significant,

- there are small differences within the CEEC group; although these differences are not significant, it is likely that economic culture is more advanced in countries that have coped better with the transition from a planned to a market economy, including the Baltic States.

Table 1: Indicators of economic culture
(indexes, a low value is positive, high negative)

State	EDS	STA	MK	RAS	PTS
Great Britain	4.68	4.77	2.41	4.00	4.43
The Netherlands	4.56	5.48	2.68	4.70	4.64
Germany	4.00	4.62	2.36	3.80	4.23
Estonia	5.81	6.10	3.15	4.39	6.09
Latvia	6.41	7.35	2.35	3.42	6.66
Lithuania	6.09	4.59	3.78	3.99	5.39
Poland	6.33	6.64	2.22	3.99	5.76
The Czech Republic	5.95	6.03	2.08	3.25	4.90
Slovakia	6.26	7.12	2.16	3.59	6.38
Hungary	5.81	6.65	2.11	3.76	6.12
Romania	6.52	6.20	2.79	2.73	4.81
Bulgaria	5.86	5.40	2.00	3.50	5.22
Slovenia	6.31	5.53	2.34	3.24	6.53

Note: EDS – "economic democratic syndrome" – the share of agreement with the statement "Democracy has a bad influence on the economy", STA – "statist syndrome" – agreement with the statement "The state should own industry and business", MK – "Martin Krpans's syndrome" – agreement with the statement "Taking the opportunity of tax evasion can always be justified", RAS – "rivals syndrome" – agreement with the statement "Competition is harmful and it brings out the worst in people", PTS – "paternalistic syndrome" – agreement with the statement "The government should take more responsibility to ensure that everyone is provided for".

Source: Zver, M., Zivko, T., Bobek, V. Is There a Gap in Economic Culture between EU Countries and the Transition Economies? Managing Global Transitions, 2(1), Spring: 31-40.

The Center for Political Studies of the Central European University has done further intense research into the economic cultures in the new member states. One of the projects (DIOSCURI) tries to predict the convergence between the twin economic cultures of the "East" and the "West". The research fields – entrepreneurship, governance and economic knowledge – were explored in four Central Eastern European countries (the Czech Republic, Hungary, Poland and Slovenia) and in four countries of Southeastern Europe (Bulgaria, Croatia, Romania and Serbia and Montenegro). The selection of fields was based on the conviction that the producers of economic culture, businesspeople, civil servants and economists exert a vast influence on the economic performance of the Union and the social cohesion between the old and the new member states.

In this way, previous research implicitly attests that there are differences in economic culture between Western European and post-Soviet economies; however, the applied methodology leaves a lot of doubt about the validity of the achieved results. Most of the research is based on sociological surveys, where answers may be compared only if questions are understood in the same way. However, answers may vary not only because of different attitudes to the explored topic, but also because of different perceptions about this topic in different societies. In other words, the results of any survey about economic culture *per se* are affected by the cultural beliefs of respondents. For instance, in transition countries, locals neglect their own values mainly because they compare their situation with an idealised, theoretical situation they have heard about in the Western Countries, rather than the real situation, which they have little knowledge about.

Assuming that divergence of economic cultures is proved, the question remains of whether there is a clash between western European and post-Soviet economic cultures that would cause conflicts in relations between societies and countries or, more specifically, within the enlarged European Union. To answer this question one must look at the areas affected by economic culture. Regarding economics, these are:

- building a democratic society – a cornerstone for development of a welfare state,
- the observance of the rule of law, fair business practices, promotion of progress,
- economic competitiveness on the basis of technological achievements, and
- consequently growth and economic stability.

There are no indications in earlier research that divergence of economic cultures may cause conflicts in any of the mentioned areas. Reasons for the lack of such indications are, first, the absence of substantial differences in empirical research results (even in cases when authors concluded that differences are important [Zver et al. 2004]), and, second, the many similarities in the basic value systems of western and post-Soviet people, such as a predisposition to peace and a better life, welfare, education and culture, high morality, and adequate intellectual levels to sustain progress.

On the other hand, the transformation of post-Soviet economies highlights two types of people – passive and active – more than stable Western economies do. Characteristic features of passive people, such as modesty about own needs, obedience towards authority and acceptance of existing conditions, whatever they are, have distorted civil society, and made it more difficult to build democracy. Weak democracy and passive civil society allow active people to derive greater gains from changes, and in a way this is sometimes described as "eastern" economic culture. This is characterised by phenomena such as unfair business practices, corruption, development of oligarchs, "the power in the state", etc. Yet, even assuming that these phenomena have a negative impact on the building of a welfare state in the long run, this concerns individual and national rather than commonwealth interests.

The importance of the economic culture is related to its impact on economic development. It is argued that the negative aspects of the post-Soviet economic culture may hinder economic development. Table 2 shows that diverging economic cultures do not prevent rapid economic development in post-Soviet countries. However, it is evident that GDP growth depends on the welfare level of countries rather than on the specific economic culture.

It is argued that high growth rates in some countries reflect a low starting point and that growth will slow as the welfare level improves. Besides, economic development cannot be measured only by GDP growth rates – according to economic theory, fast growth not necessarily means good economic development. On the other hand, in countries starting from a low level of economic development good economic development is not possible without rapid growth. As Table 2 shows, countries with a low level of welfare have high growth rates, while those with a higher level of welfare have lower GDP growth figures. The table also shows that there is no large difference in the GDP growth rates between post-Soviet and other countries with a low level of welfare (example: Turkey).

Table 2: GDP growth indicators of selected countries

	2000	2001	2002	2003	2004
ES (25)	103.7	101.8	101.1	101.1	102.4
ES (15)	103.7	101.7	101.0	101.0	102.3
Post-Socialist Countries					
Latvia	106.9	108.0	106.4	107.2	108.5
Estonia	107.9	106.5	107.2	106.7	107.8
Lithuania	–	106.4	106.8	110.5	107.0
Czech Republic	103.9	102.6	101.5	103.2	104.0
Poland	104.0	101.0	101.4	103.8	105.3
Slovakia	102.0	103.8	104.6	104.5	105.5
Slovenia	104.1	102.7	103.5	102.7	104.2
Bulgaria	105.4	104.1	104.9	104.5	105.6
Romania	102.1	105.7	105.0	104.9	108.3
Hungary	105.2	103.8	105.1	103.4	104.6
Other Countries					
USA	103.7	100.8	101.6	102.7	104.2
Japan	102.4	100.2	99.7	101.4	102.7
Canada	105.3	101.7	103.2	102.0	102.8
Turkey	107.4	92.5	107.9	105.8	107.7

Source: Statistical Yearbook of Latvia 2005. Central Statistical Bureau of Latvia, Riga, 2005, p. 275, and Eurostat, http://www.europa.eu.int/comm/eurostat (tables; structural indicators)

If we assume that economic culture has an impact on progress, and that there are several negative features in the economic culture of the transition countries, such as corruption, bribery, low incentives and old-fashioned thinking, obviously there must be something that compensates for these negative impacts. Progress has been achieved on the basis of rapid structural reforms in all transition countries. To a great extent, reforms, many of them experimental, risky and difficult for society, were possible because of characteristics of post-Soviet economic culture, such as strong allegiance to the nation-state, ability to accept enormous social and economic difficulties, enthusiasm and an ability to prioritise targets and achieve them.

There is clear evidence that society in post-Soviet countries is very open to reforms. Reforms are accepted and possible in these countries. By contrast, in Western European countries reforms are more difficult. In European countries every attempt to change pension systems meets with resistance. France was gripped by student and left-wing protests aiming at maintaining the status quo in the face of proposed reforms, even though the reforms promise better employment and higher economic growth. Every attempt to reform existing systems damages the political right and opens the door for socialist gains in elections in several western European countries. Germany, Belgium and Greece are also experiencing strong anti-reform protests, highlighting the pervasive fear of reform across much of the Europe. Analysts stress that Italy needs reforms to stop its economic and demographic decline.

Also in respect of trade and investment, the European Union is an example of economically based protectionism, versus the politically based protectionism of the United States. While politically based protectionism discriminates in favour of or against specific countries, protectionism in the EU seeks to maintain the status quo in order to preserve social benefits and jobs.[1] In contrast, CEE countries are much more likely to support right-wing governments and reforms. In the light of these facts one may ask if a belief in the role of the state, nostalgia about the past, support of protectionism and fear of reforms are typical features of only the post-Soviet economic culture. Last but not least, how sustainable are these differences? Previous research shows that some features of economic culture are based on natural factors and will not disappear, while others will change with the development of the political order, economy and society.

Finally, we have to understand how differing economic cultures will influence the further development of the EU. Their impact is likely to be rather positive than negative. Post-Soviet members of the EU are more open to liberal policies and reforms, and are now in a position to influence EU policies in the direction of a more efficient economic order. In this way, new member states may became engines of reform rather than a brake on economic progress in the EU.

3. What is the position of the Baltic States in relation to the Western European and post-soviet economic cultures?

Referring to the findings of Slovenian researchers (Table 2), the Baltic States lie between the western and the Central European countries on the one hand and the less developed south-eastern countries (Bulgaria and Romania) on the other.

---

[1] Monthly Update from ISA (International Startegic Analysis), April 2006, http://www.isa-world.com.

This assessment is clearly underestimated in some indicators ("economic democratic syndrome", the role of the state, the role of competition, and the "paternalistic syndrome") that fail to recognise that the Baltic States are among the most liberal economies in the EU. This assessment does not take into account the status quo in the Baltic States. For instance, the "paternalistic syndrome" may have a high value not only because the role of the state is overemphasised, but also because in conditions in which the state plays a small role the market dominates in highly sensitive social spheres: individual responsibility may be so high that under the existing division of responsibilities in the given welfare conditions the state does not provide vital services for the population, which contradicts all notions of the welfare state.

In addition, the Baltic States have made rapid progress in the years since the survey. Referring to the findings of political scientists (cf. Zver et al. 2004), there is a strong correlation between the development of political culture and political democracy. The evolution of industrial society, and even more the development of a knowledge/information society, tends to promote democratic political institutions because in these societies the people are increasingly likely to want democratic institutions and increasingly adept at getting them. These findings also indicate that industrial/knowledge/information societies develop increasingly specialised and educated labour forces. The emergence of welfare states leads to gradual value changes, in which the population increasingly gives high priority to autonomy and self-expression, and this changing political culture transforms, among other social and political phenomena, peoples' motivation to work. These findings relate to the development of political culture, but may be related to the economic culture as well.

Other findings indicate that economic culture (or value orientation) depends on economic status, whether national, regional or local. For instance, Zver et al. argue that the CEES, which are more successful in the structural adaptation to Western European standards reveal similar patterns in economic cultural phenomena.

From the beginning of their transition in 1990, the Baltic States have been actively involved in integration into the EU, and this development path was supported by their respective societies. This has two consequences. First, society accepted the goal of western political and economic culture. Second, society agreed that international organisations have an important impact on the integration process. As a result, the local economic culture had a very limited impact on the transition process and the economic development during the period of transition. Furthermore, the integration process fostered adaptation to the main module values of the Western European economic culture: democracy and market economy. Other factors that influence cohesion of economic culture in Western European countries and the Baltic States are openness of society and the economy, active interaction with the world economy through intense foreign economic relations with the West, and a comparatively high level of FDI from western countries.

Let us now take a look at the position of the Baltic States vis-à-vis other post-Soviet countries. Presumably, the economic cultures of the Baltic States and Central European countries do not diverge more than the economic cultures of other economic or administrative units. Greater divergence is evident in respect of the post-

Soviet countries that did not accept international supervision in the transition process (Russia, Belarus), or were not able or willing to follow these recommendations.

Despite similar transition conditions (comparable starting points, the same target and time horizons, similar international supervision), the Baltic States do not have a uniform economic culture. Each of the three Baltic States has its own history and economic culture. During the Soviet period Estonia had access to Finland thanks to information networks (TV, radio) and language. The economic culture of Latvia and Lithuania developed more independently, yet there are also differences between them. Catholic Lithuania has always been strongly protective of its identity (this policy has resulted in strong dominance of Lithuanians in the structure of population), whereas Latvia has been more open to different external powers.

Of the Baltic States, Latvia is in a special situation on account of the structure of population. As Figure 1 shows, ethnic groups of the former Soviet Union make up a significant proportion of Latvia's population. This raises the question of whether the ethnic structure of the population affects economic culture in Latvia and how? According to the existing stereotypes, the economic culture of Russian business is low not only in Russia, but also in countries where it might be important. Equally, the economic culture in FDI-financed companies is much higher than in local companies.

Statistical data show that there are no big differences by ethnicity or time-dependent specific trends in some important indicators (Tables 3 and 4) that may have an impact the formation of economic culture: education (Table 3) and employment.

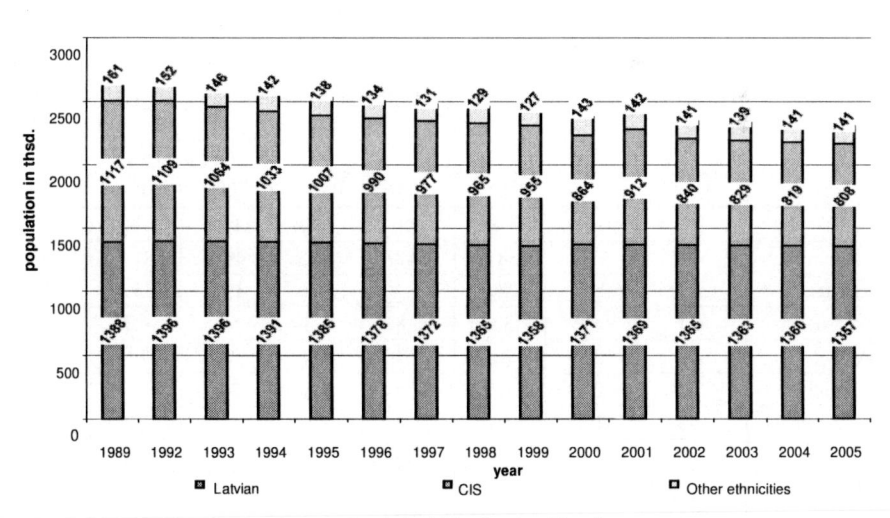

Fig. 1: Resident population of Latvia, 1989-2005

Source: Statistical Yearbook of Latvia.

Table 3: Educational attainment of population of selected ethnicities in Latvia, 2000, '000s

Ethnicity	Total population aged 15 and over	Primary	Basic	Secondary	Secondary specialized	Higher	Less than 4 grades	Not indicated
In per cent of population of selected ethnicities, in per cent								
All population	100.0	5.3	23.9	28.0	18.2	12.5	2.1	9.9
Latvians	100.0	5.0	27.1	28.4	18.0	12.3	1.7	7.5
Russians	100.0	5.3	19.3	27.9	18.6	13.6	2.4	13.0
Belarusians	100.0	8.1	21.7	26.9	19.8	8.8	4.2	10.5
Ukrainians	100.0	3.2	15.8	27.8	22.4	15.7	0.9	14.3
Poles	100.0	7.8	24.0	28.1	18.3	9.2	3.5	9.2
Lithuanians	100.0	11.3	31.4	23.5	14.0	4.8	5.8	9.2
Jews	100.0	2.1	7.4	14.9	11.7	29.8	1.1	33.0
Other ethnicities	100.0	6.2	17.1	22.6	13.4	13.0	6.5	21.2

Source: Results of the 2000 Population and Household Census in Latvia, p. 202

However, if we compare the unemployment structure by ethnicity with the ethnic composition of the population (table 4), then we see that ethnic Latvians' proportion of unemployed is slightly lower than ethnic Latvians' proportion of the total population.

Table 4: Structure of population and unemployed persons by ethnicity, in %

	Population				Unemployed			
	1995	2000	2004	2005	1995	2000	2004	2005
Total	100	100	100	100	100	100	100	100
Latvians	54.7	57.6	58.6	58.9	47.3	49.8	51.1	51.4
Russians	32.8	29.6	28.8	28.7	38.6	35.9	35.2	33.7
Belarusians	4.1	4.1	3.9	3.8	5.3	5.1	4.7	4.4
Poles	2.2	2.5	2.5	2.4	3.0	3.0	2.9	2.6
Ukrainians	3.0	2.7	2.6	2.5	2.8	2.9	2.9	2.7
Lithuanians	1.3	1.4	1.4	1.4	1.5	1.5	1.4	1.5
Jews	0.5	0.4	0.4	0.4	0.2	0.2	0.1	0.1
Other ethnicities	1.4	1.7	1.8	1.9	1.3	1.6	1.7	3.6

Source: Statistical yearbook of Latvia, 2003, p. 61; 2005, p. 68

Labour laws in Latvia prohibit any discrimination on the basis of ethnicity, which means that fewer opportunities in the labour market must be the result of personal shortcomings. One of these may well be a lack of language skills – Latvian included.

Recent research within the framework of the Global Entrepreneurship Monitor (Dombrovsky, Chandler, Kreslins 2005) shows that notably the Russian-speaking ethnic minority is underrepresented among entrepreneurs. The share of early-stage entrepreneurs among ethnic Latvian adults (between 18-64 years) is 7.95%, compared with 4.64% for ethnic Russians; the relevant figures for established businesses are 5.9% and 3.3%. However, the share for ethnic Russians who hold Latvian citizenship, and, presumably, are proficient in Latvian, is substantially higher (the same as ethnic Latvians) than that for Russian non-citizens. The authors explain this by poor knowledge of the official language, which makes it more difficult for them to communicate with state institutions. The differences in the economic culture of Latvians and Russians are not mentioned in this research.

Concerning economic aspects of ethnic diversity, two institutions, the Baltic Institute of Social Sciences and the Institute of Economics, Latvian Academy of Sciences, together carried out research on "Social Integration and Business: The ethnic dimension" (in 2004). Economic research confirmed that the share of "pure Russian" companies (companies where all employees have Russian as their native language) is not large (10-20%). These companies were mainly small enterprises, and mainly operating in the transport, trade and social and individual services sectors (Figure 2). The ethnic structure of most companies – and of all large companies – was mixed (Figure 3).

Fig. 2: Enterprise structure, in %

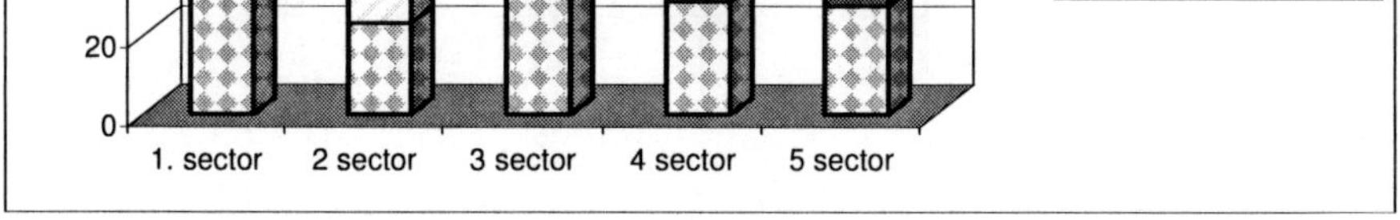

Source: Company survey; sectors see Table 5 (from Society integration ... 2004)

The researchers did not find big differences in the behaviour of "pure Russian" and "non-Russian" companies in the fields of foreign trade and investment, or in their ways of doing business. Comparing Figure 2 and Table 5, we see that there is no close connection between the "ethnic" structure of companies by sector and partner states by sector. International cooperation with western countries is much more intensive than with eastern countries across the board.

Fig. 3: Employment by ethnicity, in %

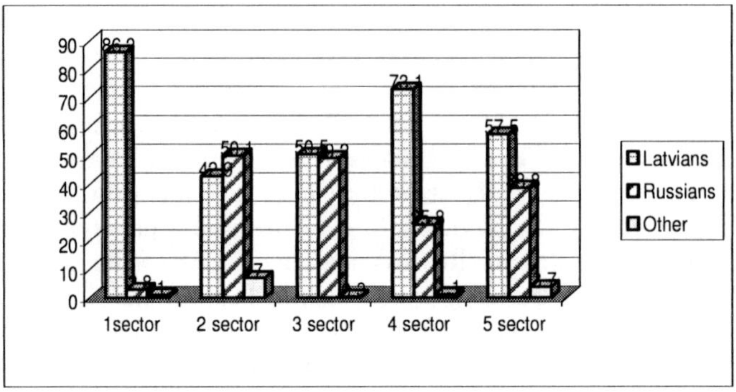

Source: Company survey; sectors see Table 5 (from Society integration ... 2004)

Obviously, there is a strong perception in Latvian society of negative traditions of Russian business and of close connections between such a business and the business environment in Russia, which could mean a strong impact of "eastern" economic culture. Economic research does not justify this perception, or a special non-Latvian way of doing business. No doubt, the impact of ethnic affiliation on economic culture needs to be investigated in greater depth.

Table 5: Market orientation of Latvian companies

Country	Agriculture, forestry, hunting, fishing	Industry and construction	Hotels, restaurants, transport, communication, finance, business services	Trade	Education, health care, other services
Russia		+	+		+
Poland	+			+	
United Kingdom	+				+
Sweden		+			
Germany	+	+	+	+	+
EU			+		
Lithuania			+	+	+
Estonia			+	+	

Source: Company survey (from Society integration ... 2004)

4. How can (if at all) the Baltic States be mediators between Western European and post-soviet economic cultures?

The role of the Baltic States in relation to the Western European and post-Soviet economic cultures may be analysed regarding publicising non-western culture in the EU and publicising western culture outside the EU, both as exercises in bridge-building between the Western European and post-Soviet economic cultures.

Zver et al. argue that the process of structural and cultural synchronisation should not be understood as general culture standardisation in the sense of unification and assimilation of different cultures, or as a one way adoption of certain cultural patterns of Western Europe. The cultural plurality of Europe should be provided with a core module of mutual democratic and modern political and economic and economic values.

Researchers of the above mentioned DIOSCURI project mention that instead of relying on a simplistic scheme, in which the "strong western" culture devours the "weak eastern" one, it is possible to find a great variety of lasting cultural hybrids in economic behaviour, which they refer to as "cultural compromise". Another research project, named DARES, on how French multinationals operating in the CEEC apply the European social model, has focused on the hypothesis that significant elements of the European social model may be found in subsidiaries located in the CEEC, but the actual organisation is a hybrid between the French and the local model. In addition, under the impact of MNC, both the European and the local social models are evolving towards an individualised neo-liberal employment relations regime rather than towards either the European social model or reinforcing the pre-1990s statist or early 1990s "cowboy" models. The development of industrial relations in Latvia within the framework of EIRO gives the impression that the described trends are very characteristic for Latvia.

In addition to normal convergence conditions, the Baltic States have a specific position in relation to the Western European and post-Soviet economic cultures:

- the Baltic States are post-Soviet economies that have been successfully transformed from planned to market economies;

- of the new EU members, only the Baltic States were constituents of the Soviet Union,

- the Baltic States have were part of the Soviet state for a shorter period than other former Soviet constituents in Eastern Europe,

- the Baltic States are open, liberal economies and close neighbours of Eastern countries, which should facilitate intense interaction between Western and post-Soviet economic cultures in business, trade and investment.

Therefore, the Baltic States and Latvia may offer an original path of change in economic culture, in which decisive elements are external impacts and a fast improving economic situation. It is doubtful whether the Baltic States could contribute to popularising EU practices in the post-Soviet economic culture. Rather, intense economic relations may contribute to the spread of characteristic features of post-Soviet culture in the western European economic culture that are currently kept severely in check, such as bribery outside EU countries or in the NMS and elsewhere. Currently the role of the Baltic States in bridging the two types of economic culture is limited due to the small scale of their economies and their limited economic relations with Eastern European countries (including Russia).

5. Conclusion

During the last decade the concept of economic culture has been used in order to explain existing or apparent divergences in the economic development of transition countries. Previous research findings affirm the divergence between Western European and post-Soviet economic cultures. However, this research is based on the provisional perception that post-Soviet economic culture is something different, even negative in terms of economic development. Besides, there are no clear definitions of Western European and post-Soviet economic cultures, or quality and impact measurement methodologies that would enable proper comparisons between them.

There are no indications in the previous research that the divergence of economic cultures may cause conflicts, first, because empirical research failed to find substantial differences (even in cases when authors viewed differences as important) and, second, because there are many similarities in the basic value systems of western and the post-Soviet people, such as a predisposition to peace and a better life, welfare, education and culture, high morality, and an adequate intellectual level to sustain progress.

The gap between economic cultures narrows in the course of economic integration; therefore existing differences cannot be classified as highly sustainable. Contrary to any previous considerations and beliefs, post-Soviet culture helps to promote social and economic reforms and rapid adaptation to the new economic order (market economy), thus ensuring rapid development of the post-Soviet countries.

In the context of EU enlargement, new member states may became engines of reform rather than a break on further economic development. The divergences between the economic cultures of the Baltic States and the Central European countries is no greater than between the economic cultures of other different economic units. Greater divergence is evident in the case of post-Soviet countries that did not accept international supervision in the transition process (Russia, Belarus), or were not able to fulfil their recommendations.

However, despite similar transition conditions (comparable starting points, the same target and time horizons, similar international supervision), the economic culture of the Baltic States is not uniform. Each of the Baltic States has its own history, which circumstance accounts for the differences between the economic cultures of the three countries. The Baltic States may demonstrate an original path of change in economic culture, in which the decisive elements are external impacts and improvements in the economic situation.

The Baltic States may be mediators between Western European and post-Soviet economic cultures in several ways:
1. the Baltic States become a location for Western European companies doing business with Russia, whereby eastern European companies use local workers who understand the economic culture of both sides;
2. the Baltic States become the location for companies from post-Soviet countries that are not members of the EU but do business with western countries, whereby the business environment in the Baltic States facilitates the adaptation of post-Soviet economic culture to the western European economic culture; or
3. the Baltic States become a laboratory for modelling changes in the post-Soviet economic culture.

In the light of new tasks laid down in the revised Lisbon Strategy, the Baltic States may serve as mediators or research laboratories for finding new aspects of economic culture – providing social comfort and at the same time promoting economic development.

References

Aleshchenko, V.V. (2008). Economic culture and competitiveness of the Russian region. Internet resource, accessed 14 March 2006.

Anderson, Gary M. (1988). "Mr. Smith and the Preachers: The Economics of Religion in the Wealth of Nations", Journal of Political Economy 96, No 5, 1066-1088.

Battente, S. (2006). The economic culture underlying the birth of the Second Republic. Internet resource: http://www.york.ac.uk/depts/poli/news/asmi/battente.pdf, accessed 14 March 2006.

Botir, V. (2000). The role of economic culture in social progress. Spiritual values and social progress. Uzbekistan Philosophical Studies, I. edited by Said Shermukhamedov and Victoriya Levinskaya. In Cultural heritage and contemporary change, Series IIIC, Central Asia, Volume 1.

Global Entrepreneurship Monitor (2005). Latvia Report. Vyacheslav Dombrovsky, Mark Chandler, Karlis Kreslins Stockholm School of Economics, Riga.

Homepage of the Centre for Policy Studies of the Central European University, accessed 14 March 2006.

Homepage of the Institute for the Study of Economic Culture of the Boston University, accessed 14 March 2006.

Noland M. (2003). Religion, Culture, and Economic Performance. Institute of International Economics Working Paper, 2003-8.

Plaschke, H. (1994). "National Economic Cultures and Economic Integration", in S. Zetterholm (ed.), National Cultures and European Integration. Berg, Oxford, 113-144.

Rohrlich, P.E. (1987). "Economic culture and foreign policy: the cognitive analysis of economic policy making", International Organisation. 41 (1), Winter.

Society integration and business: the ethnic dimension. Baltic Institute of Social Sciences, Institute of Economics, Latvian Academy of Sciences, Riga, 2004.

Zver, M., Zivko, T., Bobek, V. (2004). "Is there a gap in economic culture between EU countries and the transition economies?", Managing Global Transitions 2 (1), 31-40.

Historical and Cultural Specificity (Comment)

Karl-Heinz Schmidt

The comment refers to three contributions[1] which concern Poland, Russia and the Baltic Countries. The first contribution deals with material interests versus perception of Christian Values in Poland's road to the EU. The second article raises the problem of a "Russian economic man" and pursues the question if it is an obstacle to Russia's westernising reforms. The third contribution turns to the question if there was or is a "clash" of Western European and Post-Soviet economic cultures to be pointed out and if the concerned countries function as a "Mediator", the answer being given in a Latvian perspective. In order to comment on all of the three papers, the following discussion points are offered as a guideline and impulse for later statements: 1. Access to the papers: problems and definitions, 2. Background and framework conditions, 3. Separate views in the papers: a) Poland, b) Russia, c) Baltic Countries, 4. General views in the papers: a) Material interests vs. Christian values, b) the "economic man", c) the "clash" of economic cultures, 5. Conclusions.

1. Access to the papers

Klimczak and Klimczak start from the question, if the cohesion of formal and informal institutions is the source of Polish transition. The underlying hypothesis is: the informal background of formal change of institutions hampered the modernisation process. V. Avtonomov sets out different meanings of the term "homo oeconomicus": methodological interpretation, the role as a label for selfish persons, or a synonym for national economic mentality. The underlying hypothesis points out, that national cultural characteristics of economic agents constitute the "Russian economic man". R. Karnite emphasizes three points to be examined: the question of a "clash" of economic cultures, the position of the Baltic States in relation to the European Union and Post-Soviet States and the role of the Baltic countries as "Mediators".

---

[1] As has been mentioned in the introduction, unfortunately Vladimir Avtonomov was not able to contribute a written version if his excellent presentation "'Russian Economic Man': An Obstacle for Russia's Westernising Reforms?" (the editors).

2. Background and framework conditions

Klimczak and Klimczak review the foregone fifteen years since the transition process began in Poland. They ask: Is Poland an example of successful transformation?

V. Avtonomov distinguishes a long-run and a short-run view of the transition process in Russia. The long-run view should be focussed on the investigation of the evolution of economic mentality of the nation. The short-run view should be orientated to the effects of formal and informal changes. Rapid institutional and technological changes are characterized to need rapid informal and formal changes; old informal institutions may offer some kind of "safety-net" R. Karnita points out, that the economic systems of the past are still effective even at present, but that there are remarkable differences as to management, employees' rights and economic development of nations. The historical background and the changes of the political and social framework conditions are pointed out in all of the three contributions, though with different emphasis.

3. Separate views in the papers

The authors Klimczak and Klimczak distinguish (in case of Poland) formal and informal institutions, especially Christian and liberal values, and they emphasize the statement, that the values resulted from political compromise and interest trade-offs. As a basic problem the authors identify the relation of values and private interests. They point out the structure of the "political market" in Poland as an important reason of the ineffectiveness of values and institutions in Polish society and policymaking.

Concerning Russia, V. Avtonomov refers to theoretical terms and views. Economic rationality and ethics of rule-following are compared as for the model of a functioning market economy, the planned economy and the economy in transition. Herewith two approaches are mentioned: the "Big Bang" approach and the "Gradualists" approach; both approaches have been discussed in the literature on transition countries, whereas the author's proposal to identify a specific type of economic actor: the "homo transitionalis" seems to be a remarkable innovation in the analysis of transition processes. Of basic importance also turns out to be the range of natural and historical factors shaping the "Russian economic mentality". Moreover, the author emphasizes the role of "Orthodox values" in Russia. This statement is of special importance with regard to the long-run view of the transition process.

As to the Baltic countries R. Kainite's view of the geographical, political and economic situation of the concerned countries is important for her answer to the "clash"-problem. The author's answer seems to be well founded: no "clash", just "differences" of the countries between the Western states and the Post-Soviet states. The gap between economic cultures is identified to be narrowed, but the remaining differences are evaluated to leave impact on economic performance; therefore they should subject to further research. This statement allows for an optimistic outlook, though additional problems may turn out because of rather wide definitions of "culture" and "economic culture" being applied in the study.

4. General views in the papers

From a broader point of view three problems are focussed in the commented papers: the economic integration in Europe, the hypothesis of the "economic man" and the definition and impact of "economic cultures" and of values. Regarding the relations between the considered countries, the papers guide the reader's interest to the effects of economic integration, the role of "westernising reforms" compared to the chances of autonomous, east-oriented reforms, the reduction of "differences" or even "clash" of economic cultures, the role of specific countries as "mediators" between groups of countries, the impact of history and of old and new institutions in the considered countries during the transition process.
Several important results may be selected for further discussion:

- Concerning the statement of an "Identity crisis" in Poland: can it be solved by maintaining the tradition (fundamental Catholicism) or by imitating the West?
- "Poles lack trust" (because of corruption, scandals etc.), but how can the value-system be stabilized under the conditions of open countries?
- Are the effects of Polish transition unsatisfactory only because of the past? Comparisons with other countries should be envisaged.
- As to Russia: Is Russia's situation "unique"? Can one find the basic characteristics of the "Russian economic man" only in Russia? What about economic decisions under the conditions of "bounded rationality"?
- Importance of mutual trust and social justice as ethical foundations of a market economy, a basic problem of every economic system.
- The effects of Russian interest groups on policy-making need further research and control.
- In the Baltic countries, but not only there, the differences in economic culture should be investigated in depth.
- Latvia's special conditions between EU and Post Soviet countries should be compared with countries in similar situations.
- The restricted function of "bridging" should be pointed out, but brought forward as a promising speciality of the history and a chance of future development.

5. Conclusions

The three studies turn out to be very informative and inspiring. They are based on broad and informative empirical data and theoretical arguments. Three concluding and to some extent warning points, yet, may be emphasized:

1. The empirical data give impulses to further research. Therefore the installed channels and personal connections should be developed furthermore.

2. Some definitions of terms applied in the studies allow for simple interpretation ("clash", "mediator", "economic culture" ago.), but the terms are more complex.

3. The theoretical framework might have been intensified towards the former theory of economic systems and institutional economics and to the history of economic thought concerning Poland, Russia and the Baltic Countries.

The crucial questions of the studies like the identity crisis (Poland), the economic man (Russia) and the clash or differences of economic culture and the role Catholicism Poland) then may be brought forward to more intensive consideration and discussion in the countries of the EU and beyond.

Part 3: In Search of Empirical Evidence: Attitudes towards the Extended Order

Measuring the Attitudes towards the Extended Order in Latvia, Poland and Russia: The Extended Order Index

Joachim Zweynert & Robert Wyszyński

1. Introduction

The problem of transition has forcefully reminded the economic profession of the significance of cultural and historical factors for institutional change. The transition countries shared similar starting conditions,[1] and all of them declared the target to turn into market economies and democracies as soon as possible. Today, more than 15 years after the fall of the Iron Curtain, there are few regions in the world where the differences both in political and economic organisation and performance are greater than in Central and Eastern Europe (see Kitschelt 2003, 49). Much speaks in favour of the thesis that the explanation for the divergence in transition outcomes must be sought in the different cultural and historical legacies that shaped the values, norms and behaviour of the relevant actors (see e.g. Raiser 2001, Pejovich 2003, Gérard 2004, Winiecki 2004). If it is true that "historical specificity" (in detail see Hodgson 2001) was of decisive influence for the success or failure of transition, this raises the question to what degree it is possible to formulate general theories in the social sciences. This issue has a long tradition in our discipline that reaches far beyond the famous *Methodenstreit* between Gustav Schmoller and Carl Menger (see e.g. Richter 1988) at the end of the 19th century.[2]

This paper, as well as the research project as a whole, is based on a theoretical concept that was developed by economists like Werner Sombart, Arthur Spiethoff, Edgar Salin and Alfred Müller-Armack in the aftermath of the *Methodenstreit* – the theory of economic styles.[3] To us, it seems to be a promising approach to revive this research agenda because its basic idea is to find a 'third way' between historical and theoretical research: On the one hand, its adherents stressed the cultural and histori-

---

[1] In "transitology" the significance of the initial conditions for success or failure of reforms in different countries has been much discussed, see e.g. Krueger 1998; Stuart and Panayotopoulos 1999, Falcetti, Raiser and Sanfey 2002. The discussion now seems to approach a consensus that initial conditions had a significant impact in the early stage of transition but that their influence is negligible when it comes to explaining today's divergence between the countries concerned.

[2] The issue to what degree the economist could and should abstract from reality, had already been fiercely debated by Malthus on the one hand and Say and Ricardo on the other.

[3] For a short overview see Kaufhold 1996.

cal specificity of the economic process, on the other hand, they emphasised the importance of developing operable theories. During the last years, a number of attempts have been made to revive the concept of economic styles.[4] However, if we are not mistaken, the present paper is the first attempt at empirical research based on a style-theoretical approach. This makes it necessary to elaborate the methodological foundations of our survey in more detail than is commonly the case with empirical studies. The paper therefore has a somewhat hybrid character; it contains both a methodological proposal and the application of the suggested methodology.

The general idea behind the study is that "habits of thought" (Veblen) or "shared mental models" (Arthur T. Denzau and Douglass C. North) are an important but often neglected part of the 'soil' of informal institutions in which newly established formal rules have to strike root in order to sustain lasting changes. The times are long gone when economists measured progress in economic reforms only in quantitative terms. For example, the EBRD includes parameters of structural change into its annual *Transition Reports*. And the German *Bertelsmann Transformation Index*,[5] probably the 'broadest' of all transition indices, even tries to quantify such factors as social capital, civicness, and the degree of secularisation. None of these indices, however, includes the attitudes of the population towards the economic and political institutions of an – as Friedrich August Hayek (1988) called it – extended order. This is a severe shortcoming, for as Jean-Phillipe Platteau (1994, 795, our italics) aptly remarks,

> "to function effectively, at least in a long-term perspective, the market requires the society to be structured in a way that ensures the widespread prevalence of abstract and impersonal relationships among agents *as well as the pervasive influence of norms of generalised morality*. It is therefore wrong to assume that the market is able to deepen its virtuous mechanics in any kind of social terrain."

This paper aims at providing empirical evidence of the significance of cultural factors in transition processes by testing the degree to which "norms of generalised morality" prevail in three different societies in transition. The remainder of the paper is organised as follows: In the next section we will formulate the general theoretical framework of our research. In section three we summarise in very short terms how the transition processes in Central and Eastern Europe (in the following: CE & EE) can be described on the basis of this framework.[6] In section four we deliver a description of the main results of our survey, and in section five we develop an index that allows to rank countries according to the attitudes towards an extended order

---

[4] Ammon 1989; Klump (ed.) 1994; Schefold 1994/95; Nienhaus 1999; Zweynert 2002; Herrmann-Pillath and Hederer 2003.

[5] See the homepage of the Bertelsmann Foundation: www.bertelsmann-transformation-index.de.

[6] We would like to emphasise that sections two and three of the present paper provide a short summary of Zweynert and Goldschmidt (2006), where these ideas have been elaborated in more detail.

prevailing in them. In a conclusion we will summarise our results and give an outlook on future research.

2. The general framework: transition as extension and de-extension of social and economic relations

In accordance with the legacy of what Josef Alois Schumpeter ([1954] 1967, 815-820) called the 'youngest historical school', we start from the assumption that transition is a prime example of a social phenomenon which cannot be analysed in isolation, but only in its historical, cultural and political context. We are convinced that it is a fruitful and unwarrantedly forgotten approach to interpret the differences between economic institutions as expressions of different styles, that is, different sets of motivations, values and norms, or, in the language of older American institutionalism, "habits of thought".[7] We depart from the original style-theoretical concept, however, in two closely related assumptions. *First*, the originators of the theory of economic styles remained true to the inductivism of the younger historical school. They were convinced that it was possible to construct economic styles on the basis of building blocks derived from empirical observation (see e.g. Spiethoff 1933). We agree with Max Weber (1922, 181) that this methodological proposition has severely hampered the style-theoretical research programme: What is meaningful in the chaos of empirical phenomena can only be decided on the basis of deductively generated theories. The *second* point follows suit from this consideration: If the construction of economic styles can only be based on a prior theoretical scheme, we also must give up the idea of formulating different theories for different places and times. Quite on the contrary, the individual features of societies can be made apparent only when compared on the basis of a general theoretical framework. However, we do not claim that the approach developed here may explain institutional change in all places and at all times.[8] Rather, it is a concept at an intermediate level of abstraction that aims at highlighting some problems of CE & EE transition. And we deliberately do not make any claims about the applicability of this approach to other places and times.

Our general theoretical framework is based on the comparison between two ideal types of social and economic organisation, the extended and the holistic order. Movement between these poles can be described in terms of extension and de-extension of social and economic relations. Following Friedrich August Hayek (1988), we define the extended order as an order based on highly abstract rules with social relations being very much depersonalised. In contrast, in a holistic order social relations are strongly personalised and social interaction is based on rules that are much more

---

7 For an excellent account of "The Concept of Habit in Economic Analysis" see Waller 1988.
8 As is well known, this was precisely what Walter Eucken (1940) claimed for his theory of economic orders.

concrete and often contain moral prescripts.[9] There is a tight connection between the degree of extension of social relations and the degree of functional differentiation in a society. The fact that in 'Western' societies there exists a clearly defined (albeit not impermeable) boundary between economy and polity is an expression of the division of labour between different spheres of society, made possible by functional differentiation. Functional differentiation is a prerequisite for the emergence of different subsystems of society, each functioning according to their own functional rationality (*Zweckrationalität*) – that is, according to highly abstract and de-personalised rules. Democracy and the market are both (sub)orders of this kind. Only the politician who gets the majority of votes gains political power, and only the entrepreneur whose revenue is higher than his costs is able to survive in the market. Although both the political and the economic entrepreneur are expected to meet certain moral standards, the basic rules both in the economic and in the political system are neutral in view of moral values. And although both politicians and entrepreneurs are usually embedded in personal networks, the rules of the political and the economic game are – at least ideal-typically – neutral in view of the participating persons, for they apply to everybody independently from his or her social status, race, religious conviction and so on.[10]

In modern Western societies the existence of general, depersonalised rules makes it possible for the individual to interact in her daily business with persons far beyond her personal network(s) of personal acquaintance.[11] In a situation, in which there are no such general binding rules, the interaction with persons the individual is not personally acquainted with, bears high risks and is therefore costly. Hence, the individual is strongly dependent on and likely to restrict her social relations to the members of the community she lives in and with whom she is personally acquainted. This has two consequences: *First*, there will be a huge gap between the degree to which the individual trusts strangers (low) and the members of her own community (high). *Second*, if the individual rarely interacts with strangers, it is absolutely rational for her to behave opportunistically towards them in order to favour relatives

---

9   According to Hayek, the two types of order are not mutually exclusive. Rather, 'Western' societies are characterised by a co-existence of 'small' and 'large' society that are organised according to different patterns. To him, the problems start with the attempt to structure the whole society according to one of these patterns: "If we were to apply the unmodified, uncurbed rules of the micro-cosmos ... to the macro-cosmos ..., as our instincts and sentimental yearnings often make us wish to do, *we would destroy it.* Yet if we were always to apply the rules of the extended order to our more intimate groupings, *we would crush them.*" (Hayek 1988, p. 18) Our ideal types mainly refer to 'large' society, because a society in which the ties between kin and friends are organised according to extended patterns is simply unthinkable.
10 For a convincing critique of Granovetter's "embeddedness thesis" (1985) see Platteau (1993, 538).
11 For a thought-provoking analysis of the merits and problems of *The Company of Strangers* in modern Western societies, see Seebright 2004.

and community members. In this context, Max Weber (1958, 303-4) aptly spoke of a gap between internal and external morals (Binnen- und Außenmoral).

Viewed from our theoretical perspective, socialist transformation basically meant a de-extension of social relations. In real socialism, the degree of division of labour between the different social spheres was drastically reduced. All formerly more or less autonomous subsystems were re-subordinated to the rationality of an all-embracing political ideology. Therefore, they could only to a much lesser degree follow their own, specific logic: Highly abstract rules that had been neutral in regard to moral norms, were substituted with prescripts which were not only much more concrete (e.g. five-year-plan) but also had a strong moral impact (e.g. all economic actions had to take into account social justice). Where the impact of abstract rules decreases, that of personal relations necessarily increases.

Since the classical study of Janos Kornai (1980) it has been well known that planned economies are always economies of shortage. In market economies, the abstract medium of exchange money is the scarcest resource. In a socialist economy, this function is taken over by concrete resources and goods. As a (fairly rational) reaction to the permanent scarcity of all goods the individuals in socialist societies formed redistribution networks that were mainly based on personal relations. Within the redistribution networks the issue that decided over failure or success of a transaction was the personal relation with the potential supplier of a desired good. In addition, the only way to redirect resources into one's own network was to distract them from the official economy. Therefore, the shortage economy revived the gap between internal and external morals in which Weber had seen a typical feature of pre-modern societies. These considerations can be summarised in the following table contrasting the 'holistic' and the 'extended' order:

	Holistic society	**Extended order**
Type of ideology:	Belief in a religion or political ideology, claiming absolute and eternal truth for all areas of live.	Multitude of possible interpretations of social reality.
Degree of functional differentiation, especially between polity and economy:	No or little functional differentiation between different spheres of society, especially no clear separation of economy and polity.	Clear differentiation between the spheres of society, clear boundary between polity and economy.
Dominant type of social relations:	Dominance of personal relations within relatively small personal networks, large gap between internal and external morals.	Dominance of depersonalised relations, weakening of small networks, small gap between internal and external morals.

3. The role of history and culture: transition and the transfer of institutions

Having outlined the theoretical framework, we will now discuss the role of history and culture for processes of extension and de-extension of social relations. We start from the observation that there is an increasing gap between two groups of transition countries, with one group (the new members of the EU plus Croatia) having been successful in implementing 'Westernising' reforms and a second group (the former Soviet Republics except the Baltic States plus Bulgaria, Romania, Serbia and Montenegro), where both political and economic reforms have proceeded more slowly and where it is not yet clear which direction their development will eventually take. Our basic thesis is that an important reason behind the differences in 'transition performance' is the cultural divide between the 'Western' versions of Christianity (Protestantism and Catholicism) and the 'Eastern', Orthodox one. The following graph illustrates the connection between religious affiliation and GDP per capita in nineteen transition countries:

Country	GDP per capita	Share of Catholics and Protestants
non-Latin	3,218	3.7%
Albania	2,554	10.0%
Belarus	2,335	8.0%
Bosnia and Herzegovina	2,017	15.0%
Bulgaria	3,137	0.0%
Macedonia	2,593	0.0%
Moldova	615	0.5%
Romania	3,358	9.4%
Russian Federation	4,047	0.6%
Serbia and Montenegro	2,178	5.0%
Ukraine	1,384	9.1%
Latin	7,751	78.7%
Croatia	7,557	88.1%
Czech Republic	10,462	26.7%
Estonia	8,227	11.0%
Hungary	9,908	71.0%
Latvia	5,876	79.0%
Lithuania	6,391	79.0%
Poland	6,265	95.8%
Slovakia	7,607	87.8%
Slovenia	16,359	57.8%

GDP per capita 2004 (in US$)

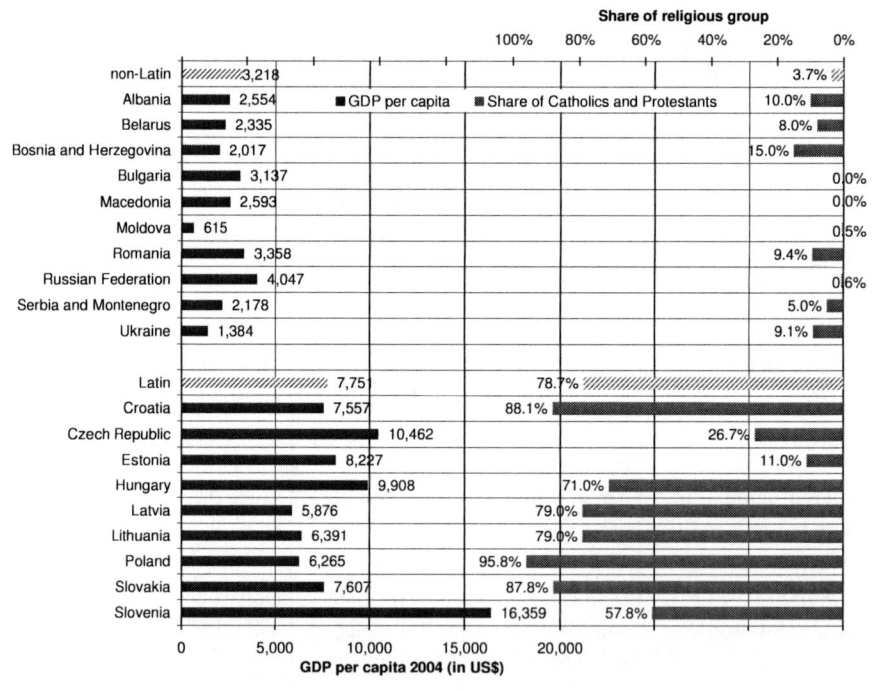

Fig. 1: GDP per capita and religious affiliation

Sources: UN Statistics Division National Accounts Main Aggregates Database (2005), http://unstats.un.org/unsd/snaama/dnltransfer.asp?fID=4 (19.01.2006), UN Statistics Division Population and Vital Statistics Report: Series A (2005), http://unstats.un.org/unsd/demographic/products/vitstats/serATab2.pdf (19.01.2006), CIA World Factbook (2006), http://www.cia.gov/cia/publications/factbook/fields/2122.html (19.01.2006), own calculations.

Now, one might argue that the GDP per capita is not the most significant indicator in transition countries. However, qualitative indicators give very much the same picture:

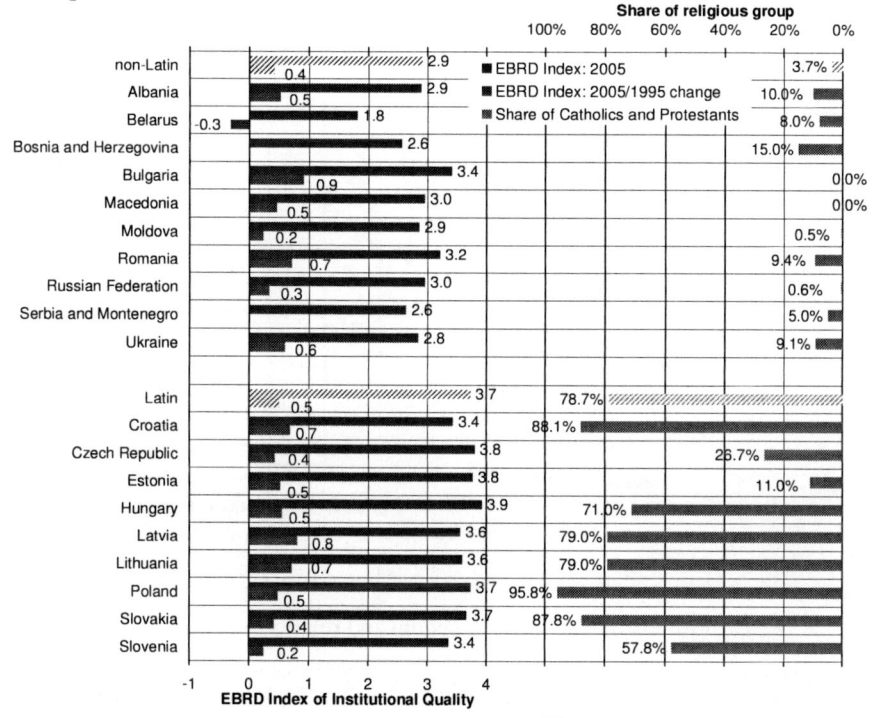

Fig. 2: EBRD Index of Institutional Quality[12] and religious affiliation

Sources: European Bank for Reconstruction and Development (various issues), Transition report, London: Europ. Bank for Reconstruction and Development, Der Fischer Weltalmanach 2006, Frankfurt a.M. 2005: Fischer Taschenbuch Verlag, CIA World Factbook (2006), http://www.cia.gov/cia/publications/factbook/fields/2122.html (19.01.2006), own calculations.

---

12 The EBRD Index of Institutional Quality is calculated as the mean of nine separate EBRD measures of the countries' different institutions. These measures range from 1 to 4 with a higher value indicating greater institutional progress. For 1995 no values for infrastructure reform were available.

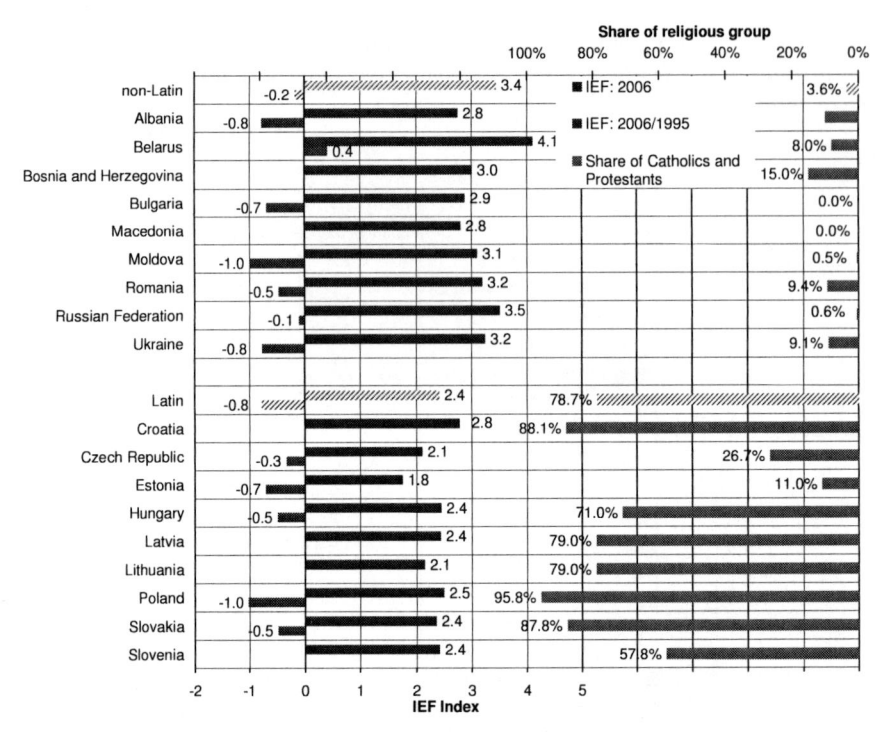

Fig. 3: Index of Economic Freedom and religious affiliation

Sources: The Heritage Foundation (2006), Index of Economic Freedom, http://www.heritage.org/research/features/index/downloads/PastScores.xls (16.02.2006), Der Fischer Weltalmanach 2006, Frankfurt a.M. 2005: Fischer Taschenbuch Verlag, CIA World Factbook (2006), http://www.cia.gov/cia/publications/factbook/fields/2122.html (19.01.2006), own calculations.

When interpreting the Index of Economic Freedom it is important to bear in mind that small index numbers stand for much freedom and vice versa.

While it is not an original idea to trace the different outcomes of transition back to the two versions of Christianity – this link has been highlighted by a whole number of social scientists and economists already (see e.g. Huntington 1993; Panther 1997, 1998, 2002; Stark and Bruszt 1998; Wallace and Haerpfer 1998; Goehrke 2000) – our explanation differs from those given by these authors: We agree that the cultural divide is central to the explanation of the gap between 'Latin winners' and 'Orthodox losers' (Panther), but in order to avoid one-dimensional culturalist explanations, we are trying to 'bring policy back in' by applying the idea of institutional transfer to CE & EE transition.[13] According to this perspective, political and military

---

13 On the problem of "institutional import" or "transfer of economic institutions" see Badie 2000; Polterovic (2001); de Jong, Lalenis and Mamadouh (2002), Djankov et al. (2003, 609-12); Oleinik 2005; Zweynert and Goldschmidt (2006).

pressure played not the smallest role in the transfer of 'Western' patterns of social organisation to the 'latecomers' of Central (Germany!) and Central Eastern Europe.[14]

The decisive feature of WE political and economic development was social differentiation. WE history since the Middle Ages has been characterised by a sequence of differentiation processes leading to a growing division of labour between the different spheres of society, with the emergence of a more or less autonomous economic subsystem at the turn of the 19th century as (for the present) the last step. The theory of institutional transplantation suggests that the success or failure of institutional transfer is determined not least by the compatibility between the informal institutions prevailing in the 'receiving' country and the formal institutions imported from abroad. Here the divide between the above-mentioned cultural divide comes into play. A decisive feature of the Orthodox legacy is a markedly holistic understanding of society. The idea that there might be a difference between religious and political truth, and that a person could act as a merchant in one way and as a believer in another, ran counter to the Orthodox religious dogma that also strongly influenced Russian secular culture (see Berdyaev [1937] 1990, 19; Buss 2003, 167). This holistic legacy is in potential conflict with the social differentiation that was basic for WE political and economic development. In our view, this may explain why the transplantation of Western, extended institutions to the countries located east of the cultural divide often led to the emergence of inconsistent hybrid settings and why many imported institutions were even rejected in the medium or long run. Although the October Revolution was by no means a pre-determined outcome of Russian culture (which of course never was homogeneous), it is also no accident that it took place in an Orthodox country. For in a way, the attempt to re-establish the unity of society by subordinating all its parts to one generally binding ideology tied in with the holistic legacy of the Orthodox Church. After the Second World War the Soviet Union managed to export her institutional settings to the Central European Countries. Even more than the 'acculturation' to WE prior to the Second World War, this transfer of institutions was politically enforced. But at the same time, the prevailing cultural traditions made the Orthodox countries more susceptive to the imported Soviet institutions which remained somewhat akin to the Protestant and Catholic societies.

Summing up, we argue that the two transitions the countries of CE & EE went through in the 20th century (with the second transition not yet being completed in all countries) can be described as processes of de-extension (socialist transformation) and extension (transition from plan to market). We emphasise that both processes were in the first order politically implemented, but we argue that the degree to which the transplanted institutions stroke roots in the receiving country, decisively de-

---

14 A typical example is that both in Germany and in Russia the decisive reforms which laid the foundation for capitalist transformations were set up after devastating defeats in wars: In Germany it was the defeat in the Napoleonic Wars that finally led to the implementation of the reforms of Stein and Hardenberg [*Stein-Hardenbergsche Reformen*], in Russia the emancipation of the serfs was accomplished after the defeat in the Crimean war (1853-56).

pended on cultural factors. The aim of our empirical research was to find out whether the divide between the Orthodox countries on the one and the Catholic and Protestant countries on the other hand finds an expression in different attitudes towards market and democracy.

4. Descriptive analysis

Our interpretation of transition towards the market and democracy as a process of extension of social and economic relations is basic to the design of our questionnaire and the choice of countries. In summer and autumn 2004 larger surveys were carried out in Latvia, Poland and Russia, the sample size being 2000 respondents in Russia and 1000 respondents in each Latvia and Poland.[15] The survey is cohort-specific with an equal share of the ten cohorts. We chose this method because in view of the future perspectives of the formerly socialist countries the attitudes of the younger generations are of special significance. We will look at these differences in the next section, in which the extended order index will be developed. The questionnaire that was developed in co-operation with Alexander Chepurenko (Higher School of Economics, Moscow) and adapted to Latvia and Poland by our regional partners (see footnote 15) consisted of 55 questions, 21 of which are of a supplementary nature (asking about the social status of the respondents, their political and religious convictions and so on). For the sake of brevity we confine our descriptive analysis to the 16 questions (out of 34) that provided the most interesting results. In accordance with our interpretation of the transition process, the main focus of these questions are the following points:

1. Exploring the ideological backing of the extended order within given societies and the evaluation of abstract and depersonalised versus moral and personalised rules respected by their members,

2. Identifying and quantifying public opinion about the relation between the political and the other subsystems of society, especially the economic one,

3. Addressing some qualities of special importance for the functioning of an extended order: the level of trust and the degree to which norms of generalised morality prevail.

The hypothesis that the differences in the attitudes towards the extended order in CE & EE are significantly due to the cultural divide between the Orthodox countries on the one hand and the Protestant and Catholic ones on the other, determined the choice of countries for the survey. Poland is one of the most successful transition

---

15 Field work was carried out by the Institute of Social Research at the Russian Academy of Sciences (Moscow, Russia), B.P.S. Consultants (Warsaw, Poland), and the Baltic Institute of Social Sciences (Riga, Latvia).

countries and is clearly located west of the cultural divide. Russia is not only a typical example of a country that until now has shown a much weaker 'transition performance' than most CE countries, it is also one of the countries with the highest shares of Orthodox believers in CE & EE.[16] Latvia is an extremely interesting case due to the fact that almost 40% of its population is of Russian, Ukrainian or Belorussian origin.[17] Therefore, the cultural boundary runs through the country, and comparing the answers given by Latvians of a 'Russian' with those of a 'Baltic' origin seems to be especially promising in order to verify the significance of the cultural divide. Indeed, if we take a look at the 'transition performance' in the three countries analysed by us, we find that – without claiming that this is solely due to the cultural divide – regarding both indicators Poland showed the best and Russia the worst performance, with Latvia taking an intermediate position:

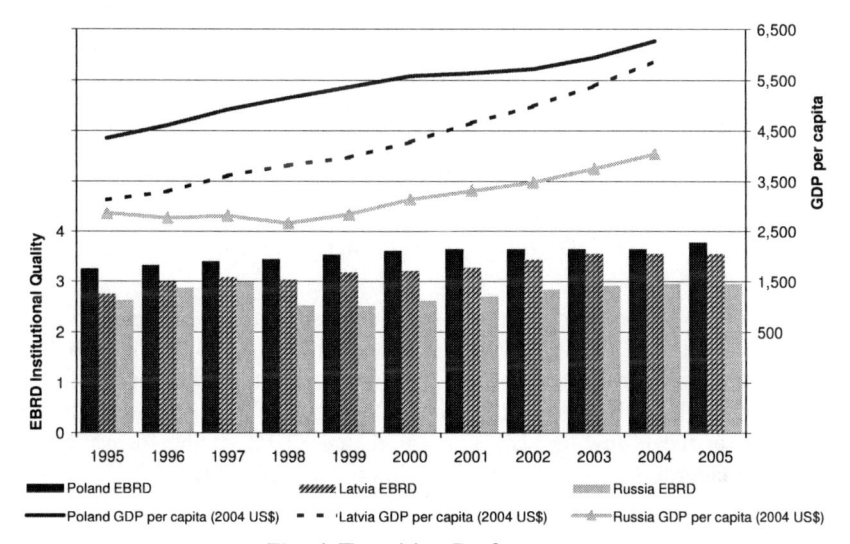

Fig. 4: Transition Performance

Sources: UN Statistics Division National Accounts Main Aggregates Database (2005), http://unstats.un.org/unsd/snaama/dnltransfer.asp?fID=4 (19.01.2006), European Bank for Reconstruction and Development (various issues), Transition report, London: Europ. Bank for Reconstruction and Development, own calculations.

Now, how do the attitudes towards the extended order relate to the developments in the real economy? Our hypothesis is that the acceptance of the extended

---

16 The share in Russia is 87%. It is only higher in Moldova (98%).
17 In Russian common speech, these Latvians are often labelled "Russians". We do not follow this classification and distinguish between "Baltic" Latvians, Latvians of Russian origin and "others". As our aim is to compare the Russian and the Latvian data, in the following we neglect the group of "others", which constitutes approximately 8 % of those questioned by us.

order should be highest in Poland and lowest in Russia, with Latvia taking a middle position. Within Latvia we would expect significant differences between the respondents of a 'Baltic' and those of 'Russian' origin.

At the beginning, we asked the respondents how they evaluated the market reforms 15 years ago (question 1) and how they judged the reforms of the early 1990s today (question 2).

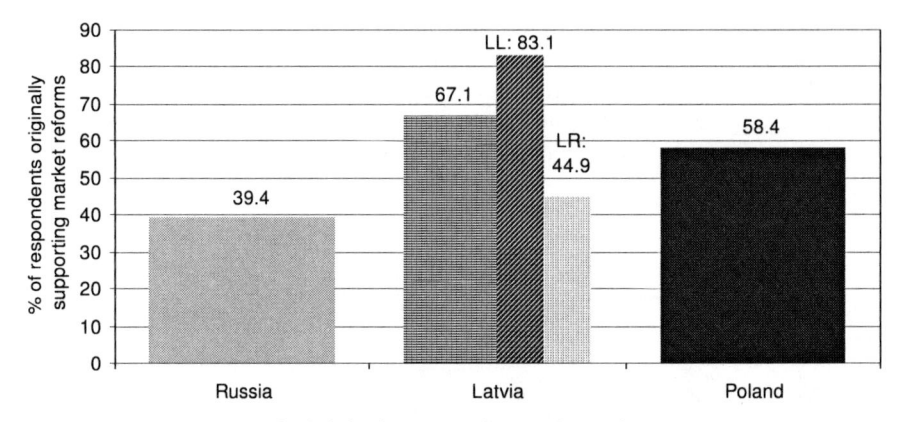

Fig. 5: Original support for market reforms

According to the memory of our respondents, support for market reforms was originally highest in Latvia (67.1%) and lowest in Russia (39.4%), with Poland (58.4%) taking an intermediate position.[18] If we differentiate the Latvian data into Latvians with a Baltic background (in the following "LL") and those of "Russian" background (in the following "LR"), we find that 83.1% of the former but only 44.9% of the latter had a pro-reform orientation in the early 1990s.[19]

---

18 The numbers in brackets are the sum of those who either said that they had "supported market reforms with vigour" and those who "had their doubts but saw more pluses than minuses".
19 This is a typical example of how careful one should be in explaining differences with cultural factors. It should not go without notice here that the 'Russian' Latvians probably were aware from the beginning that the reforms were not only likely to lead to full autonomy of Latvia from Russia, but also, that this might significantly worsen their social and political situation.

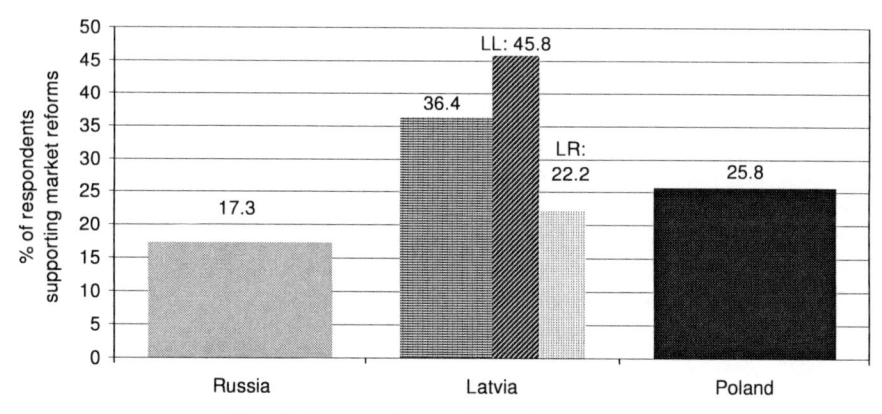

Fig. 6: Support for market reforms today

In all countries, support for market reforms has decreased by approximately 50% (R: 17.3%; P: 25.8%; L: 36.4%). Within Latvia, the relative shares have remained roughly the same; 45.8% of LL, but only 22.2% of LR still support market reforms.

Our third question concerned specific goals of development in Latvian, Polish or Russian society. We offered 19 possible answers to the respondents and asked them to choose the three they considered most important. The background to this question is that one of the basic dogmas of real socialism was to see history as a purposeful process with a well-defined final result (communist society). In contrast, Western liberal society tends not do declare overall binding goals of social development.

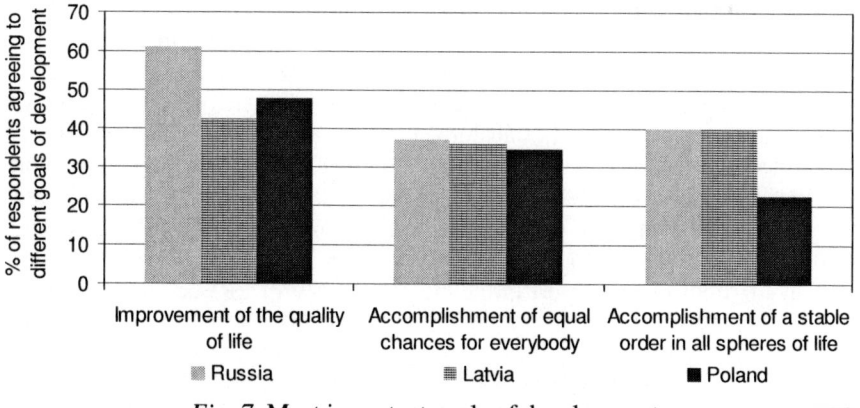

Fig. 7: Most important goals of development

161

In all countries (R 60.9%; L 42.4%; P 47.9%), an "improvement of the quality of life" was regarded as the most important goal, and in all of them between 34.8% (P) and 37.1% (R) considered the "accomplishment of equal chances for everybody" as the second most important goal.[20] If all three countries are taken together, the "accomplishment of a stable order in all spheres of life" was regarded as the third most important goal. However, there are significant differences. Stability is seen by close to 40% of the Russians and Latvians as one of the most important goals, but only by 22.6% of the Poles. This is exactly the same share of Polish respondents who hold that "the establishment of a functioning market economy" is an important goal. The share of Latvians and Poles who support this view is about the same (22.2%), but in Russia it is only 15.5 %.

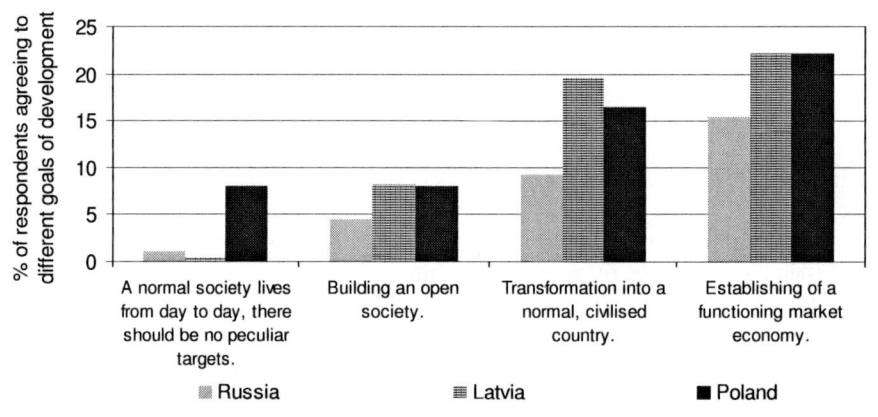

Fig. 8: Rejection of the socialist order

The most radical refusal of the socialist dogma of history as a purposeful process is the statement "A normal society lives from day to day, in it there should be no particular targets". Interestingly, it is supported by 1.1 % of the Russian and 0.5% of the Latvian respondents, but by remarkable 8.1% of the Polish ones. The targets "to build up an open society" and "transformation into a normal, civilised country" are further clear expressions of liberal values. Building an "open society" is supported by 4.4% of Russians but by 8.1% of Poles and 8.4% of Latvians.[21] Here again it is interesting that the share of LR who support the "open society" (8.9%) is significantly higher than that of LL (7.2%). The suspicion that this is due to the minority status of LR finds clear support in the fact that 36.8% of LR see the "peaceful co-

20 While all in all the differences between LL and LR were negligible for question three, this particular goal was supported by 48.4% of LR but only by 27.9% of LL. It is quite obvious that this is due to the fact that the LR see themselves as a suppressed minority that would gain by an equalisation of chances.
21 Here again it is interesting that the share of LR who support the "open society" (8.9%) is significantly higher than that of LL (7.2%).

162

existence of different nations within the country" as an important goal, in contrast to only 8.0% of LL. Only 9.2% of the Russians see the transformation into a normal civilised country as an important target, the shares in Poland (16.5%) and Latvia (19.7%) are clearly higher.

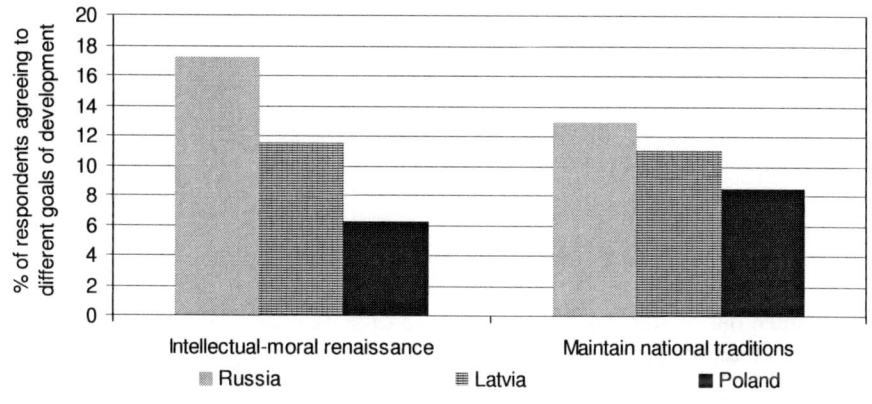

Fig. 9: Call for intellectual-moral renaissance and support for the maintenance of national traditions

Somewhat opposed to the target of becoming a "normal civilised country" is – at least in the context of a post-socialist society – the call for "intellectual-moral renaissance", which is seen as an important goal by 17.2% of Russians, 11.5% of Latvians but only by 6.2% of Poles. In all three countries it is felt that it is important to maintain national traditions, but again this share is higher in Russia (12.9%) than in Latvia (11.1%) and in Poland (8.5%).

In a next step, we asked about the relation between the political and the other spheres of society. In particular, we tried to find out to what degree the respondents still support a social order in which the political system (the government) directly interferes with the press, the law, science and private business. For this purpose we asked the respondents whether they agreed or disagreed with the following statements:

a) If the press does harm to the state interests, its freedom should be restricted.
b) The government should have the possibility to directly influence legal practice if the state interests demand it.
c) Science is not a purpose of its own. Its task is to serve the state.
d) Enterprises doing harm to the state interests should be nationalised.
e) Social justice stands higher than the entrepreneurs' striving for profit.

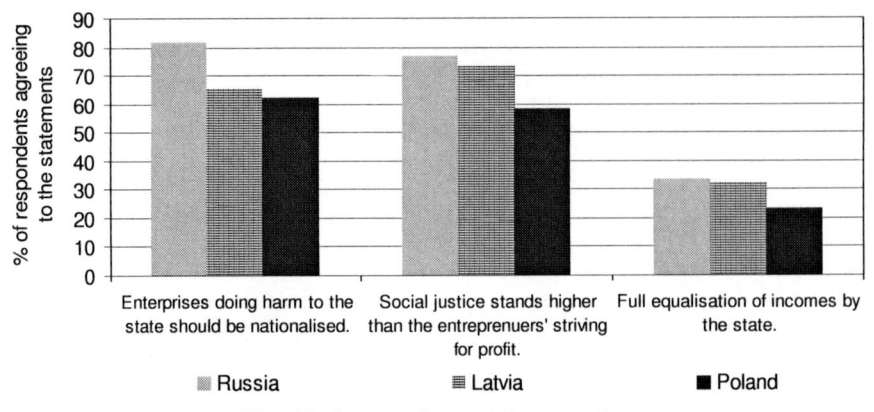

Fig. 10: Support for state intervention

In three out of five cases the acceptance of state interference (or the call for a primacy of the political system) is highest in Russia and lowest in Poland, with Latvia taking an intermediate position. However, regarding the relation between the political and the juridical system, more Poles than Latvians accept the statement that the government should intervene if the state interests seem to make this necessary, and more Latvians than Russians hold that science should mainly serve the state's interests. The last two questions more specifically concern the relation between the political and the economic sphere. 81.8% of the Russians but 'only' 65.5% of the Latvians and 62.5% of the Poles agree with statement about the nationalisation of enterprises. On this issue, the Latvian response is similar to the Polish one, but with regard to the statement that the ideal of social justice stands higher than the striving for profit, the outcome in Latvia is significantly closer to that in Russia (R 77.0%; L 73.6%; P 58.6%). We have to concede that the results of a differentiation of the Latvian data according to national origins clearly contradict our hypothesis: In the two cases where there are significant differences (questions c and d), support of holistic (or "anti-extended") patterns is higher with LL than with LR by approximately 10%.

We then focused more concretely on the relation between the state and the private sector as producers of goods and services. We confronted the respondents with 22 branches and institutions, ranging from banks to schools and theatres, and asked whether they should be managed by the state, by private business, or by both. Our findings regarding this question can be summarised in very short terms: Concerning 13 out of the 22 goods and services mentioned in the survey, the Russians preferred the strongest and the Poles the lowest participation of the state. Latvia again took an intermediate position and in most cases was closer in opinion to Russia than to Poland.[22] In view of the events around the Yukos group it deserves mentioning that 80.2% of the Russian respondents are of the opinion that oil production should be in

---

22 There were no significant differences in the answers of LL and LR.

the hands of the state. The fifth question, which is tightly connected with the fourth, is about the role of the state in the social sphere. The differences are less significant than we expected, but the share of those who desire a full equalisation of incomes by the state is slightly more than 30% in Russia (33.8%) and in Latvia (32.4%), whereas this share is 'only' about 23.5% in Poland.

In order to learn more about the values that are basic to the acceptance or rejection of the extended order, we confronted the respondents with fifteen terms[23] and asked them to qualify their associations on a scale from one (very negative) to five (very positive). The graph below gives a simplified overview of the results, with the scale points reduced from five to three.[24]

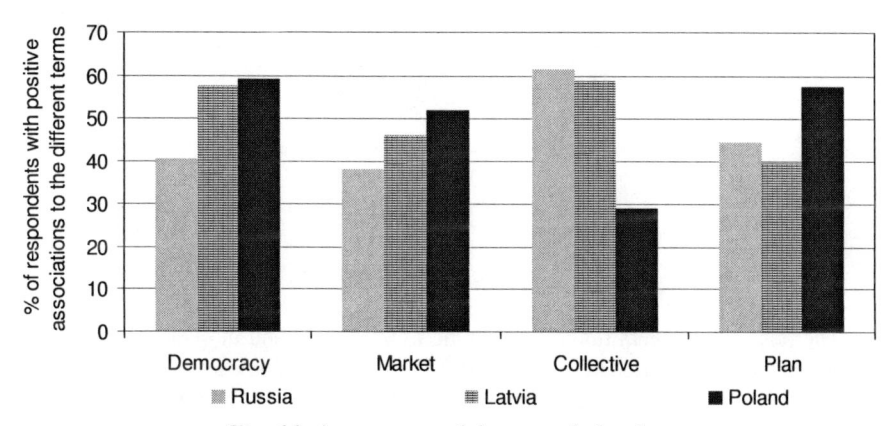

Fig. 11: Acceptance of the extended order

In general, the answers to this question also confirm the hypothesis: Both "democracy" and "market" raise the most positive associations in Poland (democracy: 59.2%; market: 52.2%) and the least positive ones in Russia (40.8% / 38.0%); as usually, Latvia (57.6% / 46.2) is located between the two.[25] The same is true for other key terms of the extended order such as "individual", "private property" and "efficiency". Particularly striking is that the term "collective" raises positive associations with 61.5% of the Russians and 58.8% of the Latvians but only 28.9% of the Poles. However, it came as a great surprise to us that the term "plan" raises posi-

---

23 These terms were: effectiveness, plan, individual, state, democracy, solidarity, market, society, competition, collective, rationality, social justice, money, profit, private property.
24 The data were aggregated by summarising scale points 5 and 4 (very positive/positive) to "positive" and the scale points 1 and 2 to "negative" respectively.
25 The differences between LL and LR with regard to both these terms are significant: "Democracy" raises positive emotions with 60.4% of LL but only 53.6% of LR, the according values for "market" are 47.3% and 42.1%.

tive associations with 57.6% of the Poles but only 44.5% of Russians and 39.6% of Latvians.[26]

The seventh question "According to your view, how must one behave towards the law?" is one of the key questions of the survey, for it directly refers to the norms of generalised morality.

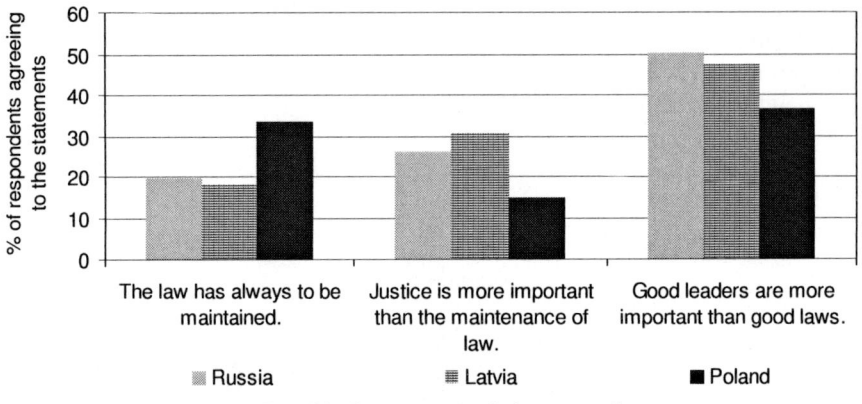

Fig. 12: Acceptance of abstract rules

The possible answers range from "One must always and in every case maintain the law, even if it is outdated or does not fully accord to today's reality" to "It is not so important if something is according to the law or not – the main thing is that it's just". The share of those who hold that the law must always be upheld is highest in Poland (33.5%) and lowest in Latvia (18.2%), but the difference between Latvia and Russia (19.7%) is not really significant. The share of those who hold that it is more important that something is just than that it is legal is again higher in Latvia (31.0%)[27] than in Russia (26,1%), but it is much lower in Poland (14,8%). Another core question regards the relative importance of abstract rules of the political process and of the individual characteristics of political leaders. Here, we get a very similar picture as with the previous question: 50.3% of Russians and 47.3% of Latvians (LL 45.7%; LR 50.0%) find good leaders more important than good laws. This share is only 35.6% in Poland, which is the only country where the majority (51.1%) holds that good laws are more important than good leaders.

Three questions concern the relative importance of the democratic order in relation to personal security, material well-being and social justice. Asked whether they would prefer to live in a society which is fully democratic but cannot guarantee per-

---

26 While the evaluation of "individual" is roughly equal with LL and LR, "private property" raises positive associations with 68.6% of LL but only 58.9% of LR; "efficiency" is an exception to the rule: this term raises positive emotions with 52.0% of LR but 48.6% of LL.
27 There were no significant differences between LL and LR here.

sonal security or in one where a strong government provides security but restricts the democratic rights of the citizens, 64.9% of the Russian, 47.9% of the Latvian and 28.7% of the Polish respondents preferred the strong state. 'Baltic' and 'Russian' Latvians are strongly divided concerning this question: The strong state is preferred by a minority of LL (41.9%) but by a clear majority of LR (56.3%). However, in none of these countries a majority voted for "full democracy" without personal security (P 39.1%; L 31.1%; R 11.1%).[28] Moreover, the share of those who found this question difficult to answer was by far highest in Poland (32.25%; R 24.0%; L 20.0%).

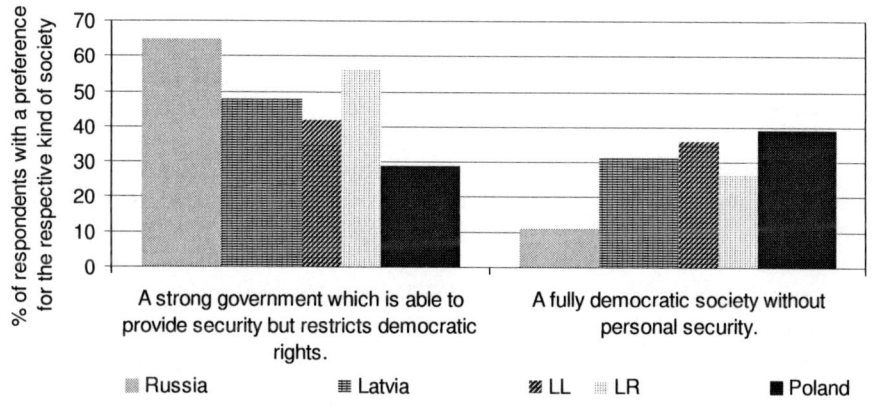

Fig. 13: Relative importance of the democratic order

36.0 % of the Russians, 29.9% of the Latvians (LL 27.4%; LR 34.2) and 28.7% of the Poles would be willing to sacrifice democratic freedom for material well-being. Consequently, if people had to choose between living in a society of individual freedom or in one of social equality, about a quarter (24.8%) of the Russians but about 35% of the Latvians and Poles (L 34.6%[29], P 34.5%) chose the society of individual freedom. Interestingly, the share of those who wish to live in a society of social equality is highest in Latvia (53.2%),[30] followed by Russia (49.5%) and Poland (37.3%). The explanation is that the share of those who find this question difficult to answer is much lower in Latvia (12.3%) than in Russia (25.7%) and in Poland (28.3%). All in all, these three question fit in nicely with our model. However, it should not be overlooked that these answers can also be seen as an expression of social reality, with Russia and Latvia being characterised by a lower level of material well-being and less personal security and social justice.

---

28 The difference between LL (35.9%) and LR (26.6%) is once more significant.
29 LL: 36.7%; LR: 29.6%.
30 LL: 50.2%; LR: 58.9%.

167

Three questions of our survey were about trust. The first one was a standard question about trust in political and economic institutions.[31] While there were no strong differences between the three countries, our two questions about the relation between personal and extended trust and the discrepancy between internal and external morals produced interesting results. In order to identify the relation between personal and extended trust, we asked the respondents which of the following statements they could agree with most:

a) I trust not only my closest friends and relatives, but also people I don't know well.
b) I trust my close friends and relatives, but I don't trust people I don't know well.
c) I don't trust anybody.

Affirmation of statement a) is lowest in Russia (7.8%) and highest in Poland (26.0%) with Latvia (13.8%)[32] taking an intermediate position. The differences are remarkable: The share of those who have an extended trust towards the society they live in is almost twice as high in Latvia than in Russia and in Poland almost twice as high as in Latvia, and it is more than three times higher in Poland than in Russia. These results also show clearly that the trust-question in the World Value Survey ("Do you think that in general people can be trusted?") is imprecise. The share of our respondents who "don't trust anybody" is not really significantly different in the three countries (R 17.2%; P 15.1%; L 13.8%). What makes the difference here, is not *if* people trust but *whom* they trust. The question about internal and external morals also delivered clear, but less definite results.

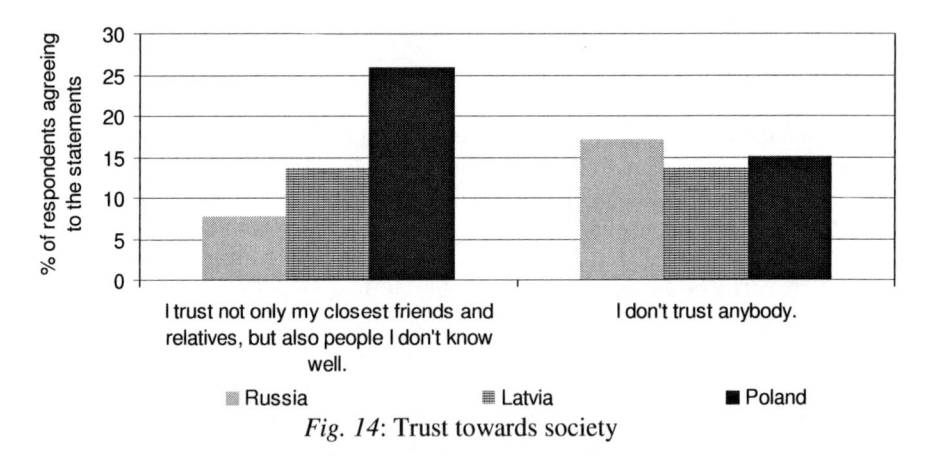

Fig. 14: Trust towards society

---

31 This question was: "To what degree do you trust the following social structures and international organisations?"; the list included 19 positions.
32 The differences between LL (13.6%) and LR (12.6%) are negligible here.

Our question was: "Some people say, it's quite okay to cheat on people you don't know well personally if this is necessary to help close friends and relatives. How do you behave?" Concerning this question, there is a clear difference between Russian and Latvia on the one hand and Poland on the other: 12.6% of the Russian respondents and 13.3 % of the Latvian, but only 7.4% of the Polish ones answered that they often behaved in this way and would continue to do so. In contrast, 41.1% of the Russian and 37.4% of the Latvian respondents but 59.8% of the Polish ones said that they never behaved in this way and would neither do so in the future.

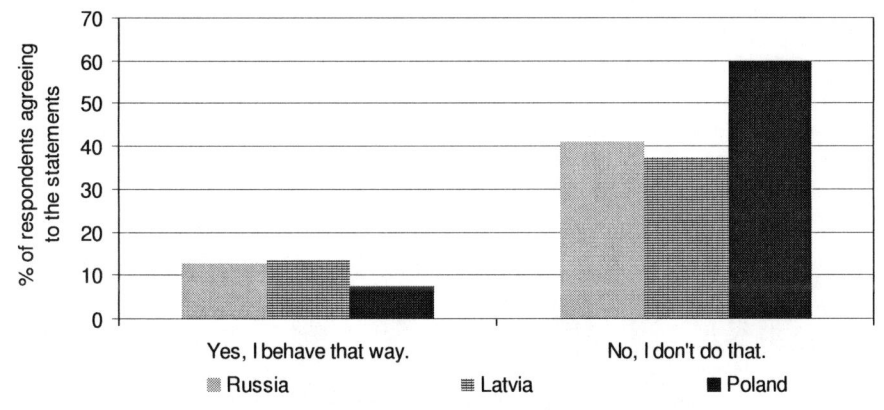

Fig. 15: Veracity in personal behaviour

It would certainly be a mistake simply to identify the Western world and the extended order. However, as this survey was carried out as part of a project that deals with the Eastern Enlargement of the EU and the interaction between the EU and its new Eastern neighbours, we included two questions concerning the evaluation of Western institutions and the respondents' understanding of how their country relates to other nations.

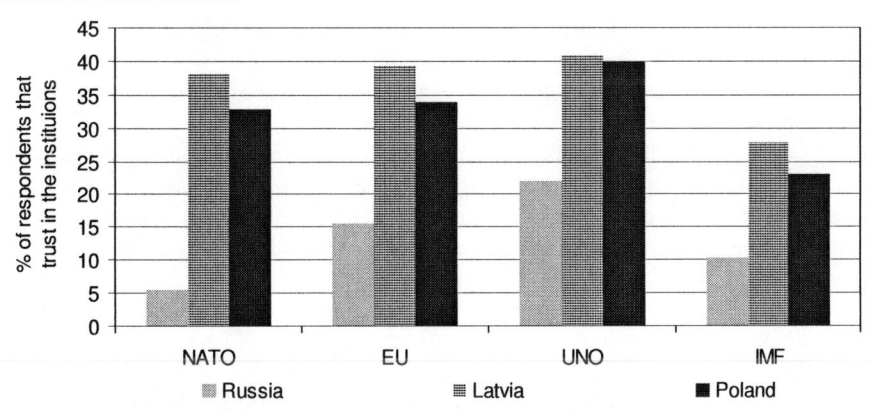

Fig. 16: Trust in international institutions

Trust in international institutions (dominated by the Western nations) is significantly higher in both Latvia and Poland than in Russia. It is interesting here that the Russian respondents do not only trust the NATO (R 5.5%; L 38.0%; P 32.9%) and the EU (R 15.4%; L 39.3%; P 33.9%) significantly less than the Latvian and the Poles, but also the UNO (R 21.9%; L 40.8%; P 40.0%) and the IMF (R 10.3%; L 27.9%; P 23.1%). In keeping with this, the share of those who welcome the enlargement of the EU is more than twice as high in Latvia (44.3%) and Poland (49.6 %) than in Russia (22.1%). Trust in the above-mentioned international organisations is significantly different between LL and LR,[33] and the gap is even greater with regard to the issue of the Eastern Enlargement of the EU, with 51.2% of LL but only 33.2% of LR being pro-enlargement.

While these are not really astonishing results, we experienced a great surprise when we asked our respondents to classify their country into a Western or an Eastern bloc with respect to cultural and economic concerns as well as mentality.

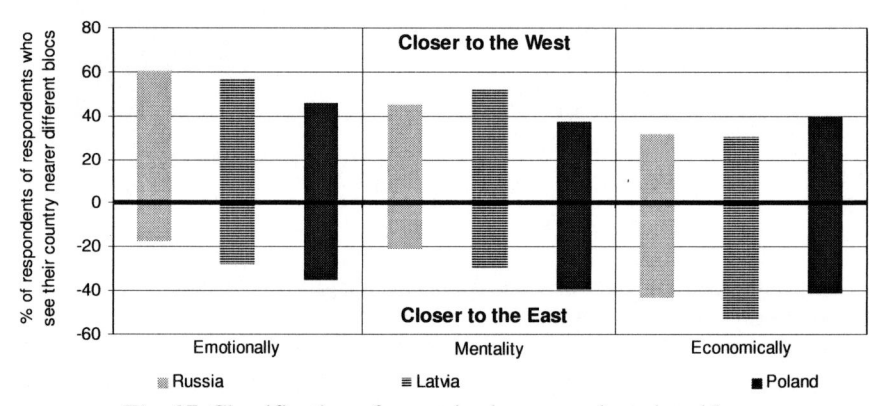

Fig. 17: Classification of countries by respondents into blocs

In order to highlight this complex issue, we grouped the USA, France and Germany together as the Western bloc, while the Eastern bloc was represented by China, India and Japan. The respondents were asked to classify the position of their country between these 'poles' on a 12 point scale with regard to each of the three aspects mentioned (culture, economy, mentality). Summarising the answers we received from our respondents, contrary to our expectations, the Poles see themselves as the most "Eastern" country. For example, 60.7% of the Russians feel nearer to the Western and only 17.1 % nearer to the Eastern bloc, whereas only 45.8% of the Poles see themselves closer to the West and 34.8% closer to the East, with Latvia (56.7% / 27.9%) taking an intermediate position. When we asked about mentality,

---

33   UNO LL: 42.6%; LR: 37.2% - EU LL 43.9%; LR 31.3% - IMF LL: 29.5%; LR: 25.0% - NATO LL: 48.1%; 21.7%.

the responses presented a similar picture,[34] and only economically the Poles saw themselves – but only slightly – closer to the West and further from the East than the Latvians and the Russians.[35] We do not have an explanation for this surprising cultural self-assessment by the Polish respondents. However, this result gives especially clear evidence that one should be extremely careful with classifying the countries of Central and Eastern Europe into a pre-occupied East-West pattern.

5. The extended order index

Having described the results of our survey in some detail, we now try to establish an index which allows to rank countries according to the prevailing attitudes towards the extended order. At first glance, this may seem a somewhat dubious endeavour. First, country rankings have an impact on the decisions of private investors and international financial institutions. Yet while it seems to be quite acceptable that a country where reforms have got stuck loses credibility, it appears to be morally problematic to 'punish' a society for its population's low acceptance of market and democracy. Second, especially the fact that countries are ranked according to the acceptance of genuine 'Western' patterns of social and political organisation might be interpreted as an expression of a rather 'imperialistic' attitude towards the transition countries.

Regarding the first objection, it must be conceded that an influence on investment decisions of private firms or funding decisions of financial institutions cannot be excluded as a negative side effect of this kind of indexing. However, in our view this can be compensated by the positive effects such an index may provide. For it might help politicians to develop reform strategies that take into account the 'soil' of informal institutions. Concerning the second objection, we would like to remind the reader that we do not declare our method to be applicable to all countries and all times. Rather, it aims at a better understanding of CE & EE transition and Eastern Enlargement of the EU. At the beginning of this process, all formerly socialist countries had announced their desire to turn into societies of the Western European type. Therefore, as far as this problem is concerned, we think our 'Eurocentric' attitude is fully justified.

In order to make indexing possible, we had to further reduce our questionnaire to the ten questions suitable for quantitative conditioning. In the case of questions 1 and 10 a short verbal explanation is necessary to clarify how the score was calculated. In all other cases the bold numbers in brackets indicate the number with which the percentage of the respective answer was multiplied. These numbers range from 2.5 to 10 and were chosen according to the relative importance of each question.

---

34   R: 45.1% closer to the West / 21.3% closer to the West; L: 52.8/29.4%; P: 37.6%/39.1%.
35   R: 31.9%/42.9%; L: 31.0%/53.3%; P: 39.6%/41.3%.

1) *What should be managed privately, what should be managed by the state?*

   The respondents were confronted with 22 branches and institutions. We measured the acceptance of private management for the different branches and institutions by calculating for each of them the mean values for the answer "should be managed privately". The resulting percentage was then multiplied with ten.

2) *What should be the role of the state in the social sphere?*
   a) The state should not interfere in the lives of its citizens, everyone should be responsible for him/herself. **(10)**
   b) The state should help only the weak and the helpless. **(5)**
   c) The state should provide all citizens with a certain minimum; anyone who wants to earn more, has to accomplish this on his or her own.
   d) The state should guarantee full equality between all citizens (material, juridical, political).

3) *How should one behave towards the law?*
   a) The law must always be obeyed, even if it is outdated or does not fully accord to reality. **(5)**
   b) Laws have to be followed even if they are outdated, but only if also the representatives of the state do so. **(2,5)**
   c) It is not so important if something accords to the law – the main issue is whether it is just or not.
   d) Don't know.

4) *What is more important for your country: Good laws or good leaders?*
   a) The law must always be obeyed, even if it is outdated or does not fully accord to reality. **(5)**
   b) Laws have to be followed even if they are outdated, but only if also the representatives of the state do so. **(2,5)**
   c) It is not so important if something accords to the law – the main issue is whether it is just or not.
   d) Don't know.

5) *What would you choose: Full democracy without a guarantee of personal security, or a strong government which is able to guarantee personal security?*
   a) Full democracy. **(5)**
   b) Strong government.
   c) Don't know.

6) *Would you be willing to sacrifice democratic freedom for an increase in material well-being?*
   a) Yes.
   b) No. **(5)**

c) Don't know.

7) *If you could live either in a society of individual freedom or in one of social justice – what would you choose?*
   a) Society of individual freedom. **(5)**
   b) Society of social justice.
   c) Don't know.

8) *With which of the following statements do you agree most?*
   a) I trust not only my close friends and my relatives, but also people I do not know well. **(5)**
   b) I trust my close friends and my relatives, but I do not trust people I do not know well.
   c) I do not trust anybody.

9) *According to a common point of view, it's okay to cheat on people you know little in order to help close friends and relatives. How do you personally behave?*
   a) I have often behaved in this way and I will do so again in future.
   b) I have never behaved in this way, but I may do so in future.
   c) I have never behaved in this way, and I will not do so in future. **(5)**

10) *Do you agree with the following statements?*
    a) If the press does harm to the national interests, its freedom should be restricted.
    b) The government should have the possibility directly to influence legal practice, if the national interests demand it.
    c) Science is not an end in itself. Its main task is to serve the interests of the government.
    d) Enterprises that do harm to the national interests should be nationalised.
    e) Social justice stands higher than the private striving for profit.

In the case of this answer we added up the percentages of the negative answers.

The following table shows each country's score for the different questions and its overall results:

Question No.	Age criterion	Russia	Latvia *All*	*Latvian origin*	*Russian origin**	Poland
1	Age under 30	0,867	1,631	1,701	1,503	1,731
	Age over 30	0,535	1,040	1,205	0,820	1,208
	All age groups	**0,631**	**1,205**	**1,351**	**0,996**	**1,377**
2	Age under 30	0,932	0,916	0,994	0,781	1,667
	Age over 30	0,747	0,776	0,883	0,629	1,445
	All age groups	**0,800**	**0,815**	**0,916**	**0,668**	**1,517**
3	Age under 30	2,023	1,934	2,023	1,675	2,699
	Age over 30	2,171	2,127	2,171	2,133	2,664
	All age groups	**2,128**	**2,073**	**2,128**	**2,015**	**2,675**
4	Age under 30	1,638	1,788	1,790	1,753	2,737
	Age over 30	2,052	2,408	2,500	2,258	2,467
	All age groups	**1,933**	**2,234**	**2,290**	**2,128**	**2,554**
5	Age under 30	0,771	1,916	1,847	2,010	1,988
	Age over 30	0,466	1,484	1,798	1,039	1,942
	All age groups	**0,554**	**1,605**	**1,812**	**1,290**	**1,957**
6	Age under 30	1,075	2,135	2,330	1,753	2,554
	Age over 30	1,218	2,330	2,417	2,204	2,949
	All age groups	**1,177**	**2,275**	**2,391**	**2,088**	**2,821**
7	Age under 30	1,837	2,190	2,273	2,010	1,835
	Age over 30	0,998	1,548	1,714	1,308	1,672
	All age groups	**1,239**	**1,728**	**1,879**	**1,489**	**1,724**
8	Age under 30	0,390	0,693	0,682	0,670	1,407
	Age over 30	0,392	0,691	0,682	0,699	1,248
	All age groups	**0,392**	**0,692**	**0,682**	**0,691**	**1,299**
9	Age under 30	1,516	1,241	1,165	1,392	2,385
	Age over 30	2,272	2,115	2,141	2,061	3,277
	All age groups	**2,055**	**1,870**	**1,852**	**1,888**	**2,989**
10	Age under 30	2,066	2,301	2,290	2,292	2,633
	Age over 30	1,541	1,923	1,825	2,079	2,318
	All age groups	**1,693**	**2,029**	**1,963**	**2,134**	**2,420**
EOI	Age under 30	13,116	16,745	17,093	15,839	21,634
	Age over 30	12,393	16,442	17,335	15,232	21,190
	All age groups	**12,601**	**16,527**	**17,264**	**15,388**	**21,334**

Certainly, one might disagree with our weighting of individual answers. And we are aware ourselves that this index is not 'perfect' in the sense that the questions were not originally developed in order to establish a ranking but rather for a descriptive analysis. However, as imperfect as this index may be, it does confirm our starting hypothesis that acceptance of the extended order is highest in Poland and lowest in Russia and that Latvia takes a middle position with significant differences between 'Baltic' and 'Russian' Latvians. However, if we differentiate the data further and distinguish two age groups – respondents under thirty and over thirty years of age – we get a more complex picture. According to our expectations, people under thirty, who have spent at least half their lives so far in a post-socialist society, score higher than people over thirty. However, in all countries the differences between the two age groups are small if not negligible. And if we quickly go through the individual questions, we clearly have to concede that in some of the very questions we hold to be central to the extended order index, younger people even scored significantly lower than the older ones. The answers to *question 1* (What should be managed by the state/privately?) show that young people are much more sceptical towards state management of enterprises and social institutions. Accordingly, they also prefer a more restricted role of the state in the social sphere (question 2). The answers to *question 3* (How should one behave towards the law?) provide a different picture. Both in Russia and in Latvia younger people show a less 'extended' attitude towards the law than people over thirty, and only in Poland the scores are about equal. A similar, but much more extreme picture is revealed with regard to *question 4* (Good laws or good leaders more important?): A much higher share of young Russians and Latvians believe that good leaders are more important than good laws, whereas in Poland there is a significant difference in the opposite direction. While the outcome of *question 5* (Reactions to trade-off between personal security and individual freedom) more or less accorded to our expectations, the answers to *question six* were 'perverse' to them: In all three countries, younger people are much more willing to sacrifice democratic freedom for an increase in material well-being than older people. In our view, there are basically two explanations for this result: Either younger people lack the experience of real socialism with its restriction of personal freedom. Or they have a stronger materialist orientation than people over thirty, because they grew up in a transition economy and were not exposed to socialist education. It is understood that these two explanations are not mutually exclusive. *Question 7* (Society of individual freedom versus social justice?) shows the highest divergence between the age groups apart from *question 1*, with the young people having a much more 'capitalist' preference structure than their older fellow citizens. While the differences are negligible in *questions 8* and *10*, we received strongly 'perverse' answers to a question which directly reflects norms of generalised morality and hence is of major importance for our concept: In all countries the young people reported on a much higher gap between internal and external morals in their personal behaviour than people over thirty. The graph above clearly shows that the correlation holds over almost all countries and cohorts. At this stage of our work, we do not have an explanation for this phenomenon. Here, it would be especially helpful to have comparative data from 'Western' countries in order to check whether this might be an age-specific result typical of other societies besides those of transition countries.

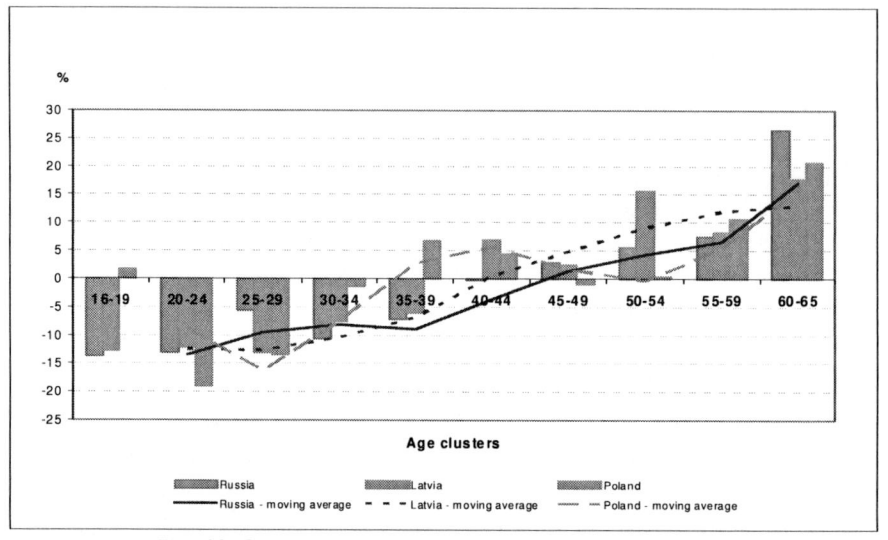

Fig. 18: Question 9 'How do you personally behave?' –
distribution of (c) answer across age clusters
(deviation from the country's average frequency of giving (c))

All in all, we might say that the extended order index roughly confirms our hypothesis, but that the cohort-specific data pose several questions we are not yet able to answer. We see this as an encouragement to continue our research in this field.

5. An outlook on future research

Much speaks in favour of the thesis that the cultural divide between 'Latin' and 'Orthodox' countries will become even more important in the further process of European integration. So far, only 'Latin' countries of Central Eastern Europe have become members of the EU – Latvia, the poorest member state, is as yet the only country of the EU in which a significant share of the population culturally belongs to the Orthodox world. What is more, the current Eastern border of the EU is identical with the cultural divide. There is only one exception: The Western part of the Ukraine is shaped by Greek Catholicism and therefore clearly belongs to the 'Western world'. In 2007 or 2008, Bulgaria and Romania, two 'Orthodox' countries will become members of the EU, and then the possible accession of the Ukraine is likely to become a major issue.

The, in our view, extremely important dimension of values and attitudes towards the extended order is hardly ever taken into account when the prospects and problems of the integration of Orthodox countries into the EU is being discussed. In our impression, the EU authorities as well as most economists tend to believe that the experience of the last enlargement round can simply be transferred to Bulgaria and Romania. At the same time, especially in the population of the EU-15 there is a widespread unpleasant feeling of the cultural differentness or even 'unrefinedness' of these accession candidates for the United Europe. If our theses are correct that

- the cultural divide between 'Latinity' and 'Orthodoxy' significantly influences the degree of acceptance of the extended order,
- the prevailing attitudes towards the extended order are a chief determinant of failure or success of the transplantation of Western European institutions,

it would be an important and promising task to carry out empirical research in these countries. However, we want to stress once more that the intention of our research is *not* to provide simple calculations that allow to divide countries into those that 'fit' market and democracy and those that do not. Rather, what it aims at is helping politicians and their consultants to improve their knowledge about an important part of the soil in which the reformed or newly formed social institutions must strike their roots in order to function in the long run. This might help them to choose the right institutions to be 'transplanted' to their society, and to modify imported rules and laws in a way that improves their cultural compatibility. Also, we should make very clear that we do not hold that the current Eastern border is a – however defined – 'natural' one. But we are convinced that the transfer of Western European institutions to the countries east of the divide will be more difficult and maybe calls for other strategies than in the 'Latin' countries of Central Europe.

The value of a country rating comparing only three countries is certainly very limited. As it did roughly confirm our starting hypothesis, however, we will now set about the task of refining the extended order index and applying it to a larger number of countries. The focus of this future research will be on the comparison between Bulgaria, Romania and Ukraine and the Central Eastern countries that have become EU members in 2004. If the method proves its worth also in the course of this larger empirical test, the next challenge would be to apply it to Turkey, where – similar to the Ukraine – the differences between the Western and the Eastern parts of the country merit particular attention.

References

Ammon, G. (1989). Der französische Wirtschaftsstil, München: Eberhard.

Badie B. (2000). The Imported State. The Westernization of the Political Order, Stanford, CA: Stanford University Press.

Berdyaev, N.A. ([1937] 1990). Istoki i Smysl' Russkogo Kommunizma, Moscow: Nauka.

Buss, A.E. (2003). The Russian-Orthodox Tradition and Modernity, Leiden et al: Brill.

Djankov, S. et al. (2003). "The New Comparative Economics", Journal of Comparative Economics 31, no. 4 (December), 595-619.

Eucken, W. (1940). Die Grundlagen der Nationalökonomie, Jena: Fischer.

Falcetti, E., Raiser, M., Sanfey, P. (2002). "Defying the Odds. Initial Conditions, Reforms, and Growth in the First Decade of Transition", Journal of Comparative Economics 30, no. 2 (June), 229-250.

Gérard, R. (2004). "Understanding Institutional Change. Fast-Moving and Slow-Moving Institutions", Studies in Comparative International Development 38 (4), 109-131.

Granovetter, M. (1985). "Economic Action and Social Structure: The Problem of Embeddedness." American Journal of Sociology 91, no. 3, 481-510.

Hayek, F.A. (1988). The Fatal Conceit. The Errors of Socialism, London: Routledge.

Herrmann-Pillath, C., Hederer, C. (2003). Wirtschaftspolitik als ökonomisches Stilphänomen. Ein evolutorischer Ansatz, in: Höhmann, H.-H., Pleines, H. (eds), Wirtschaftspolitik in Osteuropa zwischen ökonomischer Kultur, Institutionenbildung und Akteursverhalten. Russland, Polen und Tschechische Republik im Vergleich. Bremen: Temmen, 42-65.

Kaufhold, K.H. (1996)."Zur Entwicklung des Wirtschaftsstildenkens in Deutschland", in: Klump, R. (ed.), Wirtschaftskultur, Wirtschaftsstil und Wirtschaftsordnung, Marburg: Metropolis, 21-37.

Klump, R. (ed.) (1996). Wirtschaftskultur, Wirtschaftsstil und Wirtschaftsordnung. Methoden und Ergebnisse der Wirtschaftskulturforschung. Marburg: Metropolis.

Kornai, J. (1980). Economics of Shortage, 2 vols., Amsterdam et al.: North-Holland Publishing Company.

Krueger, G.J. (1998). "A Note on Initial Conditions and Liberalization During Transition", Journal of Comparative Economics 26, no. 4 (December), 718-734.

Nienhaus, V. (1999). Kultur und Wirtschaftsstil – Erklärungsansätze für die Systemdynamik und Systemeffizienz in Entwicklungsländern?, in: Cassel, D., Apolte, T. (eds), Perspektiven der Systemforschung, Berlin: Duncker & Humblot, 89-113.

Oleinik, A. (2005). Transfer of Institutions: Actors and Constraints – The Russian Case in a Global Context, HWWA Discussion Paper 320.

Pejović, S. (2003). "Understanding the Transaction Costs of Transition: it's the Culture, Stupid", Review of Austrian Economics 16, no. 4 (December), 347-361.

Platteau, J.-P. (1994). "Behind the Market Stage Where Real Societies Exist – Part I: The Role of Public and Private Order Institutions", Journal of Development Studies 30, no. 3 (April), 533-577. Part II: "The Role of Moral Norms", 753-817.

Polterovich, V.M. (2001). "Transplantatsiya·ekonomicheskikh institutov", Ekonomicheskaia nauka sovremennoi Rossii, no. 3, 24-50.

Raiser, M. (2001). Informal Institutions, Social Capital, and Economic Transition: Reflections on a Neglected Dimension, in: Cornia, G.A. et al. (ed.), Transition and Institutions. The Experience of Gradual and Late Reformers, Oxford: Oxford Univ. Press, 218-239.

Schefold, B. (1994/95). Wirtschaftsstile. 2 vols., Frankfurt/Main: Fischer.

Schumpeter, J.A. ([1954] 1967). History of Economic Analysis. 6th printing, London: George Allan & Unwin.

Seabright, P. (2004). The Company of Strangers. A Natural History of Economic Life, Princeton Univ. Press.

Spiethoff, A. (1933). Die allgemeine Volkswirtschaftslehre als geschichtliche Theorie. Die Wirtschaftsstile, in: Spiethoff, A. (ed.), Festgabe für Werner Sombart. Zur siebenzigsten Wiederkehr seines Geburtstages 19. Jänner 1933. München: Duncker & Humblot, 51-84.

Stuart, R.C., Panayotopoulos, C.M. (1999). "Decline and Recovery in Transition Economies. The Impact of Initial Conditions", Post-Soviet Geography and Economics 40, no. 4 (June), 267-280.

Weber, M. ([1923] 1958). Wirtschaftsgeschichte, Abriss der universalen Sozial- und Wirtschafts-Geschichte, 3rd ed., Berlin: Duncker & Humblot.

Winiecki, J. (2004). "Determinants of Catching Up or Falling Behind. Interaction of Formal and Informal Institutions", Post-Communist Economies 16 (2), 137-152.

Zweynert, J. (2002). "Eine systemtheoretische Neuformulierung des Wirtschaftsstilkonzepts. Geldwirtschaft und Machtwirtschaft als stiltheoretische Idealtypen", Schmollers Jahrbuch 122 (3), 415-444.

Zweynert, J., Goldschmidt, N. (2006). "The Two Transitions in Central and Eastern Europe as Processes of Institutional Transplantation", Journal of Economic Issues 40, 895-918.

Attitudes towards the Extended Order in Latvia, Poland and Russia (Comment)

Friederike Welter

1. Introduction

This paper, authored by Robert Wyszinski and Joachim Zweynert, tackles one of the "big" questions of transformation research, namely how to explain diversity in transition paths, seeking both theoretical and empirical explanations for such diversity. I particular appreciate the idea of applying 'traditional' theoretical concepts and of operationalising them, as there is a gap in transition studies: Empirical research too often is not thoroughly grounded in theory, while theoretical research alone too often is 'useless' because theories are too difficult or impossible to operationalise for empirical studies.

Overall, I enjoyed reading the paper because of this particular contribution to conceptualising and operationalising a complex phenomenon, because of the theoretical framework applied, but also because of the debate it opens up. I see the contribution of this paper as belonging to a group of a slowly growing number of studies setting economic developments in their specific contexts and understanding them as results of specific (country-specific, region-specific, culture-specific) processes. This often comes as a surprise, given the influence of the historical schools and 'good practice' examples of our discipline.

Nevertheless, there is a general problem with a 'historical' approach, using path-dependencies as one important explanation for today's developments. Such studies are walking a tight rope, which might be the reason why research paying attention to context and 'historical specificity' has lost importance over the years, only recently gaining influence again. Such studies ran the danger of over exaggerating the influence of historical influences (for an example see the discussion around Fukuyama's book on the "End of History"), as historical and path dependent processes are seen as explanation for all and everything which cannot be explained otherwise.[1]

In this comment, I will concentrate on two main issues:

First, I will present my thoughts on the theoretical concept, on some weaknesses in applying this to transition research and suggestions on how to further develop

---

[1] There is a similar problem with trust-related research analysing the role of trust in business behaviour and different cultures, where researchers are often too quick in ascribing everything which cannot be explained in entrepreneurial behaviour as being an indicator of trust.

this. Secondly, I have some thoughts regarding the operationalisation of the concept, as this is a main contribution of the paper and of value in itself.

2. Comments on the concept of a "holistic and extended order"

The authors draw on Friedrich Hayek in presenting the concept of a holistic and an extended order as two ideal type elements of a market-based economy and society. For transition research, this is of particular interest, as we can assess the transition process as a process throughout which social and economic relations change fundamentally. Moreover, for me as an entrepreneurship researcher, this concept also strongly resonates Granovetter's concept of economic actions being socially embedded (1985), which has been applied to explain individual behaviour in a multitude of contexts (e.g., entrepreneurship), although Granovetter mainly applied this on a micro level while Hayek viewed the whole economy and society.

Overall, this conceptualising is important because it draws attention to the underlying processes of change, namely transitions and changes in social and economic relations. Moreover, as the paper demonstrates we could use this concept to aptly describe what we could and can observe happening in transition countries. In this regard, the authors convincingly illustrate how this concept can explain the persisting "network culture" with both economic and social relations being (overly) dependent on networking (also cf. Ledeneva 1998; Rehn and Taalas 2004; Smallbone and Welter 2001, 2006).

However, I foresee a difficulty in applying this concept the way the authors do: Are we right in only applying this concept to "large" society? In order to understand cultural path-dependencies I see a need – as difficult as this might be – to analyse transition phenomenon on the level of both "small" and "large" societies, because it is the interplay between both levels explaining persistence, change and behavioural patterns. Interestingly, some of the empirical results presented by the authors do underline my argument. The general problem I have with this theoretical approach is grounded in (probably too many) empirical studies of transition economies in which I have participated over the past ten years. Those studies demonstrate a need to see the transition process (or socialist transformation process) on a continuum and not in terms of two ideal type order situations.

Furthermore, this raises the question of what we are talking about when applying Hayek's concept: Situations or outcomes? On a more philosophical side we come back to the question of whether there is a preferable outcome of the transition process. Transition research often assumes this implicitly, but only recently there has been a discussion started of whether our market economy model is the one to be preferred in all contexts. The authors acknowledge this discussion in stating that a Western model is the preferable one because all transition states want it, although their reasoning could be strengthened. Transition research also demonstrates more complex relations here. Donors, international organisations and single states had a major influence on the transition process in many countries, thus setting a development path which might have been different if the country governments had their "free will". Examples include the influential economic advisors in Russia (Jeffrey Sachs and his colleague Andrei Shleifer) or the German re-unification.

My suggestion would be to broaden the theoretical framework. As it stands at the moment, the authors suggest applying a static or at most comparative-static concept to a process phenomenon. I would encourage them to work on extending the extended order concept itself by bringing in dynamic elements.

3. Operationalising the concept: From too complex to too simple?

In operationalising their concept, the authors return to Max Weber's thesis of the influence of religious attitudes, setting out to researching the expressions towards market and democracy in two different contexts: an Orthodox (Russia) and a Catholic/Protestant one (Poland), and Latvia with a mixed culture.

A common problem in empirical research: We need to simplify and to construct analogies to be able to "measure" our constructs and to measure theory. The question I have here: the link between Hayek's concept and their main hypothesis is in my eyes (and I happily stand to be corrected) an artificial one I have problems in following. Let me illustrate this by an example: The empirical results presented in the paper show that 83% of 'Baltic' Latvians are pro-reform in the early 1990s, but only 45% of the Russian Latvian. This is best explained by looking at who lost most during the initial reforms, and those were mainly Russian Latvians.[2] But it does not illustrate the influence of religious attitudes on their assessment.

The authors themselves are aware of the complexities in interpreting their data. For me this suggests that we should open a methodological debate. We obviously need to question our approach to such empirical studies. How useful are questions such as the one described in broadening our understanding of the influence of cultural factors? Can they really capture path-dependencies? Or do we need a fundamentally different approach such as qualitative studies?

The extended order index: This is an interesting exercise, especially in the light of some of the results received. However, the detailed results also illustrate the problems connected to building such an index. For example, regarding the age-specific results on the high gap between internal and external morals, this obviously shows that the young generation at least has arrived in a 'wild-west' capitalistic society, as they are leaning towards a less extended order. On the one hand, I consider this score to be a result of a transition period throughout which morals and values needed to be established anew, and especially young people in Latvia and Russia have been raised in a 'lawless' period where everything was possible, pro-

---

2   Additionally, there is a methodological problem here with the retrospective approach used in the empirical study, which leads to hindsight bias of respondents.

vided one knew how the rules worked or how to bend them. On the other hand, my guess would be that results would be very similar in Western countries, and it might be interesting to additionally look at the Inglehart studies on values to ground these results. Moreover, I would expect differences also across other groups such as Caucasians in Russia, where at the level of a "small" society a holistic order prevails.

4. Conclusions

As regards future research, it certainly is interesting to include more countries, as suggested by the authors who want to broaden their study to include candidate members of the European Union such as Bulgaria and Romania. However, there also is a danger of over simplifying explanations in cross-country studies. In my understanding and based on my research experiences, valuable cross-country comparisons need to look both across and into countries to understand cross-country results better. In this I argue for a more refined empirical approach to researching the effects of the enlargement process of the EU instead of adding "simply" more countries to the sample.

References

Granovetter, M. (1985). "Economic Action and Social Structure: The Problem of Embeddedness", American Journal of Sociology 91, 481–450.

Ledeneva, A.V. (1998). Russia's economy of favours: Blat, networking and informal exchange., Cambridge: Cambridge University Press.

Rehn, A., Taalas, S. (2004). "Znakomstva I Svyazi" (Acquaintances and connections) – *Blat*, the Soviet Union and mundane entrepreneurship, Entrepreneurship & Regional Development 16, 235-250.

Smallbone, D. Welter, F. (2001). "The distinctiveness of entrepreneurship in transition economies", Small Business Economics 16 (4), 249-262.

Smallbone, D., Welter, F. (2006). "Conceptualising Entrepreneurship in a Transition Context", International Journal of Entrepreneurship and Small Business 3 (2), 190-206.

The Business Environment: Case Study Latvia

Inese Šūpule[*]

1. Introduction

This paper evaluates the business environment for small and medium-sized companies (SMEs) in Latvia, focusing in particular on various aspects of the culture of that environment. During the fifteen years of transition from a planned to a free-market economy, one of the toughest jobs has been to change perceptions about activities that were illegal in Soviet times and are now legal and desirable. Small businesspeople in the USSR had a negative image – they were known as "speculators", and their activities were either fully or partly illegal. When the economic situation changed, these attitudes had to be broken down, and people had to be encouraged to take initiative, risk and responsibility in launching business operations.

Latvia's business environment is the result of confrontation and interaction among various types of business – something that is accepted and institutionalised in the developed countries of the West on the one hand, but was a source of "speculation" and even more or less legitimised theft from the state as a part of business operations on the other. The goal of this research is to study the attitudes, behaviour and experience of Latvian businesspeople within the framework of the Latvian socio-cultural environment.

Following the breakdown of the interview questions into four sections, the results present the views of Latvian businesspeople on four major issues:

1. *Interaction between economics and politics* (the government's role in promoting economic development; assessment of national policies and the activities of the relevant institutions; expectations vis-à-vis the government's regulatory role in the economy; and assessments of the process of privatisation);

2. *Market economy institutions* (comparison between Latvia's market economy and a planned economy; ethics and the law in business; the role of the businessperson in society; comparison between the business environments of the Baltic States; contacts with the judicial system and state and local government institutions; and experiences of bribery);

3. *Changes in social relations* (changing values, mutual trust, and the importance of social networks in business); and

---

[*] I wish to thank Iveta Bebriša and Karlīna Vaivade for their input in organising interviews and the preliminary analysis of the data.

4. *Attitudes vis-à-vis the West* (a sense of belonging to Europe; changes since Latvia joined the EU; attitudes vis-à-vis EU enlargement; and views about "western culture").

The following statistical data from 2005 give the reader an overview of the business world in Latvia. In that year, there were some 53,000 economically active companies in Latvia.[1] Of these, 99% were SMEs. In addition, 76% of the companies had nine or fewer employees, i.e., they can be classified as micro companies (20% were small companies, and 4% were medium-sized companies). This means that SMEs in Latvia make up a very significant share of the national economy and play an important role in creating GDP and providing employment.

In comparison to other EU member states, the number of SMEs per 1,000 residents is low in Latvia, although the number of new companies has been rising in recent years – 4,713 companies were founded in 2002 and 10,613 in 2005. A negative factor is the enormous proportion of retail companies (40%) as opposed to manufacturing firms (just 15% of all SMEs). A comparatively positive assessment of the development of Latvia's business environment was provided in a World Bank study in 2006. Of 155 countries, Latvia ranked 26th. According to the authors of the study, Latvia is one of the 12 countries most active in introducing reforms.[2]

The aforementioned statistical trends are also reflected in answers given by survey respondents. The businesspeople and economic experts surveyed believe that Latvia is consistently improving its business environment by improving the legal framework, adapting it to European Union requirements and supervising the effect of administrative procedures on business. Shortcomings, on the other hand, include Latvia's not particularly favourable tax policy, its complicated bureaucratic requirements and insufficient support for business start-ups.

Fifteen expert interviews were conducted with the owners of small and medium-sized enterprises who are directly involved in the activities of their companies. Respondents were between 30 and 52 years old. Thirteen respondents were men and two were women. They have been active in business for between one and 13 years. In terms of staff numbers, eight were small companies (two to ten employees), while seven were medium-sized companies (12 to 50 employees).

The sectors of business represented in the interviews included construction, the timber industry, IT, bookkeeping and auditing services, translation services, consultations on management and business, advertising, sales and servicing of medial equipment, retail and packaging, water and sewage services (sales, repairs), modelling, manufacturing of technical equipment, medical sales in the field of traumatol-

---

1   Burka, A. (2006). "Uzņēmējdarbības vide Latvijā. 2006" (The Business Environment in Latvia, 2006), Ministry of Economics, Department of Business and Industry, 17 March 2006. See http://www.em.gov.lv./em/images/modules/items/item_file_12985_4ppt.
2   The International Bank for Reconstruction and Development/The World Bank. 2006. *Doing Business in 2006: Creating Jobs.* http://www.doingbusiness.org/documents/Doing Busines2006_fullreport.pdf.

ogy and orthopaedics, and services related to road paving and greenery. The interviews were conducted in February 2006.

2. Interaction between economics and politics

2.1 Evaluations of the effectiveness of government policies and institutions

Generally speaking, businesspeople's views about national policies and the institutions responsible for those policies are cautious. They do not see much support for SMEs and say that the government tends to be overbearing and not very forthcoming. Some businesspeople feel that the government's attitude is more or less negative:

> 'The environment is not the best, no. The bottom line is that taxes are fees which we pay to the state, and all of the support which a new businessperson needs when launching business – that goes missing.'

> 'Everything involves threats, not partnerships. The State Revenue Service is never your best friend. If you make a mistake, you get punished. If the State Revenue Service makes a mistake or messes up the numbers, then it will not even apologise. That is the norm.'

> 'I would like them to do more, especially in terms of lower taxes.'

> 'Businesspeople are seen as nothing, even though they pay taxes to the state and create jobs.'

> 'I think that any businessperson, beginning with me, would like to work legally, earn normal income, and see that the country is developing thanks to the taxes that we pay – benches in parks are painted, everyone has a good life. But laws are made to eliminate those businesses which engage in illegal activities. The result is that I have to go and prove that I have a clean record. The person who engages in complicated schemes does not have to do that.'

According to businesspeople, the government is particularly high-handed when it comes to drafting new laws. Guidelines related to the laws are not discussed with representatives of business. Decisions are taken in advance, and the interests of businesspeople are not respected. Laws are mostly approved up above, without respecting the interests of businesses or businesspeople. Businesses, particularly SMEs, require support from the state, but the fact is that rules and regulations issued by the government make it difficult for companies to develop and to improve their operations. Some respondents said that relevant processes in Germany are different and much more positive.

> 'We cannot see the state as a partner, because if it helps companies, particularly small and medium companies, then the assistance is very conditional. In 1993, for instance, the State Revenue Service told me that I do not need a fax machine for my operations. I think that this kind of formulation requires no further comment. ... Just look at Germany – the government is much more forthcoming there. The government helps businesspeople, particularly those who are entering the market for the first time. The state does not spend its time thinking about how to punish the businessperson over every small issue. I know of a specific example – there was a retailer who was not doing very well. He went to the tax inspectors and said that he was not

doing well – not much income, no money to pay to others. The state offered him tax discounts, additional contracts, agreements with other countries, partners – the main thing was to make sure that the guy did not go bankrupt, that his employees could keep their jobs, that the business would develop further. The government tried to stimulate growth for that company instead of trying to stamp it out.'

'The state does not care about businesspeople, there is no support at all. There are no opportunities to develop or to improve operations. Tax policies are very difficult. Businesses certainly are not interested in co-operating with the state. Businesspeople do not want to do that, and I think that there is good reason for that.'

'The government is a big machine which tortures you whenever it wants to. It is a hopeless situation – you can come up with ideas, but it is like banging your head against the wall.'

In discussing relations with those who work for government institutions and evaluating contacts with government bureaucrats, most businesspeople have the same opinion: they stress the fact that civil servants do not understand business issues, that they are not forthcoming, that there is a lack of order in the entire system, and that constant changes in laws cause all kinds of problems. Bureaucrats often have a negative attitude, or they are incompetent. They do not want to help and tend to "pass the buck" – people are sent from one civil servant to another. These are all issues which lead businesspeople to avoid contact with government institutions.

'The point is that the civil servant sits there on his throne, and I come in to beg. Instead, the civil servant should help me out.'

'The civil servants feel like they are emperors in their work, that they are superior to businesspeople. Everyone counts on that.'

'I hope that they will improve their attitude to some extent.'

'I would say that civil servants need to stop being policemen and instead become doctors. That is the quick response – bureaucrats need to stop being haughty. The general bureaucratic attitude is very formal. We can always look at the letter of the law, but this should essentially be dialogue, the civil servants should be consultants. I have lots of questions, I want to understand things, but if I ask a question now, the response is: "Oho! Perhaps he does not have something that should be there. Let us go and inspect him!"'

'We have never received any advice from civil servants. They always reject us – they just do their work, no one knows anything. You are sent from one office to the next. The next bureaucrat also does not know anything and sends you on to the next person. Finally you have spoken to six or seven people, and then you are back in the office where you began. No one is responsible for anything, no one knows anything – "Why are you here with your stupid questions? We have other functions!"'

'I hate going through that system – you are sent from one office to the next, and then you are told that you need another signature, another stamp. You have to start all over again. You have to come back the next day, you have lost an entire working day.'

It has to be said, however, that businesspeople are more critical about their experience in the 1990s, and respondents admit that the situation is gradually improving. There is praise for efforts by the State Revenue Service to improve its operations (the State Revenue Service is the government institution with which businesspeople have most contact).

'The trend is that things are improving.'

'In comparison to the previous period, we can see that laws have been improved; businesspeople are starting to understand what the Revenue Service wants of them. Bookkeeping is being simplified, rates are not constantly being changed. I now see the state as more of an ally.'

'The SRS is being improved in a humane way, and attitudes vis-à-vis businesspeople are no longer similar to attitudes toward enemies. We are increasingly treated as equal allies, because they are coming to understand that businesspeople are the ones who pay the taxes – the SRS has to be at least a little bit forthcoming. That is what is happening – the SRS is organising seminars, inviting businesspeople to attend, discussing important issues. The trend is certainly positive.'

'On a 10-point scale, I would rate the State Revenue Service, which is the institution to which you deliver documents and which you ring when you have questions, as a 9.'

'The State Revenue Service – attitudes have improved rapidly over the last five years. The quality of services has certainly improved to a significant degree. It used to be that we had to stand around in a small hallway, there were huge queues, we had to go to ten different offices, but each office door was locked, because the old women who worked there had gone off to have some tea.'

The extent to which a businessperson has to deal with government institutions depends on the sector in which s/he works. If manufacturing or services involve government procurement or imports, then the links are closer. Survey respondents said that they had few contacts with local government institutions. Businesspeople admit that when trying to resolve problems, they would prefer better rules for everyone. First of all, that creates a predictable and secure business environment, one in which the ability of a businessman to develop does not depend on the size of the bribe that is demanded by a civil servant:

'Definitely, better rules for everyone, because then it is a predictable and safe environment. It does not matter how much of a bribe one official might want.'

Second, better rules for all would guarantee uniform and clear rules of the game in business. Uniform rules are a cornerstone of stability and competition:

'Uniform rules that are mandatory for everyone are the main thing in making sure that the process is orderly. The important thing is not to pay the right bureaucrat, but rather to base your work on the rules of the game, to find your competitive advantage.'

'It is important for me to have clear rules of the game for everyone. I have spoken to other businesspeople, and this is the main thing – rules of the game which are clear, logical and do not change every day. We at least want to plan our work, to do the work.'

Some businesspeople say that direct access to high-ranking civil servants would not resolve anything in some cases. No bureaucrat wants to deal with the everyday problems of a businessperson. What is more, no businessperson can be sure that the civil servant who has been approached is competent on the relevant issue:

'How much time does the high-ranking civil servant have? We do not handle our issues at the ministerial level. The important thing is to make sure that the people who take actual decisions in terms of providing state services to businesspeople – that these people are professionals who understand the issue and are competent. I am much more interested in the masses, because that is what you encounter.'

At the same time, some businesspeople want a chance to make direct and personal contacts with high-ranking civil servants to resolve various problems:

'I definitely want direct access to high-ranking civil servants.'

'Directly, through personal contacts.'

'Definitely, and only high-ranking civil servants. Absolutely.'

'Direct access to high-ranking bureaucrats.'

'Direct access to high-ranking civil servants. If everyone goes, that will not be the best thing, because the civil servant will not be able to deal with the queue. There are lower-ranking employees for this. Those who are lower-ranking, however – they must also be accessible.'

2.2 Expectations of the government's regulatory role in the national economy

Generally speaking, businesspeople have a range of expectations when it comes to the government. Most respondents say that there is no exchange of information between them and government institutions. They want more positive co-operation, they wish to be involved in various projects, and they want information to be more readily available. Many respondents, at the same time, complain about high taxes which are a serious burden for SMEs and keep companies from growing. Others want laws to be improved and the government to leave them alone so that they can get on with their work. Respondents want to see greater understanding of the needs of businesses.

'There are many things that I expect – more understanding when you turn up with a new project. If you have a small company, then you should have better terms, lower taxes, support of some kind. The way in which information is provided – it should not be announced in the official newspaper "Latvijas Vēstnesis" alone, we should not be told that the information is in that newspaper, and so we need to go and look for it. There are many things that we do not know. When there are major projects, information is only given to certain people, although afterwards we are told that the information was freely available to everyone.'

'As far as I am concerned, the state needs to help businesspeople, it must promote the development of companies and business as such. I think that this is not really the case in Latvia at this time.'

'Let me work! Do not throw up obstacles in the way of my business! I want this to be a normal and lawful country so that I can count on the idea that if I do all of my work lawfully, then I am dealing with a lawful state in which the rule of law prevails.'

Respondents also say that there should be different rules for companies of different sizes:

'The government must differentiate between companies of different sizes and different types of business.'

'Tax policies are one thing – taxes are quite high for small companies, and particularly for small companies with a fairly low turnover. That is especially true at the beginning of operations. Launching a business is very difficult, and it is quite difficult for a small company to break into the market. The company starts to operate, it starts to work, and that is the point at which even the tiniest failure turns into a situation in which the company is threatened with bankruptcy. Taxes are too high in the early stage of a company's operations.'

Generally speaking, businesspeople want the state to allow the market to regulate itself, but they also expect a more active government role in the social sphere – they want the state to take care of people who have lower incomes:

'Social issues are the responsibility of the state. Other than that, the less interference, the better it is for businesses.'

'I think that the state has all of the levers and instruments at its disposal to improve the system. That is the main job for the government, because there are always people who are able to work, to generate ideas and energy, as well as people who cannot stand up for themselves. These are poor people – pensioners, disabled people. They cannot take care of themselves. I think that benefits must always be redistributed, but we must find the right proportions so that the system is honest, so that no one is cheated.'

'I think that the state can intervene only if something is not happening in the way which the law requires. The state must certainly intervene in the social sector. There are people, however, who tell us that we have to pay very high taxes. Pensions are low, and for me as a businessperson, that is not my issue. It is an issue for the state. I am a businessperson, I am not responsible for small pensions.'

Some respondents said that intervention by the state in economic processes is permissible only in pursuit of national goals or the public interest, e.g., to control inflation, to guarantee collection of taxes, or to avoid the emergence of monopolies:

'The state must intervene, but what are the goals? The goals must be serious and justified.'

'The state can clearly intervene in business processes when public interests are at stake – for instance, so as to make sure that taxes are paid. That is why the government intervenes in economic process.'

'The state should not intervene anywhere, but if we are talking about specific things such as inflation, then that is the competence of the Bank of Latvia. That is already being done, but only with short-term processes.'

'The state must not intervene in economic processes unless there are monopolies – balsam, oil, electricity, the railroad.'

'The state must intervene in a market economy to a sensible degree, if only to regulate inflation. If it cannot be regulated with competition, then there can be an attempt to regulate it in some other way – with social subsidies or tax laws related to the survival minimum. Other than that, the market must be allowed to do its own work – the market resolves its own problems.

The state must intervene to a greater degree to achieve social justice with respect to pensioners and the like.'

Some respondents expressed the view that government intervention in business also has negative results. Intervention in economic processes is related to lobbying, guaranteeing advantages to certain companies involved in the relevant process:

'There has always been lobbying, there will always be lobbying – there is no way to get rid of it. There should be no lobbying, but as soon as the government intervenes, that in itself is lobbying on behalf of one company or another.'

Many respondents, however, do not want the state to control businesspeople, arguing that, in that case, it is important to make sure that laws are well structured and apply to both sides – state and business world – equally. What is more, how do you evaluate various selfish interests – that is a very unclear issue:

'The idea of "harming the interests of the state" is a very, very fragile concept. Who can determine when that is happening? Who can control the situation? I think that the state certainly should not intervene in private business.'

Businesspeople are not unanimous about what the government should do if companies have selfish interests which harm the overall situation. Some respondents said that the government does have the right to control the operations of private businesses if national goals are at issue:

'I think that the state should have such rights, because public interests always stand above the interests of any private businessperson. That is clear, and then the state has the right to intervene.'

'I think that the state should be aggressive in opposing businesspeople who are harmful, who rob the state.'

2.3 Evaluations of the privatisation process

Asked about the privatisation process in Latvia, most respondents had negative things to say. People argued that many properties were privatised unlawfully. Businesspeople criticise those who managed privatisation for not knowing what they were doing. Privatisation is associated with processes such as wasting the state's resources and inappropriately taking control of properties. Respondents said that privatisation of some companies involved processes that excluded the public. Instead, the political elite and various special groups benefited. As far as the privatisation process as such is concerned, businesspeople think that the process has taken much too long and that the public does not have much information about it:

'Well, there were certain people who earned a great deal of money.'

'I am very, very sceptical about privatisation, because I think it basically involved the plundering of all of Latvia's major state-owned companies. Look at the AVELAT Group and Šķēle. There were other big companies that were privatised for a pittance and then were sold off.'

'I would like to say that those who wanted to privatise something did exactly that.'

'The things that happened just happened – privatisation could have been a better process, of course, but it could also have been worse.'

'The political elite privatised those things that were available to it.'

Asked about the scope of privatisation, businesspeople said that the privatisation process should not cover all sectors of the economy. They said that the state must retain ownership of important companies that have no competition in their sector of operations – Latvenergo (the power company), the Rīga heating company, Latvijas Balzāms (a producer of alcoholic beverages), the Latvian gas company, Latvian Railways and, to a certain extent, Lattelekom (a telecommunications company). Privatisation of such companies would have an effect on the national economy and, quite possibly, on public welfare:

'Some sectors should remain under the control of the state, because they are strategically important. Latvia is such a small country and the people who are in control are so easy to bribe that it is very risky to privatise such strategic companies.'

'Why should profitable public companies be turned over to private structures? I am talking about the big companies that we still have – Lattelekom, Latvenergo. Those are strategic companies, and they should not be privatised. The situation with Lattelekom is different, but in the case of Latvenergo and the Rīga heating company – they are the only businesses in their sector. They have to remain in the hands of the state if only for that reason.'

'The state must hang on to important things upon which the economy and the welfare of Latvia's residents are, to a certain extent, dependent.'

3. Market economy institutions

3.1 Competition

Businesspeople think that competition is an inviolable component of any market economy. Competition influences the business environment as well as the relationship between supply and demand. There must be free competition – each person must be guaranteed the right and ability to make a choice. It is also desirable that equal terms and conditions apply to all parties involved in the process. Only if there are no limitations on any of the parties involved can one speak of competition in the true sense of the word:

'There certainly has to be competition in a market economy. Before you can speak of a market, you have to have competition.'

'The cornerstone for a market economy is free competition. Each person has the right to choose what to buy and how to buy it.'

'The same conditions should apply to all competitors. There should not be any monopolies, everyone should operate on the same terms.'

Some businesspeople think that the foundation of a market economy is the free flow of capital, as well as supply and demand:

> 'The free flow of capital, human resources and all other resources. Basically this is the free flow of people and capital.'

> 'Free supply and demand. Each company manufactures and sells things, each person buys what he or she wants, each of us seeks his or her own niche.'

> 'In the market economy, there has to be supply and demand, that is the foundation of a market economy. There have to be sufficient suppliers and sufficient consumers, sufficient demand. That is the cornerstone of the market economy.'

Respondents were asked to think about competition in Latvia and to assess the government's competition policies and their influence on the business environment. Respondents said that there is strong competition. They added, however, that the government does little to regulate the process. Competition is dictated by market conditions in Latvia, not by state regulations. At the same time, however, several businesspeople said that there are a few sectors in which there is no serious competition. They add that the Latvian Competition Council and other relevant institutions cannot deal with the matter because of the problem of lobbyism:

> 'There is a lot of competition between businesses, even though the Latvian market is very, very small in comparison to the global or European market. Competition is very fierce right here in Latvia.'

> 'Yes, there are areas in which competition is fine, but there are other areas in which it has no effect at all.'

> 'The Competition Council is quite passive in its work. There is quite a bit of lobbying in politics, and so it is quite hard for the Competition Council to achieve anything.'

Some businessmen say that the procedure of national procurement processes is dishonest – businesses, as well as state and local government institutions have learned to fiddle the documentation for bids for tender so that the bidder they want wins, not the one which should, in legal terms, win the relevant order:

> 'As far as state and local government procurement is concerned, there is fairly dishonest competition here. Everything is thought out in advance, thought is given on how to arrange competitive issues in one's own favour.'

> 'All of this government procurement – it would be impossible to have even greater lobbying. If you are at the table when the bid for tenders is prepared, then the bid for tenders is prepared for you. You are the winner.'

3.2 Comparing Latvia's market economy with a planned economy

Comparing the planned with the free-market economy, businessmen said that competition is the key advantage of the latter. Competition promotes growth and development – businesspeople constantly have to think about increasing profits and ensuring that their business does better than their competitors do:

'In a market economy you have to make sure that you can compete in the market with your labour force and your goods or services.'

'A planned economy does not ensure that processes develop. You fulfil the plan, and that is all. You do not have to compete with other companies or think of anything new.'

Most interviewees said that the market economy is much better for them. They see it as an example of free interaction between supply and demand, of self-regulated markets and the ability of companies to pursue various ideas. In a planned economy, initiative is of no importance. At the same time, some respondents said that the planned economy had certain advantages for the poor – greater and more stable social benefits, for instance. Several respondents said that while there were shortcomings in the planned economy there are shortcomings in the market economy, too. In a market economy, businesspeople focus mostly on profits, and so there is a need for a regulatory institution which sets out certain guidelines for business. In a planned economy, however, there are all kinds of regulatory and supervisory institutions, but there is a lack of information about what consumers want. In the production of goods and services there is a lack of flexibility:

'In a market economy, everything is much more effective in the sense that available resources are used much more effectively. The development of all kinds of systems is facilitated, and you are forced to develop, too.'

'In a market economy, no one can feel secure about his or her job, no one knows what will happen with prices – how much will you be paying for telephone services or heat next month?'

'I think that in the market economy, the greatest benefit is freedom of thought and action. I can make plans, I can decide on one kind of business or another, I can follow my plans, I can think of a new solution and introduce it in the market. I can earn money. There are lots of challenges here. To be sure, in a planned economy, people had the sense that they were better protected – that is the perspective not of employers, but of employees.'

'There used to be plans which had to be fulfilled. You had to do this and that, you had to produce that many widgets, and you did not have to think about anything.'

'It is better now, of course, but the former system had positive elements. In any event, we now have a chance to work for ourselves, and that was not the case back then. Everything else is secondary.'

'The planned economy was absurd. Market relations are much better, because everyone has a chance. There is a lot of risk, yes, but there are opportunities to develop, to improve yourself.'

'Life in the planned economy was calmer, more stable – you could predict everything in your life. There was one option, just one.'

'In a free market, the goal is profit. If there is not a third party – the state – to tell you the rules that have to be observed, the process is quite chaotic. In a planned economy, by contrast, there are problems with information about demand. There is much less flexibility.'

3.3 Morals and the law in business

When asked whether in the present era businesspeople can turn anything into money and whether they can buy anything for money, businesspeople often said that if it comes to human relations, then no, they cannot. In business, however, money is an important driving force, and some respondents had trouble answering the question:

'This is a philosophical issue, it depends on what we are discussing. You cannot buy deeply personal things, but money is very important. Often enough, when you need to achieve a result, you look to see whether there is money there, nothing else. I suppose that is normal. That is life, that is real life – we will never be ideal.'

'We work for money and for a better future, because the main motivation in business, after all, is money. There is also the fact that you get psychological enjoyment from the fact that you are managing something, you are creating things – you are doing good work. As far as things such as love are concerned, that is, of course, a different issue.'

'Sadly, yes, the situation now is that money dictates terms, and everything can be turned into money. That is not normal, but people need money, and no one can complain if someone does something so as to get some money. I think that the overall welfare of people might change the situation – someone who has more money perhaps looks at things differently. If someone is hungry, then the only thing he thinks about is where to get money to buy some bread.'

This may also depend on a company's situation and a businessperson's ability to choose. Some respondents completely denied that money is the most important thing. Others said that money is important, but still said that not everything can be bought:

'Theoretically, there are lots of things that you cannot buy, but money can be used as a source of power so that things can be organised – there are vast opportunities in that regard. Just spend money in the system, and everything will happen.'

'No, I categorically oppose the idea that everything can be turned into money.' 'That is an extreme idea – money is your idol, your only idol. When I conclude deals, I am more interested in the results, in the team that will be needed to achieve the final results. Cash – that is not the most important thing on all occasions. There have been times when one has rejected a more advantageous deal just because one has made a promise, one has given one's word. I think that businesspeople must act in that way.'

'Money determines a great deal, but it will never be possible to transform everything into money.'

'Not everything can be bought for money, and not everything can be turned into money, but money is of importance in any corner of the world.'

'Fifty-fifty. There is a bit of deterioration here – it is not a normal phenomenon.'

Businesspeople have a variety of views on whether the ever-increasing importance of money is a normal phenomenon. Does it perhaps indicate that there has been a moral collapse in society?

'It is not normal, but it is not a matter of moral collapse. This is simply the situation which we face – no one can have a normal life if the monthly salary is 200 or 400 lats. These European prices, our European level – we have one foot in Europe, but I do not know where the other foot is. That is the situation. It is not normal, but it is not a moral collapse. I am sure that it will end sooner or later.'

'It is not normal, this is a question of ethics – people today think that everything can be bought for money, and that is not normal. That does not ensure positive relations among people.'

Asked about fraud and cheating in business relationships, businesspeople say that they do not support fraud and/or cheating, but also admit that sometimes they engage in it. That allows them to enjoy advantages in the market and to achieve the desired result more quickly or more easily. Moreover, if such behaviour yields the desired result, if it is not explicitly illegal and does not cause losses to others, then excuses are made for it:

'Well, it depends on what you consider to be fraud and cheating. I might tell someone that something will be delivered tomorrow, although I know this is not the case. Is that fraud, or is it a false statement? I think that fraud is a fairly broad concept – what does each of us think about it? We cannot be 100% honest, completely honest; that is not possible, because there are situations which demand other activities. That sounds dramatic, does it not?'

'Being cunning, I use all kinds of methods to achieve the desired result. Businesspeople have to achieve their aims in one way or another, but the difference between being sly and engaging in fraud is enormous. You can simply make use of what someone else knows or does not know, for example. Fraud is purposeful malice.'

'You can speak in categories of black and white, but if we look at our lives from that point of view, then we see that there are quite a few times when we cheat a bit. We cheat by keeping silent about things that we do not want to say and emphasising those which are more positive.'

'My experience is that fraud is impermissible. There may be cunning aspects of business, but only as long as you are thinking about your business in the long term. If you can get a new client through cunning, if you know that you will appear good because you are cunning. If, however, you use that ability to indicate that you are doing something that you do not know how to do, that you are lying ...'

'Fraud? Of course, it is never a very good thing, but it is justified if you know that the other guy defrauded you. Then you can justify your actions as cheating that person so as to recover the debt.'

'In business, there are sometimes small lies of a commercial kind, ones that do not cause any losses to anyone else while making sure that you can do your work better and more quickly. I consider that to be permissible. I do not accept fraud that causes losses to others, however.'

'There is a difference between cunning and fraud. Fraud is malice, you take advantage of someone else's trust. Cunning, however, sometimes allows you to learn about certain types of finesse, it allows you to manoeuvre. Fraud is something completely different.'

Several businesspeople say that violations of laws or regulations on an everyday basis are a fairly common phenomenon, because laws are not always precise:

'Basically, we try to act lawfully as far as we can, but there are simply situations which are not clear, and then we make use of them to our own advantage, of course. Certainly we have violated someone's rights at some point.'

'I'm not a complete gemstone.'

'Private property has to be respected, but there are all kinds of versions when it comes to observing laws and norms.'

3.4 The role of the businessman in society

The respondents were virtually unanimous on this issue. They think that their role in society is important in two respects: providing jobs and paying taxes. They also think that they help to shape, direct and develop the state, i.e., that they are the main driving force behind development:

'Businesspeople are basically locomotives which pull all of society along, because you must understand that businesspeople can be criticised about paying more or less, about the kinds of jobs that are made available – I think that this is just a matter of time. In any event, however, the businessperson is the one who enables others to work and to earn money.'

'We care about this society. We pay taxes; people have certain social guarantees.'

'Businesspeople develop, they create – jobs, if nothing else. Businesspeople – that is a good thing, a positive thing. It means accepting a great deal of responsibility, and the state should make sure that society understands this properly.'

'The employer. Without employers there would be no jobs. It all happens thanks to businesspeople, they are manufacturers, they transport goods, they sell goods – businesspeople do everything.'

'The foundation, the cornerstone for society. Businesspeople ensure jobs, work, earnings.'

'That is the segment of society which pays taxes. Even though small companies do not contribute all that much in taxes, they do offer lots of jobs. The major taxpayers are the big companies, of course. We could never make do without businesspeople, that is clear.'

'The state depends on businesspeople, but it tries to kill them in all possible ways. Businesspeople pay taxes, their money is reduced. Others are awarded money from the national budget – money that is collected through all kinds of taxes.'

'The businesspeople play a determinant role. There 650,000 pensioners, 300,000 children, 15,000 students, doctors, teachers, police officers and prisoners in this country – someone has to support all of them. Just think about the role of the businessperson who pays real taxes.'

It is clear, however, that representatives of SMEs do not see much chance of influencing market processes, nor do they feel that their role is properly understood by the public and the state:

'I think that the businessperson in Latvia is not properly appreciated, he is seen as bourgeois, even though he creates jobs.'

'The view right now is that all businesspeople are crooks.'

3.5 Comparing the business environment in the different Baltic States

Asked about the market economy in the Baltic States, several businesspeople did not agree with the statement that the market economy in the three countries is not perfect. On the contrary, businesspeople think that the situation in the different Baltic States is very comparable and that the three countries are undergoing normal development.

> 'It is hard for me to comment on the claim that "the market in the Baltic States is not perfect," because I do not see any particular problems. There are products, goods and services, I see no major differences. What does that mean – "the market of the Baltic States does not work"? I think that it works just like any other market, like the EU market. There are always normal and honest businesspeople, as well as cheats who take advantage of the weaknesses of others.'

Asked whether it is true that the market in the Baltic States is not quite perfect, other businesspeople spoke of many different factors that undermine the market economy: shortcomings in the law, incompetent and corrupt legislators, mistakes in national regulations (*"unnecessary interference by the state"*) and an unfavourable attitude on the part of government institutions.

3.6 Contacts with the courts and state and local government institutions; experience with bribery

The independence of the court system. Most businesspeople, both those who have had experience with the judicial system and those who seek to resolve their problems without involving the courts, were fairly sceptical about the independence and trustworthiness of the court system. Businesspeople with no personal experience of the court system in Latvia said that courts should be independent, but were not convinced that the judicial system in Latvia really is independent. The scepticism is supported by information in the mass media about the court system. Businesspeople who have experience with the court system do not trust it:

> 'My only personal experience involved my divorce, and I came to understand that the courts in Latvia are nothing but a theatrical performance.'

> 'The only time was when we sued a local government company. We won the lawsuit, but we did not get any money anyway, because our opponent was the state. Do I trust the system? No, I do not.'

Businesspeople spoke of several negative aspects of the court system in Latvia. First of all, the judicial system is not completely independent because of the entrenched principle of personal contacts and bribery. This reduces trust in the courts:

> 'The courts in Latvia are not independent. That is particularly true at the district level, where people know each other. Links among relatives and friends are too close for a judge to be at all independent. My personal experience has not been positive. For instance, the secretary of the court and the defendant were such close friends that on the day of the hearing someone would call the plaintiff and announce that there would be no hearing that day. It is possible not to send people elementary things such as court rulings and then pretend that nothing has happened. Never mind that after a month there can be no appeal.'

'I could sue half of my clients for work that has not been done, but that would be more expensive, at least in terms of the time we would have to spend, even if we win some of the cases. That's why none of us does this – those who know that someone else will never go to court take advantage of that fact.'

Second, the competence of some judges is questionable:

'We have incompetent judges. You cannot hear a case about which you know nothing at all. Maybe there are professionals in criminal cases, but it is clear that there are no professionals in civil cases.'

Third, it takes a long time for cases to wind their way through the courts, because there is a shortage of judges. Procedures and laws are complicated and inappropriate in the current situation:

'There are few judges, and this whole procedural order, the system, the laws – they are 30 years or so behind the times. That is why so many cases take so long to resolve.'

Fourth, businesspeople do not trust arbitration courts either, because they are private institutions:

'Basically, the banks have their own arbitration court;, any company with contracts has its own arbitration court. If something they demand is disputed, if a contract is disputed, then they immediately go to their own arbitration court, and you have no right to appeal to another court. You automatically lose – that's clear.'

3.7 Contacts with state and local government institutions and bribery

Businesspeople had fairly negative things to say about the operations and competence of local government and state institutions with regard to various issues. Most respondents think that one needs personal contacts or must pay a bribe to get a government institution to approve a request, take a decision or resolve some issue:

'If you have a personal contact, then everything is faster and more successful. You know where to go, who to see – there are no delays.'

'Yes, it is good if there are personal contacts, because I think that then you can get a fast and positive decision. Everyone, however, should have the same opportunities. Still, I am happy, of course, if I can settle things more quickly in this way.'

'I think that for big projects and big ideas, you certainly need the support of the government, the state, or politicians. Contacts can clearly speed up the taking of decision.'

'Of course a contact helps, it speeds up the whole process, it protects your nerves. I am at ease with this – I cannot change anything.'

'Contacts help a great deal. You go to see someone you know, and he looks at your differently. You are certain that you can make contact with this person, you do not have to pay him anything. To settle issues quickly, you need either a contact or money. I have a negative view of this.'

Businesspeople stress, however, that personal contacts are not necessary in resolving everyday issues, but they are needed when complicated issues arise:

'If there is a simple issue, then you do not need a contact, that is clear. Every issue has its bureaucracy, which could be less extensive, but there is nothing to do about that. If there are more complex issues, however, then personal contact could be of use.'

'I think that making use of contacts is often exaggerated.'

'If I have good intentions and operate within the law, then there is no problem whatsoever in handling formalities.'

'You do not need any personal contact for rank-and-file questions. If your work is lawful, and it has to do with business, then everything happens in a timely way.'

If, however, a businessperson wishes to get around certain aspects of the law, ten respondents think that it cannot be done without personal contacts:

'If the issue requires more than everyday work on the part of the government institution, or if another party is putting pressure on the process, then there can be problems.'

'If you plan to cheat, then you need contacts. If everything is legal, then you can do just fine even without any personal contact.'

Asked whether the Latvian economy will ever be completely rid of corruption, businesspeople had a variety of views. Some feel that any economy can exist without corruption, whereas others think that this is impossible in Latvia at this time:

'I hope that eventually that will be the case. Then we will all have excellent lives.'

'Any economy can exist without corruption. The point is not that everyone will be like a white swan. The point is that the level of corruption at this time is too high.'

3.8 Competence of local government and state institutions

Businesspeople in the survey have not, generally speaking, had particularly close relationships with local governments, but they are still critical of local government operations. They think that local governments should have less power than they have now, because local governments do not have the capacity to deal with certain issues, and there is no one to supervise the operations of local governments:

'They are not competent, they often do not know what is happening. They should be more responsible for what they do. No one can check what the local governments are doing and what they are not doing.'

'It is hard for me to comment, because I have had few contracts with local government institutions. It seems to me, however, that local governments do not need additional powers, sometimes they should fewer powers.'

4. Changes in social relations

4.1 Changes in relations and values

Businesspeople think that relations and values in Latvia have changed in recent years. As positive aspects of this process they list changes in education and labour relations. People are increasingly judged on the basis of their skills. People have greater freedom of choice and can improve their standard of living. Businesspeople think that at least some people in Latvia are becoming wealthier, and they are becoming more friendly and positive:

> 'There have been positive developments in education and labour relations. People are increasingly assessed on the basis of their skills, not on the basis of who they know. That used to be the most important thing.'

> 'There are many positive things – people are freer, they have a better sense of their rights.'

> 'There are positive trends. I think that people have overcome the initial shock which occurred during the radical changes, people have more or less found their place in society, and at least some people have better lives now. Relations are improving, but I suspect that this is more true of Rīga. It is different in the countryside.'

> 'My overall feeling is that there is progress. There are all kinds of challenges and opportunities, it is all in your own hands. There are lots more opportunities, of course, but all of that is accompanied by a variety of problems. We have to count on this.'

> 'Generally speaking, I think that people are much friendlier, they have much greater hopes with respect to the future.'

When it comes to negative factors, businesspeople speak of the dominance of materialistic values in society, and to the fact that there is less time for friends – each person tries to make more effective use of his or her time to earn money. Businesspeople also think, however, that this is a transitional situation; as the economic situation improves, other values will become more important:

> 'The standards in society right now are a good job, a good career, and the latest automobile. Tabloid magazines are full of such information, everyone is interested. You have to be merciless to achieve something like that.'

> 'The focus is on material things. Eventually this race might slow down, but right now the average person is burdened with leasing contracts and loans, he has no time to think about himself, about his health.'

> 'There are good things, too, but relationships are becoming more material. There are fewer friendly or emotional relationships. Everything is dictated by those business numbers, calculations, advantages.'

> 'I think that some people have become calmer, more friendly, more understanding, but there are also people who, on the contrary, have become more aggressive. Those who have normal lives and normal work are peaceful and friendly. Those who are always under stress and cannot fulfil their obligations, whether financial or labour-related, are aggressive and very ambitious. They show off in public with expensive toys such as cars, helicopters or other chic things to compensate for their negativism, or they are aggressive in public, they explode, they butt into queues just because they think that they can.'

> 'We are moving toward the material side we are quite materialistic, but if someone is positive

and has positive energy which sparkles, if that person is ready for normal contacts and a normal attempt to overcome problems, then let that person have the money!'

'All of these value systems are upside-down, but I think that we are in a transition period right now – people are fighting over their places in society, and when each person has won a place, there is a battle to keep that spot. Later, I think, human relationships and matters of the soul will be very important.'

'There have been fairly radical changes. You party with those friends who are in your sector, with whom it is interesting for you to talk. You talk about nothing, or about the weather – there is no time. Things are changing. I have negative views about this, but life is life.'

Businesspeople admit that the focus on material things has changed relations in society, too. People see each other more as competitors; they ignore other people's rights and their own obligations:

'People increasingly perceive each other as competitors. The reason is that people compete with each other to see who fulfils targets the best, who gets a bigger raise. That does not provide for positive relations among people. There is a constant battle, a constant fight. You cannot be convinced that when you meet a particular partner, when you talk and agree, you will not have any surprises the next day.'

'People are still not used to the fact that they have rights. People have forgotten, too, that they have obligations; they forget that they are not the only ones. Their rights are rights only insofar as they do not limit the rights of others. Others also have rights.'

'Materialism is negative. Young people are growing up and thinking only about themselves, about how to earn money. The law in business is live and let live. I have to earn, but you also have to earn. If you earn, then you will work with me, and we will both earn. Young people are just thinking, in most cases, about how to earn as much money as possible right now, without thinking about tomorrow. They do not think about long term co-operation, they are thinking about how to get your money, and that is it.'

'The negative thing is that people achieve new levels of material security; relationships with friends and acquaintances who are less well off disappear. That is the trend.'

4.2 Mutual trust

Business and friendship. Businesspeople in the survey had two kinds of views when asked about business and friendships. There are those who think that years of business contacts can lead to friendship and more, adding that transactions, too, can be based on existing friendships. Others think that business and friendship can never be combined. They think that money spoils relationships. Most of these people have had negative experiences of losing friends as a result of business transactions:

'It is hard to co-operate with friends and maintain a true friendship. Money spoils relationships. I think that friends should not establish joint business operations. There may be successful examples in the world, but there are also cases in which friends have quarrelled over business.'

'Friendship and money have little to do with one another.'

'I understood long ago that friends cannot engage in business together. That is one thing. It is clear that friendships can be destroyed because of business. Friends usually split up when it comes to business.'

'I know that it's better not to work with relatives. I have not had such experience with friends, but relatives? No.'

Others say that they have not lost friends because of business deals, but there does tend to be a gap in mutual relations, perhaps because interests are not the same:

'I have recently been so busy that I do not have time for friends, and I do not know – perhaps my friends are busy, too. We meet less often, because there is more work. That could be a gap of sorts. I might want to meet my friends more often. Companies are companies, but friends are friends.'

'When you are young, 20 years old, you have more time for friends. You do not have work. Now there is less time because of work.'

4.3 Trust in businesses

Businessmen think that mutual relations cannot exist without trust. Trust is also an inviolable component of relations with partners. Without trust, work becomes impossible, and it is trust which helps companies to handle transactions more quickly:

'If there is no trust among partners, then you cannot work. You have to trust people. If you do not trust the partner, then why is he your partner?'

'Without trust, you cannot work. You have to trust people, or you have to find new partners for co-operation. If there is trust, then you can arrange things very quickly. If your partner keeps his word, then there is a lot that you can accomplish quickly.'

'I try to trust others. I very much want to trust people, otherwise life is impossible. Quite often, however, I have been disappointed.'

'My personal principle is to trust people – when a client or someone else betrays me a few times, then I understand that I must not trust that person.'

'There is a lot of trust among businesspeople – someone's word is very important.'

'I think that we trust one another. To be sure, if we are talking about business, then sooner or later someone has been burned, and once is just enough to cancel trust.'

'People trust one another; the alternative is not really possible. To be sure, there are always control mechanisms. One thing that I know is that a good company cannot be a family. I do not mean a family enterprise – a family. There are too many rules for the relationship.'

Most businesspeople are cautious when it comes to trust. They feel that someone who is very trusting will quite often be disappointed, but they also say that they try to trust people – at least their employees and their close partners. The best pill against fraud or disappointment is information and knowing someone in advance:

'Of course there are employees who are my people – it is a very good team that I have assembled, and I absolutely trust them to the very end. To be sure, I control these people to a greater or lesser extent if I can. With other people or allies there is always the desire to believe the other person, but life is life – sometimes you are disappointed, of course.'

'I trust my employees. Partners? Around 50% of the time, because I have had different experiences. I try to trust my clients.'

'I try to do that, but often it is very expensive. In truth, I am always afraid that something will not be done as it should be done.'

'We trust our clients and our employees – not strangers, of course, but the people we know.'

'There is no trust in business. Today he is my partner, tomorrow he will be my competitor. I have seen lots of examples of this in my business.'

'There is always some mistrust, but I try to trust people. We have people who have not paid their bills, though – there are problems, too. These incidents, however, cannot affect everything.'

'You cannot trust others. You cannot say "I trust people". If I take part and monitor the situation constantly, then I trust myself, not them, because I control the situation all the time. I suppose that when I am not there, things may be done differently.'

Some businesspeople say that there are cases when they might allow someone to postpone payment for goods or services. Payment procedures and deadlines are agreed in contracts. There are two main reasons for postponing payment for goods and services. One is that the businessman cannot demand immediate payment as a result of competition, because that might mean losing a client or partner:

'Competition is a prerequisite for this. We cannot insist that people pay for our services right away.'

'In co-operation, there are personal contacts. You do not sell things over the telephone, in an impersonal way. People always call and ask whether they can pay later. To be sure, I could tell them that according to the contract, they will have to pay a fine, but I do not know whether in that case that person will ever come see me again. If I had one million clients, then perhaps I could afford to act that way.'

One businessperson said that only a company which has a monopoly in its sector or controls most of the sector can afford to demand immediate payment from partners and clients. When partners and clients have no choice, they have to observe the rules that are in place:

'Only those organisations insist on pre-payment for services which are, to a certain extent, monopolies. Try to delay payment of your phone bill for more than 30 days. The next day you will be told to pay the debt, and then your phone will be cut off.'

The second reason why companies might allow someone to postpone payment for goods or services is because the company depends on the partner or client. If it is a state or local government company, then businesspeople think that it will not disappear and payment will be made eventually. The specifics of the company can also affect payment procedures, although businesspeople prefer contractual guarantees:

'We only allow stable organisations which will not disappear to pay for goods and services later. The Rīga water company is an example. They cannot just disappear and shut down their office.'

'We always allow clients to pay later.'

What is more, companies with a long history of dealings with state and local government institutions or other partners begin to understand each individual billing system. The cash-flow of state and local government companies, for example, is different from that of private companies; the company's management itself cannot ensure faster payment. In sectors such as the building industry, companies depend on the object being built: once the work is done, salaries are paid, and only then can the companies pay their own bills:

'When it comes to state institutions, that is always the case. It is because of long-term co-operation and other factors. For instance, we respect most clients who have a different cash flow. We know very well that this does not depend on them.'

'Building firms are the poorest companies in the sense that they depend on the thing that is being built – once the work is done, they get their money. They have more money than local governments, but they regularly spend their own money on construction work. Sometimes they get their money two or three months later. The person comes to see us when he comes to see us.'

4.4 The need for contracts

Businesspeople think that co-operation is often impossible without a contract, because a contract is a legal document which confirms the co-operation that has been agreed to. It is a cornerstone for the sale or purchase of goods or services. At the same time, however, the contract is not always the primary element in a transaction, because mutual communications and advantages among partners are also of importance. Businesspeople sometimes make oral agreements before signing a written agreement, while at other times there are only written contracts. In most cases in which there is an oral agreement with a partner or client, the goal is to find out what that person wants. This is then put into a written contract. If all aspects of the process are already known, an oral agreement is not necessary, and a written contract can be drawn up immediately.

The way in which contracts are concluded also depends on whether the company and the client are acquainted, whether there is information about the specific company and whether other circumstances or conditions prevail. Virtually all businesspeople, however, stress the importance of co-operation in drawing up contracts:

'If I see this person for the first time, and I do not feel I can trust him, then of course there will be a written contract. If it is a permanent client whom I trust, then first we arrange for things in oral form, and then, when the work moves forward, then we put everything down in writing.'

'We use contracts, of course, but often we communicate with foreign partners only via e-mail, and then it is harder to conclude a contract. It is clear that we send the first samples – we trust them.'

Businesspeople do not hide the fact that they make do without a contract when a contract would only make the deal more difficult, e.g. if something has to be bought quickly and the parties are willing to make do with only a receipt confirming the transaction:

> 'A contract is not always necessary. We have serious partners as well as builders who buy equipment from us. If a building is being put up, the builder does not have time to mess around with contracts. We go over there, we see what is needed, we supply it, and that is all. They give us a receipt, and that is enough. We have not had any problems so far.'

Other situations involve bookkeeping, auditing and business consultations. In these cases, co-operation is not possible without contracts. Consultations involve long-term co-operation, and so a contract is definitely needed. What is more, the contract should be one which covers all possible situations. Otherwise co-operation between the two parties becomes difficult:

> 'Nothing specific happens until we have a written agreement on our relationship. We can agree on principles that will be the basis for our work, but we do not move until we have a signature on paper.'

In the consulting world, too, however, there is sometimes co-operation without a contract. One businessperson in the sector said that a prerequisite for providing services without a contract is long-term co-operation:

> 'There are situations where we have permanent clients with whom we do not conclude a contract at all and the service is provided anyway.'

Businesspeople say that when partners fail to satisfy the terms of an agreement, the result is usually negotiations to find a solution:

> 'If payment is not made on time, then we meet and deal with the problem. We seek a compromise and get back to work.'

> 'Usually we try to discuss the situation with the partner, see what the problem is. So far we have always found a compromise, because it is not always the case that someone is violating the terms of the contract on purpose. There are various situations. You can always talk and find solutions through negotiations.'

Even if there are contracts that include sanctions if terms are violated, businesspeople say that they usually do not insist on the penalties. Because of competition, businesspeople avoid going to court over brief delays in payment for goods and services. Second, the length of co-operation is also of key importance; if the relationship has been without complications, then long-standing clients are given a break:

> 'If the terms of the contract are violated for a known reason, then we allow the client to pay within 30 days. If there is a delay, we do not apply sanctions anyway, we forgive the other person. I am not going to go to court over a three-day delay in payment. The client will go elsewhere.'

> 'Those who are permanent clients – sure, they sometimes pay their bill too late. Our contracts speak of sanctions, but we do not want conflicts with our partners. We usually do not apply sanctions.'

4.5 Co-operation with strangers

Most businesspeople say that working with strangers is an everyday practice, because businesses are always looking for new partners and establishing new types of collaboration. They are more cautious, however, in working with new and unknown partners and clients, and usually make checks. Only then can there be trust. Most businesspeople say that in recent times they have had more transactions with strangers, and they stress that contracts are absolutely necessary in such cases. Contracts are sometimes nothing more than a formality; however, because the deal would otherwise be impossible and because the person is unknown, there can be no talk of trust:

> 'Everyone is a stranger when they first do business. The law says that when there are larger sums involved, there must be a contract if payment after the fact. How official the agreement is – that is a different thing: usually there is a contract just to have a contract. There is machinery which no one buys like bread. It is not the case that someone walks in off the street and buys equipment for 2,000 lats and says that he will come in the next day and pay. There are always receipts.'

> 'We do engage in business with strangers. Basically, we try to conclude contracts with strangers. When the person is unknown, nothing happens without an agreement.'

> 'The things is that contracts become more and more important to us each year, they become more detailed and we include things in the agreement based on things that we have learned. We also are working increasingly with foreign clients.'

> 'There are always new and, therefore, unknown partners and clients. If possible, get prepayment. If not, then prepare a contract, sign the contract.'

Some businesspeople say that they conclude contracts with unknown clients because of past disappointments with transactions that did not involve a contract:

> 'Sadly, I have bitter experience – you cannot have business relations without a contract. I have had specific cases of being disappointed. As soon as a relationship is agreed, we conclude an agreement.'

Interestingly, there are some businesspeople who use not only contracts, but also their intuition to protect themselves in deals with strangers. There are businesspeople who think that they must trust each partner unless the partner has proved that he is not trustworthy. Businesspeople also check each other out:

> 'In any new deal, people do not know each other. A new employee is always a stranger, and you always take a certain risk. We base our thinking more on intuition, as opposed to protecting ourselves in legal terms.'

> 'I am almost British in that I consider everyone to be a gentleman until he has proved otherwise.'

There are others, however, who are loath to work with strangers. Protect yourself, and then you can trust others – that is their motto:

> 'I do not really like to work with strangers. It all depends on the co-operation – how extensive it is, what we are discussing.'

'You must never tempt your employee unnecessarily to take something or steal something. Leave nothing in the open. I trust people, but I do not need to tempt them. We have many deals with strangers. Mostly we trust them.'

4.6 Trust in the state

Respondents are more cautious when talking about trust in the state. They say that there have been changes, but there is still insecurity which prevents them from trusting the state. Occurrences in the legislative and executive branches of politics and the low level of state support for small companies do not inspire trust:

'I do not really trust the state, I do not trust banks. I still shiver a bit because of Banka Baltija. We have accounts in Brussels, we do not keep our money at the Bank of Latvia.'

'My trust in the state? 10%.'

'I think that individuals cannot trust the state. Trust has to do with responsibility – if the state has no responsibility vis-à-vis me, then how can it expect trust from me? That is true of anyone.'

'I very much distrust the Latvian police, that is true, because I have had differences of opinion with other businesspeople and I have seen that they have support from the interior affairs system. You are simply pressured to step aside.'

4.7 The importance of social networks in business

Businesspeople say that contacts and networks offer certain advantages in business. When there is co-operation with an acquaintance, the businessperson knows what can be asked from the individual and what can be expected. Contacts offer some guarantee that the cooperation will be positive:

'Many transactions involve contacts. When you deal with someone you know, then you not only have the written contract, but also the fact that you are personal acquaintances. That has always been an advantage for businesspeople.'

Social networks are undeniably important in business, and in most cases these emerge from simple contacts. If a businessperson has proved to be a specialist in a specific sector, and if co-operation with that individual has been successful, then a partner or client will inform others about this fact. The emergence of such a network helps companies to develop:

'Recommendations are always the foundation of business to a greater or lesser degree. People know one another, and if one person needs something and he does not know where the office is, then he will even ask his competitors.'

'Word of mouth is the thing here – someone who knows you can then recommend you. If no one knows you, then it is probably the case that no one will want to work with you. Personal contacts are what promote development.'

One businessperson, however, said that this is not true in all sectors of the economy. In a narrow sub-sector in which everyone more or less knows everyone else the network does not ensure the accustomed functions, i.e., it does not help companies to grow:

> 'I do not think that there is a network structure in our area of business. I suspect that there are such networks in other sectors, certainly, but not in our area. Our sphere is not big enough for something of that kind.'

5. Attitudes vis-à-vis the West

5.1 A sense of belonging to Europe

Surveyed experts mostly said that Western Europe is a big marketplace for ideas and for work. Some think that the problem of "old Europe" is that everything is in place there and so, to a certain extent, things have stopped; there is a lack of new and flexible ideas. Latvian businesspeople do not complain about the absence of these qualities. On the contrary, they speak of being active, of moving towards the West and of co-operating with the West. Some Western European companies are seen as an example and as a goal for the future. Western Europe can set an example for Latvia in terms of wages, labour relations and tax systems:

> 'To a certain extent we can see Western Europe as an example. We would like to work at the level of PricewaterhouseCoopers or MG at some point. We have a goal to pursue.'

> 'No, not a competitor. We would have to be terribly conceited to say that the West is our competitor. We have a very long way to go to reach them. There are probably areas in which we are ahead of them, perhaps in terms of innovation and imagination, but they are ahead of us in terms of systems and orderliness.'

> 'They may dominate as an example, but they have become lazy. We are far superior in the sense that we are much more aggressive vis-à-vis the market, we are more fearless, we risk more. They are different – they do not need that. The innovations do not introduce anything, of course, they go forward and develop, but if we are talking about growth, then companies in Latvia are certainly growing much more rapidly than companies in other countries are.'

> 'They are more of an example. I work with clients from abroad, from the European Union on an everyday basis, and I see that they finally consider us to be a part of the same community. That was not the case in the past. That is very good.'

When it comes to businesspeople from other European countries, respondents see them as partners or as part of a market in which they can work, not as competitors or models:

> 'It is hard for me to say whether they are an example or a competitor, I think that it is something in between. You can take positive things from them to a certain extent, but we have lots of things which they do not have. We are not afraid of the West; that is not the case.'

> 'Europe and the West – that is an opportunity to grow, to expand. It may be too early to talk about branch offices, OK, but two years from now that may be realistic. That is a market into which I can expand.'

> 'I see Europe as a partner, not as a competitor, but as a market.'

Because of the differences between Latvia and Western Europe, some businesspeople see Western Europe as a competitor, not a model. They think that events in Western Europe cannot be adapted to Latvia's situation. Western Europe is also seen as a competitor because businesspeople in those countries, as in Latvia, can take part in national procurement processes:

> 'At this particular stage, we can see Western Europe more as a competitor than as an example. It is hard for Western European companies to adapt to our environment. Our environment is quite a bit different than the one in Western Europe.'

> 'They are competitors, not an example. The situation in Latvia is different.'

> 'Our market economy often has national bids for tender in which we take part. Then Western European companies are our competitors, because they take part as well.'

Asked whether they feel that they belong to Europe, most respondents are evasive in their answers. Respondents say that after the collapse of the Iron Curtain, there were idealised ideas about Europe, but today businesspeople feel a stronger sense of allegiance to Latvia:

> 'The situation has changed. Initially everyone thought that all is beautiful and wonderful over there, that they must go there. Now, however, I think that it is no longer the case; there are problems over there, as well. Life is different there, but it is hard to say whether it is better or worse.'

> 'I have always said that I am nothing but a Latvian patriot. It is accepted that Latvia is now in the European Union, but I feel more a Latvian than a European.'

> 'It depends on the moment – not so much when I am here, but OK, all is well when I travel abroad.'

> 'I do not feel a sense of belonging to Europe. When we joined the European Union, things became different, but not better.'

> 'I am a citizen of the world, why should I be a citizen of Europe. Europe as a community? That is not for me.'

5.2 Changes in attitudes vis-à-vis the West in the last 15 years

Some businesspeople think that their personal attitudes vis-à-vis the West have not changed over the last 15 years. Some feel positive about the West, others are neutral, and still others are cautious and sceptical:

> 'I have nothing against the West. Perhaps my attitude is even a bit more positive, because as soon as we became an official member of the European Union, some co-operation partners, without even asking, extended payment deadlines for us. If in the past we had to pay in ten days, we are now told that we can pay in one month.'

> 'My attitude has not changed much, it is cautious and sceptical. I do know why people like the fact that western money is used to teach them loyalty and blind trust in western values. The West has its values. The West is not Mother Teresa to come and raise us to the sky. Western Europe has its own interests of business and power.'

Some businesspeople do not deny, however, that their personal attitudes toward the West have undergone a change, whether positive, neutral or negative:

> 'I cannot compare my attitude 15 years ago and now. There are much greater opportunities now, of course. Back then we looked at them as at miracles, we thought that we would probably never have the same situation.'

> 'I think that my attitude has changed from positive to neutral. I am neither a supporter of Europe nor a sceptic about Europe. We try too hard to push our way into the European Union. We are not yet ready, and the truth is that Europe is not all that excellent. Europe wants us as a place where older people can spend their holidays. We have to emphasise the service sector, but manufacturing remains in their hands.'

> 'It has developed in the negative direction. Once upon a time Western Europe was a mythical example of the good life, of high culture. It seemed that Western Europeans are very positive and developed. When I got to know them, however, the vision collapsed. I understood that they are lower than us in terms of development and understanding.'

> 'Fifteen years ago people did not know much about the lives of people in the West. We had just left the Soviet Union, and our introduction to Western civilisation had only just begun. Now people know a lot more. They also know that not everything that glitters is gold.'

Businesspeople say that public opinion about the West has changed over the last 15 years. People no longer see each foreigner as something special, and rejoicing over Latvia's membership of the European Union has receded. People's expectations have been disappointed, which is one reason why attitudes are changing:

> 'Overall, public opinion has changed, the euphoria about being in Europe, about finally being in the European Union, about being equal – it has diminished. We will never be equal in their eyes, and we will never be a part of the same Europe as far as they are concerned. We are a part of the former Soviet Union to them. No matter where you go, no matter with whom you have contact, life experiences are quite different.'

> 'Public opinion has changed, too. A foreigner who arrives in Latvia is no longer a god. No one treats foreigners like they did ten years ago. Foreigners come here, and they are nothing, just as we are nothing over there. Who is he when he comes here? Who needs him?'

5.3 Changes since Latvia joined the European Union

Respondents think that Latvia's membership of the European Union has brought change, both positive and negative. The most important positive change noted by respondents is that customs procedures have become easier for goods and travel. Several respondents said that it took a lot of time to deal with customs formalities before Latvia joined the EU:

> 'We can do more successful business with European companies. Lots of customs formalities are no longer in place.'

> 'Customs problems are gone in our business. Customs declarations and the amount of time that we spent waiting – that required so much time and resources. We have to pay anyway, of course, but the work is now much easier.'

'Changes in customs procedures make our work easier. We used to spend half of our time at customs offices and dealing with the procedures. Goods flow more freely. For well-known companies in the export sector, these changes were very important, because they made life much, much easier.'

'Open borders – go where you want, import what you want. No customs!'

'Within the European Union there are no customs payments for transporting goods; that makes the work much easier, and it is also advantageous – you can buy services in another European Union country and do not have to pay VAT.'

'There are more tourists, and I agree that this is positive.'

Other positive changes listed by respondents include a larger market, the linkage between the Latvian lats and the euro and the concomitant exchange-rate security, and greater trust on the part of partners:

'A clear plus is that the average Latvian company can now distribute its goods more successfully in Europe.'

'We can very clearly see our expenditures and our income, because the lats is linked to the euro. We used to have currency exchange rate shifts, we concluded contracts for three years, and we often suffered great losses in many areas. In competition, if you fight over a single percentage point while the exchange rate shifts by 15%, then that is quite dangerous. Now everything is predictable. It is a greater sense of security.'

'In business, there is greater trust on the part of our partners. It used to be that others really did not want to trust us, many did not even want to talk to us. We used to be associated with Russia – that is the point.'

'Customs procedures are easier, as are purchases, mutual transactions and contacts, too. They perceive us more seriously now.'

Respondents think that another positive factor is the inflow of financial resources from various European Union funds:

'Through the EU's funds, the SAPARD programme, Latvia got quite a lot of money. That was very serious money, and to a certain extent it helped business to grow. It also created a cornerstone for agriculture and tourism.'

One negative change that businesspeople see since Latvia joined the European Union is changes in the law. Latvia's businesses had to accept countless regulations when Latvia joined the EU, and some businesses collapsed under the pressure. Businesspeople also say that the Latvian market is not yet functioning properly, with the result that labour is moving to other parts of the EU:

'One minus – the EU's regulations, which are applied to a great many companies in Latvia which were doing perfectly well before then. The regulations have caused many companies to go bankrupt, because they require enormous investments which the companies sometimes can finance.'

'I have more European Union regulations, rules and laws now for which I basically see no point at all. They disturb my work.'

'Businesses had finally started to work seriously, and then all of a sudden there was a pile of instructions and guidelines about what we were supposed to do.'

'The only change is that people are allowed to leave the country. As a businessperson, I want to say that those who have an education and who really want to work hard – I do not think that they cannot find a job and an income here, that the situation is so poor that they have to leave. Absolutely not. The movement of labour is certainly needed, but it has to be controlled. The situation in our sector is absolutely tragic at this time.'

It has to be said that respondents generally felt that membership of the EU had been beneficial rather than harmful for business operations in Latvia.

5.4 Attitudes toward EU enlargement

When asked about further eastward expansion of the European Union, respondents' views differed. Some think that it would be logical so as to avoid isolating Russia and to make sure that it does not "create a fuss". These respondents also think that Turkey is important and advantageous in terms of development. Others, however, are more sceptical about the European Union's enlargement, because they think that the situation would be too complex for the Union. For that reason, they say that for the time being and/or in the future enlargement is not necessary. Some respondents, moreover, think that enlargement harms the national interests of the state and the overall image of Europe.

Positive views about enlargement:

'Certainly Russia is an enormous country with enormous potential. I think that we cannot and must not isolate it. Nothing good will happen if it is all alone, I think.

My view is that it would be absolutely normal for Turkey to join the European Union. If Turkey satisfies all of the requirements, then it has the right to join Europe.'

Negative views about EU enlargement:

'I have never cared for big unions. It already seems that the European Union is much too large. Sooner or later the Western European countries paying for all of this will not be happy to do so. There are already quite a few dissatisfied people in old Europe. Perhaps they do not want to earn money for, maintain and feed a great many poor countries.'

'The European Union is unnecessary for me as a structure. The European Union is yet another artificial alliance. A small country cannot resolve its problems inside a union. They do not understand, we do not understand. Little countries with lots of people – do they offer any potential? Can the European Union help them? Should the European Union help them? I doubt whether they need this.'

Certain respondents said that their attitudes are not the same towards all of the countries seeking membership of the European Union: Romania, Bulgaria, Croatia, Turkey, Ukraine, Belarus and Russia. There seem to be no objections to post-Soviet countries with a Western orientation, but there are objections to the membership of Turkey and Russia. Some respondents say that this would unquestionably mean changes for the European Union:

'There will be problems with the Turks. They should not be admitted to the European Union, because theirs is a different religion. It is a mass of people, and the European Union will have to lower the bar and find that much is lost. The post-Soviet countries that are not particularly loyal to Russia, which are focused on the West – why not? But Russia and its satellites – that is a very serious question. Russia is a power which cares less about people's welfare and more about power and influence. After the accession of Russia, the European Union would no longer be the same European Union, that is absolutely clear. It may happen sooner or later, but then Russia must adapt and change.'

'I think that I would categorically reject it, because Europe would lose its physical boundaries. We are not going to bring the entire Eurasian continent – China and Russia – into Europe!'

Some respondents think that we have no right to object to the enlargement of the European Union, adding that enlargement is inevitable:

'We just joined the European Union. What moral right could we possibly have to ban others from doing the same? We have no such right.'

'It is an inevitable process. Countries improve themselves so as to join the European Union. It helps, and when everything is in order, that helps businesspeople to earn more money. Countries become rich. That is a commendable process, and if the whole world were to structure itself in that way, then we would all live wonderful lives.'

'After all, the entire world is turning into a single country, so this is inevitable. It is normal – the main thing is to stamp bar codes on people's hands.'

Few businesspeople had anything to say about Russia's membership of the World Trade Organisation; most had difficulty formulating their attitude in this regard because they did not feel competent on the issue. For others, it was a difficult question with no clear answer. Those businesspeople with an opinion supported Russia's membership of the WTO. They think that this would be an investment in natural resources and would balance out the organisation's interests.

5.5 Views about "western culture"

When asked about western culture, businesspeople were fairly evasive or else could not associate anything with the concept. Most compared western culture to eastern or Latvian culture, saying that there is not really any such thing as "western culture." Instead, it is made up of the cultures of many European countries:

'The differences between western and eastern culture are mainly in the mind. We 'probably belong to western culture, and so this concept is not particularly specific.

'I certainly think that we represent western culture, Christianity.'

'In essence, western culture is very varied, there are so many different countries.'

Interestingly, several respondents thought that western culture involves excessive concentration and consumption, as well as a failure to observe elementary standards of behaviour. Others spoke of attempts to conquer the world. Still others pointed to laziness and slowness:

'It is a consumer culture. The mission is this: the more we consume, the more we manufacture and the better it will be for everyone.'

'It is a bad culture, one which we cannot understand. Do you want examples? In public transport in Western Europe no one will get up to let an elderly person sit down. That is not accepted there, while here it is still, to a certain extent, true. I sometimes stand up. People cough in other people's face without putting a hand or a handkerchief in front of their mouth.'

'Conquering the world. Europe wants to lord it over the entire world.'

'There is laziness over there. People do not want to work, they do not have any special interests, they do not develop or improve themselves.'

'It is balanced and slow, people are stagnant when it comes to taking decisions.'

6. Main conclusions

The owners of small and medium enterprises – people who are directly involved in the activities of their companies – were asked about their attitudes vis-à-vis the environment in which they work, and responses indicate that the environment in Latvia has improved significantly in recent years. Businesspeople speak positively about changes in the services offered by the State Revenue Service and about easier customs procedures now that Latvia has joined the European Union. On the other hand, respondents were not happy about the introduction of EU regulations, which make their work more difficult. Respondents also expect the state to be more forthcoming in dealing with their needs. Businesspeople most often speak of the need for tax relief for SMEs or companies facing difficulties – respondents argue that the tax burden in Latvia is very heavy, indeed.

According to businesspeople, government institutions in Latvia should think more about supporting businesspeople and about establishing friendly partnerships with reciprocal feedback. There is also a need for higher levels of competence among civil servants, who must abandon their haughtiness and take an interest in what their clients are saying. Latvians have little trust in the judicial system. There are claims that judges are corrupt, incompetent and less than independent. Others speak of the long time that it takes to resolve court cases. Many violations do not end up in court at all because parties to the process wish to save time and money – solutions are usually sought through negotiations and compromise.

Businesspeople say that bribery and taking advantage of contacts are everyday practices, adding that these are necessary when dealing with specific issues or with matters on which the law is unclear. Contacts speed up decision-making. In everyday, lawful issues, contacts and bribery are not necessary.

When it comes to the state's role in regulating the market, businesspeople think that government should not intervene in market operations; the market can take care of itself. Businesspeople say that the role of government is to improve social policies and to control major companies of national importance – the Latvenergo power company, for instance. Businesspeople are sceptical about the process of privatisation in Latvia. They think that the public has not been properly informed about the privatisation process and its results. On the other hand, there is a clear desire among interested parties to manage the process, either to speed up or slow down the privatisation of specific objects. Respondents point to the negative effects of privatisation, such as the alienation of property, waste of resources, and accumulation of wealth by a few at the expense of everyone else. Businesspeople do not think that major state companies should be privatised, because that could harm public welfare and the national economy.

Comparing Latvia with other countries, businesspeople feel that Latvia's situation is similar to that in the Baltic States, although Estonia is a more developed. Despite this, respondents think that the business environment in Latvia is developing in the right direction. Asked about model countries in the West, respondents mention Ireland, Germany and other developed Western European countries. At the same time, however, respondents also point out that Western European countries are stagnating, while Latvia has experienced very rapid growth over the last few years. They see Western Europe as a model, but are against adopting European practices without adapting them to the Latvian situation. Businesspeople see Western Europe as a market as well as a partner.

Asked to compare the market economy with the planned economy, businesspeople speak of certain problems with the former: minimal social guarantees, poverty among some groups in society, an imbalanced market, and great risks in everyday operations. At the same time, however, they unquestionably prefer the market economy, which allows them to pursue their ideas, to take advantage of opportunities and to choose their activities. They also speak of competition as a driving force behind development.

Businessmen also were asked about competition in Latvia. They said that there is lots of competition, but the government's role in this is negligible; for the most part, the government just watches what is happening without doing much. Competition among businesspeople determines the overall level of competition. In some sectors involving state or local government procurement, however, there is no real competition.

When asked about their role in society, businesspeople mostly speak about themselves as employers and taxpayers. Businesspeople do not think that they should assume responsibility for the social security of local residents. They say that they pay taxes and play a key role in the country's development, and it is the government's responsibility to take care of the people.

Asked about possible changes in people's situations and values in Latvia in recent years, businesspeople speak of several positive trends. Better skills enable people to choose their activities and improve their standard of living. The situation of the comparatively wealthy stratum in society is also improving. Businesspeople also speak about the general emphasis on material values: the increased role of money, the way in which time is spent, and the attempt of individuals in some segments of society to focus on a improving their standard of living. Respondents think that the situation will stabilise, and people will eventually return to a system of values in which money does not play the primary role.

When asked about mutual trust, businesspeople are not unanimous about links between business and friendship. Some businesspeople think that co-operation can lead to friendship and that co-operation can be based on friendship. Others argue that business and friendship do not go hand in hand. Respondents say that trust is necessary in relations with employees, clients and partners as it brings a variety of advantages. The way in which contracts are negotiated and payments for goods and services are made is closely bound up with trust. Respondents, however, prefer the security of a written contract; some respondents say that they have been cheated in the past. Businesspeople are cautious when speaking about trusting the government. They think that constant changes in the law and the low level of support for SMEs are not things which encourage trust.

In speaking about positive and negative changes since Latvia joined the European Union, businesspeople emphasise the former rather than the latter. Positive changes include easier customs formalities, a wider market, the certainty provided by the link between the Latvian lats and the euro, EU funding, and greater trust on the part of partners in the EU. Negative aspects include the careless application of EU regulations and norms in Latvia and the outflow of labour.

Some businesspeople are frank in saying that their attitude vis-à-vis the West has changed in the last 15 years. Among the public at large, enthusiasm about the EU has diminished since joining. Businesspeople think that we have a much more realistic view of the West than was the case in the early 1990s, when the lives of people in the West were idealised. When asked about enlarging the EU and about Western culture, businesspeople offer a variety of views.

In general one can conclude that the business environment is changing rapidly in Latvia, mostly for the better. However, it is not easy to overcome the negative experiences of corruption and cheating and to start trusting business partners, clients and the Latvian judicial system.

The Approach of Russian Entrepreneurs towards the Extended Order

Nina Oding & Lev Savulkin

1. Introduction

Modern Russian entrepreneurs, encumbered with the experience of living under a command economy and in post-Soviet Russia, currently face serious difficulties in their day-to-day activities. After almost 15 years of free enterprise development in the country, the protection of private property and private business development still continues to pose an acute challenge. The results of numerous entrepreneur surveys show significant volatility, inconsistency and divergence in entrepreneurs' attitudes toward the free market, private property and competition. This can be explained by the commingling of old and new social institutions in the country. The problem has been aggravated by a series of re-nationalizations of large Russian companies. At present, even some ideologists of the liberal reforms of the 1990s express doubts as to the "legitimacy" of the privatizations in an attempt to justify the growing presence of the state in the Russian economy (Dmitriev, 2006).

The most palpable result of Russian market reforms is the emergence of independent, privately-owned companies. The compromise character of the Russian privatization model made it possible to dampen the social upheaval and protract the process of enterprise reorganization and the emergence of efficient property owners. It appears that the mass character of the Russian privatization, in which all interested parties (enterprise administrations, working collectives and the general public) followed the rules of game, legalized the divestiture process initiated by the RF "Law on Enterprise."

The results of a survey undertaken in 2005 by the IKSI RAN Institute show that over half of all Russian citizens have a positive attitude toward the institution of private property, about one third are neutral about it, and only 15.5% are definitely against private property (Andreev, 2005, p. 18). The survey also notes an improvement in the attitude to such concepts as "privatization" and "entrepreneur" (70% positive answers against 53.6% in 2000). The assessment of the entrepreneurs' role also improved: whereas in Soviet times, they were mostly slandered as exploiters of the workers, about 50% of the 2005 sample saw their main role as that of providing new jobs. At the same time, the survey notes that "in the majority of cases, though not all, Russians' views of private property depend on the circumstances under which the owners have come to possess it." Notably, this includes not only legal, but also moral and ethical circumstances (ibid., p. 21).

Despite the acceptance of the concepts of private property and free enterprise, the population continues to associate the state not with the rule of law and with democratic institutions, but with a force and state machinery designed to serve some great idea. This is particularly evident in discussions that periodically erupt on the choice of a driving force for economic modernization and growth, i.e. on the choice between liberal and dirigist economic policy models. In addition, in a situation of uncertainty and dynamism characteristic of a market economy the lack of immediate positive results of the transformations evokes nostalgic feelings about the stability and order of the socialist past.

One would think that past experience should make society aware of the necessity for government to give up its role as largest property owner and economic agent. Indeed, during the Soviet period the government tested practically all conceivable methods of state participation in the economy and of operating state enterprises. This alone should have been sufficient to convince people that the alleged viability of such economic systems is a chimera.

On the other hand, the experience of dozens of years in a command system with its repressive methods of negative selection has significantly diluted private initiative and the work ethic, encouraged double standards and a disregard for the law and contractual commitments, and created paternalistic patterns of behaviour over several generations. In addition, in contrast to other countries of the former Soviet Bloc, Russia has known only a short period of capitalism and respect for private property.

In the period since the start of privatization in Russia, public views on basic shortcomings of the process have changed drastically. While at the onset of the reforms critics mostly targeted the allegedly unjustified speed and mass character of the privatization efforts, in later years the focus shifted to the lack of efficient owners and institutional transformations, which should have taken place before privatization began. It has become evident that privatization alone is not enough for stable economic growth if other conditions (the most important of which are macro-economic stability and a propitious legal environment) are absent. However, we believe that in Russia it would have been impossible to first establish official rules or introduce a mature system of legal regulations modelled on the West, including binding contractual commitments, respect for private property, and general compliance with the rule of law (especially given the Russian inclination to nepotism and disregard for the law.)

If one agrees with S. Kirdina's view that "evolutionary updating of the modern transitional economy means developing its inherent institutional order" (Kirdina, 2004, pp. 89–98), one should acknowledge that the present stage of development in the Russian economy reproduces the generic features of the past – basic institutions and concepts propounding domination of the state in all spheres of life. However, as G. Easter pointed out (Easter, 2001, p. 58), despite the importance of the historical heritage, the transition has led to the rise of hybrid political and economic institutions, shaped by old and the new.

Aiming to analyze the existing situation by seeing it through the eyes of Russian entrepreneurs, we conducted a survey of their opinions and values based on a sample drawn from the St. Petersburg business community. We conducted in-depth interviews with 17 entrepreneurs (business owners) and top company managers in December 2005–January 2006. All our respondents have sufficient practical economic management experience under various conditions in Russia. Therefore, though our sample is not representative, the survey made it possible to collect important qualitative information on the existing political, economic and social interfaces, as well as on the entrepreneurs' attitudes toward public institutions and the West. We paid special attention to the fact that our respondent's values had been formed in the Soviet environment, while their economic activities spanned three distinct periods in modern Russian history: traditional Soviet economy, perestroika, and market-oriented reforms.

Of the 17 companies surveyed, 12 are in the top five positions by turnover in their respective industries in St. Petersburg. All companies have been operating for over 12 years. Five of the respondents were under 40, nine between 49 and 50, and three over 50. Five companies have been privatized, while the other 12 started from scratch. Eight respondents both own and manage their businesses, and nine are top managers, including five "junior" co-owners of their companies. Five companies are in manufacturing; the others operate in the services industry, with 11 companies selling their products and services directly to the public. Of these, six companies have business clients as well. The other six companies serve only business clients. Of the 17 companies, eight focus on the domestic market, while seven either sell their products/services abroad or procure goods/services from foreign companies.

The main objective of the survey was to identify the respondents' attitudes toward basic aspects of the economic environment as a means of identifying their style of economic behaviour.

2. Interplay between economics and politics

Russia's modern history includes different types of relations between the state and business. One respondent noted: "From the early 1990s until 1999, we were left to our own devices. 1999–2002 was a period of grinding in. Now state power clearly dominates."

Our set of questions was designed to depict the actual situation at the business-politics interface and seems to have produced practically unanimous answers. The respondents' emotional reaction (with confidentiality of their personal information guaranteed) shows the urgency and importance of this social aspect. At the same time, while expressing a negative view about the character of these relations, the respondents showed a fatalistic acceptance of the existing order of things and a lack of faith in the possibility of change.

Practically all respondents insist that at present the state dominates business. Owners and managers of large companies believe that government officials simply sponge on business:

"Bureaucrats view businesses as a part of the state machinery they can use at their own discretion."

At the same time, the state squeezes businesses of different sizes in different ways. One respondent (from a construction company) classified business-state relations in three types:

> "Type 1. The company is integrated into the state system and resolves all its major problems through corruption. Type 2 (non-interference). The company minimizes its contacts with the state (since they are too burdensome) and establishes contact only when it is unavoidable, including, of course, bribery. Type 3: A 'snow-white and transparent' company that strives to minimize bribery. Such a company wages active – including courtroom – battles with the state. The first type consists mostly of large businesses, the second type of small business, and the third type medium-sized businesses."

One entrepreneur said that the dependence on bureaucrats is so strong that *"large businesses simply cannot survive in Russia without 'administrative contacts.'"* Respondents stressed that the state handles small businesses *"in an absolutely ungodly way."* All respondents are convinced that such relations are unacceptable. At the same time, the respondents' answers to the question of the desirable type of business-state relations were divided almost equally, with about 50% opting for complete separation (*"everyone must take care of his own business"*), and the other 50% preferring a business-state partnership.

The majority of the sample believes that the current model of business-state relations in Russia can be best compared only to those existing in other countries of the former Soviet Union (FSU). One respondent said: *"All of us have graduated from the same Soviet greatcoat"* (an allusion to a classic novella by the famous nineteenth-century Russian author N. Gogol). Over half of the respondents view Russia as a unique country and cannot see any model of the existing business-state relations in other countries that could be adopted by Russia. The majority is convinced that Russia *"should borrow the best components of such relations from all countries and adapt them to the domestic situation."* The bulk of the respondents insist that the "uniqueness" of Russia would defeat any attempt to take over completely any existing model of the interface between the state and the business community. Only one third of the respondents named the USA as a model system of business-state relations, while the others opted for Germany, Finland, the Baltic republics or Scandinavian countries (these countries were named by one respondent each).

Only two of the 17 respondents have had occasional contacts with highly placed government officials, while the rest have to fairly frequently deal with bureaucrats *"because otherwise one could not run a business at all."* Characteristically, the respondents have no faith in any of the existing state institutions. One respondent said:

> "They should prove their credibility. One should have a sound credit history. None of our state institutions can boast a sound credit history."

In this respect, entrepreneurs differ from the majority of the Russian population. In particular, entrepreneurs do not trust the president or approve of his policies, while a population survey in the same period (December 2005) by the Levada Centre showed that 73% of the respondents approved of the president's policies and 75% trusted him.[1]

Interviewees most emotional responses were to questions about relations between the state and business. The opinions were predominantly negative:

> "The law protection bodies and the tax services are especially "delightful." They have poor qualifications, are obstinate, interpret laws arbitrarily, and use their "administrative contacts" a full 600 percent." "Our customs and tax agencies are focused not on control, but on fulfilling the budget. They operate like quasi-commercial organizations. For example, I come to a customs office in Finland. The customs declaration sits in their computer. I simply present my invoice and waybill, pay with my credit card, and the thing is done. They do not charge any VAT until the goods are sold. One cannot even imagine anything like this in Russia!"

The respondents believe that "bureaucrats and the state create unfavourable conditions for businesses and make a profit out of businesses." "One cannot deal with them without bribes. And sometimes even bribes cannot help you. I think that the distinctive feature of this period is that a business has to pay simply in order to exist." Notably, "while low-level bureaucrats are learning something and improving their qualifications, the top and the medium levels are capable only of using only their "administrative contacts".

Entrepreneurs urge the state to comply with its own laws. They find that there is no public control over state officials. One respondent gave the following example:

> "At present the city is revising its methods for leasehold rate calculation and is planning to establish new rates as of next year. Only very few business people have seen the new regulations. The majority will not see them before January 1, when they come into force. Moreover, they are so complicated that one cannot understand them easily. I have a good education in mathematics, so I could cope with them. However, not every shop owner has a good mathematical background. The majority will not understand the methods, and one will be able to cheat them any way one likes. Moreover, those who have concluded their leasehold contracts between July 1 and January 1 will get some benefits. This means that benefits are offered only to those who have taken trouble to obtain inside information and learned about the changes beforehand. Well, how can one trust the state after all this? Or, look at their decision to close retail trade in the Metro. They declared this decision only three months before the contracts were to be renewed. Why did they not do this earlier? People could have had time to look for other locations. But no, they must do this without warning in order to make people go bust."

All respondents would prefer better, reliable and stable rules of the game to maintaining direct contacts with powerful government officials. However, they believe that in modern Russia this is impossible.

> "One cannot establish or develop a business without ties to government officials. Maybe that is what they call a 'competitive' policy of the state. For example, a group of 'comrades' come to you and say: hey, this shop is not yours. The owner answers: how come? But then a gang of ruffians armed with baseball bats arrives and throw your personnel and goods into the yard. Mind you, this happens not just anywhere, but on the Nevsky Prospect (the main avenue of St. Petersburg). And the ruffians are not just gangsters from anywhere, but personnel of a security company connected with the police."

---

1   http://www.levada.ru/prezident.html.

Almost half of the respondents stress the necessity to tightly regulate and control state officials, while the rest believe that the best way is to simply loosen controls and regulations for economic activities.

A little over half of the respondents said that no goals can justify the state's interference in the economy. One third of the respondents allow for such interference in the economy if this interference is in strict compliance with existing laws. Only two respondents said that the state has the right to interfere in the economy in the interests of the state, though they noted that *"such interests have not yet been defined or reflected in legislation."*

In the opinion of 70% of the respondents, the role of the state should be reduced to the protection of human and property rights, establishment of common regulations and controls, and provision of antimonopoly regulation. Half of the respondents are convinced that the existing anti-monopoly strategy is *"inefficient and selective"* and that *"the state itself creates artificial monopolies."*

At the same time, one third of the respondents believe that "natural-monopoly enterprises must be in state ownership", while one respondent said that the state must "develop capital-intensive industries with long pay-back periods, such as nuclear power engineering or the aerospace industry." Three quarters of the respondents believe that the state must provide for education, healthcare and social protection, while the rest want only a minimal role for the state in these sectors.

One of the most sensitive issues was that of the rights and regulations of private enterprise. Of the 17 respondents, 16 believe that the state has no right to control private enterprises, let alone nationalize them. *"Who defines national interests? Whose interests are they?"* they asked and offered the following answer:

> "In our country, these are the interests of bureaucrats. One can do any mischief under the cover of national interests. Entrepreneurs always focus on their own business and egoistic interests, but the results are beneficial to everyone. The state always focuses on national and common interests, but the results are beneficial only to bureaucrats. A struggle against 'egotistic interests of individuals and businesses' may in the end cause national genocide."

They believe that any actions based on law are good for the national interest, while any actions defying law cannot serve the national interest. The majority of the sample believes, therefore, that good laws are more beneficial for a country than strong leaders, while a respondent from a retail company insists that a country needs both.

Over half of the sample are completely happy with the privatization results. They believe it to be "one of the few Russian reforms conducted on a good technical level that took into account all parties' interests."

> "It was Russia's first bloodless redistribution of property."

Five respondents were neutral to both the privatization and the way it was organized. The gist of what they say is as follows:

> "One can criticize the past privatization, but there would have been no market without it." "A market was launched in the RF only thanks to free prices and to privatization." "The transformation of property relations in our country took place normally; it might have been worse."

Three respondents give a low mark to the privatization.

"My attitude to the privatization is negative; it was organized poorly and with legal violations. Many entrepreneurs were assassinated. This will have a negative impact on the future." "The privatization should have been honest and open; the property should have been sold for money and at market prices." "I believe that the privatization was hasty, and that control in the oil sector should have been handed over to private hands at a slower pace."

Nevertheless, only one respondent believes that the privatization results may be revised, but only in those instances where "blood was shed."

The majority thinks that the privatization was carried out with sufficient speed, while a quarter of the respondents think that the privatization should have been more comprehensive. They are convinced that the privatization *"lacked sufficient depth."*

"They could privatize more, including power engineering, telecommunications, housing, and utilities."

Importantly, one third of the respondents believe that the existing social contract restricted the scale of the privatization. All respondents are convinced that at present privatization results are being revised, and the majority of them are inclined to view this process as negative for the economy.

"We are now witnessing a reverse movement (everything is being gradually nationalized), which, in my opinion, will have a negative impact on the economy in the longer term. I believe that the fewer economic sectors are controlled by the state, the better. Moreover, I do not understand why state enterprises are vested with state power functions. These include Avtodor, RAO UES, Gazprom, all sorts of water utilities, etc. This significantly undermines economic efficiency."

Interestingly, our respondents voiced no complaint about taxes, assessing them as "normal" or "fair". However, they proposed tax improvements, in particular, reducing the social tax, which forces

"companies, whose payroll exceeds 10% of the total costs, to resort to various schemes to avoid this tax. The alternative for many of them is bankruptcy".

Three quarters of the respondents are convinced that the social tax could be safely reduced. The rest think that it can be abolished altogether; instead, *"we should change over to private medical insurance and pension provision and give up social insurance. Why should the state maintain all those rest homes?"* *"Of course, VAT should be levied on the transport sector just as in the oil sector. There is no difference between exports of goods and of services."* At the same time, our respondents noted a rise in the share of bribes and the so-called "social responsibility" in the total taxes they have to pay. All respondents said they suffer from "tax terrorism" and repeated inspections by tax officials, who interpret laws arbitrarily.

Official taxation goes hand in hand with "shadow taxation"; 15 respondents believe that *"the share of the shadow taxation is growing in proportion to the strengthening of the notorious power hierarchy."* They insist that bribes, extortion and the notorious "social responsibility" are comparable in size to the official taxes.

"Bribery and extortion have expanded so that the total "tax" burden has even increased instead of contracting. We have to pay around 64% of earnings. This can drive you crazy." "The extortion by officials exceeds all conceivable limits and continues to grow. I pay them as much as I pay to the tax service. To make the picture complete, you should count in this 'social responsibility' business." "Oh, the size of extortions and bribes is fantastic. I wonder how they will grow in the next five years. If everything continues along these lines they will exceed tax collections, and significantly. We shall have to cut taxes to be able to pay off everyone." "Maybe one should cancel all wages paid to the bureaucrats so that we can feed them. Though at present their wages seem to be quite decent." "Very often one has to pay for what is one's legal right or just so that they let one work."

Notably, in compliance with the RF Law *"On General Principles of Local Self-government in the Russian Federation",* the functions of local municipalities in St. Petersburg are minimal, and only three companies from our sample deal with local municipalities. Corporate mobility is also very low. Relocation to other regions involves significant losses, and only three respondents feel they could relatively effortlessly reregister their companies in the Leningrad Oblast.

3. Free market institutions

Russian reforms established a specific economic order that is a complex mix of inherited social institutions, new formal market institutions with significantly modified content, and informal institutions that emerged when enterprises struggled to adapt to a constantly changing and uncertain environment (Kuzminov, Smirnov, Shkaratan et al., 1999, p. 17).

All our respondents describe the free market as a special form of economic and public order. One respondent added that the market is also a model for the integration of resources. Most respondents find that the free market has definite advantages over a planned economy. They are convinced that the market is more *"oriented toward human beings and their needs."*

"The free market is significantly more efficient than a planned economy." "There is not a single economic sphere where a free market system would be less efficient than a planned system." "People with initiative get a chance to show their worth, the shops are full, you can watch and read anything you choose." "Socialism had advantages for those in the military-industrial complex."

Notably, none of four respondents who used to occupy key positions in the Soviet period spoke positively of a planned economy. Here is what they said:

"I have worked all my life in international trucking, both in Soviet times and now, and what I have to say is this: one can hardly imagine a less efficient shipping system than the Soviet one." "I have worked at this enterprise all my life. And I have to say that now its operation is much more efficient than in Soviet times." "I have worked a significant part of my life in Soviet external trade organizations. I know how 'efficient' they were! Multiple routes, restricted initiative, stripping of enterprises that exported their products, concentration of resources in the centre and inefficient resource management."

Only two respondents saw the advantage of a planned economy in greater social security for the population. At the same time, all respondents declared that they liked the existing system much better than the planned economy of the past. None of them is nostalgic about the past. The most characteristic opinions:

"My only regret about those times is that I wasted so many years of my life for nothing." "How can one be nostalgic about the gray moronic past?"

A 2005 survey of the Russian population by the VTSIOM Institute shows that in this area the opinions of the Russian public and Russian entrepreneurs diverge as well. For example, 51.9% of Russian citizens between 35 and 45, 48.1% between 26 and 35, and 37.5% between 16 and 25 are convinced that the USSR was a social state that provided much better social protection than now (Gorshkov, 2005, p. 17). According to a survey by the Levada Center, 46% of Russian citizens would prefer to return to pre-perestroika times, and 54% are convinced that the Gaydar government reforms ruined the Russian economy.[2] The same proportion of Russian citizens believes that a planned economy has advantages over a market one.

All respondents believe that private property must be respected and protected.

"Private property is the nervous system of a market economy." "I believe that a market economy will not operate without private property." "Private property may be restricted by law, but it cannot be just taken away."

Ten of the 17 respondents believe that existing private property is legal, since the privatization was based on the laws that were in place at the time. The most characteristic opinions:

"The privatization was based on law. Of course, those who were closer to the powers that be got much more than others. That was unavoidable. I know no better way for privatization if one aims to legitimize private property. Show me someone who can organize fair privatization! There are no such people." "The problem was not privatization but the seizure of enterprises by all sorts of bandits and their helpmates such as the Cossacks. I mean, for example, the seizure of the LentransAgency and the Third Taxi Station. They did it in order to resell the immovable property. The authorities did nothing at all, though these actions were absolutely illegal. And now the state in the same (very strange) way is nationalizing everything that it comes across."

Forty percent of our respondents believe that "regardless of the way the privatization was carried out, the market will arrange everything as it should be" and that "private property will come into the hands of efficient owners." "One can have long and fruitless discussions on the legality or illegality of the way people have become proprietors. On the one hand, they did it based on laws and other regulations; on the other hand, the population does not recognize this and considers these people to be thieves (i.e. they think privatization was illegal). It may have been unfair: those who had connections got more. But, in any case, revision of the privatization results would ruin both the economy and the society. Many of those who got their property through loans-for-shares deals became brilliant entrepreneurs. I would very much like Gazprom to run its business at least as well as Khodorkovsky or Abramovich, but it cannot. The company is less transparent than those people's companies, the

---

2   http://www.levada.ru/files/1124718847.doc.

financial management is worse, and the tax payments are smaller. And now government drones from Gazprom and Rosneft will ruin these brilliant (for Russia) companies."

Only one respondent insisted that a partial revision of the privatization results would contribute to the legitimization of private property.

> "The result of illegal privatization is the illegality of private property in Russia. A big bomb has been planted under it that can blow the economy to pieces."

Opinions of this kind currently dominate in Russian print media and on TV. Among our respondents, 70% are convinced that private property has no real protection and that property rights are not guaranteed in Russia. The most characteristic opinions:

> "Neither the public nor the authorities show any respect for private property. No matter what you do, the public will believe that the current owners obtained their property illegally." "The authorities view private property as legal only when it serves their interests, and the public considers private property to be legal only when it is recognized by the authorities. I cannot imagine when our public will begin to respect private property, or what sort of privatization it needs. Neither have I any idea of what could make our strange and pensive people recognize the legality of privatization. But the economy cannot develop normally if the public and the state have no respect for private property rights."

At the same time, the 2005 population survey by the Levada Center showed that only 32% of the Russian citizens believe that there are no private property guarantees in Russia.

Almost half of our respondents (eight people) said that they would not risk setting up a new business now. The most characteristic opinions:

> "I will not set up a new business, because now you can be successful only if you have administrative support on your side and shadow machinery at your service. A bureaucratic crust has covered everything; they call this 'stabilization.' One cannot break through a rigid wall of state power and public opposition. Now the risks are far greater than when I began. Now it is more difficult than in the late 1980s or early 1990s. Now one has to be an adventurer through and through to do this."

The rest of our respondents are prepared to risk it, though they admit that conditions have become much "tougher" compared to when they began. However, the respondents of this group have an emergency solution in stock:

> "If the country continues in the same vein, I'll move abroad, and let them go to hell. I will never agree to be a servant or a serf again."

Based on our survey, we have drawn the following portrait of a modern Russian entrepreneur. He/she is an ambitious person with great self-respect, whose basic values include freedom, independence, self-realization, and true friendship. He/she is an individualist who can easily get on with other people and work in a team, a workaholic and a risk-taker with a broad outlook who is prepared to use any means (including illegal ones) to protect his/her business if he/she believes him/herself to be in the right; he/she is an ironic cynic and pragmatist.

All our respondents believe that entrepreneurs are the engine of a market economy. The most characteristic opinions:

> "He combines factors of production in the most efficient way, implements new ideas, offers new products and services, creates new jobs and pays taxes. This is his social function. While pursuing his egotistic interests, the entrepreneur improves people's lives. A market economy without entrepreneurs is impossible. Such people are not numerous, but without them, society stagnates. They represent a very specific type of adventurer."

At the same time, ten respondents were critical of the currently unfolding government campaign for the "social responsibility of businesses." They are convinced that charity must be organized by the business community itself, without any state management. Many of our respondents do this.

> "All these 'social responsibilities' are a bluff covering bureaucrats' avarice and their attempt to shift the burden of their own responsibility to businesses. I do charity from my own income. What else does this state expect of me? The state wants me to take on its functions, because it is incapable of performing them."

All respondents view money as a means of reaching their objectives. They are convinced that not everything is for sale. Notably, no respondents see a decline in moral values in modern Russia.

All respondents believe that the Russian market functions normally: "We have a peculiar mentality, it's true; our state is also peculiar, but I don't see what this has to do with the market." The most characteristic opinions:

> "You cannot feel offended by the readings of a meter. The market is real life. Any attempt to regulate real life smacks of stagnation. You cannot blame the market for our mentality, whatever that mentality is. The people's mentality and the bureaucrats' quirks are their own problems. If you want to live better, revise your mentality. You cannot blame the market for government failures, corruption, etc., that have a negative impact on the country's economy."

All our respondents are unhappy with the existing judicial system; the majority of them believe that Russian courts are strongly dependent on executive power, the prosecutor's office, and law-protection bodies. They think that this dependence has even increased in the past five years. Twelve of our respondents have personal experience of courtroom corruption. They note that they had to pay bribes even when they won cases. They are amazed at the "interest" judges take in the outcome of cases. A characteristic opinion of one of the respondents:

> "I can tell you: if you offer a bribe and the judge does not take it, this means that you have offered too little."

Seven respondents noted the poor qualifications of judges. Our respondents characterized the Russian judicial system as follows:

> "It is wonderful when there are many professional judges and justice is guaranteed to everyone. In our country, things are different. Our judicial system makes a negative impression on me. The courts are corrupt and strongly influenced by executive power, and this influence is increasingly. Business people in our city have courtroom pricelists on hand that say how much you must give to this or that judge. Experience shows that the pricelists accurately reflects costs. The prices depend on the influence a given judge wields. Courts, law protection bodies,

and the public prosecutor's office all depend on executive power and represent a closed caste with strong internal solidarity. Courts are under strong pressure from the public prosecutor's office and law protection bodies. The qualifications of judges are declining, and a negative selection process is underway. Though there are good professionals, professional solidarity has the upper hand. Judges in courts of first instance have especially poor qualifications. Though higher courts are more professional, they have been known to issue unlawful verdicts. Public prosecutors are even less professional. Law protection bodies are the least qualified."

"The workload of judges is tremendous: heaps of cases per judge. Judges are buried under pending cases, the proceedings move terribly slowly; sometimes they last for years. And there is a shortage of judges. Court verdicts are very often not executed at all. There are very few things that marshals would do without a bribe. If the case involves the interests of highly placed state officials at any level or the interests of very large companies, you cannot win in court even if the law is on your side. Currently it is impossible to win a case against the state if high officials' interests are at stake. Even if you are absolutely right, even if you have acted in strict compliance with the law. In the last 15 years, I have won only three cases against the state, and not a single verdict has been executed. Sometimes, though, wonders do happen in the Russian Federation as well. In other cases, you can win if you apply a lot of effort and will. But the price of victory will be unbelievably high. The costs are exorbitant. So we go to court only in extreme cases. You see, only courts can make legal decisions. This is why many people avoid taking their matters to court. However, these are the only courts that we have. The judicial system is in place, and no matter how bad a court is people go there. This in itself is good."

The respondents noted that they prefer to abide by the law. Nevertheless, 15 respondents believe that in order to act quickly and solve a problem positively, one has to have personal contacts, links, and a good knowledge of the individuals in the corresponding "authorities". This is how they describe the existing situation:

"Alas, you must have a friend in the corresponding authorities even if the law is on your side. Having an administrative contact is an 80% guarantee of success. Even if you are completely in the right. Personal ties are decisive even if you comply strictly with laws. You must have knowledge of people and know how to come to an agreement with them. Otherwise, nothing will work, and you will not get even what you are entitled to by law. If you don't know specific people, resolving any issue turns into a nightmare."

Seven respondents find the existing situation abnormal. The rest describe it as *"normal for our society"*.

4. Social relations in a period of transformation

One of the key problems in the Russian society is social capital in the form of trust, social norms and ties. Many studies of the dynamics of social capital in modern Russia have been published lately (J. Stiglitz, I. Diskin, O. Yanitsky, N. Tikhonova). In particular, the 2003–2004 study by R. Blom, H. Melin, A. Sarno and I. Sarno found that managers had very little trust in the subjects of their social environment. At the same time, trust is characteristic of the Russian business culture, being inseparable from relations between business partners. Companies that have built up relations on trust with the subjects of their social environment can derive advantage for developing their management. A low level of trust is a social anomaly in the Russian business community (Blom, Melin, Sarno and Sarno, 2005, p. 155)

The majority of our respondents (14) believe that social relations between people have changed, and that those engaged in business have become more individualistic.

> "People have learnt to be self-reliant and no longer expect any benefits from the state. They have lost all illusions. Pragmatism, positivism, and a lack of sentimentality have become the rule, especially in business. Responsibility for one's actions has increased."

Our respondents describe these changes as positive. At the same time, half of the respondents insist that such changes are mainly characteristic of the business community, while society in general still retains a *"Soviet mentality."*

> "The only change from the Soviet past is that the public has become more fragmented and aggressive," "there is more individualism and distance between people."

Three respondents do not notice any substantial change in social relations and believe that Russian society is still Soviet through and through.

> "There is simply more suspicion, aloofness, and distrust of each other." "I have a very sad view of the relations between our people. As Golitsyn once said: 'Russian people eat each other alive, and it is their only way of feeding.' Tarkovsky shows this very well in his film "Andrei Rublev." If our people could focus all the energy that they now spend on ruining each others' property on building their own good, life in our country would have been better by an order of several magnitudes."

The respondents divided into three groups on the issue of friendly relations in business. The largest group described situations in which they or their colleagues had lost old friends due to the strong social differences that had emerged between them and former friends who did not go into business. On the other hand, some of these respondents have retained old friends who are not in business.

Group two (three respondents) have lost only those friends who cheated them in business, but still maintain contacts with old friends who are not in business.

One respondent said that he has lost his old friends only because of the differences in their welfare standards. His friends found it difficult to cope with the situation.

> "This does not mean a rupture of relations; they simply distance themselves from you and try to see you less often."

One third of the respondents have not lost any friends and maintain good relations both with old friends and with new ones they have met in the business community. Their views on friendship are best reflected by the following opinions:

> "Firstly, real friends are few. Secondly, if they are real friends, they will not leave you, regardless of what your circumstances are. I can tell this from myself. If someone cheats you in business, if he envies you, he is not a friend. And you have only yourself to blame, because you have chosen that person for a friend. The majority of my friends come from my young days. They remain my friends, regardless of the difference in our incomes or social status. However, we do not meet often because there's so much to do at work and at home."

At the same time, our respondents do not show any haughtiness and prefer not to base their choice of friends on their social status.

> "I have come a long way from a simple driver to a company owner, so there's no snobbism in me. I can reach an understanding with anyone. Only one needs time for that, while the time is alarmingly short."

They prefer to have really good and true friends, and they have only a few friends: not more than two or four. Apart from two respondents, the interviewees noted a lack of trust both in interpersonal relations (toward business partners, customers and employees) and in their attitude to the state. They believe that:

> "confidence in people can be bolstered by a good up-front payment and a healthy credit history." "Take for example the beauty parlours my colleagues operate. They seem to pay good wages, the working conditions are excellent, but if you do not use video-camera monitoring, they [the employees] will invariably hide a part of the earnings. You see this everywhere."

Over half of the respondents (10) are convinced that before one deals with unfamiliar people or companies, one has to obtain detailed and complete information about them. Nine respondents prefer to demand up-front payments from individuals or companies who are new to them. The following opinion sums up the general attitude of the respondents about doing business with unfamiliar people and companies:

> "If you have no means to put pressure on a company in any way, better do not do business with it."

Three respondents never deal with individuals or companies they do not know.

Almost all respondents have been cheated recently (by the state, particular officials, partners or clients). One third of the respondents have been cheated on many occasions. They offer the following conclusions:

> "Such is life. You have only yourself to blame. In Soviet times, they cheated everyone in the same way. This is very Soviet behaviour. We are used to this. We have learnt this from our Soviet experience. Always check the other party and look out. Learn to fend for yourself. A decent person will never do any meanness for the sake of an insignificant profit."

All respondents are convinced that cheating other people is wrong under any circumstances and stated that they never cheat others. The majority do not see any difference between slyness and cheating:

> "Cheating is bad, always. I know for sure that cheating someone may turn out to be more costly for yourself, and being sly is stupid. Those who cheat never last in business for long. They have no self-respect."

They believe that their own advantages in business include high professionalism, an ability to better calculate and analyze any situation, and an ability to be better informed. At the same time they stress that their partners may have a *"different understanding"* of business methods and have different views on morality.

Only two of our respondents agree to oral contracts before they put them in writing. The rest put all agreements in writing immediately. All respondents make their contracts as detailed as possible. Two respondents hire highly professional lawyers to prepare their contracts in order to avoid misunderstanding or fraud. However, they say that despite detailed information about new partners and despite detailed contracts, they get cheated in about 10% of deals.

Generally, all our respondents grant a grace period for payment only to partners of long standing. Five respondents do this only in exceptional cases when they know the current situation of the other party. In case of a default, all respondents first try to learn its cause and seek an amicable settlement. Only when this attempt fails, do they take the matter to court.

Thirteen respondents believe that they may use any methods available against defaulters if their company's future is at stake and they have acted within the law. Such methods include using both state and non-state mediators. Only four respondents declared that they would not use all methods they have at their disposal.

No respondents believe that private parties with partners must or will lead to friendship. In general, they see no connection between friendship and business, although all entrepreneurs view such parties as a Russian tradition. Nine respondents see no real benefit in it:

> "This is widespread in Russia. This is custom. Our people like such gatherings, traditional Russian drinking bouts. One has to attend these gatherings from time to time. There is not much sense in them. Just an idiocy, but one has to respect traditions. They do not help business in any way. But if you do not turn out, some people may take offence, and this may impact business.

All other respondents find such meetings useful, since they can get to know their partners and colleagues better or obtain useful information.

> "Such gatherings have the function of a 'sarafan radio' (a source of rumours)." Though "unfortunately, such gatherings may sometimes grow out of all proportion."

All respondents admit that now, as before, many things can only be done if you have connections. But, as one respondent noted, a *"good reputation"* is necessary to use your connections. Fourteen respondents find no significant change either in the character or mechanisms of such connections. Only one respondent noted that money interests have become very prominent in this mechanism, and one respondent believes that one must have talent in one's field to be able to use one's connections.

All respondents believe that paternalistic relations with employees are characteristic of Russia. They noted that in the majority of companies official Soviet paternalism had been replaced with unofficial paternalism.

> "Both earlier and now, the problem was and is: do employees know how to use it? Not everyone could or can do it. Russia is not Japan or Korea. Russian paternalism recognizes no obligations."

The majority of respondents (15) believe that such relations *"are inefficient, interfere with work and are dangerous for business."* *"They pose a huge problem."* They *"corrode business."* This is why our respondents prefer establishing formal relations with their employees:

> "I'm trying to get rid of this, though I do not always succeed. We are working in Russia, where this is customary."

Only one respondent said that he had succeeded in formalizing his relations with his employees. In contrast, two respondents do not view paternalistic relations with employees as something detrimental to business. One respondent voiced an opinion that stands out against the others. He believes that at large companies *"people are being turned into robots,"* while at the same time they try to get illegal income, so-called kickbacks, in the course of their duties.

All respondents are convinced that under the existing system of relations between businesses and the state, the Russian economy would not be able to function without corruption. They are convinced that the state itself is instrumental in fanning corruption. They provided the following examples:

> "There are 17 traffic police stations between Moscow and the border. The applicable regulations have been designed in such a way that you simply cannot avoid a violation. They [the traffic police] immediately request a bribe. Or take the truck-weighing procedure. Four different agencies, the Transport Control Department, the Avtodor, the road police, and the Customs, are in charge of this procedure. They do this 36 times on the stretch between the state border and Moscow. The rules establish certain limits for the load on each axle. They do the weighing in dynamic conditions where it is easy to deceive the driver. If he asks to re-weigh the truck, they refuse to do it. Either you bribe them, or they impound both the truck and the driving license, which means huge losses for the company. If you take the matter to court, you can get your truck back in six weeks' time in the best case. So far, no one has succeeded in recovering such losses from the state. In normal countries, they weigh your truck only once, and they will repeat the procedure several times on your request. They have only one agency in charge of this procedure, and they issue a single weighing certificate. I am especially delighted with the rights that have been given to the Avtodor. They are just another enterprise, like mine. Why should they have executive authority? I can give more examples. Take the notorious Traffic Management Directorate of St. Petersburg. The directorate is in place; only it does not do any traffic management. Instead, it is very keen on making all truck companies purchase city-access passes from it, allegedly as a measure to save the city centre from heavy trucks. Only my trucks will never dare go onto the Nevsky Prospect anyway. They will get stuck there and lose lots of time.
>
> Now, why are St. Petersburg's roads so awful, though the city spends exactly as much as Helsinki on road construction and repairs? Why does the construction of one square meter of road cost three times in St. Petersburg as much as in Helsinki? I know the answer: because of corruption. One more remark, about toll roads. In Europe, they set up toll roads when road construction has been financed by investors who need to recover their expenses. But our toll roads have been financed from the budget. This is a scandal! The notorious public-private partnership calls for a separate remark. It is just very subtle roguery. Here is an example: the state is building a ring motorway around St. Petersburg (why should it be a four-lane road that costs heaps of money?), but the access roads are being built by private investors who will turn them into toll roads. There's partnership for you!"

Our respondents believe that the Russian public is complacent about corruption.

> "This is very bad. All these jokes about the traffic police. They show that corruption is the norm in our society, that you are a fool if you do not give bribes."

Over half of our respondents believe that corruption in Russia will only increase. The factors behind this trend include growing state interference in the economy, uncontrolled behaviour of government officials, and a public permissiveness that justifies corruption.

According to numerous population survey results,[3] corruption in Russia appears to be one-sided: respondents focus their attention only on the fact that certain individuals give bribes, while ignoring the fact that there are also individuals who take them. This belief stems from a widely spread conviction that business is the only culprit. One would think that entrepreneurs purchase illegal services from some shadowy beings without titles, family names, or physical entities. According to a population survey conducted by the Public Opinion Foundation in December 2005, 69% of the respondents have never given bribes. Only 28% of the respondents recognized that in the last year or two they had found themselves in situations when officials requested or expected from them unofficial payments or services for their work. At the same time, 64% of Russian citizens are convinced that all (or the majority of) officials are corrupt. Thus, while the Russians willingly discuss the corrupt practices of officials, they prefer, on the one hand, not to explain why they give bribes themselves, and on the other hand, to blame entrepreneurs for corrupting officials. At the same time, the business community clearly understands how and why the authorities take bribes, and why entrepreneurs have to give them.

Around 60% of our respondents believe that one of the characteristic features of Russia (both now and in the past) is the use of different moral norms for the "*external world*" (unfamiliar enterprises or individuals) and for the immediate environment (old friends, long-standing clients, employees, etc.). Half of the respondents in this group describe this as a "*normal adaptive mechanism*" found in any community.

> "Well, for example, if a friend calls me a fool, I will not be offended, but I naturally will be if you, a stranger, do the same. This is part of human nature."

Four respondents (who view the state-business relations in the USA as a model) believe that this behaviour may stem from the existence of different moral norms in different strata of Russian society.

> "It is simply that the people you know have the same approach to business and have the same faith. Moral concepts among the Russians differ drastically, and the moral values of someone who does not belong to your immediate circle may be opposite to yours."

Nine respondents are convinced that applying different moral norms to the "*external world*" and to one's immediate environment is abnormal and immoral. Eight respondents insist that they use the same moral norms in dealing with all people, which is the only correct approach.

---

3   http://www.fom.ru/topics/1045.html.

5. Attitudes to the West

For the majority of our respondents, the Western Europeans are either partners or friends. They would like Russia to be like Western Europe, but this is either altogether impossible or realizable only in some very distant future and only if the Russian community "*gets rid of corruption and chauvinism*". Ten respondents believe that Western European countries are partners for Russia, and four view them as a model for our country. Only three respondents believe that Western Europe is a "*friend*" of the RF. Only three respondents believe that

> "Russia is a European country and will inevitably succeed in having the same social, political and economic structures as Western European countries."

Six respondents are convinced that Russia will never have a social or economic structure comparable to that in Western Europe. Six respondents believe that Russia could be like Western Europe, provided it eliminates corruption and puts in place necessary reforms, but one can hardly count on this.

The prospects of Russia entering the EU are also unrealistic. Our respondents' opinion is practically unanimous:

> "They will not accept us;" "Russia's entry into the EC would throw this organization off balance;" "Russia is too large for the EC to swallow."

Only one respondent described this step as unnecessary:

> "Russia does not need the EC with all its bureaucracy."

Only one respondent voted for Russian membership of the EU if it is accepted as an equal partner. At the same time, all respondents showed reserve toward the EU as an institution; they believe it to be a bureaucratic organization. In contrast, representative St. Petersburg population surveys by the Megapolis Sociology Centre show that in 2005, 27% of the city residents viewed the EU as Russia's partner, and in early 2006, this figure grew to 32%, with another 32% declaring they had a neutral attitude to the EU. Only 7% of the St. Petersburg residents surveyed consider the EU to be an enemy, while the USA was viewed as an enemy by 22% and the NATO by 30%. Sociologists explain this attitude by the fact that the EU is viewed as community of states created for purely economic purposes (Protasenko, 2006).

Our respondents were neutral about the eastward expansion of the EU both on general grounds and from the angle of their own situation, though the majority of them believe that the EC will have difficulties in "*digesting*" Eastern European and Baltic countries.

Only the representatives of tourist and trucking companies took a positive attitude. The trucking company owner said:

> "This is a welcome development for my business. Shipments to Baltic countries have become easier. Obtaining permits to enter Baltic countries, especially Latvia, is easier. They are doing great. The custom duties went down, which is good for cargo owners. In two years' time, it will be easier to get visas and green cards (insurance policies). You pay once, and you may go ahead."

Only one respondent, who works in a construction business, assesses the EU expansion to the East negatively. He believes this move has robbed Russian companies of a significant proportion of their market.

Notably, half of the respondents have not changed their positive attitude to the West in the last 15 years. Only one respondent noted that, in contrast to his initial enthusiasm, his attitude has become more pragmatic. The rest noted a significant change in their attitude to the West following personal contacts and travels abroad:

> "Earlier, we were poisoned by the Soviet propaganda." "We began visiting Europe and have got to know it better. We used to see the West as an enemy, and now we see that they are normal people. They live well; I wish we could live like that." "I used to think of them as of enemies. Now I see that they are normal people with their own joys and problems."

However, better contact and better understanding of the western way of life do not lead our respondents to feel fully European. Only six respondents feel that they belong to Europe, since they speak foreign languages and share European values. The others feel a certain "separation:"

> "I am a different person, formed under different conditions." "I am living in a different environment with different values." "Both the living conditions and the values are different. We, living in the Northwest, are closer to them [than the rest of the Russians]. I say: they are brothers and sisters, while we are just God's slaves, alas. Former slaves have no better aspiration than to become slave-owners."

Our respondents were unanimous about the substance of the western culture. They noted such basic components as a market economy, a civil society, and democracy. In particular, they said:

> "Free people responsible for their life, democracy, strict public control over officials." "Respect for the individual. Our government officials break all speed limits on the roads and do not care a fig about laws. They are different. In Russia, an expensive car will never give way to a Zaporozhets[4] or Oka. In the West, people behave differently."

A respondent (legal services), who does not view himself as belonging to Europe, described western culture as follows:

> "A strongly stratified community of narrow-minded people with narrow specializations, a high level of training, and little need for communication with others."

When offered to select a country that could serve as a model for Russia, the break-down was as follows. Seven respondents voted for the USA, two each for Germany and the Scandinavian countries, and one respondent voted for the Czech Republic. Three respondents do not see any suitable model at all, and two respondents said the best way would be to borrow the best things from all countries. Notably, our sample found the US administrative model was more attractive than their model of relations between government and business.

Four respondents failed to define their position toward Russian membership of the WTO, despite a long history of preparation, discussion and agreement. The most

---

4 Small cars of Soviet production.

curious fact is that one of them represents an insurance company lobbying against Russian membership of the WTO without special conditions, since this move threatens Russian insurers. Six respondents are indifferent to Russia membership of the WTO. Nine respondents welcome it, with seven of them noting positive prospects for their own businesses:

> "The fewer trade barriers, the better it is for my company." "This would be great for us. This would facilitate the antidumping procedures."

The other two companies (of the nine) are focused on the domestic market, and their positive attitude toward the WTO has nothing to do with their business interests. Only two respondents were negative about WTO membership because of their business interests. The representative of a biochemical company said:

> "This is very unfortunate. The prices on analog drugs will go down, while their drugs are of a better quality than ours." The representative of a transport company said: "Things will get worse, because our trucks are worse. And our authorities will be unable to provide for a normal transition period".

The results of a survey mentioned above (Blom et al, p.144) show that entrepreneurs' trust in international organizations is lower than in most social environment subjects. They view WTO membership as a matter of prestige. Two of our respondents with positive and neutral attitudes, respectively, on the issue noted:

> "I am surprised about all this fuss around WTO membership. There is too much politics and two little economics in this. Therefore, if Russia does join the WTO, Russian economic practices will not change much." "This is just another scheme of our bureaucrats. The issue is deeply political and has nothing to do with our interests."

Such sentiments and opinions of randomly selected respondents reflect certain changes in their attitude toward new institutions and the new economic order. The business community shows no signs of either Soviet ideology or market romanticism. Naturally, one should take into account that the adherence to market liberalism shown by our respondents may be significantly influenced by their geographic location: they operate in a metropolis where the pace of modernization is fastest. On the one hand, entrepreneurs of a large city located on the EC border demonstrate acceptance of a market ideology, pragmatism, and sober analyses of the situation without nostalgic feelings about the past. On the other hand, they are convinced that Russia should go its own, special way without joining the European Union. At the same time, they demonstrate a certain fatalism and lack of faith in the possibility of changing the mentality of the population to which they belong, although they do not share its basic goals.

References

Andreev, A. (2005). Kontzept sobstvennosti v sovremennoy rossijskoy mentaljnosti. Monitoring obschestvennogo mneniia, ekonomicheskie I sotsialnye peremeny 4 (76), 17-28.

Blom, R, Melin, H, Sarno, A., Sarno, I. (2005). Sotsial'nyj capital doveriia i menedzherialnye strategii, Mir Rossii 2, 126-160.

Diskin, I.E. (2003). Sotsial'nyy capital v global'noj ekonomike. Obschestvennye nauki I sovremennost' 5, 150-159.

Dmitriev, M (2006). V zaschitu natsioalizatsii. *Kommersantъ*, January 30.

Easter, G. (2001). Networks, Bureaucracies, and the Russian State, in: Explaining Post-Soviet Patchworks.V.2 Pathways from the past to the global, 29-58.

Gorshkov, M.K. (2005). Dinamika massovogo soznania v kontekste sotsial'no-ekonomicheskoiy transformatsii // Monitoring obschestvennogo mnenia 3, VTSIOM, 17.

Kirdina, S. (2004). Institutional'naia struktura sovremennoy Rossii: evolutsionnoe obnovlenie, Voprosy Ekonomiki 10, 89-98.

Kuzminov J., Smirnov S., Shkaratan O. et al. (1999). Rossiiskai ekonomika: uslovia vyzhivania, predposylki rasvitia. – M., GU VSHE.

Protasenko, T. (2006). Rossia i Zapad. Nikogo ne liubim no v gosti zoiem, Delo. 409.

The Entrepreneurial Approach to the Extended Order: Case Study Poland

Oskar Kowalewski

1. Introduction

Despite economic and political problems in the countries of Central and Eastern Europe (CEE), there is little doubt that the region has undergone an economic transformation of historic proportions since 1990. In all countries, economic reforms have had a significant impact on politics and society. In Poland the transition period may be divided into three stages. The first stage covered the period 1989–1997 and was a time of rapid economic development and changes in the political institutions. New, public institutions were established, while the economy, after a three-year recession, was growing again. The foundation of economic growth was the privatization of state-owned enterprises and the introduction of the free-market reforms. In this period, more than 2.5 million new small enterprises were created. These new companies created new jobs, while employment in state companies continued to fall. However, after a period of fast growth the economy slowed down in 1998. The economic slow-down, which lasted till 2002, was the second stage of the transition period. In this period, many of the newly founded enterprises went out of business. Since 2003, the economy has been recovering, although unemployment is still high and remains one of the biggest problems in Poland. The recovery of the economy is the third and final stage of the transition period in Poland. Thus, overall the transition can be characterized as a full economic cycle, as also be observed in developed countries.

The consequences of this transition process are profound changes in the political institutions, economy and society. A visible side effect is growing inequality in society, social disruption and political instability. Recently criticism of past reforms has surfaced in Poland, encouraged by populist political parties.

Any evaluation of the reforms and economic and political changes depends strongly on the viewpoint of the individual. To obtain empirical results on political reforms, interviews were conducted with a group of 21 entrepreneurs. Twelve of them were owners of small companies with less than 25 employees, while the remaining respondents were owners of medium-sized companies. By business activity, the entrepreneurs were drawn mainly from the retail and wholesale sectors, manufacturing and construction. The entrepreneurs had been in business for between five and eighteen years, with an average of more than eight years. This long period is explained by the fact that even under the socialist system small businesses were allowed in Poland, although they were often harassed by state officials and the tax system was skewed against them. Most of the respondents were successful entrepreneurs. However, two of them have been struggling for some time and will probably go out of business in the near future; their opinions are often harsh and represented outliers from those of the other respondents.

The sample group of entrepreneurs was selected by age, so the interviewees would have experienced both the socialist system and the transition period. Therefore, respondents were between 35 and 65 years old. Thirteen of them were men, and eight were woman. By education, 12 had a university degree, eight a high school diploma and one had only elementary education. As will be presented later in this paper, most of them view the transition and reforms as positive, and all of them agree that it changed their lives profoundly.

The interviews were carried out from December 2005 till February 2006. All businesses were located in or in the vicinity of Warsaw. The interviews were based on an Extended Order Index constructed by the *Hamburg Institute of International Economics* in Germany.

Thoughts about economic reforms always contain strong, but largely unexamined, assumptions about the structure of the politics, economy, and society in which they take place. In this article I try to assess Polish entrepreneurs' views about democracy and political institutions and the extent to which changes in the political and economic order affect social relationships. This assessment is based on the results of a survey using the Extended Order Index and observations of changes in Polish attitudes in recent years.

The remainder of the paper is divided into five sections. Section II presents the interaction between the economy and political institutions. Section III describes entrepreneurs' opinions about market institutions based on a comparison of the present situation with the situation before the transformation. Section IV portrays the changes in social relationships since the transformation. Section V presents entrepreneurs' views and changes in attitudes toward western countries since the transformation, while Section VI presents conclusions.

2. Interaction between economy and politics in Poland

Poland's democratization was achieved mainly through political and economic reforms. In the past, politics was the preserve of one party, and the government played a leading role in the economy and strongly influenced society as a whole. The first steps toward democratization in 1989 culminated in complete reform of the state. The ongoing political changes and the issue of democracy created support for the introduction of a free-market economy. However, today Polish society is still far from having a strong value system comparable with democratic systems in western countries. According to the results of the survey, Polish entrepreneurs express low levels of tolerance and trust and a lot of respect for authority, and sometimes even support for undemocratic rule. This does not mean that democracy is not likely to endure in Poland. It means that Polish entrepreneurs and other Polish citizens are just getting used to democracy, both its virtues and its problems, and developing a real sense of it. At the same time, a condition for the survival of new democracies is the prevention of regression into authoritarianism and rejection by the polity of such a possibility. The result of the 2005 parliament elections confirms that the democracy is still unstable and that there is strong support for populist and radical parties. The strong position of populist parties may be explained by disappointment with some effects of the transformation process, such as high unemployment and growing social inequality. In the case of the entrepreneurs, their frustration is caused mainly by the inefficiency of the state and the civil service, uncertainty about regulations and corruption, as shall be discussed below.

According to the results, more than 40 per cent of the entrepreneurs describe the current government as authoritarian or dominating. At the same time, 33 per cent describe their relationship with government as a partnership, while 29 per cent are more reserved. Almost all the respondents would prefer a change in their relationship with the government, which seems surprising given the variety of answers. The entrepreneurs would prefer a more outgoing government, willing to act as a partner and consult them on decisions affecting their business operations. In their opinion, new laws often disrupt business and have a negative impact on competitiveness and cost efficiency. In the opinion of the entrepreneurs the government intervenes too much in matters concerning the business environment.

Almost all entrepreneurs in the survey emphasized that the form of government in Poland is different than in other countries. Asked about the relationship between government and business, respondents felt that other transition countries had a relationship similar to that in Poland – Ukraine (23%), Lithuania (19%), Slovakia (14%) and the Czech Republic (10%) –, whereas Germany (48%) and other old EU member states (33%) were suggested as ideal models for a relationship between government and business. The respondents favoured Germany in particular, which in their opinion has efficient government institutions and little corruption. According to the entrepreneurs, Germany offers the best government model and its social market system is also worth copying as an economic model.

The results of the survey show a strong aversion to any form of government domination, something most living Poles know from past experience. Only 15 per cent of the respondents feel that a good leader at the head of the government may be better for the country than proper enforcement of the rule of law. The results show clearly that the Polish entrepreneurs prefer a democratic and stable legal environment to authoritarian government. This is understandable, as the entrepreneurs benefited from the transition and see the civil service as repressive. In addition, entrepreneurs' recent experiences clearly show that for them a stable legal system, in particular tax regulations, is more important for business than contacts with high officials.

The entrepreneurs who described their contacts with the public service as irregular had a positive attitude. By contrast, entrepreneurs who had regular or frequent contacts with the administration, in particular in connection with taxes or permits, found these contacts troublesome and often a burden. The respondents complained in particular about the large and bureaucratic civil service. In addition, in the opinion of the entrepreneurs, civil servants are arrogant, inflexible and uninformed. As a consequence, the respondents often stressed that the one of the needed reforms is an improvement in the public service. According to the entrepreneurs, the most effective way to improve the administration is by changing the civil servants' attitudes to the public and introducing better management. In addition, in view of current time-consuming procedures, entrepreneurs often mentioned the need for quicker government decision-making and simpler procedures. Besides the improvement in administration, the respondents would like to see lower taxes in the future. The respondents emphasized the need for tax relief for new companies as well as small and medium companies if the economy is to grow fast in the next decade. They argued that taxes, and the frequent changes in tax regulations, are a heavy burden for them. As a contrast to Poland, the respondents pointed to Slovakia, where the government's decision to lower corporate taxes resulted in an increase in foreign investment and high economic growth.

To deal with problems, all the respondents would prefer clear rules that applied to all entrepreneurs in Poland instead of direct contact with high government officials. In their opinion, direct contact with high-ranking civil servants is a reflection of corruption and does not guarantee stability in the long term. The respondents emphasize that clear rules known in advance are more important than any kind of connection. Some respondents also pointed out that one way of improving the public service would be to inform people of the applicable laws in advance.

Asked about the right economic model, the majority of entrepreneurs chose the social market economy. In their opinion, government and market have common objectives that include alleviating poverty, providing affordable housing, improving employment and economic opportunities, addressing environmental concerns and providing access to services and programs that can assist individuals and groups to improve their personal circumstances. The strong sense of social responsibility among the entrepreneurs is understandable given the transition from a socialist economy to a free-market economy. In the opinion of the respondents, a model linking both economic systems would be preferable and would justify government intervention. The respondents indicated that Germany's extensive social welfare system is an ideal model that Poland should follow. It should be noted that Germany's system of government was also chosen as the perfect model for Poland. In the opinion of the respondents the German economy is both conservative and dynamic. It is conservative in the sense that it draws on that part of the country's tradition that envisages some role for the state in the economy. An area in which respondents would like to see greater state intervention was public investment in poor regions with high unemployment and serious social problems.

On the other hand, the entrepreneurs would like the Polish economy to be as dynamic as in Germany in the sense that it is growth-oriented, even if growth is slow and steady rather than spectacular. Hence, in the opinion of the Polish entrepreneurs, the government should try to combine the virtues of a market system with the virtues of a social welfare system.

Conversely, 86 per cent of the entrepreneurs emphasized that the state should neither intervene in the market nor nationalize private companies, even if the government felt this was necessary and not doing so could harm the state. The entrepreneurs think private ownership – one of the gains of the transformation – is too important and should be protected by the law at all costs.

At the same time, the entrepreneurs would like to see state intervention in some sectors of the economy. According to the entrepreneurs, the following industries should be controlled by the state: energy (71%), healthcare (48%), telecommunications (29%), transportation (24%), financial services (10%), forestry (5%) and defence (5%). The fact that the energy industry is the prime choice for state control can be explained by the current political and economic situation. In the recent months, the Polish government has often emphasized that the sovereignty of the state is in danger as it depends too heavily on the gas from Russia for its energy. In addition, the political crisis between Ukraine and Russia at the end of 2004 and the construction of the German-Russian Baltic gas pipeline has fuelled new fears. In consequence, state control over the energy sector is seen as a way of promoting the country's energy security.

Almost 50 per cent of the entrepreneurs would like also to see the state in charge of the healthcare industry. On the one hand, the respondents complain about the current state of the healthcare system in Poland. They themselves mainly use private health centres as they are more efficient and customer-oriented than the state health centres. Nevertheless, in the opinion of the respondents a state healthcare system is an important part of the social security system. Therefore, in their opinion it should be state-owned and the service should remain free, even if it does not always function properly.

In case of the remaining sectors, views about state ownership are mixed and depend mainly on respondents' personal experience and views. Moreover, respondents often could not give any reasonable arguments for state ownership in these industries.

3. Market economy institutions in Poland

Most of the entrepreneurs are glad about the transformation process and the introduction of the free-market economy. They view the country's opening toward democracy and market economy as a positive move. In their opinion, thanks to the transformation they have better access to resources and a better social standing. In addition, they associate the changes in the system with freedom, represented by the possibility of travelling in western countries.

Only entrepreneurs whose companies had financial problems would like to have the social planning back again. They emphasized that the socialist system gave them the social security they were missing now. The entrepreneurs also mentioned that since the introduction of economic reforms some state sectors, such as healthcare, reported a significant decline, which they find worrisome.

In the opinion of the respondents, private ownership is very important for the functioning of the system and should be protected at all costs. All of the respondents indicated that they try to comply with the law, even if it is sometimes inconvenient and causes additional costs for the company. The use of business software is given as an example: although it can be bought cheaply on the black market, the entrepreneurs emphasized that they buy und use only legal software solutions.

At the same time, respondents explained that the likelihood of inspections gives them a strong motive to obey the law. The entrepreneurs are especially afraid of tax inspectors, who can impose fines, possibly resulting in the liquidation of the business even if it later turns out that the fine is unjustified. Hence, entrepreneurs are frustrated with these potential arbitrary tax decisions and the difficulty of defending themselves owing to the inefficient legal system.

Some of the respondents indicated that wealthy businessman in particular may have acquired their wealth through bribery or as a result of abuses in the privatization of state-owned companies. In such cases, respondents would welcome state intervention, including justice in the form of seizing the illegal, private property. However, many of the entrepreneurs think the richest people cannot be touched as they are often protected by influential politicians and corrupt law enforcement.

Money is seen mainly as a goal and was the reason for the entrepreneurs' decision to set up business. Only a handful of the respondents saw money as a medium of the market economy. Respondents feel that morality has declined as a result of money and the free-market economy, even though they view the transformation and the political changes as positive, despite some minor flaws. According to the entrepreneurs, making money has become society's primary goal. Personal achievement or social standing in society is measured mainly by money. Consequently, traditional authority and moral values have declined significantly. However, only a few respondents had any solution for the moral decline, mainly suggestions for tougher laws and better law enforcement so as to reduce bribery, especially in politics.

Overall the entrepreneurs see themselves as positive and important members of society. In their view, their work and businesses are an important source of support in particular for their own families, but also for the company's employees, even though their employees often find them to be hardhearted. Many of their employees are people who lost their jobs in state-owned companies. In addition, they emphasized that their businesses also have an impact on the broader environment as they positively affect other stakeholders such as suppliers.

The respondents indicated that although their companies are small or mid-sized they also try to be as socially responsible as they can by e.g. supporting charities and non-profit organizations. However, when asked for more details, only a few respondents were able to identify the charities they supported. As a consequence, the level of support for charities may be exaggerated.

The entrepreneurs recognize that the transformation into a market economy is not complete. In their opinion, the main problems in the transformation have been caused primarily by the state and politicians, but there are also problems with the "socialist" attitudes and mentality of society. The most pressing problem is the public service; respondents find it to be bureaucratic and civil servants and politicians arrogant. Entrepreneurs' second complaint was with the workers, who take a lot of sick leave. According to the respondents, this popular practice is tolerated in state-owned companies, but in private companies it means additional costs and lower competitiveness. However, workers seldom understand that this behaviour may negatively affect their company and, as a result, their jobs and themselves. This behaviour makes it clear that the employees do not identify with the companies they work for, and see a poor work ethic as something that applies to other people. Finally, the entrepreneurs are frustrated by the level of corruption in the government as well as in the private sector. Giving bribes for permits or contracts is increasingly regarded as a one-time cost and a way of conducting business. Corruption is accepted by most of the entrepreneurs and does not impact their opinion of themselves as honest and law-abiding citizens.

Thus, in the opinion of the entrepreneurs, the main problem of the market economy is the high level of corruption, which is accepted throughout society. A major cause of malfunctioning in the market economy is weak enforcement of laws. Entrepreneurs who have had to deal with the courts think the legal system is corrupt and the judges subject to outside influence. Hence, the feeling is widespread that connections are needed in order to obtain a positive decision in the courts. As a consequence, most of the entrepreneurs would like to see dramatic changes in the legal and court systems.

4. Changes in social relations in Poland

Most entrepreneurs feel that the changes wrought in the society and in private life by the transformation are negative. In their opinion, social differences are widening and, as a result, 33 per cent reported that they have lost old friends. According to 43 per cent of the entrepreneurs, the cause for the changes in existing friendships is envy and jealousy. Only 10 per cent of respondents reported that the changes meant less time for themselves.

Due to the changes in society, respondents have started new relations, which more often than not are based on distrust from the beginning. In addition, entrepreneurs are more suspicious of new associates and their clients than in the past. The distrust is partially explained by the fact that more than 52 per cent of the entrepreneurs reported that they have often been affected by fraud, while no more than 19 per cent said this was seldom the case. Only 29 per cent of the respondents have not been cheated. Nevertheless most of the entrepreneurs report that they feel they are deceived mainly by the government. As a result, entrepreneurs distrust the government more than they do business partners or friends. The lack of trust is caused mainly by the stubbornness of the civil service and the unpredictability of their decisions. Part of it is caused by uncertainty about corporate and tax laws, which have changed frequently in recent years. This is an important factor as trust is fundamental for the functioning of democracy (Putnam, 1991). The combination of trust and tolerance reflects a will to understand others' preferences and build successful social relationships.

The distrust of new business partners is significant. As a result, only written contracts are accepted by the entrepreneurs. Whereas in the past oral agreements were often the rule, now they are accepted only if the parties know each other well. Nevertheless, even in such cases entrepreneurs prefer to have some guarantee as many have also been cheated by long-time business partners. Contractors, for instance, only grant loans if they have a strong relationship with the debtor. Even then, respondents will act only if both the company and its owner have solid reputations.

Despite all precautions, most of the respondents have been cheated, and in some cases debtors have defaulted on their loans. In such cases, the entrepreneurs first try to solve the problem through negotiations with the business partner. The respondents explained that this is often very difficult as the default is often caused by the insolvency of the partners' business. In some cases it involves personal insolvency and thus also affects the partners' families.

However, in most cases the fraud is such that it is hard for the entrepreneur to identify the final borrower. Nevertheless, even in such cases entrepreneurs first try to solve the problem themselves. The courts are always the last resort for entrepreneurs as they are costly and inefficient. According to the entrepreneurs, it takes years before the courts reach a decision and in the end it is unlikely that the loan will ever be recovered. In addition, regardless of the outcome, the entrepreneur will be obliged to pay court costs and the cost of the lawyer. In consequence, if negotiations fail, entrepreneurs often resign instead of suing the dishonest business partner.

Despite their great distrust of clients, 62 per cent of the entrepreneurs are willing to meet their clients privately. Entrepreneurs who meet with clients outside their business dealings report that those encounters sometimes end in friendship and can lead to new business opportunities. More than 86 per cent of the entrepreneurs reported that a business contact is more likely to result in friendship than friendship to result in a new business opportunity. Only ten per cent of the respondents indicated that both situations are possible, and only five per cent indicated that friendship may result in business dealings. Many of the entrepreneurs explained that they have already tried to involve friends in their business, but in most cases this resulted in failure and bad blood. Thus, they would prefer not to do it again, which explains why entrepreneurs would not like to enter into any new business based on an existing friendship.

Most of the entrepreneurs find that networks are important, even though 32 per cent of them would prefer not to meet with their clients outside business hours. At the same time, the entrepreneurs emphasized that in order to expand their business it is important to expand their networks. Thus, networks are seen as an important part of business as well as social life.

Finally, the respondents state that they are honest, and only a small fraction would justify fraud in an extraordinary situation. At the same time, the moral values applied to family members and close relatives are often different than those applied to the outside world. A typical situation is where the owner uses private connections in order to receive a contract or help a family member to get a job, while the same behaviour by a third person would be seen as unfair and dishonest.

5. Attitudes in Poland vis-à-vis the Western countries

Most of the entrepreneurs have a positive view of the West, particularly the old EU member states and the United States. In the survey, 86 per cent of the entrepreneurs reported that their attitudes toward the West had not changed significantly after the transformation. However, the respondents associated western culture with negative changes in Poland and Polish society. Nevertheless, 81 per cent of the entrepreneurs see western countries as good models for democracy, freedom, market changes, and economic growth. According to the entrepreneurs, examples worth following were either strongly socially-oriented countries such as Germany and Sweden or countries with transparent administrations and little corruption such as Switzerland and Singapore.

In Poland, membership of the EU is associated with greater freedom as well as bureaucracy. For the entrepreneurs, freedom means in particular the free-trade agreements, the possibility of travelling without high official barriers and of working in the EU. At the same time, the entrepreneurs also feel that Poland's membership of the EU has brought a substantial increase in bureaucracy. Furthermore, although 67 per cent of the entrepreneurs report a strong feeling of solidarity in the EU, some respondents are disappointed by the lack of support. Respondents reported that after joining the EU they expected large inflows of EU subsidies. However, it turns out that it takes a lot of time to receive any financial help from the EU and the procedures are quite complicated and require a lot of documentation, which discourages them from applying for subsidies.

Finally, dealings with Russia, such as the invitation to join the WTO, are seen as very positive. In the opinion of the entrepreneurs, the EU can help with the urgent task of stabilizing political and economic relations between Poland and Russia. According to the entrepreneurs this relationship is vital as the Russian market may play an important role in the future.

6. Conclusions

Overall the entrepreneurs take a positive view on the political and economic changes in Poland in recent years. At the same time, the survey reveals one surprising effect of the transformation for entrepreneurs. One would expect democracy and a free-market economy to result in better relations with the government. However, the results of the survey clearly show that for the most part entrepreneurs are disappointed with and distrust the government and the public service.

The entrepreneurs expected more support from the government and that the government would lay the foundations for a friendly partnership in the long term. However, in reality the public administration is overbearing and civil servants have a bad attitude toward entrepreneurs. Many respondents indicated that there is a need for government reform and greater competence in the administration.

Entrepreneurs' social relations were affected by the transformation, while views about the West seem not to be significantly affected by the changes in the political system. The western system is still seen as superior, although the economic situation has worsened for many and the state provides less security. The entrepreneurs hope that at some point the transition period will end and the existing laws will be properly enforced. This will help to stabilize the situation and will eliminate causes of the system's malfunctioning, such as corruption. The respondents hope that at some time the country will develop in the direction of countries with a strong social security system, such as Germany and Sweden, or law-abiding countries such as Singapore and Switzerland, but do not think this is likely in the near future.

References

Gérard, R. (2004). "Understanding Institutional Change. Fast-Moving and Slow-Moving Institutions", Studies in Comparative International Development 38 (4), 109-131.

Inglehart, R. (1997). Modernization and Postmodernization: Cultural, Economic, and Political Change in 43 Societies, Princeton: Princeton University Press.

North, D.C. (2005). Understanding the Process of Economic Change, Princeton and Oxford: Princeton University Press.

Putnam, R.(1991). Making Democracy Work, Princeton: Princeton University Press.

Winiecki, J. (2004). "Determinants of Catching Up or Falling Behind. Interaction of Formal and Informal Institutions", Post-Communist Economies, 16 (2), 137–152.

Zweynert, J., Goldschmidt, N. (2006). "The Two Transitions in Central and Eastern Europe as Processes of Institutional Transplantation", Journal of Economic Issues 40, 895-918.

All happy Families are happy in the same Way: Some Remarks concerning Baltic Entrepreneurs and Extended Order (Comment)

Alexander Chepurenko

One of the most popular statements in the systemic transition literature since the second half of the 1990th is that different experiences of the CEE and Baltic states, on the one hand, and the most of the CIS countries, on the other hand, are embedded in different social norms and values, encouraging efforts in the new EU member states and preventing it in some of CIS countries.

Since entrepreneurs are the trigger social group of a market transformation, the comparative study of entrepreneurial values and socio-economic attitudes after 15 years of systemic transition is of great importance.

The first impression after reading the Latvian, Polish and Russian papers was confusing: to describe this impression, one might cite the first phrase of Leo Tolstoi's "Anna Karenina" where he argued that 'All happy families are happy in the same way' – in fact, the differences in entrepreneurs' approaches to some key results of transition, basic institutions and values are more or less negligible. Any differences could be explained rather as a result of the size of businesses represented by the interviewed persons (in Russia, there were some big or medium sized companies' CEOs among the interviewed persons, whereas in Poland and Latvia the interviews were been conducted only with SMEs): for example, the bigger the firm is, the more positive is the attitude of the owner towards privatization in any (post)transitional country, and vice versa. Another important consideration: these differences are closely connected with different types of state and political institutions. Cf. Tables 1-4.

As one may see from the reports delivered by research teams, there are four contradictions which may be constructed from a comparison of statements of the interviewed entrepreneurs in the three countries:

- Between verbal goals and values (market, freedom, democracy) and the real state of institutions (frauds, bribery, bureaucracy),

- Between the values and moral norms of entrepreneurs and other groups of population,

- Between the estimations and the real state of transition to market and democracy,

- Between the general perception of the 'West' and of the EU.

(1) As regards the contradiction between verbal goals and the real state of things, entrepreneurs were talking about excessive state interference – moreover, they were stressing opportunistic and rent seeking behaviour of bureaucrats – their behaviour is not one of so called civil servants, but rather one of a good organized interest group. Such moods are common for representatives of all three countries. Not common is the fact that the dynamics are quite different – both Latvian and Polish entrepreneurs did not mention any worsening of the situation whereas most of Russian respondents clearly defined the situation becoming worse. So, the *first result is the different direction of changes*: in Latvia and Poland the situation is gradually improving, whereas in Russia the discrepancy between verbal goals and values and the real state of institutions is becoming even bigger.

(2) There were Latvian experts who sometimes referred to positive changes – especially in education level and labour relations. But general trend of observations of entrepreneurs in all three countries was negative, although these negative impressions were of different nature – whereas Latvian respondents were worried about a prevalence of materialist values (formation of a 'one-dimensional man'), Polish and Russian entrepreneurs mainly were been speaking about Socialist mentality of broad groups of the population. In fact, especially in Russia entrepreneurs are worried about the co-existence of two totally different and contradicting moral systems, which is a big constraint to the development of market relations. From that point of view it is not surprising that Russian respondents had no trust in employees and clients as representatives of population groups with clearly different moral systems. The *second difference* between the three states could be formulated as follows: whereas Latvian small entrepreneurs are worried about too much materialism and need for achievement among their countrymen, Polish and Russian entrepreneurs are missing this bourgeois spirit among the population. In fact, on the one side it is too much marketization of mentality and common day-life strategies, whilst on the other side – too little.

(3) Most disillusioning impressions concerning the real state of transformation were connected with the development and results of privatization (Latvia and Poland) and the State interference in economic process (especially in Russia). Latvian experts often argued that privatization was unfair, a lot of assets have been privatized with big contradictions to the legal base. Moreover, privatization is associated with a waste of state resources and inappropriate control take-over. Besides, it was a much too long process even if people didn't have enough information about it. In fact, it is very interesting that being dissatisfied with the privatization, no one of Latvian or Polish respondents raised the problem of illegitimacy of the property rights in their countries. However, they would support a formation of a state owned sector in their economies – for instance, in the sector of energy production and distribution etc. On the contrary, Russia experts mainly adopted the privatization model and results in Russia, didn't insist on any forms of state ownership in the economy, but several times mentioned that property rights were not secured in their country. Here, we maybe have the *third big distinction between Baltic states and Russia*: in the former group we have to do with a social acceptance of results of the privatiza-

tion, despite of all the failures and legal gaps (positive social contract concerning the property rights system), whilst in Russia it is still a lack of legitimacy of property rights system (negative social contract). It is the State in Russia, which raises this question again and again.

(4) The West was a shop-window for many of nowadays entrepreneurs in all three countries before the breakdown of the old planned economy. So, it is hardly surprising that the general attitude towards the West – as an economic, moral and political system – was initially very positive. After several years of transition, both Latvian and Polish entrepreneurs have now more practically based perception, whilst for many Russian entrepreneurs it is still another part of the world. Becoming a member-state of the EU, Latvia and Poland joined – with some exceptions – to the legal system (complicated EU law), the administrative system (anonymous Brussels' bureaucracy) and the common market (competition on the larger scale). It made them less idealistic, but on the other hand, unification of customs procedures, stronger law enforcement, broader chances to find clients on the European market made their attitude to the EU well balanced and generally positive. As regards Russian entrepreneurs, they clearly accept the fact that Russia will never become a part of the EU and 'the West' in a broader sense. Only few of them regard themselves as Europeans, EU is a neighbour, business partner, but not a desirable community to join. So, the *fourth distinction* between both new EU member states entrepreneurs and Russians is the fact that Baltic states' entrepreneurs are on the way of internalization of norms and values of the EU, whilst Russian entrepreneurs regard it as an external system, partly practicable, but not in all compatible with their own practices.

Hence, the shared values of entrepreneurs on both sides of the invisible border between EU/non-EU are more or less the same; all of them believe in market and competition, all of them are against a state interference in economic process – with an exception of competition protection; all of them prefer to do business without frauds etc. On the other side, fragile environment – slightly improving in the new EU countries – led to the formation of a certain "zones of low trust" – that is, systemic trust, collective trust and individual trust. Corrupt state institutions, including the juries, weak enforcement of legal norms contribute to bribery and dualism of business moral (the rules to deal within networks and on the "open market" are still different). A third important result is the fact that even under more or less unified conditions there are some differences in the state of mentality of non-entrepreneurial groups of population in Latvia and Poland – the former seems to be 'over-marketized' whereas the latter one – still overloaded by socialist norms and values.

Table 1: Comparative results of in-depth interviews with entrepreneurs in Latvia, Poland and North-Western Russia: attitude e to Economy and State

Item	Latvia	Poland	NW Russia
Respondents N and firms size	N = 15, SMEs	N = 21, rather small	N = 17, rather medium and big
Institutional trust to the State	Lack of trust	Lack of trust	Distrust
Law	Important, but corrupt courts and bad enforcement	Important to follow	Important, but corrupt courts and bad enforcement
Enforcement	Inefficient	Inefficient, briberies	Selective, oppression
State 'interface' to business	Bureaucracy, corruption, frauds	Bureaucracy, corruption, frauds	Bureaucracy, corruption, frauds, business capture
Private property	No statement	No statement	Not secured
Positive economic consequences of the transition	Free competition	Private ownership, free market, wealth creation	Private property, market
Perception of privatization	Sceptical	Often - negative	Mainly positive, the social contract as its main constraint and the policy of the State as its main threat
Any desirable exceptions from privatization?	Energy, infrastructure	Energy	No statements
The main cause of transition problems	No statements	State and politicians as well as 'Socialist' mentality of population	Society and bureaucrats as well as old mentality of population

Table 2: Comparative results of in-depth interviews with entrepreneurs in Latvia, Poland and North-Western Russia: statements on Economy and Entrepreneurship

Item	Latvia	Poland	NW Russia
Respondents N and firms size	N = 15, SMEs	N = 21, rather small	N = 17, rather medium and big
Comparison 'planned economy – market economy'	In favour of market, however, planned economy was good for poor people	In favour of market, however, planned economy was good for poor people	In favour of market without exceptions
Money	Money – more a medium than a target	Money – more a medium than a target	Only medium, not a target
Entrepreneurs role	Locomotive of the economy, paying salaries and taxes	Positive people, supports his/her family and stakeholders	No statements
Social responsibility of business	To pay taxes and salaries	To pay taxes and salaries	To pay taxes and salaries, extremely negative attitude to the State organized campaign on the 'social responsibility of business' as a form of oppression
Trust in the sphere of B2B relations	Written contracts preferred, oral contracts – only after long business relations	Written contracts preferred, oral contracts – only after long business relations	Written contracts and informal enforcement
Business – friendship relation	Partly – friendship can rely on steady deals, partly – vice versa	Friendship rely on steady deals	Written contracts and prepayment from unknown firms
Networking	Important	Important	Important, despite often a waste of time
To become entrepreneurial again?	No statements	Partly no	Up to 50 % - no

Table 3: Comparative results of in-depth interviews with entrepreneurs in Latvia, Poland and North-Western Russia: observations on Society in transition

Item	Latvia	Poland	NW Russia
Respondents N and firms size	N = 15, SMEs	N = 21, rather small	N = 17, rather medium and big
Description of the moral state of society	Negative - prevalence of materialist values in the society, people treat each other as competitors, ignore rights of each other	Negative - moral degradation as a consequence of opportunistic behaviour of civil servants	More individualistic, bigger distance between people; however, the society as a whole still a 'Soviet' one
Ties between people	Weak, no time for friends	Weak, no time for friends	Weak, less time for friends, widening social distance
Interpersonal trust	No trust	No trust	No trust
Connections	Needed in local institutions and courts	Needed in courts	Extremely needed in everyday entrepreneurial practice
Moral values in communication with close relatives and outsiders	Different	Different	Different

Table 4: Comparative results of in-depth interviews with entrepreneurs in Latvia, Poland and North-Western Russia: attitude to Western Europe

Item	Latvia	Poland	NW Russia
Respondents N and firms size	N = 15, SMEs	N = 21, rather small	N = 17, rather medium and big
General attitude to Western Europe	Positive, less idealism after the years of transformation	Positive, no significant changes after the years of transformation	Positive, not changed after the years of transformation
General attitude to the EU	Positive	Positive	Neutral, to bureaucratic
In which country the situation is comparable to yours?	Baltic states	Ukraine, Lithuania	CIS
Model for own country is...	Ireland, Germany	Germany, Sweden	If any USA
EU enlargement: own experience	Gen. pos., complications w. EU law in the initial stage	Generally positive, more EU bureaucracy	Not applicable
EU enlargement in future	Positive as regards CEE and SEE countries	Positive as regards CEE and SEE countries	Neutral
Russia's access to WTO	Positive	Positive	Mainly positive or neutral, no understanding of the consequences

Some conclusions:

(1) The shared values of entrepreneurs on both sides of the border between EU/non-EU are more or less the same; all of them believe in market and competition, all of them are against any state interferences in economic process – with an exception of competition protection; all of them try to do business without frauds etc.

(2) Fragile environment – slightly improving in the new EU countries – led to the formation of certain "zones of low trust" – that is, systemic trust, collective trust and individual trust. Corrupt state institutions, including the juries, weak enforcement of legal norms contribute to bribery and dualism of business moral (the rules to deal within networks and on the "open market" are still different).

(3) Even under more or less unified conditions there are some differences in the state of mentality of non-entrepreneurial groups of population in Latvia and Poland – the former seems to be 'over-marketized' whereas the latter one – still overloaded by socialist norms and values.

Part 4: Economic and Cultural Integration in the Baltic Sea Area

Factors influencing Integration of the Baltic Sea Region. With special Focus on the spatial and economic Dimensions

Jacek Zaucha

1. Introduction

According to Domański (2002, 109) "a region in spatial management, like in geography, is an area, in which the character of the components and spatial relations forms a certain uniform or cohesive whole." A single Polish voivodship (province) or the whole of Baltic Europe may be regarded as the "Baltic region". In order to understand the essence of the Baltic Sea Region (BSR), which comprises parts or all of several Baltic countries, it is thus necessary to identify the mechanisms that distinguish it from the surrounding area. The following criteria may be helpful:
a) natural criteria – river basins, catchment areas for lakes, mountain massifs, similar climate, flora and fauna, etc.;
b) socioeconomic criteria – a similar level of socioeconomic development (i.e. a uniform economic region) or strong functional connections illustrating economic and social interdependencies (i.e. a functional region);
c) political criteria - legal acts, conventions and treaties;
d) spatial criteria (cooperation among cities and regions, infrastructural connections, etc.);
e) cultural, historical, ethnic criteria – self-determination of regional communities, a feeling of belonging to a particular region, common religion, common language, etc.

This paper will analyse points "b" and "d", although the remaining factors also seem important for the formation of the BSR. For example, cultural and economic matters were the basis for the creation of the Hanseatic League or the Scandinavian co-operation, so intensely pursued in the twentieth century. On the other hand, the physiographic factors have played an important role in the environmental protection sphere (the Helsinki Commission). It is also difficult to imagine the formation of the Baltic Sea Region without the political factor, which is *de facto* the driving force of this process. As Deike (2000, 9) has remarked, perceiving the development opportunities of the Region in institutional and economic cooperation between the Baltic Sea countries without counting on trade with central regions of Europe is a specific feature of the Baltic Sea Region. It is, to a large extent, the political will that led to the realization of the Baltic Sea Region concept in the 1990s.

2. Integration based on economic interactions

This chapter will concentrate on the concept of a functional region. Trade flows (international trade) and foreign direct investments (FDI) are mentioned most often among the economic mechanisms conducive to this type of integration.

Due to the fact that the Baltic Sea Region is not a uniform economic region, selection of functional links is the main element of the analysis. It is, to a certain extent, obvious, considering the scale of well-known discrepancies in the Region illustrated by differences in such indicators as GDP per capita (see Tab.1), GDP growth rate, employment level or the shift to the knowledge-based economy. However, the situation does not necessarily have to adversely affect the economic integration of the region, i.e. the creation of a functional region. Many researchers emphasize that it is not the differences, but the development potential of the region that determines its future; see e.g. Ketels and Sölvell (2004, 10), who indicate that the eastern part of the Region is quickly catching up as regards research and numbers of scientific papers. Human capital is one of the Region's most essential resources.

Table 1: GDP per capita (PPS) in current prices in 2005 in thousands (estimates)

	Dk	EST	FIN	GER	LV	LIT	NOR	PL	SWED	RUS
Euro	28.9	12.8	26.3	25.3	10.9	11.9	36.0	11.6	27.0	-
USD [1]	34.6	16.7	30.9	30.4	13.2	13.7	42.3	13.3	29.8	11.1

(-) no data; Source: Eurostat, CIA

The differences are also interpreted in a positive way by Kisiel Łowczyc (2000, 62), who underlines the phenomenon of paracomplementarity, and in documents of the World Bank, the European Bank for Reconstruction and Development and the International Monetary Fund (De Broeck and Koen 2000; Fischer and Sahay 2000; Denizer 1997; EBRD 1997; EBRD 2000).[2]

Orłowski (1997, 82) is similarly optimistic, mentioning, who indicates a considerable range of complementarity between the economies of the Baltic Sea Region countries in the area of services exchange and flow of capital. In these factors he perceives an opportunity for deepening economic integration around the Baltic Sea.

2.1 Pan-Baltic Trade

There is a dominating opinion in the literature that according to empirical data (see e.g. Groth and Cornett 2001, 17) that "the Baltic Sea Region to only a very limited

---

1 Euro by Eurostat; USD by CIA World Factbook;
   https://www.odci.gov/cia/publications/factbook/docs/profileguide.html.
2 The chapter titled "Recent developments in the transition process" in particular.

extent constitutes a functional or integrated region with regard to trade." The most intensive trade relations take place within countries in western part of the region, and also between Russia and Germany, Russia and Belarus, and Germany and Poland (Tab. 2).

Table 2: Bilateral flows of intraregional trade as a share of total intraregional trade in 2003 (%)

Country	BELA	DK	EST	FIN	LIT	LAT	GER	NOR	POL	RUS	SWE	TOT
BEL		0.01	0.00	0.01	0.07	0.02	0.35	0.01	0.15	2.96	0.03	3.62
DK	0.03		0.27	0.48	0.13	0.08	5.03	1.00	0.45	0.16	2.71	10.33
EST	0.03	0.06		0.50	0.10	0.07	0.33	0.03	0.07	0.44	0.25	1.90
FIN	0.01	0.88	0.47		0.04	0.03	2.82	0.45	0.14	1.80	2.30	8.93
LIT	0.08	0.11	0.07	0.11		0.08	0.66	0.04	0.36	0.84	0.14	2.48
LAT	0.11	0.07	0.15	0.15	0.23		0.36	0.03	0.12	0.30	0.13	1.65
GER	0.16	4.38	0.20	2.38	0.30	0.18		4.65	6.85	4.95	4.08	28.13
NOR	0.01	1.34	0.07	0.51	0.06	0.03	2.03		0.33	0.22	2.93	7.53
POL	0.16	0.40	0.02	0.39	0.11	0.02	6.85	0.32		1.92	0.68	10.86
RUS	1.91	0.29	0.15	1.13	0.22	0.07	4.22	0.14	0.63		0.50	9.26
SWE	0.02	3.09	0.30	1.94	0.15	0.15	6.19	2.28	0.75	0.43		15.30
Total	2.51	10.64	1.70	7.60	1.42	0.73	28.84	8.95	9.84	14.03	13.75	100.00

Source: IMF (2004)

Further analysis of the data (Tab. 3-4) shows that only Lithuania, Latvia and Estonia trade predominantly with other Baltic countries. At least 50% of their exports go to and over 60% of their imports come from countries in the Region.

Their regional connections are multilateral that are not dominated by bilateral relations (perhaps with the exception of Estonia, which has strong relations with Finland). At the other extreme is the Hamburg sub region, which is weakly connected with the Baltic Sea Region (Tab. 5-7). St. Petersburg, strongly connected only with Germany and Finland, has a slightly bigger, yet still relatively small share of intraregional trade.

Table 3: Imports from selected countries /sub regions of the Baltic Sea Region from all countries of the Baltic Sea Region as a share of the total imports of the country/sub region in question in the years 1993-2000

Country importer / Year	Estonia	Lithuania	Latvia	Hamburg	Mecklenburg-West Pommerania	Denmark	Finland	Norway	Sweden	Poland	Kaliningrad Region	Leningrad Region	Murmansk Region	St. Petersburg
1993	74	73	64	10	51	45	44	41	40	44	52	58	-	57
1994	73	70	66	10	55	45	44	43	41	44	66	51	46	47
1995	75	65	72	9	50	46	45	43	43	42	50	-	40	-
1996	69	64	71	11	49	46	44	43	43	39	60	-	62	-
1997	65	66	71	10	52	46	44	43	42	38	62	66	64	40
1998	62	67	67	8	49	45	44	41	39	39	60	54	51	38
1999	64	65	66	8	48	44	44	42	40	39	67	52	33	34
2000	64	68	66	8	58	45	46	41	43	41	71	44	53	31

(-) no data

Source: Own calculations based on Hedegaard and Lindström 2003 statistical annex

Table 4: Exports from selected countries /subregions of the Baltic Sea Region to all countries of the Baltic Sea Region as a share of the total exports of the country/region in question in the years 1993-2000

Country exporter / Year	Estonia	Lithuania	Latvia	Hamburg	Meck.-Pom.	Denmark	Finland	Sweden	Poland	Kaliningrad Region	Leningrad Region	Murmansk Region	Petersbug
1993	77	61	55	13	42	46	38	36	49	41	38	-	59
1994	78	62	60	13	21	45	41	35	50	24	88	39	45
1995	76	55	66	11	23	46	39	34	53	18	81	45	28
1996	74	58	62	11	30	47	40	35	51	32	-	37	-
1997	74	56	62	10	32	46	40	25	51	41	75	28	30
1998	75	54	60	8	32	46	40	34	51	47	67	38	25
1999	74	55	57	8	27	38	39	32	48	45	83	45	22
2000	75	56	55	7	18	44	37	33	48	50	89	42	33

(-) no data

Source: Own calculations based on Hedegaard and Lindström 2003 statistical annex

The remaining countries/sub regions lie in the middle. They can be divided into three subgroups: (a) Nordic countries, (b) countries/sub regions with a relatively big share of the Baltic trade and strong bilateral relations with neighbours and Germany, and (c) countries/sub regions with a relatively smaller share of intraregional trade and strong bilateral relations with neighbours: Poland, the Murmansk district and (with some reservations) Mecklenburg-West Pommerania. Poland trades mainly with Russia and Germany, and the Murmansk district has trade relations with Norway and Finland (Tab. 6, 7). Although the exports of Mecklenburg-West Pommerania (Tab. 7) to countries of the Baltic Sea Region are relatively limited, its imports from them are quite big (about 50%) (Tab. 6), both as regards those from neighbouring countries and from Russia and Norway; hence, it is characterized by multilateral relations.

Belarus (connections with Russia dominate), the St. Petersburg district (strong connections with Sweden) and the Kaliningrad district (connections with Poland, Lithuania and Germany) can be assigned to the second group. It is hard to perceive both groups of countries/sub regions as integrated by the regional trade.

The Nordic countries trade mainly among themselves, and also with Germany and Russia (Finland). Kisiel Łowczyc (2000, 70) has pointed out that Sweden, which trades intensively with all Nordic countries, is the keystone in that respect. The remaining Nordic countries have selective connections, i.e. intensive trade relations with two or – less frequently – three countries of the Region; the specific relations are usually based on the neighbourhood factor.

Table 5: Main trading partners of the Baltic Sea Region countries in 2003

Baltic Sea Region Countries	Export targets	Origin of imports
Estonia	**1. Finland** 19.1% **2. Sweden** 13.1% **3. Germany** 8.9% **4. Latvia** 7.5%	**1. Russia** 18.2% **2. Finland** 18.3% **3. Germany** 11.2% **4. Sweden** 9.6%
Latvia	1. Great Britain 20.2% **2. Germany** 12.1% **3. Sweden** 11.4% 4. USA 9.8%	**1. Germany** 17.4% **2. Russia** 15.5% **3. Lithuania** 7.6% **4. Finland** 6.1%
Lithuania	**1. Germany** 11.2% **2. Latvia** 10.1% **3. Russia** 7.4% **4. Sweden** 6.7%	**1. Russia** 22.0% **2. Germany** 19.1% 3. Italy 5.9% **4. Poland** 4.3%
Norway	1. **Germany** 20.2% 2. Great Britain 14.6% 3. France 8.3% **4. Sweden** 9.0%	**1. Sweden** 22.4% **2. Germany** 13.2% 3. Great Britain 8.2% **4. Denmark** 7.7%
Germany	1. France 10.6% 2. USA 9.3% 3. Great Britain 8.4% 4. Italy 7.4%	1. France 9.2% 2. Netherlands 8.3% 3. USA 7.3% 4. Netherland 6.3%
Poland	**1. Germany** 33.0% 2. Italy 5.7% 3. France 5.0% 4. Great Britain 4.8%	**1. Germany** 28.8% 2. Italy 8.1% **3. Russia** 7.5% 4. France 6.9%

Denmark	**1. Germany** 16.2% **2. Sweden** 12.0% 3. Great Britain 7.4% 4. **Norway** 7.0%	**1. Germany** 24.2% **2. Sweden** 12.4% 3. Netherlands 7.5% 4. Great Britain 6.4%
Sweden	1. USA 11.5% **2. Germany 10.1%** **3. Norway** 8.4% 4. Great Britain 7.8%	**1. Germany 18.7%** **2. Denmark** 9.0% 3. Great Britain 8.0% **4. Norway 8.0%**
Finland	**1. Germany 11.8%** 2. Great Britain 9.9% 3. USA 8.2% 4. Great Britain 8.0%	**1. Germany** 16.2% **2. Sweden** 4.1% **3. Russia** 1.7% 4. Netherlands 6.3%
Russia	1. Netherlands 6.6% 2. China 6.2% **3. Germany** 5.0%	**1. Germany** 15.5% 2. Ukraine 8.4% 3. China 6.3%

Source: Eurostat, WTO internet data base, Market Information and Analysis Section of the Australian Department of Foreign Affairs and Trade.

Table 6: Imports of selected Baltic countries/sub regions from individual Baltic Sea Region countries as a share of total imports of a given country/sub region in 2000

Imports from \ Imports to	St. Petersburg	Leningrad Region	Karelia Republic	Kaliningrad Region	Poland	Sweden	Finland	Denmark	Mecklenburg-West Pommern	Hamburg	Lithuania	Latvia	Estonia	Belarus (2004)
Finland	8.2	14.8	23.5	1.2	1.8	5.5		2.7	2.2	0.4	3.5	8.6	23.8	-
Sweden	2.6	4.9	4.0	1.8	2.9		10.4	12.3	10.2	0.7	3.6	6.7	8.8	0.6
Denmark	1.6	1.3	0.1	1.7	1.6	7.6	3.9		9.9	1.7	4.2	3.6	2.2	-
Germany	15.1	21.1	7.3	36.9	23.9	17.6	14.3	21.0			17.0	15.7	8.8	6.6
Poland	1.3	0.8	0.0	17.1		1.3	0.9	1.8	8.0	1.2	6.3	4.8	1.0	2.9
Lithuania	0.4	0.1	0.2	8.0	0.6	0.3	0.1	0.5	0.7	0.1		7.6	1.5	0.7
Latvia	0.2	0.1	0.1	1.7	0.1	0.5	0.2	0.3	0.8	0.1	3.9		2.4	0.5
Estonia	0.2	0.1	12.0	0.6	0.1	1.2	2.8	0.3	0.8	0.1	2.3	6.2		-
Russia					9.4	0.8	9.4	0.9	16.6	1.9	26.7	11.6	14.1	68.2

(-) no data

Source: Own calculations based on Hedegaard and Lindström (2003) statistical annex and data from Министерство статистики и анализа of the Republic of Belarus

Table 7: Exports of selected Baltic countries/sub regions to individual Baltic Sea Region countries as a share of total exports of a given country/sub region in 2000

Exports to	St. Petersburg	Leningrad Region	Karelia Republic	Kaliningrad Region	Poland	Sweden	Finland	Denmark	MeckWestPomm	Hamburg	Lithuania	Latvia	Estonia	Belarus (2004)
Finland	10.3	12.5	29.0	1.6	0.7	5.6		3.4	0.8	1.6	1.3	1.9	27.1	-
Sweden	5.6	65.8	3.0	0.5	2.7		9.3	13.0	2.7	1.2	4.4	10.8	17.3	1.0
Denmark	0.1	0.2	0.3	1.0	2.7	5.8	2.5		3.0	1.4	4.9	5.8	2.9	-
Germany	11.6	2.0	3.3	10.2	34.9	11.0	12.5	18.9		14.3	17.2	7.6	3.7
Poland	0.6	0.5	4.7	29.7		1.7	1.6	1.7	5.4	1.7	5.5	1.6	0.6	5.3
Lithuania	0.5	0.4	1.0	5.7	1.8	0.2	0.4	0.4	0.5	0.1		7.6	3.1	2.6
Latvia	2.1	2.7	0.8	0.6	0.7	0.2	0.6	0.2	0.2	0.1	15.0		7.2	2.4
Estonia	1.3	4.4	7.2	0.4	0.3	0.5	3.1	0.2	0.5	0.1	2.3	5.3		-
Russia					2.7	0.6	4.4	1.1	3.2	0.9	7.1	4.2	6.8	47.0

(-) no data

Source: Own calculations based on Hedegaard and Lindström (2003) statistical annex and data from Министерство статистики и анализа of Republic of Belarus

The analysis presented above, using absolute values, is not free from simplifications arising from the ignoring differences in the scales of economies of the Region's countries. In order to eliminate this shortcoming, a simulation of the volume of exports and imports for individual countries was carried out using openness to BSR trade and GDP as a proxy of the economic potential of each country. The model variable obtained in this way X'_{kj}[3] was compared with actual imports and exports. The results of the analysis are presented in Tables 8 and 9.[4]

---

[3] $X'kj = (\sum xkj/\sum xki)*(PKBj/\sum PKBj)* \sum xki$
where
i = all the countries to/from which the "k" country/subregion exports (imports)
j = the Baltic countries to/from which the "k" country/subregion "k" exports(imports).

[4] Excluded from the analysis are subregions loosely connected by trading ties with other Baltic countries (Hamburg, St. Petersburg and Mecklenburg West Pommerania as regards exports).

Table 8: Exports of selected Baltic countries/sub regions in 2002, compared to model figures

Exporter / Export to	Murmansk	Leningrad Region	Karelia Republic	Kaliningrad	Poland	Sweden	Norway	Finland	Denmark	Lithuania	Latvia	Estonia
Finland	*	*	**			*						**
Sweden		**		\			*	*	*		*	*
Norway	*	\\\		\		*						
Denmark		\\\	\			*						
Germany	\	\\\	\\	\								\
Poland		\\\		*				\			\	\\
Lithuania	**			**	*						**	*
Latvia	Li	*								***		***
Estonia	Li	**	****			*			***		**	***
Russia					\	\\	\\\		\\		\	\

Explanations:
* - Real exports 2.5-9.0 times higher than predicted by model
** - Real exports 10 -20 times higher than predicted by model
*** - Real exports more than 20 times higher predicted by model

\ - Exports should increase by 2.5-9.0 times to be equal to the model value
\\ - Exports should increase by 10-20 times to be equal to the model value
\\\ - Exports stout increase by more than 20 times to be equal to the model value
Li – Lack of exports

Source: Calculations based on IMF (2004) and Hedeg aard and Lindström 2003 statistical annex

The analysis reveals strong mutual relations among Nordic countries and very weak relations between subregions of Baltic Russia and other countries of the Baltic Sea Region, with the exception of the neighbours. One can also notice the unused potential for Polish imports to Nordic countries and weak relations between those countries (except Finland) and Russia. Additional conclusions include a harmonious and well-balanced structure of Mecklenburg-West Pommerania's imports, and Poland's exports to and imports from other countries of the Region, which contradicts to some extent Peschel's assumption (1998, 33) that sub regions of north-eastern Germany and Poland are not, in fact, Baltic entities according to the concept of the economic region. On the other hand, Latvia and Estonia, regarded as models of Baltic economic integration, are characterized by considerable disequilibrium as regards their trade relations with the BSR.

Table 9: Imports of selected Baltic countries/sub regions to individual countries of the Baltic Sea Region in 2002, compared to model figures

Import from \ Importer	Murmansk Region	Leningrad Region	Karelia Republic	Kaliningrad Region	Poland	Sweden	Norway	Finland	Dania	Mecklwestpom	Lithuania	Latvia	Estonia
Finland	*	*	*			*						*	**
Sweden				\			*	*	*				
Norway		\				*					\		
Denmark			\\\			*	*						
Germany	\		\										\
Poland	\	\	li			\	\	\	\				\
Lithu	\	\	\	**				\			**		
Latvia	Li	\	\	*						*			*
Estonia	Li		***			*					*	***	
Russia						\\	\		\\				

Explanations:
* - Real import 2.5-9.0 times higher than predicted by model
** - Real import 10-20 times higher than predicted by model
*** - Real import more than 20 times higher than predicted by model

\ - Import should increase 2.5-9.0 times to be equal to the model value
\\ - Import should increase 10-20 times to be equal to the model value wej
\\\ - Import should increase more than 20 times to be equal to the model value
Li - Lack of imports

Source: Own calculations based on IMF (2004) and Hedegaard and Lindström 2003 statistical annex

The special role of the German economy (and to a certain extent the Russian economy, too) in the Region should be noted. Russia and Germany are important trading partners for the remaining countries (Tab. 2), but among their key trading partners there are no countries from the Baltic Sea Region (Tab. 5). This is due to the scale of their economies and historical developments. Some researchers are of the opinion that the economic role of Russia in the Region (with GDP comparable to the GDP of Finland and Norway together, i.e. the countries whose population is about 3/4 of the population of Moscow) is underestimated, and Russia constitutes potentially the biggest Baltic economy (Cornett and Iversen 1997; Callsen and Jäger-Roschko 1996). One should also notice the great openness of the economies of the small Baltic countries. The share of exports and imports in the GDP is very high (over 50%) and they have one of the highest regional indicators of foreign trade per capita (Cornett and Iversen 1998, 6).[5] In addition, the three countries and Poland are characterized by very high rate of growth in foreign trade volume.

The East-West trade relations in the Baltic Sea Region are based, to a large extent, on interindustry trade (Groth and Cornett 2001, 20), whereas intraindustry trade which promotes integration far more strongly. Intraindustry trade is based on competitive advantages, results from the existence of economies of scale and usually involves highly processed products with high value added (Zielińska 1996, Chapter 2), thereby promoting an integrated economic and professional *milieu* in the countries connected through it. As a result, a common production system (cluster) is created. Therefore the proportions of intraindustry and interindustry trade may indicate the level of trade-driven regional integration.

At present, intraindustry trade in the Baltic Sea Region accounts for about 40% of the trade between countries in the eastern and western parts of the Baltic Sea Region and almost 100% of the trade between countries in the western part. However, the significance of intraindustry trade has been growing steadily. This would indicate potential integration possibilities. However, so far

> The adjustment of structures of exports from the western Baltic countries to structures of imports demand of the eastern part of the Baltic was higher than the rate of adjustment of structure of export supply of the eastern Baltic countries" (Kisiel Łowczyc 2000, 100).

In the opinion of Cornett and Snickars (2002, 41), one can expect a normalization of the structure of intraindustry trade and equilibrium at a low level of that trade between countries of the eastern and western parts of the Region.

According to Kisiel Łowczyc (2000, 100) the existing model of specialization seems to be stable (countries in the eastern part of the Region export mainly labour-consuming, raw materials-consuming and time-consuming goods to countries in the western part). Ketels and Sölvell (2004), too, indicate different export specializations of individual sub regions in the Baltic Sea Region (e.g. see. Ketels and Sölvell 2004, 17). Actual specialization is focused on different goods at different stages of the production chain. The modern (knowledge-consuming) manufacturing and service clusters are concentrated in the Nordic and German parts of the region. Extending them to the East and South is currently one of the main development challenges in the BSR.

In such a situation, different scenarios of the development of Baltic trade relations are possible. For example Kisiel Łowczyc (2000, 73) envisages a more equal distribution of trade streams. The Germany-Poland pair will be joined by Nordic countries and/or Russia, creating the core of the Baltic economic integration. One can also expect integration at the sub regional level based on the existing crystallization centres of integration, leading to overlapping trade integration areas: the Polish-German one (including Kaliningrad and Lithuania) and the Scandinavian are (including Estonia), for which areas Germany will be the keystone.

---

5   Save for the exports of Latvia.

2.2 Foreign Direct Investment (FDI)

Generally there is an opinion that foreign direct investment is the economic factor that integrates economies more strongly than trade does.[6] The Baltic Sea Region in the broad meaning of the term is an important area of inflowing foreign direct investment (about 12.3% of the inflowing global FDI in 1990-2001). As table 10 shows, the main importers (recipients)[7] of FDI in the Region were the most developed countries, particularly Sweden and Denmark (in absolute terms and per capita) and Germany. They have absorbed nearly 80% of the FDI flowing into the Region.

Table 10: Net inflow of foreign direct investment at current prices (BoP) 1990-2003

Country	Cumulated inflow of FDI in current prices (BoP)1990-2003 Million USD	%	USD capita	Stock of inward FDI in current prices 2003 year Million USD	USD capita
Belarus	1,779	2.12%	180.10	1,897	191.99
Denmark	92,563	10.80%	17,182.09	76,195	14,143.71
Estonia (1990-2000)	2,645	0.31%	1,954.92	2,645	1,954.92
Finland	48,761	5.69%	9,355.59	46,400	8,902.53
Germany	401,534	46.84%	4,864.67	544,604	6,597.98
Latvia	3,320	0.39%	1,430.42	3,320	1,430.42
Lithuania	4,960	0.58%	1,436.02	4,960	1,436.02
Norway	36,004	4.20%	7,892.30	45,010	9,866.29
Poland	52,125	6.08%	1,364.67	52,125[8]	1,364.67
Russia (1990- 2000)	27,695	3.23%	193.10	27,695	193.10
Sweden	177,988	20.76%	19,873.70	143,230	15,992.63
BSR[9] total	857,201	100.00%	2,807.84	862,296	2,824.53
USA	1,507,966		5,185.40	1,553,955	5,343.54
World	7,507,899		1,196.95		
EU (euro zone)	2,575,284		8,392.12		

Source: World Bank and UNCTAD 2004

---

6 See Klein and others 2001, in particular the annex containing discussion of 119 results of empirical research in recent years on the influence of FDI on economic growth, income inequalities, political system, natural environment, positive technological external effects, combating of corruption, level of salaries, working conditions, etc.).
7 Also the FDI exporters.
8 According to PAIZ (Polish Agency of Foreign Investments), FDI in Poland in 2003 amounted to USD 7,2705 m.
9 All countries including all of Russia and Germany.

Table 11: Indicators of openness of countries to FDI, 1900-2003

Country	1990-2003 FDI inward flows as a proportion of gross fixed capital formation - annual average in %	FDI inward flows as a proportion of GDP -annual average in %s	FDI inward stocks as % of GDP 2003	FDI outward stocks as % of GDP 2003	UNCTAD Inward FDI Performance Index 2000-2002 Value[10]	Ranking among 140 countries	UNCTAD Outward FDI Performance Index 2000-2002 Value[11]	Ranking among 128 countries	Inward FDI Potential Index 2000-2002 Value[12]	Ranking among 140 countries
Belarus	3.73	0.92	11.		0.570	99	-0.236	126	0.213	56
Denmark	20.08	4.07	36	37	3.545	11	1.921	12	0.387	19
Estonia	17.77	5.07	78	12	4.149	10	1.207	22	0.275	38
Finland	14.08	2.76	29	42	1.718	43	1.069	23	0.409	13
Germany	6.90	1.46	23	26	0.554	102[13]	0.396	44	0.432	9
Latvia	17.27	3.42	35	1.1	1.760	41	0.105	63	0.234	49
Lithuania	10.58	2.37	27	0.7	1.517	55	0.072	71	0.223	52
Poland	11.91	2.50	25	0.9	1.188	68	0.046	76	0.256	44
Sweden	29.90	5.21	47	63	1.745	42[14]	2.329	7	0.427	10

Source: www.unctad.org and World Bank

10   The ratio of a country's share in global FDI inflows to its share in global GDP.
11   The ratio of a country's share in global FDI outflows to its share in global GDP.
12   The ratio ranges from 0 (minimum) to 1 (maximum) and is calculated as the average of 12 macroeconomic indicators of the country investigated. The indicator does not take into account spatial, political or social factors, which results, for instance, in Belarus and, say, Lithuania, having a similar potential, or Russia and Estonia. Hence, the ratio should be applied with caution.
13   A drop from 40th in 2002, with a ratio of 1.491.
14   A drop from 23rd in 2002, with a ratio of 2.233.

The inward flow of FDI to the economies of the eastern part of the Baltic Sea Region (Tab. 10), in absolute values and per capita, is still relatively small in comparison with more developed countries (the biggest countries in eastern part of the Region, i.e. Poland and Russia, receive most in absolute terms), partly due to low absorption ability of these countries, partly due to their limited attractiveness for potential investors (see Kisiel-Łowczyc 2000, 110) and initial resistance of local communities and elites to foreign property (see Lönnborg, Olsson, Rafferty 2003, 8; Sinn Weichenrieder 1997; Fabry 2000, 4). This inward flow is much smaller than was expected in the early 1990s (Lönnborg, Olsson, Rafferty 2003, 5). The literature, however, is unambiguous as regards the assessment of the scale of the phenomenon. The data presented in UNCTAD report (2004, Annex B) concerning the share of inward flow of FDI in GDP (Tab. 11) shows, for example, Estonia (with Sweden) as regional leader in that sphere and indicates a high level of FDI absorption with regard to existing economic potential.[15] This has been confirmed by Hanell and Neubauer (2005, 220), who have calculated that in the years 1997-2001 Estonia annually absorbed FDI at the rate of about 8% of GDP. Also the compared UNCTAD indicators of potential to absorption and actual FDI absorption present optimistic perspectives with regard to countries in eastern part of the Baltic Sea Region. Only Russia and Belarus (see Tab.10-11) do not use their potential for FDI absorption (see also UNCTAD 2002, 71).

The data in Tables 12 and 13 show, as in the case of international trade, that the Baltic integration through FDI takes place mainly in the group of the more developed Baltic countries. This concerns both the mutuality and absolute values of the FDI streams. In countries of the eastern part of the Region, on the other hand, unilateral relations dominate. Owing to their economic conditions, these countries are primarily recipients of FDI.

---

15 Even though Estonia trailed far behind China (with its 256%) or Singapore (98.8%) in this respect.

Table 12: Ranking of Baltic countries as exporters of direct foreign investments to individual countries of the Baltic Sea Region in the years 1995-1999

FDI inward flows, the countries of origin		Germany	Denmark	Sweden	Finland	Estonia	Latvia	Lithuania	Russia	Poland
Recipients	Germany		12	7	13	-	-	-	19	28
	Denmark	5		2	8	-	-	-	-	-
	Sweden	4	7		3	-	-	-	-	-
	Finland	5	3	1		-	-	-	-	-
	Estonia	7	5	1	2		11	10	-	-
	Latvia	3	1	4	7	8		12	6	13
	Lithuania	8	4	1	2	9	12		11	10
	Murmansk Region	-	-	4	3	-	-	-		-
	Karelia Republic	2	-	4	3	-	5	-		-
	Leningrad Region	2	6	9	7	-	-	-		-
	St. Petersburg	4	9	6	2	-	-	-		-
	Kaliningrad Region	1	8	3	10	13	12	6		4
	Poland	2	6	5	8	-	-	-	-	

Source: Groth, Bourennane, Snickars, 2001, 26

The intraregional inward flow of FDI is relevant with regard to Finland, Lithuania, Latvia and Estonia (see Tabs. 13 and 14). The situation is different in Poland and Russia, but also in Germany and to some extent in Sweden and Denmark. Partners from outside of the Region dominate there.

Table 13: The three main partners as regards inflow and export of FDI in the Baltic Sea Region countries in 2001

Baltic Sea Region countries	The countries of origin of FDI inflows for the given BSR country in 2003	Countries of destination of FDI outflows for the given BSR country in 2003
Estonia	1. **Sweden 39%** 2. **Finland 26%** 3. USA 10%	1. **Lithuania 44%** 2. **Latvia 36%** 3. Italy 7%
Latvia	1. USA 13% 2. **Germany 11%** 3. **Denmark 11%**	No data
Lithuania	1. **Denmark 19%** 2. **Sweden 16%** 3. **Estonia 10%**	1. **Estonia 22%** 2. **Russia 20%** 3. **Latvia 19%**
Norway	1. **Sweden 19%** 2. Netherlands 18% 3. **Denmark 11%**	1. USA 17% 2. **Denmark 15%** 3. **Sweden 14%**
Germany[16]	1. USA 19% 2. Netherlands 18% 3. Belgium and Luxemburg 16%	1. USA 41% 2. Great Britain 9% 3. France 6%
Poland[17]	1. France 19% 2. Netherlands 13% 3. USA 12%	1. China 14% 2. Belgium and Luxemburg 13% 3. Great Britain 12%
Denmark	1. USA 30% 2. **Sweden 14%** 3. Belgium and Luxemburg 13%	1. Belgium and Luxemburg 19% 2. USA 17% 3. Switzerland 7%
Sweden	1. USA 23% 2. **Finland 15%** 3. Great Britain 12%	1. USA 20% 2. **Finland 13%** 3. Great Britain 9%
Finland[18]	1. **Sweden 56%** 2. Netherlands 17% 3. Great Britain 6%	1. **Sweden 25%** 2. Netherlands 17% 3. USA 12%
Russia	1. USA 21% 2. Cyprus 19% 3. Netherlands 12%	lack of data

Source: UNCTAD and PAIZ for Poland

The countries in eastern part of the Region also invest among themselves, but to a limited extent. Lithuania and Estonia, for example, make most of their foreign direct investments in the Baltic Sea Region (Tab.14). Also Russian investments have some significance for Latvia, Latvian investments for Karelia, and Polish and Lithuanian investments for the Kaliningrad district. In absolute terms these are, at best, mid-sized amounts.

To sum up, FDI flows indicate sub regional integration within Nordic countries and Nordic countries with Lithuania, Latvia and, above all, Estonia. An important integration role may also be played by FDI flows between the less developed Rus-

---

16 As of 2001.
17 As of 2004 for inflows (PAIZ data) and 2000 for exports of FDI (UNCTAD data).
18 As of 2001.

sian sub regions and their closest neighbours. As with trade, the German economy, thanks to its size, is the regional keystone.

Table 14: The share of intraregional (Baltic) streams of foreign direct investment in FDI inflows and outflows for the selected countries of the BSR in the period 1994-99

Country	Inflows of FDI from the BSR in 1994-2000 as a % of total inflows			Outflows of FDI to the BSR countries in 1994-2000 as % of total outflows		
	Baltic Sea Region	Baltic Sea Region, west part[19]	Baltic Sea Region, east part	Baltic Sea Region	Baltic Sea Region, west part	Baltic Sea Region, east part
Estonia	79.9	79.0	0.5	86.9.8[20]	-1.4[21]	88.3[22]
Latvia[23]	60.2	46.4	13.8			
Poland	24.0	24.1	-0.1[24]	7.5	7.7	-0.2
Lithuania	72.2	62.5	9.7	77.7	4.6	73.1
Denmark	25.9	25.9	0.0	18.5	14.9	3.6
Finland	72.0	71.8	0.2	51.3	50.4	0.9
Sweden	28.4	28.4	Lack of data	31.5	28.6	2.9
North-western Russia[25]	28.2	27.5	0.7	lack of data	lack of data	lack of data

Source: Own calculations based on Hedegaard and Lindström 2003 statistical annex

The data for inward and outward flows of FDI are incomplete: they do not include information on FDI structure, and therefore do not allow us to specify more precisely the role FDI plays in the economic integration of the Baltic Sea Region.

19 Sweden, Germany, Norway, Finland, Denmark.
20 In 2003, the share was 76.5% (Eesti Pank data).
21 In 2003, the share amounted to 2% (Eesti Pank data); the negative figure is owing to Estonian FDI withdrawn from the western part of the Region.
22 In 2003, the share amounted to 74.5% (Eesti Pank data).
23 The percentage data refer only to foreign capital in companies registered in Latvia.
24 The negative figure is owing to Polish FDI withdrawn from the eastern part of the Region and the withdrawal of that part of the Region's FDI from Poland.
25 Data for the years 1995-2001 for the districts of Murmansk, Kaliningrad, Leningrad, Karelia and St. Petersburg.

Table 15: Economic sectors to which FDI flowed in Lithuania, Latvia, Estonia, Poland Russia and Sweden

Baltic Sea Region Countries	Three top destination sectors of FDI in a given country
Estonia	1. banking and finance 2. transport 3. retail
Latvia	1. retail 2. banking and finance 3. other services
Lithuania	1. retail 2. telecommunications 3. intermediaries
Poland[26]	1. banking and finance 2. retail 3. food and beverages
Sweden	1. chemical industry 2. automotive industry 3. other services
Russia	1. transport 2. mining 3. food and beverages

Source: Own calculations based on the UNCTAD data base

In the eastern part of the Region FDI flowed mainly in sectors with a relatively small catch up effect (Tab. 15). It is hard to regard such flows as highly integrating, i.e. supporting intraindustry exchange. There is also notice a tendency for FDI to concentrate in capital cities (Cornett and Snickars 2002, 53). The higher the status of the capital, the greater its relative attraction for FDI, e.g.– Riga 82%, Tallinn 72% and Vilnius 66% (Cornett and Snickars 2002, 47). This fact has considerable significance for creating geographically defined systems of production in the Baltic countries that are new EU members.

2.3 Summary

The analysis of economic relations shows that the Baltic Sea Region is not a functional region according to the generally accepted meaning of the concept. The external connections are stronger than internal ones. This is true, in particular, for Russia, Poland and Germany (Peschel 1998, 33). This does not mean that integration processes do not occur. There is evidence of a geographic concentration of connections in sub regions and strong cooperation in certain sectors (Cornett, Snickars 2002, 33).

---

26 As of 2004 for the inflow (PAIZ data) and 2000 for the outflow of FDI (UNCTAD data).

Orłowski has pointed out (1997, 80-81) that the share of the Baltic intraregional trade over the last 100 years has remained fairly stable, despite various political shocks. However, one can accept the argument that the Baltic Sea Region is rather a part of a bigger economic system than a system in itself (Cornett and Snickars 2002, 38, Orłowski 1997, 80). Some countries in the Region have strong economic relations (trade and FDI) with countries outside the Region. The cooperation of individual industries and sectors and the sub regional clustering of business activity in the Region are complementary factors that do not replace integration within a wider European system and global economy, much as happens in other parts of the world (Cornett, Snickars 2002, 54).

According to Groth and Cornett (2001, 24), economic integration around the Baltic Sea requires a policy of competitive production based on endogenous resources, strengthening strong sub regions, and, parallel with this, a policy of subsidizing production in weaker sub regions, so as to strengthen the sub regions and ensure self-sustaining growth mechanisms in them. Outsourcing may serve as a good example of this kind of mechanism.

3. Spatial factors influencing integration around the Baltic Sea

3.1 The similarities and differences between spatial integration and cohesion

The Third Cohesion Report (European Commission 2004, 27) and Art. I-3 of the unratified European constitution both defines spatial cohesion, alongside social cohesion and economic cohesion, as a main objective of the European Union. In the former document the category is connected with spatial integration and cooperation between sub regions. Szlachta has pointed out (2004, 4) that „the problem of territorial cohesion has been so far a lack of such precise measures as in the case of economic and social cohesion." Similar statements concerning the lack of precise definition of spatial cohesion can be found in ESPON reports, e.g. in project 3.1. (ESPON 2004b, 118). It has been pointed out that the category in question does not simply mean equalization of social and economic differences, but rather a cohesive development of Europe as a single mechanism (mega region) (EU Ministerial Conference on Territorial Development 2004, 16-17). Emphasis is placed on the equalization of development opportunities in space (e.g. as regards accessibility to transport and communication, accessibility to research infrastructure and results of research). Other elements mentioned as creating spatial cohesion include spatial integration (network ties between settlement units such as companies, inhabitants, NGOs, etc.), identification and identity at sub region level (cultural, historic, linguistic heritage), ability of territorial units to anticipate asymmetric economic shocks and to cope with global economic challenges, the extent of coordination and integration of policies of public authorities. Thus, spatial cohesion means a coordination of sector policies in their spatial dimension (i.e. in the scope in which they contribute to cohesive development of Europe) and coordination of spatial development in the vertical dimension (EU working group on Spatial and Urban Development 2003, 32).

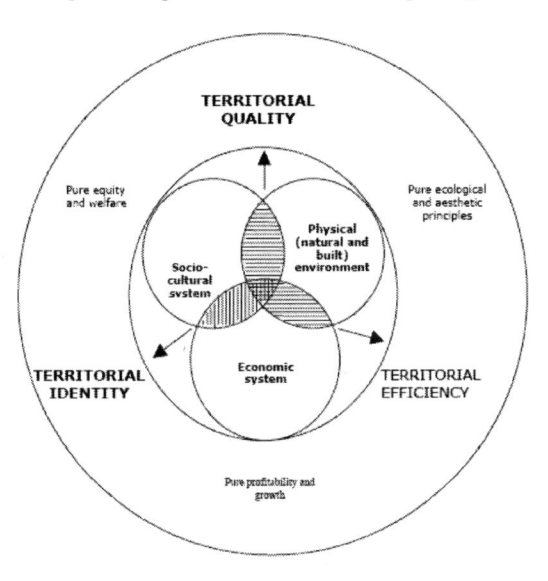

Figure 1: Spatial cohesion – concept diagram

Source: Espon 2005b, Part 2, 78

In the ESPON 3.3 project (ESPON 2005b, Part 2, 77), the following components of spatial cohesion (see Fig. 1) are specified: quality of space (quality of the working and domicile-related environment, access to services and knowledge), effectiveness of space (effectiveness of use of natural resources, power resources and land, effectiveness of economic fabric and attractiveness and accessibility of local space for business) and spatial identity (presence of social capital, ability to create development visions, local know-how, competitive advantages and specific production predestinations).

In the literature, there is considerable confusion about and lack of agreement on the definition of spatial cohesion. Nor has the concept of spatial integration and its relation to spatial cohesion been fully defined. In the ESPON 3.1. project, territorial integration is defined as:

A system of economic, social, political, cultural and personal relationships between territories, which relies on links, complementarities and co-operation opportunities between them, and which may express itself in concrete patterns such as flows, mixes, similarities and cooperative initiatives" (ESPON 2004b, 132).

Therefore integration may take the form of connections (physical links), processes and joint projects. Such integration is composed of a social component and area-related component (spatial integration) probably denoting a system of spatial relations (i.e. connections among spatial structures). In the discussed project, spatial integration constitutes an element of spatial cohesion. This kind of approach raises many doubts. Firstly, integration may lead not only to network connections (an element of spatial cohesion), but also to monocentric connections, thereby enhancing spatial polarization. In extreme cases, integration may lead to a greater degree of peripherality of part of a bigger whole. Hence, spatial integration need not be identical with spatial cohesion. Secondly, spatial integration also contains an economic thread, and not only a social or area-related one. This aspect has been pointed out by Cornett and Snickars (2002). According to them (see Fig. 2) the spatial integration category includes:

- the development of specific geographically defined systems of production such as industrial districts, clusters of industries or systems of innovation;
- a system of urban networks defined according to specific functional links;
- the availability of a regional infrastructure linking the analysed areas together;
- the intensity of intraregional flows relative to the outside flows."

Figure 2: Spatial integration – concept diagram

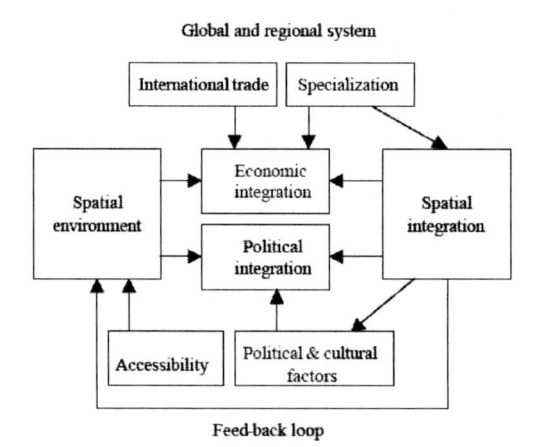

Source: Cornett and Snickars (2002, 37)

The notion of spatial integration has to be understood as:

> the most far-reaching concept of integration. In such an analysis the spatial concept is not merely a consequence of the physical environment, but also the result of economic and political integration. In a continental or regional perspective we have strong evidence that political and economic integration is powered by spatial proximity and adjacency, but at the same time political, economic and social integration reinforce the central aspect of spatial integration, accessibility" (Corentt, Snickars 2002, 37).

In this meaning, the phenomena of polarisation and convergence (cohesion) interpenetrate each other.

In the light of the existing divergence of opinion and disputes it is hard to clearly define the relationship between cohesion and integration. It seems that cohesion and spatial integration are different concepts, although they have many elements in common. These include polycentricity (with regard to spatial structures and business entities), accessibility, natural connections among biocoenosises, identity and cultural identification, and also cooperation between the public sphere, private sphere and non-governmental organisations. A specific part of spatial cohesion is convergence (of opportunities and situations) and the ability to stay on the chosen development path (absorption of shocks). On the other hand, the specific element of integration is monocentric ties in both economic systems and spatial ones.

3.2 Spatial integration of the Baltic Sea Region

In the Connecting Potentials document (VASAB 2005) three factors are considered as crucial for the spatial integration of the BSR: polycentricity, accessibility and spatial development on the sea.

3.2.1 Polycentricity

The degree of polycentricity of the Region's settlement network grows as we move from the north southwards. In the Nordic part of the Region it is particularly low (save for Denmark), owing to the low population density (see ESPON 2004a, 7). The ESPON studies (2004a, 124-162) have confirmed that the Baltic Sea Region has relatively limited potential for developing polycentricity based on morphological factors, particularly in its eastern and northern parts. This is indicated both by the map of PUSH areas[27] (map 5.5 in ESPON 2004a, 127) and the map showing results of the PUSH transformation in PIA[28] (map 5.17 in ESPON 2004a, 150). To strengthen Baltic polycentricity, pressure needs to be put on its functional aspects.

---

27 Potential Urban Strategic Horizons (PUSH) or areas situated not more than 45 minutes by car from the nearest FUA (functional urban area) created by the city (at least 15,000 inhabitants) and functionally (e.g. via commuting to work) tied with their hinterland, or FUA. ESPON (2004a, 257-293) identifies 1,595 FUA.
28 Potential Polycentric Integration Areas (PIA) created by overlapping of areas bordering on each other (PUSH). Creation of such areas would allow individual cities to improve their demographic potential and, thereby, according to the authors (ESPON 2004a, 15), enhance their position and role in the European settlement hierarchy.

Compared to the western part of the Continent, the structures of metropolises around the Baltic Sea is insufficiently developed for the cities to play an important and independent role in the world economy. This is confirmed by results of the research done by ESPON (2004a, 8-12) indicating that the Region lacks metropolises (MEGA)[29] of global functions, and that only four of the metropolises can be counted among the most important in Europe (map 5.2, in ESPON 2004a, 118): Hamburg, Berlin, Stockholm and Copenhagen. Besides St. Petersburg, they are the Region's largest urban centres (in terms of population). They can be matched only by Minsk, Warsaw and the conurbation of Upper Silesia, the functions of which centres, however, do not correspond with their demographic potential (Fig. 7 and map 5.2, in ESPON 2004a, 118).

The VASAB project "Urban Systems and Urban Networking - USUN", which studied the profile of co-operation between Baltic cities (see Groth 2001, 38, Fig.16) revealed the contemporary structure (hierarchy) of individual urban centres important for the spatial integration of the Region.

Compared with the assumptions made in 1994 (VASAB 1994), the minor role of Warsaw, Minsk, Szczecin and Kaliningrad for BSR integration is striking. Due to their population and economic potential, in VASAB (1994) Warsaw and Minsk were classified as cities with European significance in the Baltic Sea Region with only a limited presence in the system of Baltic connections and relations.[30] In Poland, the leader in Baltic cooperation is the Tri-City, not Warsaw. Other Russian and Belarus cities not mentioned earlier, also play a minor role in Baltic integration, particularly Kaliningrad, in which great hopes were placed in the early 1990s, so that this town was made equal to the Tri-City, Vilnius and Tallinn in the VASAB classification (VASAB 1994).

There are also examples of faster development than expected. For instance, the Tri-City was classified as two separate centres (Gdańsk and Gdynia) of diversified Baltic cooperation (Groth 2001, 38), whereas in 1994 in the VASAB report the role of Baltic centre was assigned to the whole agglomeration. Furthermore, developments in Schwerin, Kalmar, Karlskrona, Rönne and Pärnu, which began to play the role of supraregional centres, exceeded expectations. There has also been an improvement in the network connections of small and medium-sized Baltic towns in Nordic countries and Estonia, giving them greater significance in the spatial development of the Baltic Sea Region. Their influence is, however, primarily sub regional. There is, however, a deficit in respect of regional (Pan-Baltic) connections.

In addition, polycentricity was adversely affected by demographic processes (see Tab.16). The population has been falling in all towns; the decline is slowest in metropolises and the capitals of the Baltic countries and fastest in big non-metro-

---

29 Metropolitan European Growth Areas. Their typology was developed in ESPON (2004a).
30 However, in Hanell and Neubauer's research Warsaw scores much better (Hanell and Neubauer 2005, 16).

politan towns, i.e. those with over 200,000 inhabitants. Hanell and Neubauer (2005, 4) have also indicated that

> out of 521 towns of the Baltic Sea Region which recorded a decrease in population in the years 1995-2001, as many as 80%, i.e. 406 towns, were located in the eastern part of the Region. This is much more than the 70% share of towns in this part of the Region in the overall number of towns around the Baltic.

The population in towns and small towns around metropolises and capitals of countries is growing, even in countries that recorded a fall in overall population, such as Latvia, Estonia and Russia. According to Balerino, Johansson and Well (2005, 9), in much of the Region the structure of towns is dominated by capitals at national level, and development goals at the national, sub regional and local levels have not been clearly defined.

Table 16: Population changes in Baltic Sea Region countries in the period 1995-2001, separately for towns and rural areas
(villages and towns up to 10,000 inhabitants)

	Entity	Mean annual change of population 1995-2001				Notes on the rate of changes in individual types of cities[31]
		absolute values	in %	as the result of migrations in %	as the result of natural growth increase in %	
Denmark	National	19,555	0.37	0.22	0.14	Fastest growth in the metropolis (Copenhagen) and big cities; Rate of growth declines with drop in size of the cities in the analysis.
	Town	14,300	0.41	0.22	0.18	
	Country	5,255	0.29	0.22	0.07	
Estonia	National	-10,658	-0.76	-0.51	-0.42	Similar pace population decline in all types of cities.
	Town	-7,700	-0.93	-0.81	-0.39	
	Country	-2,959	-0.52	-0.08	-0.47	
Finland	National	13,013	0.25	0.07	0.17	Fastest growth in the metropolis (Helsinki) and big cities, rate of population growth decreases with drop in size of the cities.
	Town	25,038	0.76	0.40	0.34	
	Country	-12,026	-0.65	-0.54	-0.14	

---

31 Comments should be treated with some reservation; e.g. in the Baltic part of Russia, Denmark, Finland or Norway not many big cities (i.e. 200,000 – 1,000,000 inhabitants) are left once the capitals are classified as metropolises.

Germany Baltic part	National	10,544	0.07	0.26	-0.19	Fastest decline in population in medium-sized towns and a small increase in population in small towns.
	Town	-39,490	-0.39	-0.20	-0.20	
	Country	50,034	1.10	1.26	-0.17	
Latvia	National	-20,627	-0.85	-0.58	-0.28	Fastest decline in population in the metropolis (Riga).
	Town	-13,151	-0.93	No data	No data	
	Country	-4,823	-0.50	No data	No data	
Lithuania	National	-12,223	-0.35	-0.07	-0.29	Fastest decline in population in big cities (except Vilnius, where the drop in population was the slowest).
	Town	-7,514	-0.36	-0.22	-0.14	
	Country	-4,709	-0.34	0.17	-0.51	
Norway	National	25,685	0.58	0.25	0.33	Fastest growth in the metropolis (Oslo).
	Town	21,333	0.84	0.42	0.43	
	Country	4,352	0.23	0.04	0.19	
Poland	National	3,842	0.01	-0.04	0.05	Fastest decline in population in the metropolis; population growth in small towns.
	Town	-13,352	-0.06	-0.03	-0.03	
	Country	17,194	0.10	-0.05	0.15	
Russia Baltic part	National	-62,890	-0.59	0.19	-0.95	Fastest decline in population in big cities and small towns.
	Town	-57,050	-0.67	0.22	-0.94	
	Country	-5,840	-0.27	0.17	-1.25	
Belarus	National	-37,722	-0.37	0.14	-0.44	Fastest growth in population in the metropolis, rate of growth decreases with a drop in size of the cities in the analysis.
	Town	9,657	0.15	0.19	-0.05	
	Country	-47,379	-1.30	-0.37	-1.15	
Sweden	National	11,939	0.13	0.17	-0.03	Fastest growth in the metropolis (Stockholm) and big cities; decline in the population of small towns (rate of growth decreases with a drop in size of the cities in the analysis).
	Town	25,737	0.37	0.33	0.05	
	Country	-13,799	-0.07	-0.39	-0.32	

Source: Hanell and Neubauer, 2005, 55-77 and 42

The analyses presented above do not indicate univocally that the settlement network is a factor enhancing dynamic growth in the Region (mainly due to agglomeration benefits) and increasing its spatial integration. On one hand, the significance of specific immobile endogenous factors (including knowledge, research) promoting growth has been improving in some Baltic towns. Moreover, as the number of sub regional network connections grows, they may, taken together, begin to have influence at regional level. On the other hand, there is no obvious value added of this cooperation so far, and a large part of it lacks a strategic, pro-development, pro-Baltic character. In many cases, the scale of the problems involved in running towns in the eastern part of the Region leads to these towns focusing on local problems.

The analysis of the interaction between settlement network and spatial development in the Region or its spatial integration produces more questions than answers, e.g. which market mechanisms condition polycentric growth around the Baltic Sea (in the functional dimension), and how can these mechanisms be supported and promoted (see VASAB 2005).

3.2.2 Accessibility

Transport. Only Denmark, Germany and the western and south-western parts are regarded as well connected with the rest of the continent. The eastern part of the Region suffers from transport deficits in both major traffic arteries and sub regional infrastructure.[32] According to ESPON (2004c, 175) the road infrastructure in the Region, with some exceptions in Lithuania and Scandinavia, is inadequate for the needs. Many connections between towns in the Region are substandard. Some of these are direct connections between big metropolises, i.e. cities of more than one million inhabitants. Proper rail and air connections exist only between major towns in Scandinavia and Germany. In 2004, low cost airlines were introduced in Lithuania, Latvia and Estonia. However, they have improved mainly the external accessibility of the Region and its capitals. Inhabitants of eastern part of the Region do not have access to rail transport at all (apart from suburban trains and connections to Russia). The highway network in the eastern part of the Region is oriented towards domestic traffic and does not promote the spatial cohesion of the Region. The potential multimodal accessibility in the Baltic Sea Region is below the EU mean value (ESPON 2004 e, 285, 450 and 460).[33]

The planned priority regional investments on an international scale (see van Miert's report[34] and European Union 2004) do not improve the situation in the Region.[35] They will improve the accessibility of eastern part of the Baltic Sea Region only to a very small extent (see ESPON 2004d, 125).

The EU investment proposals do not execute the important part of the VASAB's vision (1994, 59-60 and 2001, 29); the Via Hanseatica corridor, for instance, has not even been included in the section from Gdańsk to Germany. A real improvement in the accessibility in the Region would require greater emphasis on developing regional connections of a Baltic character as identified by the JASON project and other relevant studies.

---

32 See also in CPI of BSR INTERREG III B.
33 One should note that the potential multimodal accessibility in the formula applied by ESPON is the result of the quality of transport infrastructure and density of population. Therefore, the Baltic Sea Region, which is characterized by low density of population cannot in this approach count on a significant improvement of accessibility even if the condition of its infrastructure improves.
34 High Level Group on the trans-European transport network, 2003.
35 In the decision, 28 projects, which should all have started by 2010, are mentioned. They include six projects for the Baltic Region: Nordic Triangle (railway and roads), a railway bridge over Belt, a highway and railway line from the Tri-City to Vienna and Bratislava, a Baltic railway from Tallinn to Warsaw, and sea highways in the Baltic Sea.

This situation requires particular consideration, because in the coming years one can expect the south-eastern part of the Baltic Sea Region to experience one of the biggest increases in cargo streams in relative terms, with a 70% increase in road haulage between 2000 and 2020 (ESPON 2004d, 228). Already haulage in the Region is growing at a rapid 15-20% per year, in particular the carriage of general (unit) cargo.

Accessibility - Telecommunications

The countries and sub regions of the Baltic Sea Region are very different as regards the number of stationary and mobile-phone subscribers per 1000 inhabitants (see Tab. 17).

Table 17: Telephone subscribers per 1000 inhabitants in 1990, 2001, 2003

Countries	1990	2000	2003
Belarus	154.48	280.41	424.31
Denmark	595.75	1345.77	1552.55
Estonia	203.69	750.29	1118.61
Finland	585.75	1270.76	1401.56
Germany	444.58	1196.48	1442.48
Latvia	233.84	468.63	811.23
Lithuania	211.81	463.49	868.93
Norway	548.16	1480.99	1622.37
Poland	86.39	457.83	769.65
Russia	139.95	240.47	362.3[36]
Sweden	734.51	1475.17	1624.53[37]
USA	568.52	1053.51	1164.29
World	101.84	284.03	405.67
EU euro zone	419.41	1148.5	1385.81

Source: World Bank Internet database

For many years the Nordic countries have been among the world most saturated telecommunications markets. Although countries in the eastern part of the Region are still far behind in terms of telecommunications services saturation, growth in the number of stationary and mobile-phone subscribers[38] is impressive, e.g. a doubling of the number of mobile-phone subscribers in a year. Furthermore, technological

---

36 2002.
37 2002.
38 With the exception of Russia and Belarus, which mandate the development of stationary telephony infrastructure.

solutions in wireless communications in these countries are among the most advanced in the world.

With regard to Internet use (Tab.18), the situation is similar to that concerning mobile phones. Apart from Ireland, Sweden has a most technically advanced system of Internet access to public services in Europe.[39] Estonia is also among the European leaders in Internet use. According to the e-Forum Public Services Requirements Survey on electronic access to public services in countries of the Eastern Europe, 90% of employees in the public sector have access to the Internet, whereas in the old EU countries the figure is between 74% (southern countries of the EU) and 81% (northern countries of the EU).

Table 18: Internet users per 100,000 inhabitants

	1997	1998	1999	2000	2001	2002	2003
Belarus	50	75	499	1,872	4,324	8,157	14,098
Denmark	11,374	22,645	30,601	39,212	42,950	51,282	..
Estonia	5,487	10,347	13,866	27,210	30,046	32,768	44,412
Finland	19,429	25,407	32,274	37,230	43,028	50,970	53,382
Germany	6,703	9,874	20,812	30,148	37,603	43,617	47,255
Latvia	2,016	3,254	4,304	6,188	7,231	13,310	40,359
Lithuania	945	1,891	2,785	6,093	6,792	14,440	20,190
Norway	29,425	35,993	40,192	43,300	29,164	30,723	34,565
Poland	2,070	4,083	5,421	7,246	9,837	23,000	23,245
Russia	475	815	1,019	1,974	2,971	..	..
Sweden	23,735	33,441	41,370	45,583	51,627	57,307	..
USA	22,126	30,809	36,696	44,062	50,149	55,138	..
World	2,479	3,899	5,868	8,470	10,714	13,087	14,988
EU Monetary Union	6,834	10,738	17,433	24,988	30,658	33,610	37,823

Source: World Bank

The analyses of ESPON project 1.2.2. confirm the domination of the Nordic countries in Europe, and consequently the existence of differences between the north-western and south-eastern parts of the Region (in the EU) as regards telecommunications infrastructure, its accessibility and use (ESPON 2005a, 10, 17). The most dramatic differences concern use of personal computers, permanent telephone lines, broadband Internet access and use of mobile phones (ESPON 2005a, 22, 50, 68, 83). Differences of this kind are much smaller with regard to use of telecommu-

---

39 Result of a survey conducted by Cap Gemini Ernst & Young in 15 EU Member States and Switzerland, Ireland and Iceland between October 2001 and 2002 on electronic access to public services as part of the programme assessing progress of the EU "E-Europe" initiative.

nications IT tools. For example, use of these tools by firms is relatively less advanced only in Lithuania and Latvia (as in Spain and Portugal), whereas Estonia and Poland, on a par with France, are close to European mean value (ESPON 2005a, 8). With regard to the number of Internet users per 100,000 inhabitants, Estonia and Latvia are among leaders in Europe (ESPON 2005a, 96). ESPON also points out that countries that joined the EU in 2004 are quickly closing the gap with regard to access to the Internet or mobile phones.

To sum up, there is a need for a Baltic model to promote accessibility which takes into account the existing backwardness, specific features of natural conditions (climate, low density of population) and development conditions (e.g. human capital as the leading resource in the Region) and is oriented towards promoting integration within the Region. This model should be able to avoid the well-known "pump effect" of new infrastructure. The focus on IT development and public passenger transport seems the proper direction for improving the BSR accessibility. In addition, sea transport is crucial for diminishing number of substandard cross-Baltic connections in the Region.

3.2.3 Transnational development zones

In the BSR, further progress has been made with a concept to promote the integration of the Region in larger territories that cover parts of several countries and extend beyond typical crossborder areas. This concept was implemented under the name of transnational development zones, and its implementation has had a considerable impact on the geography of cooperation within the Region. It is characterised by the integration of all spatial development issues from city networking to accessibility in a larger sub-area of the BSR. The concept is process-oriented, based on political networking, and comprises the elaboration of spatial development perspectives, the definition of key development themes and the generation of concrete pilot projects.

In the Region at present there are nine international development zones in operation. These are: Baltic+, String II, Seagull DevERB, South Baltic Arc, Via Baltica Nordica Development Zone, Baltic Palette II, South Baltic Four Corners, Strategy and Action Plan for the Barents region up to 2010 and Sustainable Development in the Mid Nordic Region (ProMidNord). These projects cover nearly the whole Baltic Sea Region. The only gaps are zones integrating southern Poland, southern Norway and Belarus with the Region.

The activities undertaken in the zones are varied and multi-aspect, and their international and multi-sector character is their common denominator. In accordance with definitions of a zone (VASAB 2005, 12), within these seven projects joint, i.e. international, development priorities were formulated and accepted (vision and strategic documents, often also including plans for joint activities). Once these priorities gained the formal support of local and regional politicians (formal international cooperation agreements), implementation began by establishing more or less stable structures for the project purpose. When we compare the amount and intensity of cooperation within international development zones with the goals and intentions in this sphere formulated in VASAB documents (VASAB 2001, 26), we can conclude that these goals have been accomplished, with some minor exceptions (absence of a zone linking Estonia with Russia, and Norway with Denmark). Questions concern the permanent character of this phenomenon of sub regional integration, the extent to which it depends on external financial support, and whether it will be continued to an extent that continues to provide tangible benefits for the parties involved.

4. Conclusions

1. The Baltic Sea Region is not a functional region with regard to economic links. There are also no autonomous economic mechanisms which might lead to this.
2. Economic integration around the Baltic Sea has, however, considerable growth potential.
3. A policy of combining this potential and reducing the transaction costs of initiating Pan-Baltic cooperation is necessary. Inclusion of the eastern part of the BSR in strong Nordic and German clusters constitutes an important element of building a functional polycentricity in the Region.
4. This indicates the importance of spatial factors for the Baltic integration.
5. Among these factors, the major ones include: functional polycentricity, accessibility and cooperation within development zones.
6. Functional polycentricity is in its infancy. There is no unanimous agreement on which market mechanisms condition polycentric growth around the Baltic Sea (in the functional dimension) and how to support and promote these mechanisms. Further research is required on this topic.
7. Accessibility in the Region is poor due to past shortcomings in the development of infrastructure and physical and natural factors (climate, low density of population, geomorphologic barriers). In this situation, it seems reasonable to give priority to eliminating bottle-necks and creating channels for the flow of ideas and knowledge (ITC). This last issue is particularly important as it takes into account the strength of the Region's human capital. A real improvement of accessibility in the Region would place greater emphasis on the development of regional connections of a Baltic character.
8. The development zones are well developed, with the exception of those covering southern Poland and Belarus. Institutionalization of this kind of cooperation and its utilization in the spirit of the Lisbon Agenda for strengthening human capital in the Region is a challenge.
9. The Baltic integration, in spite of the benefits which it offers, is not an autonomous natural process arising from the free operation of market forces. It requires the support of public administrations both in the form of investment projects (infrastructure of accessibility) and lower transaction costs, i.e. creating the climate for Baltic cooperation, branding and an institutional network supporting contacts among firms, urban areas, NGOs and educational institutions. A long-

term strategy for building the Region with specific tasks at specific stages and specific goals is necessary.

References

Balerino, C. C. and Johansson, M. and VanWell, L. (2005): Polycentric Development and Territorial Cohesion in the BSR: Strategies and Priorities. Stockholm: The Swedish Institute for Growth Policy Studies, The Royal Institute of Technology in Stockholm.

Callsen, S. and Jäger-Roschko, O. (1996): Langfristige Entwicklungspotentiale für die Regionen des Ostseeraums, in: Beiträge aus dem Institut für Regionalforschung der Universität Kiel, Beitrag Nr. 22 Kiel, English summary: On potentials for long term development and policy options in the Baltic Sea region.

Cornett, A., and Iversen, S. P. (1997): The Baltic Rim in the European Trade System, in: The Nordic-Baltic Europe: Integration Risks, Barriers and Opportunities edited by J. W. Owsiński and A. Stępniak. Warszawa-Sopot, 131-164.

Cornett, A., and Iversen, S. P. (1998): The Baltic States in a European and Baltic Perspective: Trade and Transition in the Baltic Rim. http://www.geo.ut.ee/nbc/paper Paper presented at the 5th Nordic-Baltic conference in Regional Science, Global-Local Interplay in the Baltic Sea Region, Pärnu, Estonia, October 1-4, 1998. (Published on CD-proceedings, Pärnu 1998).

Cornett, A., and Snickars, F. (2002): Trade and foreign direct investments as measures of spatial integration in the Baltic Sea region, in: Geographica Polonica, 75, 33-55.

Cornett, A. (2002): Spatial Development – Regional and Global Specialization, in: Facing ESPON, Nordregio Report 2002:1 edited by C Bengs. Stockholm: Nordregio.

De Broeck, M, and Koen, R. V. (2000): The Great Contractions in Russia, the Baltics and the Other Countries of the Former Soviet Union - A View from the Supply Side. International Monetary Fund Working Paper no. 00/32.

Deike, P. (2000): Center-Periphery Dynamics in the New Europe and Their Impact on Transport Infrastructure Planning in the Baltic Sea Region. Paper presented at the International Planning History Conference in Helsinki, August 20-23, 2000: Department of Urban Planning and Policy Development Rutgers University.

Denizer, C. (1997): Stabilization, Adjustment and Growth Prospects in Transition Economies. World Bank Working Paper no. 1855.

Domański, R. (2002): Gospodarka Przestrzenna. Warszawa: PWN.

EBRD (1997): Enterprise performance and growth. Transition report. London: European Bank for Reconstruction and Development.

EBRD (2000): Annual Report 2000. London: European Bank for Reconstruction and Development.

ESPON (2004a): The role, specific situation and potential of urban areas as nodes in a polycentric development. Luxembourg-Stockholm: Project ESPON 1.1.1. Potentials for polycentric development in Europe.

ESPON (2004b): Part C: New tools and instruments for European spatial Analysis. Luxembourg: ESPON Project 3.1. Integrated Tools for European Spatial Development.

ESPON (2004c): Final Report. Luxembourg: ESPON Project 1.2.1 Transport services and networks: territorial trends and basic supply of infrastructure for territorial cohesion.

ESPON (2004d): Territorial Impact of EU Transport and TEN Policies. Luxembourg: ESPON Project 2.1.1 Territorial Impact of EU Transport and TEN Policies (2002-04).

ESPON (2005a): Amended Final Report. Luxembourg: ESPON Project 1.2.2 Telecommunication Services and Networks: Territorial Trends and Basic Supply of Infrastructure for Territorial Cohesion.

ESPON (2005b): Third Interim Report. Luxembourg: ESPON Project 3.3 Territorial Dimension of the Lisbon-Gothenburg strategy.

EU Ministerial Conference on Territorial Development (2004): Draft Conference Report.

EU working group on Spatial and Urban Development (2003): Managing the territorial dimension of EU policies after enlargement. Expert Document, (http://www.bth.se/tks/ctup.nsf/(WebFiles) /2836F1D1B9B3F5A7C1256F4A0055C89B/$FILE/esdpemlargement.pdf.

European Commission (2004): A new partnership for cohesion. Convergence competitiveness cooperation. Third report on economic and social cohesion. Luxembourg: Office for the Official Publications of the European Communities.

European Union, 2004: Decision No 884/2004/Ec Of The European Parliament And Of The Council of 29 April 2004 amending Decision No 1692/96/EC on Community guidelines for the development of the trans-European transport network, in: Official Journal of the European Union L 167/1-38.

Fabry, N. (2000): The Role of Inward FDI in the Transition Countries of Europe: An Analytical Framework. Working Paper no. WP 2000-4, Université de Marne-la-Vallée, Département Aires Culturelles et Politiques,Laboratoire GREET – ICARIE.

Fischer, S. and Sahay, R. (2000): The Transition Economies After Ten Years. International Monetary Fund Working Paper no. 00/30.

Groth, N.B. (ed.) (2001): Cities and Networking The Baltic Sea Region, in: Reports no. 8-2001. Hørsholm: Danish Centre for Forest, Landscape and Planning.

Groth, N.B. and Cornett, A. (2001): Economic Integration, in: Cities and Networking edited by N.B. Groth. The Baltic Sea Region Reports no. 8-2001. Hørsholm: Danish Centre for Forest, Landscape and Planning, 17-24.

Groth, N.B. and Bourennane, M. and Snickars, F. (2001): Industrial Networking, in: Cities and Networking edited by N.B. Groth. The Baltic Sea Region Reports no. 8-2001. Hørsholm: Danish Centre for Forest, Landscape and Planning, 25-32.

Hanell, T. and Neubauer, J. (2005): Cities of the Baltic Sea Region - Development Trends at the Turn of the Millennium, in: Nordregio Report 2005:1, Stockholm: Nordregio.

Hedegaard, L.and Lindström, B. (ed.) (2003): The NEBI Yearbook 2003. Berlin-Heidelberg: Springer.

High Level Group On The Trans-European Transport Network (2003): Report.

IMF (2004): Direction of Trade Statistics Yearbook. Washington: International Monetary Fund.

Ketels, C. and Sölvell, Ö. (2004): The State of the Region Report 2004 An Assessment of Competitiveness in the Baltic Sea Region: VINNOVA and the Baltic Development Forum (BDF).

Kisiel Łowczyc, A.B. (2000): Bałtycka integracja ekonomiczna. Stan i perspektywy do 2010r. Warszawa: PWE.

Klein, M. and Aron, C. and Hadjimichael, B. (2001): Foreign Direct Investmnent and Poverty Reduction. World Bank Working paper no.2613.

Lönnborg, M. and Olsson M. and Rafferty M. (2003): The Race for inward FDI in the Baltic States and Central and Eastern Europe. Paper presented at the 5th annual SNEE (Svenska Nätverket för Europaforskning i Ekonomi) conference on European integration, European Integration in Swedish Economic Research, Mölle, May 20-23 2003.

Orłowski, W. (1997): The Baltic Economy: Did It Exist? Does It Exist? Will It Exist?, in: European Space Baltic Space Polish Space Part One edited by A. Kukliński. Warsaw: European Institute for Regional and Local Development University of Warsaw, 71-87.

Peschel, K. (1998): Will the Baltic Sea region become an economically highly integrated area?, in: Searching and Researching the Baltic Sea Region. Proceedings from an international research seminar on Bornholm. Research Centre of Bornholm, Report 17, edited by J. Manniche. Bornholm: Research Centre of Bornholm, http://www.crt.dk/Pdf/Rep/0056.pdf, pp.31-34.

Platz, H. (ed.) (2001): Background documents for VASAB 2010 Plus Spatial Development Action Programme. Gdańsk: Vision and Strategies around the Baltic Sea 2010.

Sinn, H.W. and Weichenrieder, A. J. (1997): Foreign Direct Investment, Political Resentment and the Privatization Process in Eastern Europe. CES Working Paper. Series 129. Munich: Center for Economic Studies.

Szlachta, J. (2004): Wnioski dla Polski wynikające z raportu kohezyjnego Komisji Europejskiej: Nowe partnerstwo dla spójności. Konwergencja, konkurencyjność, współpraca. Trzeci raport na temat spójności gospodarczej i społecznej Luksemburg 2004. Warszawa: Ministerstwo Gospodarki i Pracy, ekspertyza.

UNCTAD (2002): The World Investment Report 2002. Transnational Corporations and Export Competitiveness. New York - Geneva: United Nations.

UNCTAD (2004): The World Investment Report 2004. The Shift Towards Services. New York - Geneva: United Nations.

VASAB (1994): Towards a Framework for Spatial Development In the Baltic Sea Region. Denmark: Vision and Strategies around the Baltic Sea 2010.

VASAB (2001): VASAB 2010 Plus Spatial Development Action Programme. Gdańsk: Vision and Strategies around the Baltic Sea.

VASAB (2005): Gdańsk Declaration and Policy Document Connecting Potentials Gdańsk: Vision and Strategies around the Baltic Sea, 6th Conference of Minister for Spatial Planning and Development.

Zaucha, J. (1998): *Integracja wokół Bałtyku,* in: Podstawy reformy samorządowej, edited by E. Toczyska. Gdańsk: Uniwersytet Gdański, 93-108.

Zielińska-Głębocka, A. (1996): Handel krajów uprzemysłowionych w świetle teorii handlu międzynarodowego. Gdańsk: Wydawnictwo Uniwersytetu Gdańskiego.

Cultural Factors of Competitiveness in the Baltic Sea Region (BSR)

Anna Barbara Kisiel-Łowczyc

The modern definition of competitiveness and the factors shaping it are rooted in the development of economic thought. This starts with classical economics, which identifies four factors of production – land, capital, natural resources and labour (Adam Smith, *The Wealth of Nations*, 1776) – and the theory of comparative advantage, which shows how countries should compete with one another (David Ricardo, *Principles of Political Economy and Taxation*, 1817).

Pure economic theory was broadened to include sociological elements dealing with the system of values shared by society, religion and economics in nations (Max Weber, *The Protestant Ethic and* the *Spirit of Capitalism*, 1905). At the same time, the special role of the entrepreneur in introducing innovation and technological progress – major factors of competitiveness – was acknowledged (J. Schumpeter, "Capitalism, Socialism, and Democracy," 1942).

The significance of management in shaping competitiveness (A.P. Sloan and P. Drucker) and the broad understanding of the notion "knowledge" emerged in increasingly comprehensive research in the early 1990s. In studying economic growth in the USA between 1948 and 1982, Robert Solow (e.g. 'A Contribution to the Theory of Economic Growth', 1956) demonstrated the significance of education and technological innovation for US competitiveness in the global economy. By putting the above concepts into a systemic model, Michael E. Porter built the so-called Competitiveness Diamond (*Competitive Advantage of Nations*, 1990); its composition is based on a country's economic situation, government efficiency, business efficiency and infrastructure.

Nations' international competitiveness, i.e. their ability to compete, in other words, the conditions that support the competitiveness of enterprises, develops in a complex social, political and cultural environment (Bossak and Bieńkowski 2004, 139 ff.). National competitiveness largely depends on the shape of the business environment that supports and will continue to support value generation. In fact, it is not just the factors determining current competitiveness that matter, but the quality of the business environment: the quality of the factors determining the long-term development capability.

The World Competitiveness Yearbook (WCY)[1] divides countries into four groups, according to their national competitiveness (cf. Table 1).

---

1 The World Competitiveness Yearbook (WCY) published annually since 1989 by IMD is the oldest comparative study of national competitiveness. The latest report (for 2004) covers 60 nations (OECD, NIC, emerging markets) and highly developed competitive regions of selected countries.

Table 1: Factors affecting national competitiveness

Economic performance (82 factors)	Government efficiency (77 factors)	Business efficiency (69 factors)	Infrastructure (94 factors)
Domestic economy	Public finance	Productivity	Basic infrastructure
International trade	Fiscal policy	Labour market	Technological infrastructure
International investment	Institutional framework	Finance	Scientific infrastructure
Employment	Business legislation	Management practices	Health and environment
Prices	Societal framework	Attitudes and values	Education

Source: 2004 IMD Competitiveness Yearbook, Lausanne, 2004

Fig. 1: The Competitiveness Cube

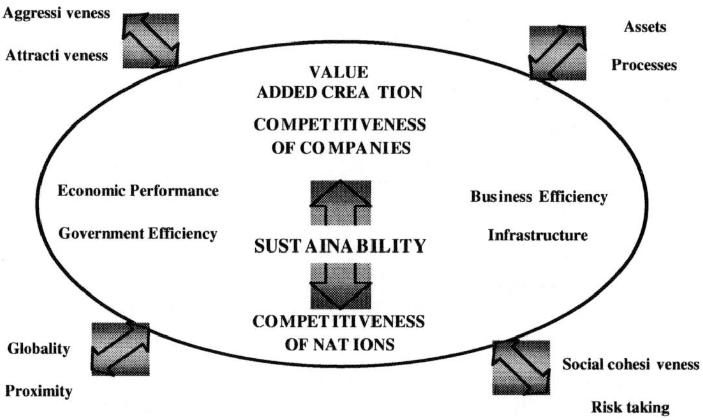

Source: IMD World Competitiveness Yearbook, 2005 Lausanne

WCY introduces a distinction between the competitiveness of supply of goods and services (the so-called aggressive competitiveness); the competitiveness of attractiveness (to investors); the competitiveness based on resources (natural and human) and the competitiveness based on organisation, economic system and broadly understood institutions (cf. the competitiveness diagram).

Knowledge of competitiveness, i.e., the ability to compete – its factors, how competitiveness should be measured and how it is affected by individual determinants – is relatively broad and is growing fast. Innovation, technological progress and science have repeatedly been shown to be major boosters of economic growth and competitiveness, and are, in turn, affected by many factors. The scale and extent of their impact is presented by the quality framework of the IMD 2004 World Competitiveness Yearbook.

The ranking of 60 national and regional economies for 2004 based on 323 criteria (competitiveness factors) is presented in Table 2. The 323 criteria have been grouped in 4 sections:

- economic performance (83 criteria / factors),
- government efficiency (77 criteria / factors),
- business efficiency (69 criteria / factors),
- infrastructure (94 criteria / factors).

Each section is broken down into five sub-sections, each with between 5 and 20 criteria. Each sub-section, irrespective of the number of criteria, has the same weight in the final score. As the whole of the environment is described by 20 sub-sections (4 sections broken down into 5 sub-sections each), the weight of each is 5 percent. This measurement allows us to determine a somewhat general competitive standing that is more comprehensive than consideration of only a narrow specialisation.

The criteria used reflect reality, institutions and business climate. Countries now compete not only in terms of goods and services, but increasingly, and increasingly effectively, in terms of systems, like education or attitudes and values. Within the four groups of competitiveness factors, subgroups may be identified which measure the role of culture (as it is defined today) and affect the business environment and management and, therefore, competitiveness.

Culture is defined as the complex of lifestyles of various social groups, relations within these groups, attitudes of their members and the values, beliefs and norms they adhere to (Fryzel 2004, 21-24). It is a specific model of development, reflected by the system of knowledge, ideology, values and laws. The evolution of corporate culture follows the functioning of the organisation because it correlates with the attitudes and behaviour of its employees. In this way it becomes an integral element of organisation and as such can be managed. Although a product of organisation itself, corporate culture is fundamental to efficient organisation and may foster structural maturity. Corporate culture is a dynamic phenomenon and an instrument consciously used by management to achieve specific objectives by stimulating certain attitudes and activities among employees.

As human capital becomes increasingly important for economic growth and competitiveness, the evolution of value systems and patterns of social behaviour correlating to competitiveness becomes more important. Evolution of value systems is sequentially correlated with national development, from complete commitment to work and common goals (as in Korea) to a stage where work remains intensive, but income becomes more relevant (e.g. in Singapore). The next stage in the evolution of value systems is growing involvement in the shaping of society (USA and Europe in the 1960s) and then greater attention to individual rather than social change (USA and Europe today). The natural evolution of attitudes from collectivistic to individualistic is a process of transformation that can be managed. Value systems in Southeast Asia today are reminiscent of nineteenth-century value systems in the USA and in Europe; the Confucian principles of hard work, loyalty, discipline and education are similar to the Protestant working ethic in Europe and the USA, which are rooted in the industrial revolution.

The different patterns of social behaviour correspond to the evolution of value systems; in contemporary Europe three systems of attitudes can be identified:

- southern European: low labour costs, limited infrastructure and parallel economy, which stimulate determination;

- northern European: the long-term pursuit of stability, consensus and regulation, which favours long-term prospects;

- Anglo-Saxon: deregulation, privatisation, flexibility of employment and higher acceptance of risk, which stimulate entrepreneurship.

The BSR is a special region, not only within the enlarged European Union, but within the global economy as well (Cf. Kisiel-Łowczyc 2000; Kisiel-Łowczyc 2004). It is a region in which the Baltic Sea has an important integrating function – nearly an EU *mare nostrum*. For centuries, the Baltic Sea uniquely affected relations between the nations around it. This includes the care of the environment of the coast and the sea itself as a source of food and wealth. Thanks to a shared Baltic identity, initiatives and institutions emerged to protect Baltic natural resources, despite artificial political and ideological divisions along the Iron Curtain (e.g. the Warsaw Convention or Helcom).

The unique nature of economic relations in the BSR and between the countries of the region is also due to the strong and lasting position of this group of countries in the world economy (cf. Table 2). BSR countries produced 9.17% of global GDP in 2004, compared with 21% for the enlarged EU. BSR accounted for 16.8% of global exports (12.6% of EU exports) and for 13.3% of global imports (12.8% of EU imports), although the BSR population was only 4.6% and 7.1% of the respective global and EU figures in 2004.

For more than a decade, economic ties between BSR countries have been growing stronger. These relationships are reflected in the trade figures. Baltic trade (trade between BSR countries) in the last decade accounted for about 40% of the foreign trade of Poland, Sweden, Finland, Norway and Denmark, 20% of Russia's trade and 10% of Germany's. This structural development is owing to both geography and the dynamic of renewed trade relations since the CEE countries began opening their economies to global economic influences. The significant economic disparities that prevailed between countries of the Baltic region in the early 1990s triggered paracomplementarity, which stimulated the development of the region as a whole.

Table 2: Basic economic indices of BSR countries in 2004

Country	GDP USD bn	GDP per capita USD bn	GDP growth %	Inflation rate %	Unemployment rate %	Exports USD bn	Imports USD bn	Population m
Global	55 500.0	8 800	4.9	-	-	8 819.0	8 754.0	6 446.2
Denmark	174.4	32 200	2.1	1.4	6.2	73.1	63.4	5.4
Finland	151.2	29 000	3.0	0.7	8.9	61.0	45.2	5.2
Germany	2 362.0	28 700	1.7	1.6	10.6	893.3	716.7	82.4
Norway	183.0	40 000	3.3	1.0	4.3	76.6	46.0	5.6
Sweden	255.4	28 400	3.6	0.7	5.6	121.7	98.0	9.0
Estonia	19.2	14 300	6.0	3.0	9.8	5.7	7.3	1.3
Lithuania	45.2	12 500	6.6	1.1	8.0	8.9	11.0	3.6
Latvia	26.5	11 500	7.6	6.0	8.8	3.6	6.0	2.3
Poland	463.0	12 000	5.6	3.4	19.5	76.0	81.6	38.6
Russia	1 408.0	9 800	6.7	11.5	8.3	162.5	92.9	143.4
Σ BSR	5 087.9	21 840*	4.62*	3.04*	9.0*	1 482.4	1 168.1	296.8
Σ EU	11 650.0	26 900*	2.4*	2.1*	9.5*	1 109.0	1 123.0	456.1

* Averages for the BSR and the EU, respectively
Source: The Global Competitiveness Report 2004-2005; World Economic Forum, Geneva, 2004

Cluster analysis, which was used to investigate the pattern of trade relations between countries around the Baltic in the last decade, demonstrates that trade ties were strongest between Germany and Poland, Estonia and Finland, and within the Nordic triangle of Denmark, Sweden and Norway (Kisiel-Łowczyc, Owsiński, and Zadrożny 2004). The BSR has been a globally significant FDI recipient and exporter; its share of global FDI flows between 1991 and 1998 averaged 7%, which rose to 12.7% after the 1995 enlargement. According to UNCTAD investment report 2004, FDI flows into and between the BSR countries picked up between 1995 and 2003. Investors from the north-western Baltic – the Danes, Finns, Swedes and Germans – are most active, while investors from Russia and Poland are less expansive and limit their activity to their neighbouring countries (Liuhto 2005). Competitiveness rankings for BSR countries, taking all 323 measurable factors into account, are presented in Table 3.

Table 3: Global competitiveness ranking of BSR countries (by 323 criteria)

year Country	2000	2001	2002	2003	2004
Poland	40	47	45	55	57
Denmark	12	15	6	5	7
Estonia	-	22	21	22	28
Finland	6	5	3	3	8
Germany	13	13	17	20	21
Norway	16	19	14	15	17
Russia	47	43	44	54	50
Sweden	14	11	12	12	11

Source: as in Table 1

The global competitive position of the BSR countries correlates positively with selected cultural sub-factors at both the macro and the micro levels that determine the countries' ex-post and ex-ante competitiveness (Table 4). This correlation is evident in the Nordic countries, in particular in systems of education and management in Finland and Denmark and in attitudes of societies in which opinions in the past were shaped by the Protestant ethic. In these respects, the new EU countries are clearly lagging.

Table 4: Global competitiveness ranking of BSR countries by selected sub-factors (2004)

Country	*Management practices*	*Attitudes and values*	*Education*
Denmark	3	14	3
Estonia	37	28	20
Finland	6	11	1
Germany	32	46	33
Norway	26	47	6
Poland	60	57	30
Russia	49	49	26
Sweden	15	24	5

Source: as in Table 1

A country's ability to compete globally strongly depends on the quality of the institutional environment of business: the rule of law and public institutions to enforce it. The institutional environment extends beyond the legal framework to include issues such as transparency, red tape, regulation and corruption. They not only mean extra costs for business but also hamper development and adversely affect competitiveness.

Tables 5 and 6 below, based mainly on surveys, assess the transparency of general economic policy and the effectiveness of government offices responsible for assisting business activity and encouraging foreign investment. The level of corruption is subjective. In Table 5, Estonia ranks relatively high (owing to its open policies), similar to earlier rankings of Nordic countries (Denmark, Finland), despite their scarcity of classically defined production factors. This can be attributed not only to systemic conditions, but also to human capital in the broad sense, which directly and indirectly affect a country's competitiveness.

Table 5: Selected institutional competitiveness factors of policies towards business in BSR countries (2004); Source as in table 1

Country	Transparency Rank	Transparency Weight	Red tape Rank	Red tape Weight	Corruption Rank	Corruption Weight
Finland	(1)	7.66	(3)	6.09	(1)	9.38
Denmark	(2)	7.63	(1)	6.41	(2)	9.12
Norway	(5)	7.02	(13)	4.56	(9)	7.48
Sweden	(15)	6.21	(8)	4.85	(10)	7.47
Estonia	(17)	5.96	(9)	4.84	(29)	4.96
Germany	(42)	4.16	(43)	2.10	(19)	6.38
Russia	(50)	3.55	(50)	1.85	(52)	1.45
Poland	(59)	2.21	(57)	1.42	(53)	1.39

Source: As in table 1.

Table 6: Societal framework and competitiveness of BSR countries (2004)

Country	Labour legislation Rank	Labour legislation Weight	Social cohesion Rank	Social cohesion Weight	Discrimination (race, gender) Rank	Discrimination (race, gender) Weight
Denmark	(1)	7.79	(5)	8.21	(23)	6.76
Estonia	(11)	6.29	(55)	4.25	(9)	7.60
Finland	(20)	5.32	(2)	8.49	(9)	7.60
Russia	(23)	5.05	(57)	4.00	(56)	5.03
Norway	(27)	4.70	(7)	8.15	(21)	6.78
Sweden	(33)	4.03	(14)	7.31	(38)	6.14
Poland	(52)	2.64	(59)	2.88	(52)	5.33
Germany	(60)	1.88	(12)	7.42	(8)	7.62

Source: As in table 1.

Differences in attitudes and values and in patterns of behaviour translated into attitudes to work, cooperation, rivalry and motivation, apply to both employers and employees (Tables 7 and 8).

Table 7: Attitudes and values towards competitiveness in BSR (2004)

Country	Management credibility Rank	Weight	Social responsibility of business leaders Rank	Weight	Social support for competitiveness Rank	Weight	Recognition of need for social and economic change Rank	Weight
Finland	(1)	7.85	(8)	6.78	(9)	7.38	(16)	6.52
Denmark	(2)	7.55	(2)	7.69	(21)	6.36	(26)	6.24
Norway	(25)	6.30	(4)	7.15	(52)	4.72	(40)	5.55
Sweden	(34)	6.00	(5)	7.10	(38)	5.62	(34)	5.80
Germany	(40)	5.69	(29)	5.78	(49)	5.03	(43)	5.38
Estonia	(43)	5.60	(45)	4.76	(27)	6.15	(22)	6.36
Russia	(47)	5.32	(58)	3.48	(44)	5.35	(11)	6.85
Poland	(60)	4.00	(59)	3.42	(57)	4.52	(58)	3.94

Source: as in Table 1

Table 8: Competitiveness by selected management practice sub-factors in BSR countries (2004)

Country	Staff motivation Rank	Weight	Market change responsiveness Rank	Weight	Business ethic Rank	Weight
Denmark	(2)	7.83	(10)	7.38	(5)	7.81
Finland	(5)	7.63	(9)	7.45	(3)	7.97
Sweden	(16)	6.68	(8)	7.46	(9)	7.46
Norway	(26)	6.33	(37)	5.85	(6)	7.67
Germany	(33)	5.90	(44)	5.45	(17)	7.01
Estonia	(34)	5.89	(30)	6.18	(47)	5.13
Russia	(47)	4.97	(55)	4.69	(49)	4.82
Poland	(57)	4.09	(58)	4.61	(59)	3.67

Source: as in Table 1

The approval of the activities of business leaders in Nordic countries (in terms of employer–employee relations, ethics and adaptability to change, especially market change) is an example of positive interaction in establishing the competitive position of nations characterised by an open market economy and a traditional model of attitudes and values. As far as general economic attitudes and values are concerned (e.g. recognition of the need for change or support for measures aimed at improved competitiveness), BSR nations do not differ much from one another. This is probably a function of their interactions.

The empirical material presented above indicates that, despite economic globalisation, differences in the disposition and behaviour of societies (people in their capacity as consultant, employee, investor or employer) still have a significant impact on national competitiveness. This impact correlates with the growing importance of human capital in every activity, not only business.

References

Antola E. (2005). One Voice for the Baltic Sea Region in the EU?, in "Baltinfo Newsletter", May 2005.
Bossak J.W., Bieńkowski W. (2003). Konkurencyjność gospodarki Polski w dobie integracji z Unią Europejską i globalizacji (Competitiveness of Poland's economy during its EU integration and globalisation), SGH, Warsaw.
Bossak J.W., Bieńkowski W. (2004). Międzynarodowa zdolność konkurencyjna kraju i przedsiębiorstw. Wyzwania dla Polski na progu XXI wieku (International competitive ability of nations and businesses. Challengers for Poland at the onset of 21st century) SGH, Warsaw.
Fryzeł B. (2004). Kultura a konkurencyjność przedsiębiorstwa (Culture and business competitiveness), Toruń.
The Global Competitiveness Report 2004–2005, World Economic Forum, Geneva 2004.
IMD Competitiveness Yearbook, Lausanne 2004.
Kisiel-Łowczyc A. B. (2000). Bałtycka integracja ekonomiczna. Stan i perspektywy do r. 2010 (Baltic economic integration – the present and prospects till 2010), PWE, Warsaw.
Kisiel-Łowczyc A. B. (2004). Poland's competitiveness and Finnish-Polish economic relations, in Jan W. Owsiński (ed.), MODEST 2004: Integration, Trade, Innovation & Finance: From Continental to Local Perspectives, Warsaw, 73-83.
Kisiel-Łowczyc A. B., Owsiński J. W., Zadrożny S. (2004). Baltic Rim – The information technology region? Paper presented at the Fifty-seventh International Atlantic Economic Conference, Lisbon, March 2004.
Liuhto K. (2005). A Common Baltic Sea Investment Agency could attract new capital into the region, in "Baltic Rim Economies", 28 April 2005.
UNCTAD (2004). World Investment Report 2004, Geneva.
Ziemiecki J., Żukrowska K. (2004). Konkurencja a transformacja w Polsce. Wybrane aspekty polityki gospodarczej (Competition and transition in Poland. Selected aspects of economic policies), SGH, Warsaw.

Latvia and the Baltic Sea Region: The Historical Context of Trade and Investment

Viesturs Pauls Karnups

1. Introduction

This paper examines the historical roots of foreign trade with and investment in Latvia and analyses foreign trade and investment during the interwar period and the period after the restoration of independence.

'Trade' within the context of this paper refers to merchandise exports and imports, while 'investment' refers to foreign investment stock, i.e. investments made by non-residents as direct and portfolio investment in the company capital of Latvian enterprises. The trade statistics analysis for the interwar period has been limited to the period 1925-1939 to coincide with available data on interwar investment.

During the interwar period Latvia was a successful exporter of agricultural products to industrialised Western Europe. Despite external constraints to trade, Latvia's trade pattern reflected inter-industry specialisation along the lines of classic comparative advantage. Latvia exchanged food and natural resources such as wood and wood products for manufactures such as consumer goods and machinery with Western Europe. Regional trade in the interwar period, however, was limited due to the similarity of exports (except to Germany and to a limited extent Sweden). Nevertheless, regional trade was important to the manufacturing sector of the Latvian economy: in 1937, some 20% of the total value of Latvia's industrial production was exported (*Latvian Economist*, 1938, 93).

In the broader context, since Latvia regained independence in 1991 there have been a number of studies of Latvia's reintegration into the Baltic Sea Region and European trade as a whole utilising the analytical framework known as the "gravity model" to evaluate the current trade patterns of the Baltic States, including Latvia (e.g. Byers et al. 2000; Cornett and Iversen 1998; Lasser and Schrader 2002).

The gravity model attempts to explain trade between two market economies in terms of the distance between them, their population and their income levels. In the context of this article the work by Eichengreen and Irwin (Eichengreen and Irwin 1996) and, in particular, Lasser and Schrader (2002) are of relevance. Eichengreen and Irwin made the point that history plays a role in shaping the direction of international trade, or, put another way, "past trade patterns influence current trade flows in a way that a passing historical event causes lasting cost reductions" (Eichengreen and Irwin 1996, 5). Within the gravity model framework, Eichengreen and Irwin found that historical factors, which are associated with the reduced costs of market entry and exit, exercise an important influence on trade flows.

Thus, history matters. Moreover, in their recent (2002) paper, Lasser and Schrader have provided some historical data within a gravity model framework on Baltic regional trade patterns and have attempted to integrate the ideas of Eichengreen and Irwin into the analysis (Lasser and Schrader 2002, 5). They suggest that "history may play a special role for current Baltic trade relations", and that "the changes in regional trade patterns following [the regaining of] independence show parallels to the development of Baltic trade after World War I" (ibid., 12-13). Indeed, the results of their analysis show that the process of EU association was not reflected in the regression analysis, but that in fact "the process of European integration mainly runs [for the Baltic States] via their Baltic Rim neighbours" and, thus, "in this respect EU integration means reintegration into regional markets to which a historical affinity exists" (ibid., 44-45). Certainly, for Latvia, trade with the countries of the Baltic Sea region has been of paramount importance in the period after the restoration of independence.

2. Latvia as an entrepôt prior to WWI

In the second half of the nineteenth century the importance of Latvia's larger ports in the foreign trade of the Russian Empire grew rapidly. By 1913, Rīga was the largest trading port in the empire with total exports and imports of some 405 million roubles (Skujenieks 1927, 663). Latvia had three main ports: Rīga, Liepāja and Ventspils. In 1913, 28.2% of total exports and 20.6% of total imports of the empire went through these three ports (ibid., 677). Although they mainly handled exports, Rīga and Liepāja also received a large import trade, due to their rapid industrialisation at this time.

Table 1: Imports and Exports from Latvian Ports prior to WWI (million roubles)

	Rīga		Liepāja		Ventspils	
	Exports	Imports	Exports	Imports	Exports	Imports
1911	186.8	147.3	61.4	31.9	22.3	24.4
1912	224.8	145.9	72.0	32.1	19.4	28.1
1913	226.3	178.6	48.6	33.6	23.4	18.8

Source: Skujenieks, M., *Latvija: Zeme un iedzīvotāji* (Latvia: Land and People) 1927, 663-665

The main exports were flax, hides, butter, timber, eggs and grain. The main imports were industrial and agricultural machinery, rubber and raw cotton, coal and herring. Foreign trade through the ports was mainly with Great Britain, Germany, Belgium, France, USA, the Netherlands and Denmark.

Of course, much of the trade was for the rest of the empire, rather than for the territory of Latvia itself. Thus, in this sense the ports were also transit ports. It was only after it gained independence that Latvia became an importing and exporting nation in its own right.

3. Latvian foreign trade 1925-1939

Latvia's foreign trade in the 1920s was based in large measure on a system of commercial and trade treaties. By 1929, Latvia had concluded commercial treaties with all major European states, including its two most important trading partners – Great Britain (22 June 1923) and Germany (28 June 1926), as well as with its regional neighbours Norway (14 August 1924), Finland (23 August 1924), Denmark (3 November 1924), Sweden (22 December 1924), Russia (USSR) (2 June 1927) and Poland (12 February 1929). Latvia concluded a provisional commercial agreement with Estonia in 1928, and a commercial agreement between Latvia and Lithuania was concluded in 1930.[1] They provided the regulatory framework for Latvia's obligations in its foreign trade relations with its main and regional trading partners, at least until 1930.

Table 2: Latvian Exports to its Regional Trading Partners 1925-1939

Selected years	Germany (1000 lats)	% of total exports	Nordic countries[1] (1000 lats)	% of total exports	Baltic States[2] (1000 lats)	% of total exports
1925	40636	22.6	7543	4.3	10591	5.9
1926	45837	24.3	7189	3.9	9016	4.8
1929	72442	26.5	9738	3.5	10546	3.9
1932	25287	26.2	2510	2.7	5462	5.7
1934	25185	29.5	4235	5.0	3520	4.2
1936	42665	30.8	8487	6.2	3669	2.7
1937	92374	35.1	10500	4.1	4080	1.6
1938	76001	33.5	8258	3.6	3709	1.6
1939	82949	36.5	15956	7.5	2537	1.2
Av. % of total exports for 1925-1939		28.7		4.3		3.8

Notes: [1] Finland, Denmark, Sweden, Norway; [2] Estonia, Lithuania

---

1 Prior to this, Latvian-Lithuanian trade was governed by a special law granting most-favoured-nation treatment to Lithuanian imports.

Table 2 (continued): Latvian Exports to its Regional Trading Partners 1925-1939

Selected years	Poland (1000 lats)	% of total exports	Russia (USSR) (1000 lats)	% of total exports
1925	3903	2.2	7519	4.2
1926	3367	1.8	10240	5.4
1929	3771	1.4	40079	14.6
1932	1174	1.2	14222	14.7
1934	347	0.4	1913	2.2
1936	686	0.5	4140	3.0
1937	800	0.3	6645	2.6
1938	609	0.3	7634	3.4
1939	261	0.1	11588	5.1
Av. % of total exports for 1925-1939		1.2		7.0

Source: *Latvijas Statistiskā gada grāmata. 1925-1939* (Latvian Statistical Yearbooks 1925-1939), Rīga: Valsts Statistiskā Pārvalde; *Strukturbericht über das Ostland. Teil I: Ostland in Zahlen,* Rīga: Reichskommissar für das Ostland, 1942: 57; and *Historisk Statistikk 1968,* Oslo: Statistisk Sentralbyrå, 1969: 325.

With the onset of the Great Depression in Latvia in 1930, the country, following the lead of the rest of Europe, did all it could to reduce imports and halt the outflow of foreign currency, including establishing a currency commission and imposing import credit restrictions, suspending the gold standard with respect to the lat (while retaining the gold parity), establishing a contingent (quota) system for imports, increasing import duties and promoting import-substitution. The most successful import-substitution was in the area of cereals and animal fodder imports, which by 1933 had almost disappeared as an import item.

In 1932, Latvia signed a so-called bilateral "clearing" agreement with Germany. The basic idea behind bilateral clearing agreements was to even out or "balance" trade between two countries, while at the same time conserving scarce foreign currency and gold reserves. In 1935, Latvia also signed clearing agreements with Sweden, Lithuania, Estonia and Russia (USSR). Poland, Finland, Denmark and Norway remained 'hard currency' countries and as a result trade with these countries actually declined. On the other hand, although the United Kingdom was also a "hard currency" country, after the signing of a new trade agreement in 1934 exports to Britain increased almost every year until the outbreak of the Second World War.

Latvian exports to its regional trading partners in the period 1925-1939 (Table 2) were dominated by Germany with an average share of total exports for the period of 28.7%, while the average for the Nordic countries together was only 4.3% of total exports, Poland 1.2%, the other Baltic States (Estonia and Lithuania) 3.8% and Russia (USSR) 7%. As can be seen from Table 2 above, the trade agreements and bilateral clearing agreements signed during this period had only a small effect on Latvian exports to its main trading partners, except for exports to Russia (USSR) during the life of the 1927-1932 trade agreement.[2]

Latvia's main exports to Germany were butter, pigs, seeds, timber materials, plywood, flax yarn and flax.

Latvian imports from its regional trading partners in the period 1925-1939 (Table 3) were dominated by Germany with an average share of total imports for the period of 36.6%, the Nordic countries together accounted for 6.7%, the Baltic States 4% and the USSR 5.2%. By comparison, in 1938 only 19.3% of all Latvian imports came from Great Britain. Again, as can be seen from Table 3 below, the trade agreements and bilateral clearing agreements signed during this period had only a small effect on Latvian imports from its regional trading partners.

Table 3: Latvian Imports from its Regional Trading Partners 1925-1939

Selected years	Germany (1000 lats)	% of total imports	Nordic countries[1] (1000 lats)	% of total imports	Baltic States[2] (1000 lats)	% of total imports
1925	116319	41.5	28487	10.2	18482	6.5
1926	103886	40.0	28659	11.0	15883	6.1
1929	149177	41.2	19856	5.6	17077	4.7
1932	30140	35.6	3769	4.4	2696	3.2
1934	23206	24.5	3958	4.2	5429	5.3
1936	46785	38.4	7057	5.8	2870	2.4
1937	62595	27.1	16688	7.2	3179	1.3
1938	88659	39.0	11599	5.0	4574	2.0
1939	100318	44.7	13081	6.2	3348	1.5
Av. % of total imports for 1925-1939		36.6		6.7		4.0

Notes: [1] Finland, Denmark, Sweden, Norway; [2] Estonia, Lithuania

---

2   Latvia concluded a particularly advantageous trade agreement with Russia (USSR) in 1927, in terms of which Russia (USSR) would import from Latvia some Ls 40 million of mainly manufactured goods annually. This provided a short-lived stimulus to Latvia's industrial sector and delayed the onset of the effects of the Great Depression by one year. When the agreement expired in 1932, it was not renewed and Latvia's trade with Russia (USSR) returned to the previous low levels.

Table 3 (continued): Latvian Imports from its Regional Trading Partners 1925-1939

Selected years	Poland (1000 lats)	% of total imports	Russia (USSR) (1000 lats)	% of total imports
1925	10262	3.7	10638	3.8
1926	16381	6.3	11703	4.5
1929	33158	9.2	17022	4.7
1932	5063	6.0	8506	10.1
1934	3802	4.0	2767	2.9
1936	1928	1.6	3558	2.9
1937	4559	2.0	8679	3.8
1938	3282	1.4	8382	3.7
1939	1693	0.8	14213	6.3
Av. % of total imports for 1925-1939		4.8		5.2

Source: *Latvijas Statistiskā gada grāmata. 1925-1939* [Latvian Statistical Yearbooks 1925-1939], Rīga: Valsts Statistiskā Pārvalde; *Strukturbericht über das Ostland. Teil I: Ostland in Zahlen,* Rīga: Reichskommissar für das Ostland, 1942: 58; and *Historisk Statistikk 1968,* Oslo: Statistisk Sentralbyrå, 1969: 325.

Latvia's main imports from Germany were industrial machinery and motors, wool yarn, dyes and dyestuffs, pig iron, various kinds of tin, coal and coke, sulphate ammoniac, textiles, artificial silk thread and pipes for various industrial purposes.

Taking both tables together, it is striking that, apart from Germany, Latvia's trade with its regional neighbours was relatively marginal. Only an average of 16.3% of Latvia's export trade went to its other regional trading partners, and only 20.7% of Latvia's imports came from them. Imports and exports from Poland, other Baltic States and Russia (USSR) in fact declined in the 1930s. In general, Britain and Germany dominated Latvia's foreign trade throughout the interwar period.[3] Other important export partners were Belgium, the Netherlands and the USA. Latvia's exports to her regional neighbours (except for Germany) were small and negligible compared to Britain and Germany: in 1937, total exports to Estonia, Lithuania, Poland, Denmark, Sweden, Norway, Finland and Russia (USSR) were only 8.6% of all exports (*Latvijas ārējā tirdzniecība un tranzits* 1937, 1938: X-XI). Exports to Germany and Great Britain in 1937 made up 73.5% of all exports. In 1937, some 48% of all imports came from Great Britain and Germany, while imports from regional neighbours (except for Germany) made up 12.6% of all imports (*Latvijas*

---

3   This was of course due to the operation of the "triangle of trade", where Latvia sold more to Britain than it purchased from it and used the surplus to purchase manufactured goods from Germany (Hiden and Salmon 1991, 86).

ārējā tirdzniecība un tranzits 1937, 1938: X-XI). Thus, Latvia's near neighbours were more significant as sources imports than destinations for exports. Other important countries for imports were Belgium and the Netherlands.

In 1937 Latvia exported mainly raw materials, and agricultural and forestry products to industrialised or industrialising countries such as Germany, Great Britain, Sweden, Denmark, Norway, Finland and Russia; to other agricultural countries and countries that exported similar products (such as Poland and the other Baltic States) Latvia exported mainly manufactured goods. However, the manufacturing sector in Latvia was small (in 1926 19.7% of total exports, which increased (thanks to the trade treaty with Russia (USSR)) to 30% of total exports in 1929, but fell again to 18.2% of total exports in 1938 (Zālīte 1999, 84). Nevertheless, the regional trading partners were also important for many individual sectors of the Latvian economy (see Karnups 2004, 245-246).

4. Foreign investment in Latvia 1925-1939

Even before the end of the Latvian War of Independence against Soviet Russia, foreign companies had established branches in Latvia. For example, in 1919, some Scandinavian trading houses established branches in Rīga, Liepāja and Ventspils and a lively trade was maintained through the establishment of steamship lines between Scandinavia and Latvia (*Economist*, 1920, No.1, 13). Many investors hoped to use Latvia as a base from which they would be able to expand into the huge Russian market. These hopes were not fulfilled and soon the branches closed. Foreign capital started to flow into Latvia on a larger scale after the stabilisation of the lat in 1922.

Foreign capital was invested mainly in banking, industry, transport and trade. By 1927, over 60% of the equity capital of all Latvian joint-stock banks[4] was foreign owned, while foreign capital comprised 27.8% of aggregate capital in insurance, 33.9% in trade, 63.1% in transport and about 50% in industry (*The Latvian Economist* 1928, 24). Up until the beginning of the Great Depression the largest investor was Germany, closely followed by Great Britain and the Nordic countries.

As can be seen in Table 4, German capital in 1927 was invested mainly in the textile industry, chemical industry, metallurgy, timber and paper industry and commerce, in particular, banking. For the Nordic countries, the main field of investment was the chemical industry,[5] followed by trade and banking, while for the other Baltic States the main area of investment was the paper industry,[6] followed by the chemical

---

[4] For a brief overview of banking in Latvia in the interwar period see Hiden, J., On Banks and Economic Trends in Latvia 1918-1940, in Falk, P. & Krantz, O. (eds), *Transformation and Integration in the Baltic Sea Area*, Umeå: Umeå University 2000, 133-149.
[5] That is, mainly Danish capital investments in the margarine industry.
[6] That is, mainly Estonia capital investment.

industry and textile industry. Polish capital in 1927 was mainly invested in the chemical and textile industries, food, trade and real property.

Like many other European countries, Latvia also introduced exchange controls in the wake of the stock market collapse and later, the 1931 British devaluation of the pound, in an attempt to prevent capital flight. Whilst suspending the operation of the gold standard, Latvia maintained nominal gold parity for the lat. Foreign investment from Latvia's main and regional trading partners increased over the period until the 1934 coup d'état.

The nationalistic Ulmanis regime began to systematically reduce the amount of foreign investment. Foreign investment in all Latvian enterprises fell from 50.4% in 1934 to 25.4% in 1939; in industry it fell from 52.4% in 1934 to 31.9% in 1939, in commerce from 35.9% to 28.2% and in finance and banking from 62.4% to 9.7% (*Finanču un kredita statistika* 1939, 172). Nevertheless, with the exception of Russia (USSR) (whose investments fell dramatically in 1936 with the liquidation of the *Kooperatīvā transitbanka* [Co-operative Transit Bank], a bank wholly owned by Russian (USSR) interests, including the Moscow Narodnyi Bank), the reduction in most foreign investments was gradual, and in the case of the Nordic countries even increased slightly in this period, due mainly to Swedish investment in the building of the Ķegums hydro-electricity station on the Daugava River. German capital investment also increased slightly overall. Russia, the Baltic States and the Nordic countries were pushed out of the banking industry and Germany out of the metallurgy industry in this period.

Table 4: Foreign Capital of Latvia's Regional Trading Partners in Latvian Joint-stock Companies in 1927 and 1939 by Main Sectors of Investment

Main foreign investment sectors	Germany 1927	Germany 1939	Poland 1927	Poland 1939	Russia (USSR) 1927	Russia (USSR) 1939
Ceramics	39	185	0	192	27	64
Metallurgy	2158	102	0	0	0	0
Chemical	1879	2308	356	113	0	0
Textile	1976	2837	316	103	0	63
Timber	1045	509	0	5	0	12
Paper	335	834	0	0	0	0
Foodstuffs etc.	295	237	250	496	0	118
Trade	750	1696	193	150	133	43
Real Property	253	398	115	0	0	0
Transport	173	76	0	0	0	0
Banks	2000	2862	0	0	2000	1
Total	10903	12044	1230	1059	2160	301

Table 4 (continued): Foreign Capital of Latvia's Regional Trading Partners in Latvian Joint-stock Companies in 1927 and 1939 by Main Sectors of Investment

Main foreign investment sectors	Baltic States[1] 1927	Baltic States[1] 1939	Nordic countries[2] 1927	Nordic countries[2] 1939
Ceramics	0	0	0	320
Metallurgy	50	50	374	216
Chemical	925	117	6672	5925
Textile	726	1383	0	50
Timber	75	51	377	1593
Paper	1560	237	0	0
Foodstuffs etc.	94	1	345	1
Trade	620	122	619	832
Real Property	456	17	165	1540
Transport	490	75	76	5
Banks	244	3	855	5
Total	5240	2056	9483	10487

Notes: [1] Finland, Denmark, Sweden, Norway; [2] Estonia, Lithuania

Source: *Latvijas Statistiskā gada grāmata. 1927-1939* (Latvian Statistical Yearbooks 1927-1939), Rīga: Valsts Statistiskā Pārvalde; *The Latvian Economist,* 1928: 26; and *Statistikas tabulas,* 1940: 170.

German capital in 1939 was invested mainly in the textile industry, chemical industry, metallurgy, trade and banking. For the Nordic countries, the main area of investment was the chemical industry,[7] followed by timber and real property, while for the other Baltic States the main area of investment was the textile industry.[8] Polish capital in 1939 was invested mainly in the food, chemical and textile industries and trade.

7   That is, mainly Swedish capital investment in the match industry.
8   That is, mainly Estonia capital investment.

Fig. 1: Foreign Capital of Latvia's Regional Trading Partners in Latvian Joint-stock Companies in 1927 and 1939 by Main Sectors of Investment (% of total investment)

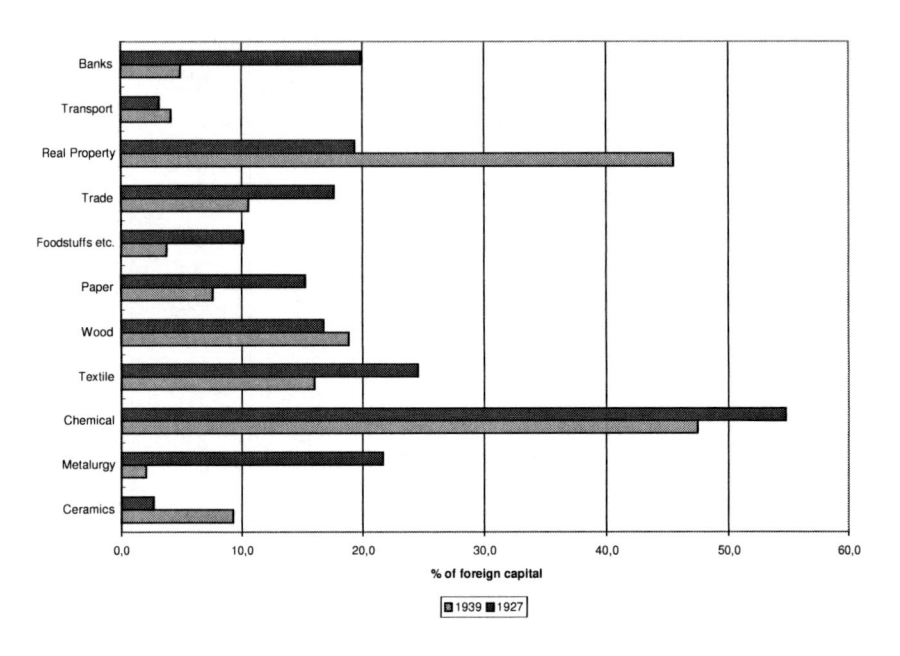

Table 5: Foreign Investment of Latvia's Regional Trading Partners in Latvian Enterprises (as at 1 January) 1925-1939

Selected years	Germany (1000 lats)	Germany % of total investment	Nordic countries[1] (1000 lats)	Nordic countries[1] % of total investment	Baltic States[2] (1000 lats)	Baltic States[2] % of total investment
1925	5828	10.4	7629	13.6	3752	6.7
1926	9509	12.8	9144	12.3	4922	6.6
1929	18124	19.2	12443	13.2	6333	6.7
1932	27110	27.7	14525	14.9	7860	8.0
1934	23045	25.7	14190	15.8	7958	8.9
1936	19324	26.9	14587	20.3	5540	7.7
1937	13895	21.7	14055	21.9	5176	8.1
1938	12194	19.9	13072	21.3	2717	4.4
1939	13395	22.3	11110	18.5	2515	4.2
Av. % of total investment for 1925-1939		21.1		15.4		7.0

Notes: [1] Finland, Denmark, Sweden, Norway; [2] Estonia, Lithuania

Table 5 (continued): Foreign Investment of Latvia's Regional Trading Partners in Latvian Enterprises (as at 1 January) 1925-1939

Selected years	Poland		Russia (USSR)	
	(1000 lats)	% of total investment	(1000 lats)	% of total investment
1925	471	0.8	1054	1.9
1926	1163	1.6	2166	2.9
1929	1527	1.6	2869	3
1932	1685	1.7	4153	4.3
1934	1555	1.7	3553	4
1936	1024	1.4	427	0.6
1937	909	1.4	394	0.6
1938	696	1.1	381	0.6
1939	1075	1.8	305	0.5
Av. % of total investment for 1925-1939		1.5		2.6

Source: *Latvijas Statistiskā gada grāmata. 1929, 1939* (Latvian Statistical Yearbooks 1929,1939), Rīga: Valsts Statistiskā Pārvalde; Statistikas tabulas (Statistical Tables), Rīga: Latvijas PSR Tautsaimniecības Statistikas pārvalde, 1940.

As can be seen in Table 5, foreign investment in Latvian enterprises by most of Latvia's regional trading partners continued to increase throughout most of the interwar years, despite the effects of the Great Depression. The main exceptions were the other Baltic States and Russia.

After the occupation of Latvia and the other Baltic States by Russia (USSR) in 1940, the Nordic countries (particularly Sweden, Denmark and Norway) applied to Russia (USSR) for compensation for their nationalised investments. For different reasons the other Baltic States, Germany and Poland were not in a position to ask for compensation from Russia (USSR) at this time.

In relation to Swedish investment, in May 1941 the Swedish and Soviet governments signed a treaty on mutual economic claims regarding the Baltic States, including Latvia. The final official calculation of Swedish economic assets in Latvia as presented to the USSR by the Swedish Foreign Office was SEK 38.1 million. Of the companies named by the Swedish Foreign Office, Swedish Match was involved in the chemical industry (matches) and wood industry (matchsticks), Svenska Entreprenad AB (Ķegums HES), Wingårdh in the chemical industry (super phosphate), Skånska Cement in the construction industry (cement), Wicander in the chemical industry (linoleum) and AGA in the chemical industry (gas and gas equipment).

The Danes also presented a claim for compensation for former Danish assets in the Baltic States, some DKK 16.5 million for nationalisations and DKK 2.5 million in commercial claims. The official calculation of Danish economic assets in Latvia as presented to the USSR came to DKK 3.5 million. In addition, there was a claim from Vacuum Oil Co. Ltd., for branches in Rīga and Tallinn (DKK 0.7 million). The company Aarhus Oliemølle Ltd partly owned a vegetable oil factory in Liepāja, a Mr. Haagensen had a business and property in Latvia and a Mr. Klingenberg had a factory in Rīga.

Compensation claims from Sweden in respect of nationalised assets in the Baltic States were basically settled by Russia (USSR) in 1946, but commercial claims only in 1964. Sweden received only some SEK 11 million from Russia (USSR) for the nationalised assets and SEK 60 000 for commercial claims (Kangeris 1998, 208-209). Denmark received DKK 2.6 million from Russia (USSR) in 1964 as settlement of all claims, and even Norway received NOK 500,000 from Russia (USSR) in compensation for lost assets in the Baltic States in 1959 (Kyn 1998, 233-234).

5. Latvian foreign trade 1992-2005

After the restoration of independence in 1991, Latvia faced the same task as in 1920: to re-integrate into the European economy and, in particular, restore trading links with the countries of the Baltic Sea Region.

Table 6: Latvian Exports to Latvia's Regional Trading Partners 1992-2005

Selected years	Germany		Nordic countries[1]		Baltic States[2]	
	(1000 lats)	% of total exports	(1000 lats)	% of total exports	(1000 lats)	% of total exports
1992	45492	7.9	70333	12.2	28268	4.9
1993	44548	6.3	65362	9.3	41930	6.0
1994	58271	10.5	63650	11.5	45054	8.1
1995	93662	13.6	112004	16.3	59577	8.7
1996	109575	13.8	105388	13.3	88235	11.1
1997	133793	13.8	139073	14.3	113560	11.7
1998	166822	15.6	195657	18.3	127851	12.0
1999	169984	16.9	196570	19.5	123101	12.2
2000	194288	17.2	219514	19.4	145825	12.9

p.t.o.

Table 6: Continued

Selected years	Germany (1000 lats)	Germany % of total exports	Nordic countries[1] (1000 lats)	Nordic countries[1] % of total exports	Baltic States[2] (1000 lats)	Baltic States[2] % of total exports
2001	209501	16.7	239090	19.0	174058	13.9
2002	218269	15.5	285081	20.2	202203	14.4
2003	245313	14.9	349616	15.8	243596	10.5
2004	267472	12.4	440544	20,4	383733	17.9
2005	294500	10.3	533605	18,6	620800	21.6
Av. % of total exports for 1992-2005		13.2		16.7		12.1

Notes: [1] Finland, Denmark, Sweden, Norway; [2] Estonia, Lithuania

Selected years	Poland (1000 lats)	Poland % of total exports	Russia (USSR) (1000 lats)	Russia (USSR) % of total exports
1992	12923	2.2	148737	25.8
1993	19960	2.8	200105	28.5
1994	8988	1.6	155719	28.1
1995	17191	2.5	174386	25.3
1996	10962	1.4	181603	22.8
1997	11789	1.2	203587	21.0
1998	18836	1.8	129007	12.1
1999	17887	1.8	66412	6.6
2000	18204	1.6	47266	4.2
2001	24102	1.9	73506	5.9
2002	22034	1.6	82546	5.9
2003	24565	1.5	88797	5.4
2004	79597	3.7	137467	6.4
2005	151510	5.3	228336	8.0
Av. % of total exports for 1992-2005		2.2		14.7

Source: Latvijas statistikas gadagrāmata. 1993-2002. Rīga: LR Centrālā statistikas pārvalde and Rīga: LR Centrālā statistikas pārvalde; Latvijas ārējā tirdzniecība. Ceturkšņa biļetens (2004) (Foreign Trade of Latvia. Quarterly Bulletin) #4, 2003, Rīga: Latvijas Republikas Centrālā statistikas pārvalde and Latvijas statistikas ikmēneša biļetens (Monthly Bulletin of Latvian Statistics), 2006, No.1, Rīga: LR Centrālā statistikas pārvalde.

In the period 1992-2005, Latvian exports to the countries of the Baltic Sea Region (Table 6) have become more 'multi-polar', that is, unlike the interwar period, when Germany alone dominated, today other countries of the Baltic Sea Region have also become important, in particular the Baltic States, the Nordic countries and Russia. Germany had an average share of total exports for the period of only 13.2%, while the average for the Nordic countries together was 16.7%, the Baltic States (Estonia and Lithuania) 12.1%, Poland 2.2% and Russia 14.7%, i.e. an average share for the countries of the Baltic Sea Region as whole of 58.9% of total exports, an increase of some 23.6% over the comparative figure for the interwar period.

Table 7: Latvian Imports from its Regional Trading Partners 1992-2005

Selected years	Germany (1000 lats)	% of total imports	Nordic countries[1] (1000 lats)	% of total imports	Baltic States[2] (1000 lats)	% of total imports
1992	81176	14.9	39270	7.3	51695	9.5
1993	63679	9.8	73363	11.3	86477	13.4
1994	94011	13.5	123359	18.0	65655	9.4
1995	147825	15.4	212094	23.2	101753	10.7
1996	176880	13.8	286167	23.7	153444	12.0
1997	253201	16.0	353849	22.4	195479	12.4
1998	315547	16.8	414319	22.0	243345	12.9
1999	261297	15.2	378341	21.9	236570	13.7
2000	302601	15.7	388898	20.1	266975	13.8
2001	374863	17.0	429116	19.5	325497	14.8
2002	429459	17.2	475821	19.1	399672	16.0
2003	479788	16.1	548778	18.4	481448	16.1
2004	556884	14.5	640735	16.8	748898	19.7
2005	669262	13.8	729178	15.0	1043452	21.6
Av. % of total imports for 1992-2005		15.0		18.5		14.0

Notes: [1] Finland, Denmark, Sweden, Norway; [2] Estonia, Lithuania

Table 7 (continued): Latvian Imports from its Regional Trading Partners 1992-2005

Selected years	Poland (1000 lats)	% of total imports	Russia (USSR) (1000 lats)	% of total imports
1992	6774	1.3	150825	27.8
1993	6254	1.0	181941	28.1
1994	11115	1.6	164178	23.6
1995	18234	1.9	208335	21.7
1996	32772	2.1	258416	20.2
1997	50781	2.7	246946	15.6
1998	66212	3.8	221290	11.8
1999	75587	4.4	180971	10.5
2000	91900	4.8	224459	11.6
2001	110210	5.0	202152	9.2
2002	125763	5.0	218750	8.8
2003	152702	5.1	260718	8.7
2004	213744	5.6	332034	8,8
2005	307002	6.3	413802	8.6
Av. % of total imports for 1992-2005		3.6		15.4

Source: *Latvijas statistikas gadagrāmata* (Latvian Statistical Yearbook) 1993-2002, Rīga: LR Centrālā statistikas pārvalde; Latvijas ārējā tirdzniecība. Ceturkšņa biļetens (2004) (Foreign Trade of Latvia. Quarterly Bulletin) #4, 2003, Rīga: Latvijas Republikas Centrālā statistikas pārvalde and Latvijas statistikas ikmēneša biļetens, (Monthly Bulletin of Latvian Statistics), 2006, No.1, Rīga: LR Centrālā statistikas pārvalde.

Latvia's imports (Table 7) reflect much the same pattern as its exports in that Germany is no longer dominant and there is a greater emphasis on all her Baltic Sea Region neighbours. Germany had an average share of total exports for the period of only 15%, while the average for the Nordic countries together was 18.5%, the Baltic States (Estonia and Lithuania) 14%, Poland 3.6% and Russia 15.4%, making an average share for the countries of the Baltic Sea Region as whole of 66.5% of total imports, an increase of 13.8% over the comparative figure for the interwar period.

Up to the end of 1991, practically all of Latvia's foreign trade (in fact inter-republican trade) took place within the Soviet Union (Van Arkadie and Karlsson 1992, 172).[9] At the beginning of 1992, all import controls were lifted. Export quotas and

---

9   They estimate that 82% of the imports of the Baltic States and 91% of their exports in 1987 were trade flows between the republics of the Soviet Union.

licences were eliminated in June 1992 and replaced with an export tariff system. Monetary reform and liberalisation of internal prices also took place at this time.

Latvia's foreign trade policy during this period was based upon liberalisation of foreign trade on the basis of bilateral and multilateral trade agreements, taking into account the trading policies of the EU. The liberalisation of foreign trade has in fact meant the gradual reduction of tariff and non-tariff barriers. In 1999, Latvia became a full member of the WTO. Latvia has also entered into free trade agreements with 28 states, including all EU and EFTA member states. An integral part of Latvia's foreign trade policy in this period included several agreements with the Baltic States – free trade agreements for both manufactured and agricultural goods, as well as an agreement to remove non-tariff barriers (for an in-depth analysis of inter-Baltic State trade see Spīča 2000; for a more detailed analysis of the structure of Latvian exports to and imports from the Baltic Sea region countries see Karnups 2004). On 1 May 2004, Latvia became a member state of the European Union; with the exception of Russia and Norway, all of Latvia's regional trading partners are also member states of the EU.

In general terms, since regaining independence, Latvia's trade with her nearest neighbours (excluding Germany) has increased dramatically: in 2005 exports to Estonia, Lithuania, Denmark, Sweden, Norway, Finland, Poland and Russia were 45.7% of total exports (over 5 times the figure for 1937), while imports were 51.5% of total Latvian imports (over 4 times greater than the figure for 1937).

6. Investment in Latvia by Latvia's regional trading partners 1992-2005

The level of foreign investment in Latvia has increased significantly since regaining independence in 1991. The rapid privatisation of former state-owned enterprises during the 1990s was a significant factor behind the inflow of foreign investment.

Table 8: Foreign Investment Stock of Latvia's Regional Trading Partners in the Company Capital of Latvian Enterprises (as at 31 December) 1992-2005

Selected years	Germany		Nordic countries[1]		Baltic States[2]	
	(1000 lats)	% of total investment	(1000 lats)	% of total investment	(1000 lats)	% of total investment
1992	595.8	2.6	3588.1	15.9	67.8	0.3
1993	3663.4	7.3	7802.2	15.5	350.9	0.7
1994	12002.1	6.9	54544.8	31.5	937.2	0.5
1995	16369.9	6.0	86757.2	31.6	1512.4	0.6
1996	17791.0	4.7	129743.7	34.3	6016.2	1.6
1997	48422.3	8.8	144227.4	26.1	22453.6	4.1
1998	56662.6	8.6	201795.5	30.5	27293.6	4.1

Table 8: (continued): Foreign Investment Stock of Latvia's Regional Trading Partners in the Company Capital of Latvian Enterprises (as at 31 December) 1992-2005

Selected years	Germany (1000 lats)	% of total investment	Nordic countries[1] (1000 lats)	% of total investment	Baltic States[2] (1000 lats)	% of total investment
1999	65475.2	8.8	238925.7	32.1	41300.4	65475.2
2000	105859.0	12.7	280277.2	33.7	53647.1	105859.0
2001	135195.2	12.7	379765.9	35.6	67277.1	135195.2
2002	129310.3	11.0	434909.6	37.1	78891.8	129310.3
2003	126725.5	9.9	451719.4	35.3	87549.4	126725.5
2004	130208.8	10.1	457539.9	35.4	124818.4	130208.8
2005	90030.8	6.5	508980.2	36,7	197983.3	90030.8
Av. % of total investment for 1992-2005		15.0		18.5		14.0

Notes: [1] Finland, Denmark, Sweden, Norway; [2] Estonia, Lithuania

Selected years	Poland (1000 lats)	% of total investment	Russia (USSR) (1000 lats)	% of total investment
1992	169.4	0.8	2102.2	9.3
1993	861.9	1.7	5391.6	10.7
1994	851.3	0.5	10288.6	5.9
1995	562.6	0.2	51280.5	18.7
1996	835.5	0.2	50757.8	13.4
1997	307.0	0.1	52665.1	9.5
1998	186.4	0.0	56954.8	8.6
1999	260.3	0.0	56380.2	7.6
2000	276.5	0.0	60593.5	7.3
2001	530.6	0.0	66666.9	6.3
2002	466.0	0.0	68733.0	5.9
2003	553.3	0.0	79179.0	6.2
2004	743.0	0.1	83797.4	6.5
2005	1385.4	0.1	95008,2	6,9
Av. % of total imports for 1992-2005		0.3		8.8

Source: Investīcijas Latvijā. Ceturkšņa biļetens. (Investment in Latvia. Quarterly Bulletin) #4/1997, #4(24)/2001, #4(32)/2003 and #4(40)/2005, Rīga: LR Centrālā statistikas pārvalde.

Privatisation started soon after regaining independence and is now essentially complete, except for large infrastructure positions (especially the energy sector). Thus, the focus of and need for foreign investment is rapidly shifting to greenfield investment.

As can be seen from Table 8, investment from the Baltic Sea Region countries has in general steadily increased, despite the various shocks such as the collapse of the Russian rouble in 1998, with its corresponding effect on trade. The exception is Germany, whose investment fell substantially in 2005, and Poland, whose has remained static in percentage terms, but increased in absolute amounts. Latvia is now among the top five former Soviet republics in terms of foreign direct investment per capita. Two free seaports, a low corporate tax rate, membership of the EU and NATO and a skilled labour force make Latvia an attractive country for investors.

According to the Bank of Latvia, in 2005, Estonian, Danish, Russian, Lithuanian, Swedish and Norwegian companies were the most significant sources of foreign direct investment in Latvia (mainly in financial intermediation, wholesale and retail trade, utilities, construction and manufacturing).[10] Thus, the Baltic Sea Region countries continue to be major investors in Latvia. The proportion of investments by regional trading partners is shown in Fig. 2.

Fig. 2: Foreign Investment by Latvia's Regional Trading Partners in Latvian Enterprises as a Percentage of Total Investment by Regional Trading Partners (average % 1992-2005)

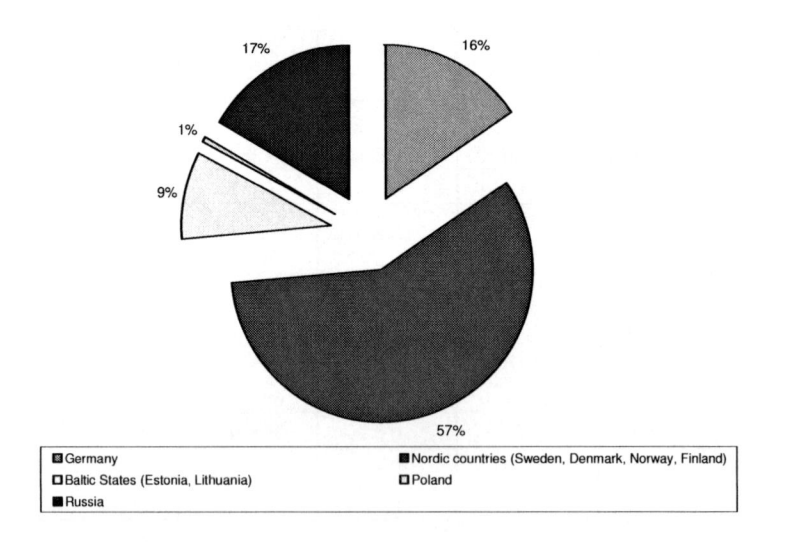

---

10   *Bank of Latvia Press Release:* "Latvia's Balance of Payments in the Fourth Quarter of 2005 and in the Year 2005", 31 March 2006.

As can be seen from Fig. 2, foreign direct investment by the Nordic countries in Latvia far exceeded FDI from other Baltic Sea Region countries in the period 1992-2005; Germany and Russia invested more or less the same amounts, which was still nearly twice that of the other two Baltic States.

In 2005, German capital was invested mainly in finance and banking, energy, textiles and insurance. The main investors were companies such as Ruhrgas AG, Norddeutsche Landesbank Girozentrale, P-D Glasseiden GmbH Oschatz and Vereins- und Westbank AG. Other major investors by country, favoured sectors and companies are as follows: Denmark: telecommunications, followed by real estate, insurance and minerals industry (Tilts Communications A/S, Hydro Texaco A/S and Torpgard Holdings); Norway: real estate, petrol stations and retail trade (Linstow Senterutvikling AS, Statoil ASA and Linstow International AS); Sweden: commerce, finance and banking (Tele2 Sverige AB, Skandinaviska Enskilda Banken AB and Rimi Baltic AB); Finland: petrol stations, retail trade, real estate and insurance (Fortum Oil and Gas Oy, Kesko Oyj and Stora Enso Oyj); Estonia: finance and banking, food and real estate (Hansapank AS, Stora Enso Timber AS and Rakvere Lihakombinaat AS); Lithuania: wholesale and retail trade (Paulauskas Vytautas); and, finally, Russia: oil pipelines, energy and finance and banking (Transnefteprodukt AO, Gazprom and Moscow Municipal Bank-Bank of Moscow).

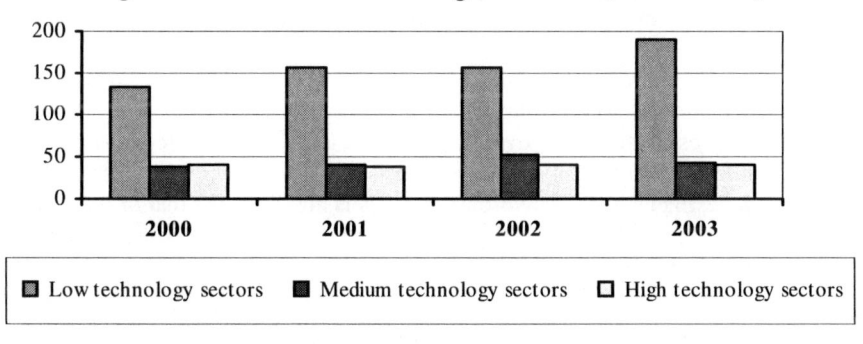

Fig. 3: FDI Stock in Manufacturing (end of 2003, LVL million)

Source: Economic Development of Latvia Report, June 2004: 51

In terms of qualitative investment flows into manufacturing, the largest investments were mainly made in the low technology sector (Fig. 3). Of the countries of the Baltic Sea Region, Germany made the biggest investment in manufacturing, equal to 17.4% of total manufacturing investment in 2005, most of it in low and medium technology sectors. These sectors have also absorbed Estonian and Swedish investment. One of the largest investors in the medium technology sector in 2005 was Sweden: 30.3% of the total.

With respect to greenfield projects involving new and modern technologies, in the sectors with the highest potential for such projects, only work that requires relatively low labour qualifications is currently being performed in Latvia. Latvia needs to create the preconditions for foreign investors to invest in knowledge intensive and high technology sectors by continuing to develop infrastructure and invest in education.

7. Conclusion

The above brief analysis of the two time periods would seem to confirm Lasser and Schrader's findings that the reorientation of Latvian trade after the country regained independence has taken place largely through her Baltic Sea Region neighbours and the reintegration into historical markets. Certainly, this time round the scale and the export product mix are different (although the import product mix remains substantively the same). Whereas Latvia in the interwar period was largely a primary producer with a small industrial sector, today Latvia's main exports to the Baltic Sea Region countries reflect the importance of her manufacturing and industrial sector. In other words, in contrast to the pre-war period, Latvia's main commodity exports to the Baltic Sea Region countries since regaining independence are forestry, metal industry and light industry products. In terms of more recent history, despite some fifty years of Soviet occupation, Latvia has managed to disengage its trade from Russia to a remarkable degree. Whereas in 1992 25.8% of exports went to Russia, by 2005 the percentage had fallen to 8%, and imports fell from 27.8% to 8.6%. Thus, the task of re-integrating into the European economy has been achieved, and regional trade flows reflect this.

In terms of investment, Germany is no longer the largest investor in Latvia: its average percentage has fallen from 21.1% in 1925-1939 to only 8.3% in 1992-2005. Baltic States investment is now over half of what it was in the interwar period and growing, while Polish investment is five times less now than it was then. On the other hand, investment from the Nordic countries is almost twice that of the interwar period, up from 15.4% to 30.7%. Similarly, Russian investment is more than three times that in the period 1925-1939.

With membership of the EU, some 76% of Latvia's foreign trade (2005 figures) has become domestic trade within the European Union (15 old plus 10 new member states). Of the remaining 24%, which now constitutes Latvia's foreign trade, some 10% in 2005 was with the remaining countries of the Baltic Sea Region – Iceland, Norway and Russia. The importance of the Baltic Sea Region countries, which account for some 64.5% of total investments in 2005 compared to 58.2% in 2003, for Latvia's economic development has increased since accession to the EU in 2004.

References

Byers, D.A. et al. (2000). "New Borders and Trade Flows: A Gravity Model Analysis of the Baltic States", Open Economies Review 11 (1), 73-91.

Cornett, A.P. & Iversen, S.P. (1998). The Baltic States in a European and Baltic Perspective: Trade and Transition in the Baltic Rim, Paper presented at the Fifth Nordic Baltic Conference in Regional Science, 1998 http://www.geo.ut.ee/nbc/paper/cornett_iversem.htm.

Eichengreen, B. & Irwin, D.A. (1996). The Role of History in Bilateral Trade Flows, NBER Working Paper 5565, National Bureau of Economic Research.

Finanču un kredita statistika 1939.g (1939) [Financial and Credit Statistics 1939], Rīga: Valsts statistiskā pārvalde.

Hiden, J. & Salmon, P. (1991). The Baltic Nations and Europe. London: Longman.

Kangeris, K. (1998). Sweden, the Soviet Union and the Baltic Question 1940-1964 – a Survey, in Hovi, K. (ed.), Relations between the Nordic Countries and the Baltic States in the XX Century. Turku: University of Turku, 188-211.

Karnups, V.P. (2004). The Northern Dimension of Latvian Foreign Trade: Historical Continuity and Future Prospects, in Jundzis, T. (ed.), Latvia in Europe: Visions of the Future, Rīga: Baltic Centre for Strategic Studies, 238-257.

Kojima, K. (1975). "International Trade and Foreign Investment: Substitutes or Complements", Hitotsubashi Journal of Economics 16, 1-12.

Kyn, P. (1998). Aspects of Recognition. Denmark's Relations to the Baltic States and Non-Recognition 1940-1991, in Hovi, K. (ed.), Relations between the Nordic Countries and the Baltic States in the XX Century. Turku: University of Turku, 1212-255.

Lasser, C-F. & Schrader, K. (2002). European Integration and Changing Trade Patterns: The Case of the Baltic States, Kiel Working Paper No. 1088, Kiel Institute of World Economics.

The Latvian Economist (1928), Rīga: Ministry of Finance.

The Latvian Economist (1938), Rīga: Ministry of Finance.

Latvijas ārējā tirdzniecība un transits 1937 (1938) [Foreign Trade and Transit of Latvia], Rīga: Valsts Statistiskā pārvalde.

Skujenieks, M. (1927). Latvija: Zeme un iedzīvotāji [Latvia: Land and People], Rīga: A. Gulbja apgāniecība.

Statistikas tabulas (1940). [Statistical Tables], Rīga: Latvijas PSR Tautsaimniecības Statistikas pārvalde.

Van Arkadie, B. & Karlsson, M. (1992). Economic Survey of the Baltic States, New York: New York University Press.

Zālīte, E. (1999). "Ekonomiskā politika un rūpniecības reorganizācija pēc 1934.gada 15.maijā "[Economic Policy and Industrial Reorganisation after 15 May 1934], Latvijas vēstures institūta žurnāls 3 (32), 74-106.

Russia and the Baltic Sea Region: Perspectives for the Integration of Kaliningrad

Gennadiy Fedorov & Valentin Korneyevets

1. Introduction

The Kaliningrad region (15,125 sq. km, 937,000 inhabitants) is an *oblast* (administrative subdivision) and exclave geographically separated from the rest of Russia (Fig. 1). It is bordered by Poland and Lithuania, which have been member states of the European Union (EU) since May 1, 2004. Under the present circumstances, it is important to work out a coherent strategy for regional development. Social, demographic and environmental issues require special attention. But it is important to sustain the regional and federal interests, taking into account the interests of the foreign partners as well. We believe that the Kaliningrad region could become a region of co-operation between the Russian Federation (RF) and the EU.

The main direction in the current development of relationships between the RF and the EU is the implementation of the concept of the Common European Economic Space. This concept is based on the Partnership and Cooperation Agreement between Russia and EU. This does not imply full integration, but a policy of rapprochement, i.e. implementing in Russia a system of technical control that is harmonized with the European system and parts of the EU financial legislation. The development of the Kaliningrad *oblast* strongly depends on relations between Russia and the EU. The *oblast* could reflect the success or failure of the development of these relations. Our group of experts from Kaliningrad State University believes that by extending the EU to Russia's borders, the recent enlargement should stimulate greater co-operation.

Kaliningrad *oblast* will increasingly become an indicator of the relations between Russia and the European Union. Everything in its development depends on the strategies Russia and the EU adopt towards each other. The experience of relations in the Baltic Sea region shows that mutually beneficial co-operation is possible. The main threat, we suppose, is insufficient understanding of the strategy of the other partner, insufficient knowledge of the situation, and a lack of mutual trust. In our opinion, EU enlargement is a factor influencing the formulation of the strategy for the Kaliningrad region. The "strategy for the region of co-operation" could be an example of the regional initiative to integrate the *oblast* (as a part of the RF) into the Baltic economic space.

2. The economic situation in the Kaliningrad oblast

The geographical position determines the regional development strategy. The following SWOT analysis is useful for the development of the strategy for the Kaliningrad *oblast* (see Table 1).

Table 1: Strengths and weaknesses, opportunities and threats of economic development in the Kaliningrad region

Strengths:	**Weaknesses:**
1. Similarities with the developed regions of Russia.	1. Spatial isolation.
2. Similarities with the developed countries of Europe.	2. Differences in conditions of land utilization.
3. Mild climate (as compared to some other parts of Russia).	3. Cold climate (as compared to the European average).
4. Access to the sea.	4. Lack of deep-water ports.
5. Availability of mineral resources (amber, oil).	5. Poor energy supply.
6. High intensity of land utilization.	6. High power load.
7. Dense transport network.	7. Poor quality of transport connections.
8. Well-developed market conditions (as compared to the other regions of Russia).	8. Poorly developed market conditions (as compared to European countries).
9. High level of public education.	9. Imbalance between specialist training and the needs of the economy.
10. Availability of scientific and research potential.	10. Low demand for science.
11. Regulations of the Special Economic zone and the Federal Special Program of regional development	11. Unstable conditions of economic activity.
12. Partnership with NATO.	12. Geopolitical inconsistency.
Opportunities	**Threats:**
1. Access to the Russian market.	1. Autarchy.
2. Development of external relations.	2. Difficulties in entering the EU market.
3. Low salaries and wages.	3. High costs.
4. Use of cheap marine transport.	

Opportunities (continued):	**Threats (continued):**
5. Exploitation of local raw materials. 6. Intensification of social and economic relations in the region. 7. Gateways to the European transport network. 8. Rapid development. 9. Integration in the European education system. 10. International scientific and research projects. 11. External relations development. 12. Baltic Sea – "sea of peace".	4. Competition from other Baltic ports. 5. Potential obstacles in the energy delivery. 6. Acute ecological problems. 7. Region cut off from the European transport network. 8. Pace of development slowing. 9. High unemployment rate and low labour productivity. 10. Decrease of scientific and research potential. 11. Economic stagnation. 12. Potential threat of conflicts.

There are two realistic possibilities. However, possible regional economic self-sufficiency thanks to large federal subsidies does not mean development. The development of the Kaliningrad region can be ensured only by implementing the optimistic strategy of the "region of cooperation". This strategy of international co-operation is based on the creation of a free economic zone. Let us discuss its perspectives.

What is the free (or, since 1996, special) economic zone in the Kaliningrad *oblast*? From 1996 to 2005, the special economic zone (SEZ) was, first of all, a duty-free zone that granted exemption from all payments on the import and export of goods. It aimed at both stimulating exports and import-substitution to replace old enterprises and create new ones, primarily with foreign capital. Goods imported for re-export to the rest of the Russian Federation are liable to all import duties. Goods are considered as produced in the SEZ only if the value added through processing or treatment is not less than 30%, or 15% in the case of electronic goods and household appliances.

Owing to the duty-free zone, the role of the *oblast* in the Russia's foreign trade (especially imports) has increased dramatically. But the volume of industrial and agrarian output in the Kaliningrad *oblast* decreased dramatically in 1991-1998. The recession was deeper than in Russia on average. The volume of industrial output in Kaliningrad *oblast* in 1998 was only 29% of the level in 1990, and the volume of the agricultural production 46%, compared to 46% and 56%, respectively, in the Russian Federation.

Import substitution did not work, because there was no demand for this production in other Russian regions. The situation changed qualitatively after the financial crisis 1998. The overall tendencies of economic growth in Russia since 1999 were also noticeable in the Kaliningrad region. Since 2000, investment and industrial growth in the Kaliningrad *oblast* have been higher than the average in the RF (Table 2). The situation in transport, construction, tourism and external trade is also optimistic, whereas agriculture remains the most problematic branch of the regional economy. But many problems have also been identified in the sphere of social development.

Table 2: Dynamics of Investment and Industry

	1999	2000	2001	2002	2003	2004	2004 in % to 1998
Investment							
Kaliningrad region	122.0	139.7	137.1	122.2	150.5	114.9	494
Russian Federation	105.3	117.4	108.7	102.6	112	110.9	171
Industry							
Kaliningrad region	103.9	132	112.5	110.2	114.8	125.8	245
Russian Federation	108.1	109	104.9	103.7	107	106.2	145

In 2002, the gross regional product grew by 9.5%; in 2003, the growth rate was 11.5%, in 2004, 12%. Average annual GDP growth rates are higher in the Kaliningrad region than the national average (NB: GDP growth in the Russian Federation is higher than in the Baltic States, Poland, and the EU countries).

The main factor driving economic growth after 1998 has been the improvement in the economic situation in the RF as a whole. In this situation, the SEZ mechanism benefits import-substituting production. Non-taxable imports of spare parts and technological equipment has increased significantly. A number of import-substituting production plants have been set up, including, for example, about 160 meat-proceeding plants, dozens of furniture enterprises, and new factories for instrument manufacturing, machinery, light industry, and fish processing.

Deliveries of goods to mainland Russia increased from $424 million in 2000 to $619 million in 2001 $759 million in 2002, $1120 million in 2003, $1.8 billion in 2004 and $ 5.4 billion in 2007. In 2004, the region accounted for 48% of the Russian production of TV sets and 66% of vacuum cleaners, 23% of tinned meat, 37% of tinned fish, 11% of fish and seafood industry, 6% of furniture, 5% of cellulose, and 2.7% of vodka and other alcoholic beverages. In 2002, the region produced 24% of the total Russian export of vodka (in value).

The low-priced, high-quality products of the Kaliningrad region take precedence over the production of Russian and foreign manufacturers thanks to the modern range of goods and the use of new technologies, realized with the help of active international commercial links and the participation of foreign partners in funding some enterprises.

The market infrastructure of the region is developing faster than in most other Russian regions. The system of higher education is being modernized. International links are expanding and numerous international programs are being implemented. At the same time, many traditional industries in the region are marking time (agriculture, amber extraction and processing, some types of mechanical engineering). The engineering infrastructure is in a critical situation. Ecological problems are becoming more acute. An underground economy is developing. Social inequalities are huge and the unemployment rate is still high.

One of the peculiarities of the Kaliningrad region is its strong dependence on the provisions of the Special Economic Zone regime. At the same time, the regional economy depends on the demand for Kaliningrad goods on the Russian domestic market. Abolition of the privileges, granted to the region by the law on the Special Economic Zone, or a falling demand for Kaliningrad goods will inevitably result in a drop in industrial production. Nowadays, the economy of the region remains "vulnerable, i.e. failing to provide sustainable development of the region", just as it was described by Ivan Samson (France) in his book "Kaliningrad region: the diagnosis of a crisis" (1998). The global financial crisis, which began in 2008 and is now hitting all countries including Russia, will have far more serious consequences for Kaliningrad. However, the demand for consumer goods manufactured in the Kaliningrad region (TV sets, cars, meat and fish products) will be less affected by the crisis. This will be an alleviating factor for the regional economy.

The situation of the new strategy for Kaliningrad is very complicated, because of competing interests in the Kaliningrad *oblast*. There are federal, regional and municipal authorities, Russian (from Kaliningrad, Moscow and other regions of Russia) and foreign businesses, the very diverse population of the region, etc. It is a very difficult task to balance all these interests.

The regional strategy of development must contain three compulsory components: *regional, federal and international*. The *regional component* is actually the development of market conditions in the region. Taking into consideration the geographical proximity of the EU countries with their developed market economies, this process can develop faster in this region than in other Russian regions. The enclave position of the region makes it easier to introduce new essential elements of the market economy, which can later be utilized by other Russian regions. The *federal component* presupposes that development in the Kaliningrad serves the interests of the Russian Federation; it has considerable significance for the RF with respect to foreign relations. This factor, and Kaliningrad's exclave position, means that the Russian power centre gives the region special attention, which might manifest itself in direct control over the key elements of the regional economy. Realization of the federal program is now based on the SEZ mechanism and the federal task program "Development of the Kaliningrad *oblast* until 2010" (with the significant federal investments and guarantees for private investors).[1] The *international aspect* of the regional strategy requires both sides – Russia and the West – to acknowledge that the Kaliningrad region plays a special role in the mutual co-operation and in the deepening of this co-operation in the interests of both sides. The *oblast* will become a Russian contact territory in Europe, a testing ground for the mechanisms of integration and interaction between Russia and the European Union in the 21st century.

The essence of the strategy is to turn the Kaliningrad region into a Russian-EU "region of intense co-operation", the place where new forms of co-operation are tested and from where the positive experience would spread to the other regions of Russia. In the framework of regional development, it is advisable for Russia and the EU to sign a special agreement on the Kaliningrad *oblast*. As a pole of international integration, the *oblast* will be a catalyst for positive change and will be able to play a more important role in the all-European co-operation (including Russia).

There are two possibilities for overcoming the difficulties of socio-economic development in the Kaliningrad region. The first is connected with greater interaction between Russia and the EU. This is enhanced by the complementarity of the economies of the two large economic areas along with some common features of a cultural nature and common political interests in military security.

The second possibility is conditioned by the top-down development of the regionalism, from the macro level to the meso and micro levels. The EU states at the macro level are unifying their economic space in accordance with the common requirements. However, regional organizations play an increasingly important role in the European sub-regions, at the meso-level, in coordinating joint activities in the sphere of economic, social, and ecological policy (in the Baltic Sea Region this role is played by the Council of the Baltic Sea States, the Nordic Council). There are also non-state initiatives ("Northern Dimension").

---

[1] The new Law on the Special economic zone (signed January 10, 2006) seeks to replace the duty-free zone with the tax privileges. The enterprise could select:
tax privileges for investor if it invests more that 150 million rubles in manufacturing in a period of three years;
or duty-free privileges (available only to enterprises, not to individuals) for a period of 10 years – before 2015.
Taxation privileges have already attracted large investors to the region. At the end of 2008, there were 55 residents of the Special Economic Zone, boasting more than 30 billion roubles of investment. These residents are large industrial, construction and transport companies.

3. Co-operation between Russia and the EU

The cooperation between the EU and Russia does not start from scratch. In fact, being first a *free*, and then a *special* economic zone, the Kaliningrad region has become a testing ground for economic co-operation, where new integration patterns are being experimented on.

The same role is played by cross-border co-operation. The last decade has seen a number of significant joint projects in various spheres, including environmental protection, energy saving, education (including conversion training of the military personnel), healthcare, transport and social issues. The international research projects on the Kaliningrad region mainly involve transport, telecommunications and energy issues. Another big issue is the development of industrial infrastructure as an indispensable foundation for attracting investments and, consequently, establishing specialized regional industries. These projects are chiefly financed by the EU through the Tacis program, as well as by Denmark (ecological projects) and Sweden (anti-AIDS program).

Thus, the region has a lot of international contacts. International co-operation will promote the formation of an effective regional economic structure suitable for the significant economic co-operation between Russia and the EU. But the development of co-operation in the region is hampered by the lack of federal and local legislation to regulate the overarching liberal economic development of the enclave, the support of the structural reforms in the region, and the patterns of complex interaction with the European Union. Therefore, in the regional development framework it is expedient for Russia and the EU to prepare and sign a special agreement on the Kaliningrad Region.

The agreement should seek to solve two issues:

- Facilitation of the rapprochement of the RF and the EU through the development of the new mechanisms of co-operation in the Kaliningrad region and the transfer of positive experiences to the rest of Russia (Kaliningrad *oblast* as the "pilot region" of co-operation).

- Creation of the conditions for the socio-economic development of the Kaliningrad region, which has become a Russian enclave within the enlarged EU, by promoting the region's integration as a Russian vanguard into the Baltic Sea Region and the European market.

The agreement should include arrangements on the following issues:

- ensuring free transit of cargo and passengers between the Kaliningrad region and the rest of Russia across the territories of the neighbouring EU countries by sea, air, and land in both directions (including the provisions for cargo transit in emergency cases);

- maintaining (as an exception to the Schengen rules of EU) the visa-free regulations for people from Kaliningrad visiting Poland and Lithuania;

- simplifing procedures for issuing visas for foreigners visiting the Kaliningrad Region and for issuing work permits;
- combining the fishing quotas and fish catching zones of the new EU member states bordering the Kaliningrad region with the corresponding quotas and zones of EU to avoid the damage to the fishing industry of the region;
- participation of the Kaliningrad Region in the "Northern Dimension" and the EU programs aimed at regional development, transfrontier co-operation, environmental protection, health protection, and cultural, educational, and scientific exchange.

4. Kaliningrad oblast and co-operation in the Baltic Region

Co-operation between Russia and the EU also could be stimulated by deepening their interaction in the Baltic Sea Region; the Kaliningrad *oblast* should play an active role in this process. The well-known project "The Northern Dimension of the EU" is now transforming into the greater project "The Baltic Dimension". The Baltic dimension project includes the northern countries as well as Poland, Lithuania, Latvia and Estonia. Germany can also play an active role. Northwest Russia, including the Kaliningrad *oblast*, could be involved in this project, too. Russian participation in this project would allow for more effective integration with the EU (40% of Russia's trade with the EU is with the Baltic countries). Certainly, Russia is interested not only in trade. Other economic aspects of high importance include foreign investment, tourism, telecommunications, etc. Cooperation could be very useful in other spheres of the Baltic dimension project, such as science and education, culture and sport, security and politics.

Kaliningrad *oblast* is an active member of many organizations promoting co-operation in the Baltic Sea Region. Participation in these programs encourages practical co-operation, improves contacts, promotes different regions, and attracts investment. Unfortunately, Russian funding of co-operation projects (including research projects) is insufficient.

The list of projects of the Baltic countries and regions that are being actively implemented also includes the following:
- "Via Baltica", "Via Hanseatica" – motorway projects to connect the countries of the region;
- "The Baltic gateway" – a project to create a network of motorways and ferries;
- "The Baltic energy ring" – a project to develop an energy system;
- programs of co-operation between the Baltic Sea cities;
- ecological programs focused on the Baltic Sea basin;

- educational programs ("Erasmus Mundus", "The Eurofaculty", "The Baltic University Programme" – the Immanuel Kant State University of Russia, Kaliningrad actively participates in these programs).

Kaliningrad is involved in many projects, but often only nominally. One of the projects that might be of interest is VASAB – 2010 ("Vision and strategies around the Baltic – 2010"), which is based on such values as development, environmental sustainability, freedom and solidarity. The document consists of four spatial elements, which could be studied and implemented for the Kaliningrad region as well:

- cities and urban networks;
- power system and transport networks;
- areas supporting dynamism and the quality of life (such as the border zones as an instrument of international exchange; tourist areas; coastal zones worthy of special attention; natural and cultural landscapes of special importance);
- comprehensive spatial planning.

To reduce the drawbacks of the exclave character of the Kaliningrad region it is necessary to include it in the *new spatial forms of international economic integration*. These are structures at the sub-national level, including regions of different states and featuring active cross-border and interregional cooperation and on-going socio-economic integration. These include "large regions", "triangles of growth", "working communities" (associations, etc), and Euroregions. *Euroregions,* which are especially active, also function in the Baltic Sea region. They develop joint strategies, collect the financial means for solving common problems and implementing interregional projects. The establishment of Euroregions with Russia's participation started as early as the second half of the 1990s. The participation of Russian regions in the Euroregions certainly differs from that of the regions of the EU countries (since Russia is not a member of the EU, and seems unlikely to join it). Nevertheless, we hope that in the course of time the differences will be eliminated.

The Kaliningrad region and its municipalities are members of 5 Euroregions: Baltics, Neman, Sheshupe, Saule, Lyna-Lava. The region most actively participates in the Euroregion "Baltic" (Figure 1). Its national secretariat is in Baltiysk. The Council and Presidium have been established, and three working groups (for environmental protection, spatial planning and social issues) have been formed. Future joint projects have been planned, including the following: SEBTrans-Link connecting Russia to the EU countries, projects for tourist and resort infrastructure development, security in the Baltic Sea region, networks of analytical and information centers, and a public health service. There are projects for the reconstruction of the old part of Baltiysk and building a new international multi-purpose centre on the Curonian Spit. The implementation of the "Seagull project" (aimed at the elaboration and development of the Euroregion strategy), launched in 2001, is in progress. This project is financed by European programs such as Interreg, Phare, and Tacis.

Fig. 1: The *"Baltic" Euroregion*

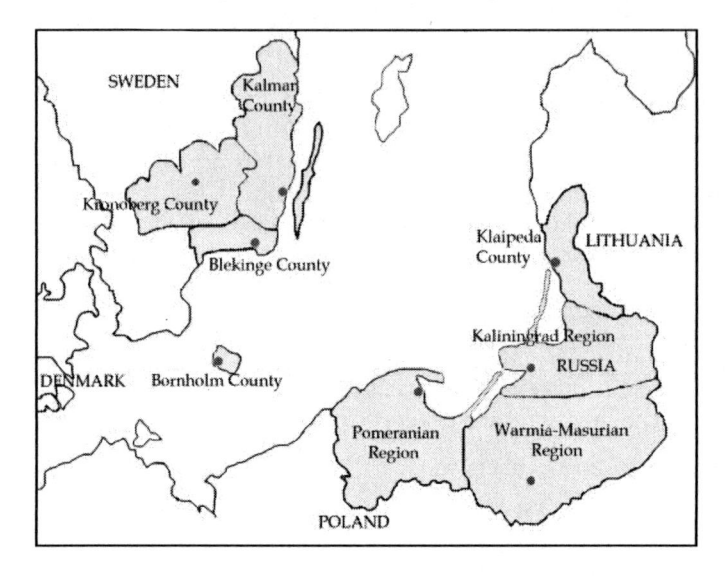

An interesting concept by Urpo Kivikari (Finland) for "the South Baltic growth triangle" proposes using:

- investment from Sweden, Denmark, Germany;
- labour from Poland, Lithuania, Latvia; and
- raw materials from Russia transported through the Kaliningrad *oblast*.

The combination of these three elements could have a significant effect. This idea is quite attractive for the Kaliningrad region because the project includes its territory.

Fig. 2: Co-operation in the Baltic region

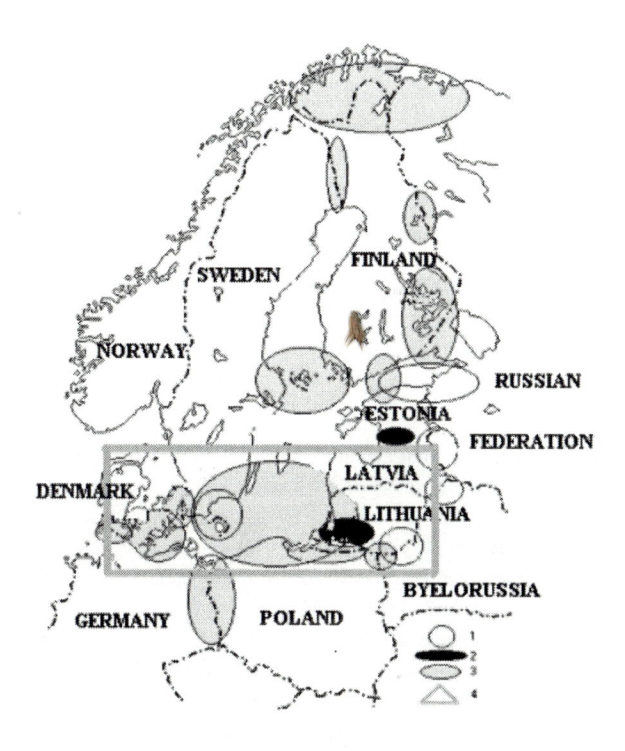

1. Co-operation in the Soviet period; 2. Idem, but developing now; 3. Euroregions; 4. South-Baltic Growth Triangle.

5. Conclusion

The Baltic Sea Region is a region of intense international co-operation (including EU-Russia). The region is gradually expanding beyond a geographical concept to become an economic, social and even political entity. The integration processes in different areas are especially active in the region, supported by the federal government as well as by the region's administration, business community and non-governmental organizations. The EU-Russia co-operation in the Baltic Sea Region is currently under development and will certainly expand in the future.

Both the Russian Federation and the European Union, as reflected in various legal documents, regard the Kaliningrad region as a "pilot" region of international co-operation. The strategy of developing the Kaliningrad region as a region of co-operation presupposes greater co-operation between Russia and the EU as a fundamental measure for overcoming the drawbacks and for utilizing the advantages of its geopolitical location.

The realization of the outlined strategy in the sphere of co-operation would enhance the region's economic security, which is by no means identical to self-sufficiency of the regional economy and consists of:
- effective specialization of the national economy and a high level of development in the regional market;
- reliable and cheap communications with the mainland;
- mutually beneficial relations with the neighboring countries.

References

Actual issues for development of semi-medium cities in Kaliningrad region // Immanuel Kant State University of Russia / Kaliningrad, 2008, 205 pages.

Economic, geopolitical and social problems of co-operation between Kaliningrad and Poland // Coastal Regions, N6. Gdynia – Peplin 2003, 141 pages.

Fedorov, G., EU Enlargement and Perspectives of the Kaliningrad Exclave. - Helsinki, Internatum, N1, 2000, Pp. 15-20.

Fedorov, G., Kaliningrad Alternatives Today. - ZEI, C80, 2000, 21 pages.

Kaliningrad 2000-2010: Diagnosis, Concepts and Proposals for Future Development / Université Pierre Mendés-France – Kaliningrad State University. – TACIS, Grenoble, 2000, 21 pages.

Kaliningrad 2010: Concepts, prospects and recommendations for a global development plan / Université Pierre Mendés-France – Kaliningrad State University. – TACIS, Grenoble, 2000, 319 pages.

Kaliningrad Region: The Diagnosis of a Crisis. Kaliningrad: TACIS-KSU, 1998. 271 pages.

Kaliningrad Region of Russia and EU Enlargement. Issues of the Pan European Integration. Analytical Report // Kaliningrad State University / Kaliningrad, 2003, 47 pages.

Kivikari, U., Lindström, M., Liuhto, K., The External Economic Relations of the Kaliningrad Region. Turku: Turku School of Economics, 1998. 84 pages.

Klemeshev, A., Fedorov, G., From an Isolated Exclave – to a "Development Corridor". Alternative Development Strategies of the Russian Exclave on the Baltic Sea. – Kaliningrad: Kaliningrad State University, 2005. 194 pages.

Klemeshev, A., Fedorov, G., Regional Strategy for Kaliningrad // Russia and the European Union / Ed. by O. Antonenko, K. Pinnick. – London and New York: Routledge, 2005, Pp. 243-252.

Klemeshev, A., Kozlov, S., Fedorov, G., The special region of Russia // Kaliningrad State University / Kaliningrad, 2003, 285 pages.

Korneevets, V., Buchhover E., Einzelhandel in Grenzstädten der russischen Exclave Kaliningrad // Europa Regional. 1998. N1. S. 25.

Perspectives for development of interregional cooperation: Kaliningrad region within Euroregion Baltic. Kaliningrad: European Commission, 2005. 353 pages.

Possibilities for co-operation between Kaliningrad Region of Russia and Northern Poland within the EU Enlargement Process // Kaliningrad State University / Kaliningrad, 2003, 75 pages.

Strategy of the social and economic development of the Kaliningrad region for the period to the Year 2010. Kaliningrad: Administration of Kaliningrad region, 2003. 100 pages.

Vision and Strategies around the Baltic Sea 2010 // MATROS Seminar Report. - Gdansk: VASAB Secretariat, 2000.

Comment on Country Studies:
Poland, Latvia, and Russia in the Baltic Sea Area

Konrad Lammers

The structure of my comment is as follows: At first I will try to catch the main conclusions provided by the three case studies. Then I will make some critical remarks in regard to these conclusions. I will do that for each case study separately. At the end I will be in search of some general conclusions which may be taken considering the three papers together.

Anna Barbara Kisiel-Łowczyc: Cultural Factors of Competitiveness of Baltic Sea Region (BSR) Countries

A main statement of the paper is: "The BSR (*Baltic Sea Region*) is a special region... It is a region in which the Baltic Sea has an important integrating function." The paper tries to underline this statement by providing several figures which shall show that integration among the countries around the Baltic Sea is deeper than in other regions of the world and that the BSR has an extraordinary economic importance within the world economy. Furthermore the paper presents several rankings which shall reflect the competitiveness of the countries of the Baltic Sea Region in a global context. The rankings are taken from the World Competitiveness Yearbook which is yearly published by the International Institute for Management Developments. The purpose of these rankings is, according to the publishing institute: "To establish a ranking how a nation's economic, cultural, social environment creates and sustains the competitiveness of enterprises." What do the rankings show, as they are presented in the paper? Regardless whether the indicators which shall reflect the nation's environment for the competitiveness for firms are considered separately or taken together, the rankings, as presented in the paper, are always as follows:

- On the top are the Scandinavian countries;
- Estonia and Germany are in an intermediate position;
- Poland and Russia are at the bottom.

In my opinion the paper raises several questions. Indeed, I share the statement that integration among the (most) countries around the Baltic Sea is, compared with other regions, rather deep although the figures provided in the paper do not support this view in a convincing manner. In order to underline this issue it would be helpful to consider the relevant literature, for example the research done by Paas/Tafenau (2005) and Laaser/Schrader (2003). As far as the rankings for the economic, cultural, social environment of the Baltic Sea Countries are concerned the presented results which reveal large differences among the countries (country groups) are not very surprising. However, the question arises what the paper intends to show by these results. In fact, of some interest would be whether the paper assumes any link between the stated deep integration among the Baltic Sea Countries and the revealed large differences in the rankings regarding their environment for the competitiveness for firms. Provided the paper assumes such a link, the most important question would be what the hypothesis in this context is. Without any discussion of these issues it is not easy to understand the message of the paper.

Viesturs Pauls Karnups: Latvia and the Baltic Sea Region: The Historical Context of Trade and Investment

The paper analyses Latvia's integration in the European economic space during the last hundred years. Prior to the First Word War Latvia was mainly a transit region for imports to and exports from Russia. During the interwar period – after the country had gained independence – Latvia established strong trade relations with the countries around the Baltic Sea, especially with Germany. Firms from Baltic Sea countries invested also a lot in Latvia. Within the period 1940-1991 Latvia was cut off from the trade and investment relations built up in the interwar period and the economy was adjusted to the Comecon. After the fall of the iron curtain and regaining independence in 1991, Latvia restored trade and investment relations with the countries around the Baltic Sea: Poland, Germany, Russia, the Scandinavian Countries, Estonia and Lithuania. Compared with the interwar period the dominance of Germany as an economic partner is not longer valid. Instead, the Scandinavian countries and the direct neighbours have gained importance.

The paper shows in a very illustrative way using many interesting details Latvia's trade relations as well as the engagement of foreign investors in Latvia during the last hundred years. What could be missed is that only little explanations are provided for the described developments. What are the causes that Latvia, under more or less free market conditions, had and has had developed strong economic relations with the countries around the Baltic Sea? What does play a role: short distances, language similarities, low transaction costs, a similar culture, or something else? It seems also important to account for the size of the partner countries, the stage of their economic development as well as for changes in these variables in order to explain trade and investment patterns among countries. The inclusion of explanations for the described trade and investment relations would increase the insights of the paper not insignificantly.

Gennadiy Fedorov, Valentin Korneyevets: Russia and the Baltic Sea Region: Perspectives for the Integration of Kaliningrad

The paper shows very impressively:

- The sharp decline of economic activities after the fall of the iron curtain in the period 1990-1998 and the recovery after 1999;

- The institutional situation of Kaliningrad as a part of Russia surrounded since 2004 by EU member states;

- The attempt in order to overcome the difficulties of the isolated location by establishing a special economic zone;

- The dependence of Kaliningrad's economic development from the development in Russia with the consequence that the economic recovery after 1999 is only due to the favourable development in Russia;

- Other severe problems of economic development in Kaliningrad such as a growing shadow economy, ecological grievances and generally a high rate of unemployment.

Furthermore, the paper discusses two possible ways to overcome or, at least, to mitigate the economic problems of the region. The first one is an "EU-Russia cooperation", so to say a special agreement between Russia and the EU concerning the status of Kaliningrad. The second one ("Kaliningrad Oblast and cooperation in the Baltic Region") consists of an active participation of the region in projects and cooperation below the national level which are – without doubt – numerous in the Baltic Sea Region.

Coming to some critical remarks, it is not quite clear for me whether the paper regards the two proposed ways as alternatives or as additional measures. Furthermore, it would be helpful to know what the material content of a special agreement between Russia and the EU should be in order to improve the economic situation in the region. What are the crucial issues to be agreed upon which can really improve the conditions for economic activities in Kaliningrad? Unfortunately, the paper is not very precise in this respect. As far as the participation of Kaliningrad in projects and cooperation in the Baltic Sea Region is concerned I have some doubts whether they are able to make a substantial contribution to the economic and social performance of the region. Surely, such projects and cooperation are helpful to establish and improve contacts among institutions and persons, and it might be that those contacts are especially important for Kaliningrad because of its isolated location since the fall of the iron curtain. But they are often labels and their material content in economic terms is limited. They never can overcome or compensate for the main obstacles for economic development in Kaliningrad which in my opinion have to be seen in the institutional conditions of the region (as part of Russia) as well as in the impediments for cross border activities which simply exist for the reason that Kaliningrad on the one side and the surrounding countries on the other side belong to different economic areas (Russia and the EU).

Is it possible to extract any conclusion taken the three papers together?

This is not an easy task. Each of the paper presents different facts and raises other questions. But perhaps an impressive, very subjective, conclusion could be: It seems that the process of integration among the EU15 and the Eastern European countries has functioned very well. New and old member countries now belong to one economic area which is formed by the EU. But there is still a border in economic terms as well as in a political sense between the EU on the one side and Russia on the other side. In so far the continent is still divided; only the borders were shifted. The existence of this border becomes very evident by the special case of Kaliningrad. There is no easy solution on the table to overcome this issue.

References

Tiiu Paas, Egle Tafenau (2005), European trade integration in the Baltic Sea Region – A gravity model based analysis. HWWA Discussion Paper No. 331, Hamburg.

Claus-Friedrich Laaser, Klaus Schrader (2003), Knocking on the Door: The Baltic Rim Transition Ready for Europe? In: L. Hedegaard, B. Lindström (Eds), The NEBI Yearbook 2003 – North European and Baltic Sea Integration, Berlin/Heidelberg, pp. 21-45.

Affiliations

Prof. Dr. Alexander Chepurenko
Chair of Economic Sociology
Faculty of Sociology
State University Higher School of Economics
achepurenko@hse.ru

Prof. Dr. Gennadiy Fedorov
Immanuel Kant State University of Russia (Kaliningrad)
Department of social-economic geography and geopolitics
Faculty of Geography and Geoecology
gfedorov@kantiana.ru

Prof. Dr. Carsten Herrmann-Pillath
Frankfurt School of Finance & Management
Sino-German School of Governance
Witten/Herdecke University, Chair of Evolutionary and Institutional Economics
c.herrmann-pillath@frankfurt-school.de

Dr. Raita Karnite
Latvian Academy of Sciences
Institute of Economics
raita@economics.lv

Prof. Dr. Viesturs Pauls Karnups
University of Latvia, Riga
Faculty of Economics and Management
viesturspauls@gmail.com

Prof. Dr. Anna Barbara Kisiel-Łowczyc
University of Gdańsk
Faculty of Economics
Institute of International Business
abkl@gnu.univ.gda.pl

Prof. Dr. Bozena Klimczak
Wroclaw University of Economics
Department of Microeconomics and Institutional Economics
bozena.klimczak@ue.wroc.pl

Dr. Mikolaj Klimczak
Wroclaw University of Economics
Department of Microeconomics and Institutional Economics
mikolaj.klimczak@ue.wroc.pl

Prof. Dr. Rainer Klump
Johann Wolfgang Goethe-University Frankfurt/Main
Chair of Economic Development and Integration
klump@wiwi.uni-frankfurt.de

Dr. Valentin Korneyevets
Immauel Kant State University of Russia (Kaliningrad)
Department of social-cultural service and tourism
Faculty of Service
vkorneyevets@kantiana.ru

Dr. Oskar Kowalewski
World Economy Research Institute
Warsaw School o Economics (SGH)
okowale@sgh.waw.pl

Dr. Konrad Lammers
Institute for European Integration
Europa-Kolleg-Hamburg
k-lammers@europa-kolleg-hamburg.de

Dr. Nina Oding
International "Leontief Centre" for Social and Economic Research, St. Petersburg
Head of Research Department
oding@leontief.spb.su

Dr. Lev Savulkin
International "Leontief Centre" for Social and Economic Research, St. Petersburg
Senior Researcher
savul@leontief.spb.su

Prof. Dr. Dres. h.c. Bertram Schefold
Johann Wolfgang Goethe-University Frankfurt/Main
Faculty of Economics and Business Administration
schefold@wiwi.uni-frankfurt.de

Prof. Dr. Karl-Heinz Schmidt
University of Paderborn
Faculty of Business Administration and Economics
Karl-Heinz_Schmidt@notes.uni-paderborn.de

Inese Šūpule
University of Latvia, Riga
Baltic Institute of Social Sciences
inese.supule@biss.soc.lv

Prof. Dr. Hans-Jürgen Wagener
Europe-University Viadrina Frankfurt (Oder)
wagener@euv-frankfurt-o.de

Prof. Dr. Friederike Welter
Jönköping International Business School (JIBS) CISEG (Center for Innovation Systems, Entrepreneurship and Growth) / RUREG (Research Unit for Research on Entrepreneurship and Growth) Jönköping, Sweden
friederike.welter@ihh.hj.se

Robert Wyszyński
National Bank of Poland
Economic Institute - Bureau of Corporates,
Households and Markets (Labour Markets)
robert.wyszynski@nbp.pl

Dr. Jacek Adam Zaucha
University of Gdansk
Economics Department
Macroeconomics Chair, Economics, Regional Development, Spatial Planning
jacek.zaucha@gmail.com

PD Dr. Joachim Zweynert
University of Hamburg
Economics Department
und Hamburg Institute of International Economics (HWWI),
Thuringia Branch (Erfurt)
zweynert@hwwi.org